ENGLISH FUNDA

ENGLISH FUNDAMENTALS

TENTH EDITION

Form C

Donald W. Emery

Late of University of Washington

John M. Kierzek

Late of Oregon State University

Peter Lindblom

Miami-Dade Community College

ALLYN AND BACON

Boston   London   Toronto   Sydney   Tokyo   Singapore

Vice President, Humanities: Joseph Opiela
Editorial Assistant: Susannah Davidson
Marketing Manager: Lisa Kimball
Composition and Prepress Buyer: Linda Cox
Manufacturing Buyer: Aloka Rathnam
Cover Administrator: Suzanne Harbison
Production Administrator: Deborah Brown
Editorial Production Service: Saxon House Productions

Copyright © 1996 by Allyn and Bacon
A Division of Simon & Schuster, Inc.
Needham Heights, Massachusetts 02194

English Fundamentals, copyright © 1935, 1942, and 1951 by Macmillan Publishing Co.
English Fundamentals, Form C, copyright © 1971, 1977, 1981, and 1986 by Macmillan Publishing Co.
Portions of this book are reprinted from *English Fundamentals, Tenth Edition, Form B,* copyright © 1995.

Library of Congress Cataloging-in-Publication Data

Emery, Donald W. (Donald William), 1906–1993
    English fundamentals, form B / Donald W. Emery, John M. Kierzek,
Peter Lindblom.—10th ed.
      p. cm.
    Includes index.
    ISBN 0-02-332920-3 (pbk.)
    1. English language—Grammar.   I. Kierzek, John M., 1891– .
II. Lindblom, Peter D., 1938– .   III. Title.   IV. Title: English
fundamentals.
PE1112.E472   1996
428.2′4—dc20   93-49853
                                      CIP

Printed in the United States of America

10 9 8 7 6 5 4 3 2   00 99 98 97 96

Contents

Preface

A new edition of any textbook prompts both a look back and a look ahead. A look back at the history of *English Fundamentals* reveals a book that has changed edition by edition, changed to serve students better, and changed to keep pace with new developments in teaching. A look ahead into this tenth edition of *English Fundamentals* will reveal a book much the same as the ninth edition, but one that has once again incorporated many small but significant changes to make it work better for students and teachers. The purpose and the audience, however, remain the same as they have been since the first edition. All students who need to improve their control of the basic principles for using the English language in speaking and writing can profit from working in *English Fundamentals,* tenth edition. The book is used in classes in developmental composition, freshman composition, journalism, advanced grammar, and grammar review at all levels.

Organization of the Text

Certain important qualities have always been characteristic of *English Fundamentals:* clear, effective instruction in the fundamental principles of English; carefully crafted exercises designed to illustrate those principles; and a comprehensive testing system to diagnose problems and measure progress. The first lessons introduce students to the basic system of the language and provide carefully chosen examples of verb connections, basic sentence patterns, and the internal workings of the sentence. Simplified presentations make the book accessible both for developmental students and for those who have advanced in their study of the language. Because the first sections are cumulative, building step by step a foundation in the operating principles of the language, these early lessons should be studied first. Once the foundation is laid, the order for studying the remaining units is flexible. Work on spelling and capitalization, for example, can be undertaken at almost any point, even during study of another unit.

Building on the foundation of the early lessons, subsequent lessons explore the more complex structures and relationships of the language. Students examine the function of various clauses and phrases, first learning to recognize their structures, and then learning to use them by practicing with sentence combining, and embedding and transformation drills. The drills are proven methods for helping students to develop flexibility and sophistication in their writing and to recognize effective, correct constructions when they revise.

The last instructional section surveys college writing. Students study the writing process, with special emphasis on techniques of invention, and then learn to apply that process to a wide range of writing assignments typical of college courses. These assignments range from personal essays to academic papers, with an additional focus on paragraph development. The section closes with an examination of essay tests and test-taking. The examples and exercises throughout the book come from a number of disciplines, including science and business, to accommodate the interests of a wide range of students.

The text concludes with a set of twenty Progress Tests and three appendixes. The first appendix discusses study skills and focuses on reading, note-taking, and time management. A dictionary usage section completes this appendix; explanations and exercises ask students to look at several excerpts from widely used desk dictionaries so that the students will learn how to use a dictionary to full advantage. The second appendix offers diagnostic tests to analyze students' abilities in spelling, punctuation, sentence structure, and usage. The third appendix contains the answer key to the Practice Sheets. The book concludes with an index to help students use the text for references to specific concepts.

New to This Edition

Those familiar with previous editions will note an important new feature in the tenth edition: short summaries of important concepts appended to selected lessons. Teachers surveyed prior to publication of the tenth edition made favorable mention of the short Summary of Punctuation Rules added to the ninth edition. Taking this cue, we have added brief surveys of the main points in several lessons including basic sentence patterns, adverb clauses, adjective clauses, noun clauses, gerund and infinitive phrases, participial and absolute phrases, punctuation, correct use of verbs, and correct use of pronouns. We hope that these condensed statements of important concepts will be helpful as a review during the work on the Practice Sheets and Exercises. In addition, we hope that students can learn to use these brief summaries as an easy reference guide for correcting writing assignments.

We have also added significant new work on dictionary skills (Appendix A). Since the publication of the ninth edition of *English Fundamentals,* three of the four most popular college-level desk dictionaries have appeared in new editions, with one of them, *Random House,* adding the word *Webster's* to its title. The publishers of these dictionaries have kindly allowed us to use facsimiles of selected sections to introduce students to these new publications. These excerpts were chosen to illustrate the wide variety of information available in a good dictionary. This section also includes a set of exercises that ask students to use their dictionaries to find interesting and unusual material. We hope that students following these exercises will develop sound skills, and we hope that they will also develop a deep appreciation of the rich resources offered to them in a good dictionary.

Finally, in our attempts to help students grasp language concepts easily, we have made hundreds of small changes that might not be immediately evident even to regular users of *English Fundamentals.* We have made many short rewrites, compressions, and insertions, and we have replaced hundreds of example sentences with new examples that we think present the concepts more effectively. And we have renumbered the Practice Sheets and Exercises to correspond with the lessons where they occur.

Practice Sheets

The tenth edition continues the use of Practice Sheets introduced in the ninth edition. After every lesson there is at least one easy-to-understand worksheet that provides examples of and practice with the concept introduced in that lesson. The sentences in the Practice Sheets are usually shorter and somewhat simpler than those in the Exercise worksheets that follow. Thus the Practice Sheets provide a starter exercise, a warm-up for students to begin work on each new concept. The Practice Sheets also allow teachers to use the book with students whose reading levels might require simplified material.

Practice Sheets are followed in Appendix C by an answer key for every Practice Sheet, which allows students to use *English Fundamentals* independently as a drill and practice book. Students in composition classes who, for example, might need extra work on punctuation for compound sentences can find that section in the index, read the instruction and commentary, work through the Practice Sheets, and correct their work by referring to the answer key in Appendix C.

Variety in Exercises

In the minds of some, English texts that focus on the fundamentals of the language often limit student work to recognition, identification, and correction—a sort of fill-in-the-blanks scheme that doesn't require much actual writing. *English Fundamentals* requires such work as is necessary to build certain skills, but also incorporates a large number of exercises that require active production of sentences. Students will practice sentence combining and reducing independent clauses to various dependent clauses and phrases. They will learn to embed independent clauses in sentences and will rewrite sentences. They will transform active expressions to passive ones and vice versa, and change from direct to indirect quotation and from indirect to direct. They will write sentences to practice using various constructions. Research has shown, and we are convinced, that such active manipulation of the structures of language will greatly improve students' ability to write effectively and correctly.

Optional Testing Program

The tenth edition, like the ninth, offers additional tests. The Optional Testing Program is a package of thirty tests sent to instructors on request. These tests, not bound into the text, are printed on plain bond paper so that instructors may make copies, transfer tests to ditto masters, and make acetates for use with an overhead projector. These tests differ from the Progress Tests in the text in that they generalize, focusing on major concepts (for example, introductory subordinate elements) rather than specific constructions. The tests first ask for recognition of correct forms, then ask for generation of the new structure out of the basic parts. There is an answer key provided with the tests so that, in addition to use in evaluation, they can be used as higher-level practice exercises.

Additional Text Forms

As always, the tenth edition appears in three forms: A, B, and C. All three forms contain the same instructional material, but each comes with a different set of Practice Sheets and Exercises. The Practice Sheets and Exercises can be removed from the book without damaging the instructional sections, which can then be used as a comprehensive handbook for easy reference.

Acknowledgments

I am, as always, extremely grateful to the editor, Joseph Opiela, for good advice and continued encouragement, and to his fellow workers at Allyn & Bacon for their timely assistance. My thanks go out also to all those who offered advice and suggestions for improving the tenth edition. The following people gave opinions which were considered while developing the tenth edition: Edwin J. Blesch, Jr., Nassau Community College; Ladson W. Bright, Cape Fear Community College; Bernadine Brown, Nassau Community College; Kitty Chen Dean, Nassau Community College; Neil G. Dodd, East Los Angeles College; Loris D. Galford, McNeese State University; Harold J. Herman, University of Maryland; William T. Hope, Jefferson Technical College; Sue D. Hopke, Broward Community College; Clifford J. Houston, East Los Angeles College; George L. Ives, North Idaho College; Edward F. James, University of Maryland; Thomas Mast, Montgomery College; Walter Mullen, Mississippi Gulf Coast Community College; Mary E. Owens, Montgomery College; Crystal Reynolds, Indiana State University; Albert Schoenberg, East Los Angeles Community College; Ines Shaw, North Dakota State University; Barbara Stout, Montgomery College; and Robert S. Sweazy, Vincennes University Junior College.

P. L.

PART I · Basic Sentence Patterns

Lessons, Practice Sheets, and Exercises

LESSON 1 ·

The Simple Sentence; Subjects and Verbs

One way of defining a **sentence** is to say that it is an orderly arrangement of words that makes sense. If we wish to be more technical, we can say that a sentence is a self-contained grammatical unit, usually containing a subject and a verb, that conveys to the listener or the reader a meaningful assertion, question, command, or exclamation.

Despite the difficulty of producing a satisfying definition, we must acknowledge the importance of the sentence as a basic unit of written or oral expression. In the first few lessons of this book, we shall examine the parts that make up a sentence and the distinctive characteristics of a few basic types of sentences that are the underlying structures of more complicated grammatical units.

To begin our work, we must be sure that we can recognize the two indispensable parts of a sentence, the **subject** (the unit about which something is said) and the **predicate** (the unit that says something about the subject). Although the predicate usually includes other units such as modifiers and complements, which we shall examine later, the indispensable part of a predicate is the **verb.** Here are a few things to remember about the subject–verb relationship:

1. When the sentence is one that reports a specific action taking place, the verb usually displays itself prominently and is easily recognized. For instance, in "The rusty bumper on the front of my truck *rattles* noisily," the verb tells what happens—it is, unmistakably, *rattles*. Then, by asking the question "Who or what rattles?" we come up with the subject, *bumper;* notice that neither "Front rattles" nor "Truck rattles" tells us exactly what the sentence means.

2. The function of many sentences, however, is not to report that the subject *does* something. Instead, the purpose is to say something about the *condition* of the subject: to point out a descriptive quality of it or to say that something else resembles or is the same thing as the subject. In this kind of sentence you must look for verbs like *am, are, is, was, were, seem,* and *become,* words that are almost impossible to define because they lack the concrete exactness and action of verbs like *rattle, throw, injure,* and *explode.* In the descriptive type of sentence, the subject usually reveals itself easily. For example, in "The long first *chapter* seemed particularly difficult," the *who* or *what* about which the statement is being made—in other words, the subject—is *chapter.*

1

"Chapter particularly" or "Chapter difficult" in no way resembles a statement. But "Chapter seemed," although incomplete, does sound like a statement, or at least the nucleus of a statement; therefore the verb is *seemed.*

3. Very often the true subject has material intervening between it and its verb:

The *price* of potatoes *is* high. [The subject is *price,* not *potatoes.*]
Each of my sisters is *blonde.* [The subject is *each,* not *sisters.*]
Only *one* of these watches *works.* [The subject is *one,* not *watches.*]

4. The normal order of the modern English sentence places the subject before the verb. We sometimes use sentences, however, beginning with some kind of adverbial modification, in which the verb precedes the subject:

Behind the house *stood* [verb] an old *mill* [subject].

A very common type of sentence with the inverted subject–verb arrangement uses *here* or *there* preceding the verb:

There *are* [verb] three willow *trees* [subject] in our yard.
Here *is* [verb] the *list* [subject] of candidates.

5. To represent casual, informal language, we often combine short verbs and subjects, with apostrophes representing the omitted letters:

I'm (I am)   It's (It is)   You've (You have)   They're (They are)

For our first practice work we shall use only one-word subjects. With this limitation the subject is always a noun or a pronoun. We should now remind ourselves of a few facts about the *form* of nouns, pronouns, and verbs, so that we can easily recognize them.

A **noun** is a word that names something, such as a person, a place, a thing, a quality, or an idea. A noun is called a *common noun* and is not capitalized if it names just any member of a group or class *(man, city, school, relative)*; it is called a *proper noun* and is capitalized if it names a particular individual in a group or class *(Albert Lawson, Toledo, Horace Mann Junior High School, Aunt Louise).*

Most nouns have two forms; they show whether the noun is naming one thing (singular number) or more than one thing (plural number, which adds *s* or *es* to the singular): one *coat,* two *coats;* a *lunch,* several *lunches.* Proper nouns are rarely pluralized, and some common nouns have no plural form, for example, *honesty, courage, ease,* and *hardness.* (Lesson 28 examines in detail the special spelling problems of plural nouns.)

Nouns often follow *the, a,* or *an,* which are called **articles.** A descriptive word (an adjective) may come between the article and the noun. But the word that answers the question "What?" after an article is a noun:

A (*or* The) happy _____ (The space must be filled with a noun.)

Another aid in identifying nouns is the recognition of certain suffixes. (See Supplement 1.)* Here are some of the common suffixes we find on hundreds of nouns:

age [break*age*]; ance, ence [resist*ance*, insist*ence*]; dom [king*dom*]; hood [child*hood*]; ion [prevent*ion*]; ism [national*ism*]; ment [move*ment*]; ness [firm*ness*]; or, er [invest*or*, los*er*]; ure [expos*ure*]

A **pronoun** is a word that substitutes for a noun. There are several classes of pronouns. (See Supplement 2.) The following classes can function as subjects in the basic sentences that we will be examining in these early lessons:

- Personal, used to substitute for definite persons or things: *I, you, he, she, it, we, they.*
- Demonstrative, used to substitute for things being pointed out: *this, that, these, those.*
- Indefinite, used to substitute for unknown or unspecified things: *each, either, neither, one, anyone, somebody, everything, all, few, many,* and so on.
- Possessive, used to substitute for things that are possessed: *mine, yours, his, hers, its, ours, theirs.*

A **verb** is a word that expresses action, existence, or occurrence by combining with a subject to make a statement, to ask a question, or to give a command. One easy way for you to identify a word as a verb is to use the following slot test:

Let's _____ [something].

Any word that will function in this position to complete the command is a verb: "Let's *leave.*" "Let's *buy* some popcorn." "Let's *be* quiet." This test works only with the basic present form of the verb, not with forms that have endings added to them or that show action taking place in the past: "Let's *paint* the car." (not "Let's *painted* the car.").

Supplement 1

A **suffix** is a unit added to the end of a word or base, making a derived form. A similar unit added to the beginning of a word is called a **prefix.** Thus, to the adjective *kind,* we add a prefix to derive another adjective, *unkind,* and a suffix to derive the nouns *kindness* and *unkindness.* An awareness of how suffixes are used will do far more than aid you in your ability to recognize parts of speech: Your spelling will improve and your vocabulary will expand as well.

Hundreds of nouns have distinctive suffix endings. The definitions of some of these suffixes are rather difficult to formulate, but you can quite readily figure out the meanings of most of them: *ness,* for instance, means "quality or state of" (thus *firmness*

---

*In some lessons of this book you will find notations referring you to a supplement that is appended at the end of the lesson. Read the supplement *after* you have thoroughly studied the lesson. The lesson contains the essential information that is vital to your understanding of subsequent lessons and exercises. The supplement presents material that has relevance to some points of the lesson but has only incidental application to the lessons and exercises that follow. The supplements at the end of this lesson are found on pages 3–4.

means "the state or quality of being firm"); *or* and *er* show the agent or doer of something (an *investor* is "one who invests").

Supplement 2

Two classes of pronouns, the **interrogative** and the **relative,** are not listed here. Because they are used in questions and subordinate clauses but not in simple basic sentences, they will not be discussed until later lessons.

Another type of pronoun that you use regularly (but not as a true subject) is the **intensive** or **reflexive** pronoun, the "self" words used to add emphasis:

You *yourself* made the decision.

or to name the receiver of an action when the doer is the same as the receiver:

The boy fell and hurt *himself.*

The first example is the intensive use; the second is the reflexive. Pronouns used this way are *myself, yourself, himself* (not *hisself*), *herself, itself, ourselves, yourselves,* and *themselves* (not *themself, theirself,* or *theirselves*).

The "self" pronouns are properly used for only these two purposes. They should not be substituted for regular personal pronouns:

Mary and I [not *myself*] were invited to the dance.
Tom visited Eric and me [not *myself*] at our ranch.

Practice Sheet 1
Subjects and Verbs

NAME _____ SCORE _____

Directions: In the space at the left, copy the word that is the verb of the italicized subject.

_____ 1. *Another* of her many virtues is her delightful sense of humor.

_____ 2. *One* of Peg's best friends accompanied her to the courthouse.

_____ 3. From the inner office came the staccato *rattle* of typewriters.

_____ 4. Only *two* of the incumbents sought reelection.

_____ 5. *Mother,* along with three of her old friends, attended the recital.

_____ 6. Within walking distance of our house are three *theaters.*

_____ 7. And there in the lobby of the theater stood an old college *chum* of mine.

_____ 8. *Either* of those two applicants seems qualified for the job.

_____ 9. Behind the city hall stands our recently built *jail.*

_____ 10. The *report* from the investigative committee whitewashed the county officials.

_____ 11. Not *one* of my algebra problems was correct.

_____ 12. Nearby was an untended, weed-choked apple *orchard.*

_____ 13. A *few* of the young people helped in the kitchen.

_____ 14. Deep down in the heart of even the most timid person is a *desire* for approval.

_____ 15. There are *murmurs* of disapproval from the rural voters.

_____ 16. Only a *few* of our group found seats on the crowded bus.

_____ 17. *One* of my classmates taped Dr. Trump's lecture for me.

_____ 18. Directly behind us was a small foreign-made *car.*

_____ 19. The *tallest* of the three boys approached the car.

_____ 20. On this delicate matter there is no *possibility* of compromise.

5

Directions: In the space at the left, copy the word that is the subject of the italicized verb.

_____ 1. Neither of these remedies *proved* helpful.

_____ 2. From the rear of the auditorium *came* a few boos.

_____ 3. One of the major networks *televised* the trial.

_____ 4. The shorter of the two men *waved* to the passing motorists.

_____ 5. High on the list of legislative problems *is* tax reform.

_____ 6. Every morning one of the children *brought* Ms. Simms a flower from the garden.

_____ 7. After the long and tedious lecture there *was* no time for questions.

_____ 8. All of the visiting relatives *departed* on the ten-o'clock bus.

_____ 9. At the other gate *stood* a tall and ominous looking guard.

_____ 10. There *goes* Mrs. Stewart's teenage daughter with her two admirers.

_____ 11. One of the hunters cautiously *entered* the abandoned cabin.

_____ 12. There very likely *is* some logical explanation for Terry's odd behavior.

_____ 13. Most of the county roads badly *need* resurfacing.

_____ 14. The three of us *thumbed* our way back to the campus.

_____ 15. One of our regular clerks *is* always on duty in the office on Saturday mornings.

_____ 16. Here *are* a few foreign stamps for your daughter's collection.

_____ 17. Behind the main house *stands* a small cottage for guests.

_____ 18. From these cottages *comes* some of the finest lace in the country.

_____ 19. After a slow start, the series of lectures *proved* instructive and entertaining.

_____ 20. Our guide, along with three of the boys, *explored* the cave.

EXERCISE 1

SUBJECTS AND VERBS

NAME _____ SCORE _____

Directions: In the first space at the left, copy the subject of the sentence. In the second space, copy the verb.

_____   1. After the holiday, all of the children returned to school.
_____

_____   2. To everyone's surprise, the coach benched our star fullback.
_____

_____   3. Either of these government bulletins is available now.
_____

_____   4. The possibility of additional funding is quite remote.
_____

_____   5. Many of the caged animals seemed restless.
_____

_____   6. The older of our two sons works in San Antonio.
_____

_____   7. From a side passage in the mine came a faint moan.
_____

_____   8. Most of the chairperson's remarks were humorless.
_____

_____   9. Four of our district managers retired last year.
_____

_____   10. There is always a place for constructive criticism in our office.
_____

_____   11. And in this corner is the defending middleweight champion.
_____

_____   12. At a table close to ours were several noisy German tourists.
_____

_____   13. The last of the skiers returned to the chalet shortly before
_____   nightfall.

_____   14. Not one of the standard American tires fits my car.
_____

_____   15. At the dictator's side stood a burly guard.
_____

_____   16. A shipment of badly needed medical supplies left Baltimore
_____   yesterday.

_____   17. One of Mr. Jackson's proudest possessions is his collection of
_____   old railroad timetables.

_____   18. Almost half of the freight cars left the tracks on the sharp
_____   curve.

_____   19. And thus ends the sad story of my career in banking.
_____

_____ 20. A period of tension and mistrust followed the election.
_____

_____ 21. The lure of sudden wealth drew thousands to the gold fields.
_____

_____ 22. Near my aunt's farm lived a retired FBI agent.
_____

_____ 23. Only the presence of the National Guardsmen prevented further trouble.
_____

_____ 24. Most of these interesting religious pamphlets are no longer in print.
_____

_____ 25. No person in that unhappy country is safe from arrest.
_____

_____ 26. On the mantel in the living room was an old-fashioned cuckoo clock.
_____

_____ 27. Here's a corrected copy of the chairperson's speech.

_____ 28. A bank of ominous black clouds moved in from the south.
_____

_____ 29. Some of the older boys obviously shirked their responsibilities.
_____

_____ 30. Someone in the editorial office blue-penciled my manuscript unmercifully.
_____

_____ 31. The cut in the state appropriation bill worries all educators.
_____

_____ 32. Next on the agenda is a report from the capital spending committee.
_____

_____ 33. There's only one appointment available this morning.
_____

_____ 34. At the head of the lake lies a small fishing resort.
_____

_____ 35. Here comes the town bully with two of his henchmen.
_____

_____ 36. Both of those payments are now long overdue.
_____

_____ 37. The mayor, together with two of her assistants, met with the delegation.
_____

_____ 38. In the basement, next to the furnace room, is an unfinished recreation room.
_____

_____ 39. We're no longer on speaking terms.
_____

_____ 40. Among our fondest memories is our visit with you last year in Vancouver.
_____

LESSON 2 ■
Verbs, Adjectives, Adverbs, and Prepositions

In Lesson 1 you learned how to recognize a verb. The verb form that you examined then is called the **base** or **infinitive;** it is the form that "names" the verb. Verbs change their form according to various conditions, three of which are person, number, and tense. (Two other conditions that can affect the form of a verb, *voice* and *mood,* will be called to your attention in later lessons after we have studied the basic sentence patterns.) You should learn the most important of these forms, the ones that occur in nearly every sentence that you speak or write.

Person distinguishes the person(s) speaking (first person: *I, we*), the person(s) spoken to (second person: *you*), and the person(s) or thing(s) spoken about (third person: *he, she, it, they*). **Number** shows whether the reference is to one thing (singular number) or to more than one thing (plural number). **Tense** refers to the time represented in the utterance, whether it applies to the present moment (I *believe* him) or to some other time (I *believed* him, I *will believe* him). (See Supplement 1.)

To demonstrate these changes in form, we can use a chart or arrangement called a *conjugation.* In the partial conjugation that follows, three verbs are used: *earn, grow,* and *be.* The personal pronoun subjects are included to show how the person and number of the subject affect the form of the verb.

Indicative Mood
Active Voice

	Singular Number	*Plural Number*
	Present Tense	
1st Person	I earn, grow, am	We earn, grow, are
2nd Person	You earn, grow, are	You earn, grow, are
3rd Person	*He earns, grows, is	They earn, grow, are
	Past Tense	
1st Person	I earned, grew, was	We earned, grew, were
2nd Person	You earned, grew, were	You earned, grew, were
3rd Person	He earned, grew, was	They earned, grew, were

*The pronoun *he* is arbitrarily used here to represent the third-person singular subject, which may be any singular pronoun *(she, it, who, nobody);* singular noun *(girl, neighbor, elephant, misunderstanding, Alice, James Archibald Peabody III);* or word groups constituting certain types of phrases or clauses that will be studied in later lessons.

Future Tense

1st Person	I shall earn, grow, be	We shall earn, grow, be
2nd Person	You will earn, grow, be	You will earn, grow, be
3rd Person	He will earn, grow, be	They will earn, grow, be

Present Perfect Tense

1st Person	I have earned, grown, been	We have earned, grown, been
2nd Person	You have earned, grown, been	You have earned, grown, been
3rd Person	He has earned, grown, been	They have earned, grown, been

Past Perfect Tense

1st Person	I had earned, grown, been	We had earned, grown, been
2nd Person	You had earned, grown, been	You had earned, grown, been
3rd Person	He had earned, grown, been	They had earned, grown, been

Future Perfect Tense

1st Person	I shall have earned, grown, been	We shall have earned, grown, been
2nd Person	You will have earned, grown, been	You will have earned, grown, been
3rd Person	She will have earned, grown, been	They will have earned, grown, been

Notice that in the past tense *earn* adds an *ed* ending but *grow* changes to *grew.* This difference illustrates regular and irregular verbs, the two groups into which all English verbs are classed. *Earn* is a regular verb and *grow* is an irregular verb. Lesson 21 lists many irregular verbs and examines certain usage problems that come from confusion between regular and irregular verbs. Notice also that some of the verb forms consist of more than one word *(will earn, have grown, will have been).* In such uses, *will* and *have* are called **auxiliary verbs.** More auxiliary verbs are examined in Lesson 5.

With the "naming" words (nouns and pronouns) and the "action" words (verbs), we can construct true sentences:

Harriet arrived.
He laughed.
Power corrupts.

But for the production of more varied and complete sentences we rely on the "describing" words (adjectives and adverbs) and on prepositional phrases.

An **adjective** is a word that describes or limits—that is, gives qualities to—a noun. The positions in which adjectives are found within the sentence are (1) preceding a noun that is in any of the noun positions within the sentence (The *small* child left. He is a *small* child. I saw the *small* child. I gave it to the *small* child); (2) following a describing (linking) verb and modifying the subject (The child is *small.* Mary looked *unhappy.* We became *upset*); and, less often, (3) directly following the noun (He provided the money *necessary* for the trip. The hostess, *calm* and *serene,* entered the hall).

Certain characteristics of form and function help us to recognize adjectives. There are several suffixes that, when added to other words or roots of other words, form adjectives. Here again, an understanding of the meaning of a suffix can save trips to the dictionary. For instance, in the hundreds of adjectives ending in *able (ible)*, the suffix means "capable of" or "tending to"; thus *usable* means "capable of being used" and *changeable* means "tending to change."

> able, ible [read*able*, irresist*ible*]; al [internation*al*]; ant, ent [resist*ant*, diverg*ent*]; ar [lun*ar*]; ary [budget*ary*]; ful [meaning*ful*]; ic, ical [cosm*ic*, hyster*ical*]; ish [fool*ish*]; ive [inven*tive*]; less [blame*less*]; ous [glamor*ous*]; y [greas*y*]

(One word of warning: Many other words in English *end* with these letters, but you can easily see that they are not employing the suffix. T*able*, ferm*ent*, arr*ive*, d*ish*, and pon*y*, for instance, are not adjectives.)

Nearly all adjectives, when they are used in comparisons, can be strengthened or can show degree by changing form or by using *more* and *most:*

> *great* trust, *greater* trust, *greatest* trust
> *sensible* answer, *more sensible* answer, *most sensible* answer

The base form (*great* trust, *sensible* answer) is the **positive degree.** The second (*greater* trust, *more sensible* answer) is the **comparative degree.** It compares two things. The third (*greatest* trust, *most sensible* answer) is the **superlative degree** and distinguishes among three or more things. (See Supplement 2.)

Another modifier is the **adverb,** a word that modifies anything except a noun or a pronoun. Most adverbs modify verbs (He returned *soon*); others modify adjectives and other adverbs (The *very* old man walked *quite* slowly); and some modify whole sentences (*Consequently,* we refused the offer).

Adverbs tell certain things about the verb, the most common being:

1. Manner: John performed *well.* We worked *hard.* The child laughed *happily. Gladly* would I change places with you.
2. Time: I must leave *now.* I'll see you *later. Soon* we shall meet *again.*
3. Frequency: We *often* go on picnics, *sometimes* at the lake but *usually* in the city park.
4. Place: *There* he sat, alone and silent. *Somewhere* we shall find peace and quiet.
5. Direction: The police officer turned *away.* I moved *forward* in the bus.
6. Degree: I could *scarcely* hear the speaker. I *absolutely* refuse to believe that story.

This classification gives a helpful clue to the recognition of the most frequently used adverbs, which supply the answers to such questions as "How?" (manner), "When?" (time or frequency), and "Where?" (place).

Adverbs of a subclass called **intensifiers** modify adjectives or adverbs but not verbs: a *very* good meal, his *quite* surprising reply, *too* often, *somewhat* reluctantly, and so on.

Many adverbs change form the way adjectives do to show degree:

> to drive *fast,* to drive *faster,* to drive *fastest*
> to perform *satisfactorily,* to perform *more satisfactorily,* to perform *most satisfactorily*

(See Supplement 3.)

A **preposition** is a word that introduces a phrase and shows the relationship between its object and some other word in the sentence. Notice that many prepositions show a relationship of space or time. Here are some common prepositions; those in the last column are called *group prepositions:*

about	beside	inside	through	according to
above	besides	into	throughout	because of
across	between	like	till	by way of
after	beyond	near	to	in addition to
against	by	of	toward	in front of
around	down	off	under	in place of
at	during	on	until	in regard to
before	except	out	up	in spite of
behind	for	outside	upon	instead of
below	from	over	with	on account of
beneath	in	since	without	out of

Every preposition has an object; with its object and any modifiers, the preposition makes a prepositional phrase. You can easily illustrate the function of prepositions by constructing sentences like the following:

After breakfast I walked *to* town *without* my friend. [Objects: *breakfast, town, friend.*]
On account of the rain, I canceled my plans *for* a game *of* tennis *at* the park *with* John.
  [Objects: *rain, game, tennis, park, John.*]
The trees *outside* the window *of* the kitchen are full *of* blossoms *during* the spring. [Objects: *window, kitchen, blossoms, spring.*]

Supplement 1

An awareness of the changes in verb forms is necessary before you can understand why certain of these forms are preferred over others in given sentences, why a careful speaker is expected to say, for instance, "The price of eggs *is* (not *are*) rising" or "I *saw* (not *seen*) him recently." Usage problems of this type are examined in Lessons 21 and 22.

Supplement 2

There are other classes of words that modify nouns but differ somewhat in form and use from the true adjectives. But when we concentrate on the *functions* of the various kinds of words, we can safely classify as adjectives all words that precede nouns and limit their meaning, including articles, numerals, and possessives (*an* apple, *the* weather, *my three* roommates); modifiers that can be used also as pronouns (*these* people, *some* friends, *all* workers); and nouns that modify other nouns (*basketball* players, *summer* days, *crop* failures).

Many words can be used as adjectives or as pronouns; the position of a word within the sentence determines which part of speech it is:

Several [*adj.*] classmates of mine [*pron.*] read this [*adj.*] report.
Several [*pron.*] of my [*adj.*] classmates read this [*pron.*].

Supplement 3

A few commonly used modifiers form their comparative and superlative degrees irregularly:

good *(adj.)*,   better,   best
well *(adv.)*,   better,   best
bad *(adj.)*,   worse,   worst

Practice Sheet 2
Parts of Speech

NAME _____ SCORE _____

Directions: In each space at the left, write one of the following numbers to identify the part of speech of each italicized word:

1. Noun	3. Verb	5. Adverb
2. Pronoun	4. Adjective	6. Preposition

_____   1. We should *next* discuss the changes in the time *schedule.*
_____

_____   2. The chairperson *scheduled* a meeting for *next* Friday.
_____

_____   3. The attorney was *openly* hostile *toward* the first witness.
_____

_____   4. Two prisoners *opened* a window and were *able* to escape.
_____

_____   5. *Most* of the volunteers performed *ably.*
_____

_____   6. *Most* critics praised the aging actor's *performance.*
_____

_____   7. Theatergoers greeted the star *most enthusiastically.*
_____

_____   8. I faced the opening of winter term *without* much *enthusiasm.*
_____

_____   9. *Each* member of the local fire department received *some* of the reward
_____   money.

_____ 10. The storekeeper *rewarded each* of the boys with some jelly beans.

_____ 11. I *sometimes* question Jensen's *willingness* to work hard for our cause.
_____

_____ 12. *During* these war years, citizens *willingly* gave up luxuries.
_____

_____ 13. Many of *these* high officials led *luxurious* lives.
_____

_____ 14. *These* could be the most *productive* years of your life.
_____

_____ 15. Attempts to settle the *warfare between* the two provinces were unproduc-
_____   tive.

_____ 16. Our office *received* a notice *about* your promotion.
_____

_____ 17. Radio *reception* was affected *noticeably* by the tropical storm.
_____

_____ 18. The committee will be *receptive* to any new *proposals.*
_____

_____ 19. *Peggy* stood up and *straightened* her tie.
_____

_____ 20. The road *over* the mountain is narrow but quite *straight*.
_____

_____ 21. Bernard *thumbed* a ride back to the campus with a *talkative* truck driver.
_____

_____ 22. The nurse handed *me* a bandage for my injured *thumb*.
_____

_____ 23. Some economists *gloomily* predicted a period of economic *chaos*.
_____

_____ 24. The first few days of a new school term are *usually* quite *chaotic*.
_____

_____ 25. For the next week the soccer team *practiced* long and *hard*.
_____

_____ 26. The team put in a week of long and *hard practice*.
_____

_____ 27. The tourists were not *happy* about the long *wait*.
_____

_____ 28. A *few* of the tourists *waited* for the next bus.
_____

_____ 29. *Few* graduate students will accept this new regulation *happily*.
_____

_____ 30. Jerry's *helpful* neighbor made a *fast* trip to the bus depot.
_____

_____ 31. John sometimes drives too *fast for* his passengers' comfort.
_____

_____ 32. The nurse *comforted* the *other* patients.
_____

_____ 33. *Others* have noticed the *change* in Betty's behavior.
_____

_____ 34. The weather *changed noticeably* in the next week.
_____

_____ 35. *Before* the end of the month, a *notice* will be sent to all subscribers.
_____

_____ 36. The water level *behind* the dam rose *alarmingly*.
_____

_____ 37. The sudden *rise* in prices *alarmed* some economists.
_____

_____ 38. The *playful* kitten ran *away* from the noisy youngsters.
_____

_____ 39. A pantomime might be called a *noiseless play*.
_____

_____ 40. The team played *best during* the final month of the season.
_____

EXERCISE 2
PARTS OF SPEECH

NAME _____ SCORE _____

Directions: In each space at the left, write one of the following numbers to identify the part of speech of each italicized word:

1. Noun	3. Verb	5. Adverb
2. Pronoun	4. Adjective	6. Preposition

_____ 1. "I've been waiting *here* for nearly an hour," *complained* Mr. Smiley.

_____ 2. Her *complaint surely* seems justified.

_____ 3. "Are you *fully aware* of your legal rights?" asked the judge.

_____ 4. *By* two o'clock the auditorium was almost *full*.

_____ 5. Imagine my *surprise* at seeing a *roomful* of people.

_____ 6. The *elders* of the tribe were *surprisingly* agreeable to the plan.

_____ 7. Many *elderly* people were left *without* adequate housing.

_____ 8. "*Patience* is not one of my husband's virtues," she replied *sorrowfully*.

_____ 9. "I'm truly *sorry* about *that*," replied the cashier.

_____ 10. "*That* briefcase is not *mine*," replied the young man.

_____ 11. Your essay *needs* a *more* effective opening paragraph.

_____ 12. The mayor's remarks seemed *needlessly apologetic*.

_____ 13. The flight attendant *apologized* for the *delay*.

_____ 14. Mark *delayed* his return to Chicago *until* two days after Christmas.

_____ 15. *Most* of *these* problems have been solved.

_____ 16. *These* are our *most* urgent problems.

_____ 17. *Some* of the protesters stayed in the hallway *throughout* the lunch hour.

_____ 18. It was his *custom* to eat lunch with *other* managers in the company
_____   cafeteria.

_____ 19. Jensen *customarily lunched* in the company cafeteria.

_____ 20. *Others* have *occasionally* complained about the slow service.

Directions: Each of these words is labeled as a noun, verb, adjective, or adverb. In the spaces following each word, write related words of the part of speech indicated. (Do not use adjectives ending in *ing* or *ed*.)

Example: wide (adj.)   width (n.)   widen (v.)

 1. activate (v.)   _____(n.)   _____(n.)

 2. agreeable (adj.)   _____(n.)   _____(v.)

 3. competition (n.)   _____(v.)   _____(adj.)

 4. conclusive (adj.)   _____(n.)   _____(v.)

 5. creativity (n.)   _____(adj.)   _____(v.)

 6. defense (n.)   _____(adv.)   _____(v.)

 7. delight (n.)   _____(adv.)   _____(v.)

 8. doubt (n.)   _____(v.)   _____(adj.)

 9. falsify (v.)   _____(adj.)   _____(n.)

10. freshly (adv.)   _____(n.)   _____(v.)

11. gladness (n.)   _____(v.)   _____(adv.)

12. hunger (n.)   _____(v.)   _____(adv.)

13. informal (adj.)   _____(n.)   _____(adv.)

14. largely (adv.)   _____(adj.)   _____(v.)

15. mad (adj.)   _____(n.)   _____(v.)

16. probably (adv.)   _____(n.)   _____(adj.)

17. progress (v.)   _____(adj.)   _____(n.)

18. satisfy (v.)   _____(n.)   _____(adv.)

19. scandalous (adj.)   _____(n.)   _____(v.)

20. scarce (adj.)   _____(n.)   _____(adv.)

EXERCISE 2A
SUBJECTS AND VERBS

NAME _____ SCORE _____

Directions: In the first space at the left, copy the word that is the subject of the sentence. In the second space, copy the verb. Many of the verbs consist of more than one word.

_____ 1. Neither of her parents had graduated from high school.
_____

_____ 2. There were, unfortunately, no really rich alumni among the
_____ school's graduates.

_____ 3. You should, of course, have answered the note.

_____ 4. There followed an honest but useless summary of our past
_____ mistakes.

_____ 5. Either of these two policies should lead to a peaceful settle-
_____ ment.

_____ 6. In recent years the increase in enrollment in adult-education
_____ classes has been great.

_____ 7. And there, in the middle of the bare stage and with a look of
_____ bewilderment on her face, stood our new drama coach.

_____ 8. Some of these fraudulent schools actually sold diplomas.
_____

_____ 9. One of the tires on the truck had developed a slow leak.
_____

_____ 10. There very likely is a good reason for his refusal.
_____

_____ 11. On the gate was a small typewritten note.
_____

_____ 12. Only a few of Tucker's friends attended the graduation
_____ ceremony.

_____ 13. One of the best displays at the museum is a collection of
_____ ritual masks from Africa.

_____ 14. On a shelf at the rear of the store stood a keg of pungent dill
_____ pickles.

_____ 15. The presence of a neutral mediator at the conference pre-
_____ vented the outbreak of violence.

_____ 16. And over here, near the cashier's desk, is a supply of extra
_____ application forms.

_____ 17. After the first lecture, a few of the new students asked
_____ Dr. Ashe for a conference.

_____ 18. Onto the dusty plains of Oklahoma surged the throngs of
_____ homeseekers.

_____ 19. At the end of the convocation, each of the flag bearers
_____ marched to the center of the stage.

_____ 20. On the scarecrow's head rested a tall, black hat.
_____

_____ 21. Not one member of the tour group could speak Italian.
_____

_____ 22. By this time some of Herb's creditors were becoming insistent.
_____

_____ 23. From the debris of the wrecked house came the faint sound of
_____ a dog's whimpering.

_____ 24. The stack of unanswered letters on my desk is slowly dimin-
_____ ishing.

_____ 25. There will probably be the usual delay at the license counter.
_____

_____ 26. By nine o'clock the last of the guests had departed.
_____

_____ 27. The youngest of their four daughters will soon be leaving for
_____ college.

_____ 28. Neither of these two models has found favor with the buying
_____ public.

_____ 29. Both of you should have apologized for your rudeness to the
_____ host.

_____ 30. In all of his later plays, a theme of world-weariness recurs.
_____

_____ 31. The first draft, along with your outline and bibliography, will
_____ be due next Thursday.

_____ 32. The first of Jackson's many interviews with the dictator took
_____ place in July.

_____ 33. This could very well mean the end of our long friendship.
_____

_____ 34. A few of the last withered leaves of the season were still cling-
_____ ing to the boughs.

_____ 35. Sitting in the rear seat of the limousine was a haughty Persian
_____ cat.

_____ 36. Neither of us has ever questioned your motives.
_____

_____ 37. One out of every three of our graduates will work toward an
_____ advanced degree.

_____ 38. The remaining part of the special order of embossed cards
_____ should arrive before the end of the month.

_____ 39. The absurdity of the situation soon became clear to all of us.
_____

_____ 40. Not many of the students in the class had taken notes on the
_____ lecture.

LESSON 3 ∎

Basic Sentence Patterns with Intransitive Verbs

You may be surprised to learn that, in spite of the apparent complexity of English sentences, there are only a few *basic* patterns into which words can be arranged and still make sense. In this lesson and the following lesson, we shall examine five basic sentence patterns, which you should think of as the simplest units of communication. If you learn to recognize these five basic patterns, you will feel more secure later in your study of more complicated sentences, most of which are combinations of basic sentences or well-defined and orderly alterations of them.

Each of the five basic sentence types is distinguished from the others by the nature of the verb, that is, (1) whether a complement ("completer") must be added, and (2) the kind of complement that must be added if the subject–verb combination by itself does not make a complete statement. The first determination must be whether a verb use is transitive or intransitive.

A **transitive** verb names an activity performed by the subject *on* something. A transitive verb requires the addition of a direct object, the receiver of the action:

Today I *saw* _____. (A "something" is required.)
I *found* _____. (A "something" is required.)
All of us *appreciate* _____. (A "something" is required.)

As we shall learn in the next lesson, where we examine transitive verbs and the direct object in detail, these subject–verb combinations make sense only when some noun is added to show what received the action:

Today I saw a *bear.*
I found some *money.*
All of us appreciate your *kindness.*

An **intransitive** verb does not require a direct object; in other words, an intransitive verb does not name an activity that is carried over to or performed on something. In this lesson we shall study the two basic sentence patterns that use intransitive verbs.

Sentence Pattern 1 contains an intransitive verb and is the only basic sentence that does not require a complement.

Sample Sentence: The child runs.

This pattern can be represented as follows:

S.—V.i.,
N.—V.i.

with the *V.i.* standing for "intransitive verb," the kind of verb in which no action is performed on or transferred to anything. Pattern 1 sentences nearly always contain modifiers:

Yesterday the neighborhood children played noisily in the vacant lot.

Notice that the material associated with the verb is all adverbial: *Yesterday* (When?), *noisily* (How?), *in the vacant lot* (Where?). All of these additions, of course, augment the total meaning of the verb, but the important characteristic of a Pattern 1 sentence is that there is no noun answering the question "What?" after the verb. Spotting the lack of a noun answering the question "What?" after the verb is the best way to recognize an intransitive verb.

In some Pattern 1 sentences, the purpose of the statement is to say no more than that the subject exists. Usually some adverbial material is added to show the place or the time of the existence:

The glasses *are* in the cabinet.
Flash floods often *occur* in the spring.
There *were* several birds around the feeder.

In most Pattern 1 sentences, however, some activity takes place, but no completer is needed because the action is not transferred to anything:

The tree *fell.*
The customer *complained* loudly.
The professor *walked* into the room unexpectedly.

Sentence Pattern 2 includes two closely related kinds of sentences. The purpose of the first type is to say that the subject is the same as something else, in other words, to rename the subject:

Sample Sentence: The child is a genius.

The noun or pronoun that renames the subject is called a **subjective complement,** because it completes the verb and renames the subject. The special type of intransitive verb that is used in Pattern 2 sentences is called the **link** or **linking verb** (V.lk.).

$$\text{S.} \quad \text{— V.lk. —} \quad \text{S.C.}$$
$$\text{(child)} \qquad \text{(is)} \qquad \text{(genius)}$$

Or we can also represent this sentence as follows:

$$N_x \text{ — V.lk. — } N_x$$

This kind of representation can be helpful; it shows that both of the noun units (*child* and *genius*) refer to the same thing. (See Supplement 1.)

In the second type of Pattern 2 sentence, the subjective complement is an adjective; it relates to the subject as a describer rather than as a renamer:

Sample Sentence: The child is clever.

S.   — V.lk. —   S.C.
(child)   (is)   (clever)
N.   — V.lk. —   Adj.

There are comparatively few verbs that have the linking function. We can conveniently think of them in three closely related groups:

1. *Be,* the most commonly used linking verb, and a few others meaning essentially the same thing: *seem, appear, prove, remain, continue,* and so forth.

John *is* a talented musician.
The performer *seemed* nervous.
He *remained* calm.
His *words proved* meaningless.

2. *Become* and a few others like it: *turn, grow, work, get, wear,* and so forth.

Later she *became* an accountant.
Soon he *grew* tired of the game.
Billy *turned* red from embarrassment.

3. A few verbs referring to the senses *(look, smell, taste, feel, sound),* which can be followed by adjective subjective complements that describe the condition of the subject. Ability to recognize this kind of N. — V.lk. — Adj. sentence pattern will help you understand a few troublesome usage problems that will be examined in a later lesson—to understand why, for instance, careful writers use "feel bad" rather than "feel badly."

The roses *look* beautiful in that vase.
This milk *tastes* sour.
I *feel* bad about the election results.

Supplement 1

A note about grammatical terminology is needed here. The noun following a linking verb and renaming the subject is sometimes called a *predicate noun* or a *predicate nominative;* and the adjective following a linking verb and describing the subject is sometimes called a *predicate adjective.*

Practice Sheet 3
Sentence Pattern 2

NAME _____   SCORE _____

Directions: Each of the following sentences is a Pattern 2 sentence containing a noun (or pronoun) subjective complement. In the space at the left, copy the subjective complement.

_____ 1. The three girls remained close friends for years after graduation.

_____ 2. The concert by the famous quartet will undoubtedly be the outstanding social event of the season.

_____ 3. The French-speaking bus driver proved a great help to all of us tourists.

_____ 4. The committee's usual meeting time is the second Wednesday of each month.

_____ 5. One of Bill's great-grandfathers had been a stagecoach driver in Nevada and California.

_____ 6. Cartwright eventually became a power in the local Teamsters' Union.

_____ 7. Psychology 212 is no longer one of the prerequisites for Psychology 450.

_____ 8. A pair of sturdy pack horses will be an absolute necessity for a trip over these rugged mountain trails.

_____ 9. The best-kept lawn on Maple Lane is yours.

_____ 10. This investment will, in time, prove a wise one.

_____ 11. In spite of his alibi, Lambert remains a suspect in the case.

_____ 12. To everyone's surprise, Ted became a moderately successful insurance salesman.

_____ 13. This seems the best time for a short vacation for the entire office force.

_____ 14. That jacket in the hallway is not mine.

_____ 15. My answer to the fourth problem on the test proved a lucky guess.

_____ 16. Your nephew has proved a valuable addition to our sales force.

_____ 17. The old man's four cats are a great comfort to him.

_____ 18. After that first game, Mother became a fanatic soccer fan.

_____ 19. In the face of all of these problems, my business partner remains an optimist.

_____ 20. Before long Seaview became one of the most popular resorts in the state.

25

Directions: Each of the following sentences is a Pattern 2 sentence containing an adjective subjective complement. In the space at the left, copy the subjective complement.

_____ 1. The new apartment will not be ready for us until next month.

_____ 2. The leaves of many of my house plants are turning brown.

_____ 3. At this high altitude, you will get tired after the slightest exertion.

_____ 4. Lucy appears shy in the presence of groups of older people.

_____ 5. He's much too inexperienced for this important position.

_____ 6. During the testimony of the first witness, the accused man looked completely relaxed.

_____ 7. Cravens Creek stayed frozen until mid-April last year.

_____ 8. Mr. Larkins keeps active in spite of his injured back.

_____ 9. This will be your last chance at these tremendous bargains.

_____ 10. Your behavior after your defeat at the polls was unworthy of you.

_____ 11. Because of its polluted condition, the beach is no longer usable.

_____ 12. With a few simple repairs, the old piano will not sound so tinny.

_____ 13. The soup tasted much too salty for me.

_____ 14. The air certainly smells fresh after that rainstorm.

_____ 15. During the winter, Grenfall grew more and more suspicious of his new partner's methods.

_____ 16. The boy's explanation for his absences from class sounded implausible.

_____ 17. Even after my long explanation, Laurie still seemed puzzled.

_____ 18. On a day like this, most of the children will feel listless.

_____ 19. Your candidate is, in my opinion, barely qualified for the job.

_____ 20. The weather continued cold for the next five days.

EXERCISE **3**

SENTENCE PATTERNS WITH INTRANSITIVE VERBS

NAME _____ SCORE _____

Directions: Circle the subject and underline the verb in each of the following sentences. If the sentence is a Pattern 2 sentence, copy the subjective complement in the space at the left. If the sentence is a Pattern 1 sentence, leave the space blank.

_____ 1. The last bus for Oakville had just pulled out of the station.

_____ 2. An ocelot is a medium-sized American wildcat with a tawny yellow or grayish coat.

_____ 3. To us trainees, the procedure looked hopelessly complicated.

_____ 4. By nightfall the mood of the mob had turned ugly.

_____ 5. With a barely audible snort of disgust, the receptionist turned away.

_____ 6. The weather is usually pleasant for our annual family-reunion picnic.

_____ 7. Halfway through the trial, Ben's chances looked somewhat better.

_____ 8. This is just another one of Aunt Beth's gloomy predictions.

_____ 9. Here are your assignments for the coming week.

_____ 10. This class looks more than usually bored this morning.

_____ 11. In time you'll get accustomed to our changeable weather.

_____ 12. By nightfall the weather had turned uncomfortably chilly.

_____ 13. The pictures on the front page of the old newspaper had faded badly.

_____ 14. The print on the front page of the old newspaper was barely readable.

_____ 15. All of us in the office have become quite tired of the boss's indecision.

_____ 16. Next week at this time the boss will be in Hawaii.

_____ 17. Next week at this time the boss will be incommunicado.

_____ 18. From the adjacent kitchen came the annoying sound of a steady drip from a leaky faucet.

_____ 19. Betty could become one of the best computer programmers in our class.

_____ 20. Behind the barn stand three tall fir trees.

_____ 21. Despite these pressures, Senator Burton stood firm in his opposition to the amendment.

_____ 22. A few of the apricots on my tree have ripened already.

_____ 23. A few of the apricots on my tree look ripe already.

_____ 24. That last remaining raincoat in the cloakroom is probably yours.

_____ 25. There is an interesting new movie at the Strand.

_____ 26. That was one of the best movies of the entire season.

_____ 27. The surface of the recently varnished bench still feels sticky.

_____ 28. Grandfather always has been an extremely gullible person.

_____ 29. Rusted hulks of landing craft from the war remain on the beach.

_____ 30. I still remain unconvinced of your new friend's motives.

_____ 31. No, I hardly feel well prepared for the final examination.

_____ 32. The western sky darkened ominously.

_____ 33. The western sky became ominously dark.

_____ 34. There's enough room in the back seat for two more passengers.

_____ 35. The old house stayed unoccupied for three years.

_____ 36. The evening paper was full of news about the invasion.

_____ 37. From his perch on the balcony, the officer looked intently through his binoculars.

_____ 38. The officer looked worried about something.

_____ 39. Her next scholarly project will be the translation of two modern Japanese novels.

_____ 40. I'm really upset about Mayor Tadwell's statement to the press.

LESSON 4 ∎

Basic Sentence Patterns with Transitive Verbs

In **Pattern 3** sentences, the verb names some activity and the subject is, of course, the doer of that activity, as it is in many Pattern 1 sentences. But in a Pattern 3 sentence, the subject and the verb, even with the addition of adverbial material, do not give a complete statement because the activity named in the verb is performed *on* something. This kind of verb is a transitive verb, for which we shall use the symbol *V.tr.*

Sample Sentence: The child plays a game.

The complement (completer) required with a transitive verb is the **direct object.** It names the receiver of the action; in other words, a transitive verb *trans*fers the action to an object. The direct object is always a noun or a noun equivalent, such as a pronoun, and we find it by asking the question "What?" of the transitive verb:

I broke my *glasses.* [What names the activity? *Broke* is the verb. Who did the action? *I* is the subject. What was broken? *Glasses* is the direct object.]
Someone threw *stones* at us. [What was thrown? *Stones* is the direct object.]

(See Supplement 1.)
We can represent this sentence pattern as follows:

$$\text{S.} \quad - \quad \text{V.tr.} \quad - \quad \text{D.O.}$$
$$\text{(child)} \qquad \text{(plays)} \qquad \text{(game)}$$

Another helpful representation is as follows: $N_x - V.tr. - N_y$. *N* stands for a noun or for a noun equivalent such as a pronoun. The small letters x and y show that the nouns refer to separate things: *I* and *glasses* are obviously not one and the same, nor are *someone* and *stones*. Contrast this formula with the formula for a Pattern 2 sentence with a noun subjective complement (The child is a genius: $N_x - V.lk. - N_x$). The Pattern 2 formula shows that the two noun units refer to the same thing (see the previous lesson).

Sentence Patterns 4 and 5 are alike in that both patterns require two complements to give meaning to the subject–verb unit. They differ quite distinctly, however, in the functional nature of the verb and the resultant structure of the sentences.

Pattern 4 sentences contain two complements, the indirect object and the direct object. The direct object, the receiver of the action, answers the question "Who?" or "What?" after the transitive verb. The **indirect object** answers a question such as "To whom (or which)?" or "For whom (or which)?" Thus, in the sentence "She sang a lullaby," we have a Pattern 3 sentence, but in "She sang the children a lullaby," we have a Pattern 4 sentence:

Sample Sentence: The child gives the parents pleasure.

$$\text{S.} \; — \; \text{V.tr.} \; — \; \text{I.O.} \; — \; \text{D.O.}$$

We can also chart this pattern as follows:

$$N_x \quad — \quad \text{V.tr.} \quad — \quad N_y \quad — \quad N_z$$
$$\text{(child)} \qquad \text{(gives)} \qquad \text{(parents)} \qquad \text{(pleasure)}$$

By this method we get a very important structural clue: all three of the noun elements refer to different things.

A typical verb for Pattern 4 is *give,* as in "The clerk gave me a refund." You can easily see why the two complements are used here: The sentence mentions the thing that is given (*refund,* the direct object) and also the person to whom the direct object is given (*me,* the indirect object). Although the indirect object usually names a person, it can name a nonhuman thing, as in "We gave your *application* a careful reading."

Other verbs that are commonly used this way and therefore produce a Pattern 4 structure are *allow, assign, ask, tell, write, send, show, pay, grant,* and so on. Nearly all sentences using such verbs can make essentially the same statement by using a prepositional phrase, the preposition usually being *to* or *for.* When the prepositional phrase is actually present in the sentence, it is a Pattern 3 sentence.

The postman brought me a letter. [Pattern 4; *me* is an indirect object.]
The postman brought a letter to me. [Pattern 3; me is the object of a preposition.]

Mother bought us some taffy. [Pattern 4.]
Mother bought some taffy for us. [Pattern 3.]

Pattern 5 consists of two closely related types of sentences. There are two complements in Pattern 5 sentences. The one closer to the verb is the direct object, and the second one is the **objective complement,** which we can define as a noun that *renames* the direct object or an adjective that *describes* the direct object:

Sample Sentences: The parents consider the child a genius.
The parents consider the child clever.
$$\text{S.} \; — \; \text{V.tr.} \; — \; \text{D.O.} \; — \; \text{O.C.}$$

In our method of representing sentences to show the parts of speech and the reference of the noun elements, these sentences would appear this way:

$$N_x \quad — \quad \text{V.tr.} \quad — \quad N_y \quad — \quad N_y$$
$$\text{(parents)} \qquad \text{(consider)} \qquad \text{(child)} \qquad \text{(genius)}$$
$$N_x \quad — \quad \text{V.tr.} \quad — \quad N_y \quad — \quad \text{Adj.}$$
$$\text{(parents)} \qquad \text{(consider)} \qquad \text{(child)} \qquad \text{(clever)}$$

The reference of the two nouns following the verb is a key to the difference between this type of sentence and a Pattern 4 sentence: In a Pattern 4 sentence, the two noun complements refer to separate things, but in a Pattern 5 sentence, they refer to the same thing. (See Supplement 2.)

Mother made us some fudge. [Pattern 4; *us* and *fudge* refer to separate things.]
This experience made John an activist. [Pattern 5; *John* and *activist* refer to the same thing.]

Because the objective complement renames or describes the direct object, we can use a handy ear test to help us recognize this pattern: The insertion of *to be* between the complements will give us an acceptable English idiom:

We appointed Jones [to be] our representative.
I thought this action [to be] unnecessary.

Sometimes the word *as* is used between the direct object and the objective complement:

We appointed Jones as our representative.

Some adjective objective complements are very important to the meaning of the verb. It is sometimes effective to place these objective complements immediately after the verb and before the direct object:

He set free [O.C.] the caged animals [D.O.].

Usual order: He set the caged animals free.

The following verbs are among those most commonly used in Pattern 5 sentences: *consider, call, think, find, make, elect, appoint,* and *name.*

Supplement 1

With one special kind of verb, there is a problem distinguishing between a direct object and the object of a preposition. Here are two examples:

Harry jumped off the box.
Harry took off his raincoat.

The first sentence is Pattern 1. *Off* is a preposition, *box* is the object of the preposition, and the prepositional phrase is used as an adverbial modifier, because it tells *where* Harry jumped. The second sentence is Pattern 3. The verb, with its adverbial modifier *off,* is the equivalent of the transitive verb *remove. Raincoat* is the direct object.

There is another way to distinguish between the adverbial use and the prepositional use of such a word as *off* in the preceding examples. When the word is a vital adverbial modifier of the verb, it can, in most cases, be used in either of two positions: immediately following the verb or following the direct object:

Harry took off his raincoat.
Harry took his raincoat off.

But when the word is a preposition, the alternate position is not possible: "Harry jumped the box off" is not an English sentence.

Here are some other examples of this kind of verb with adverbial modifier. Notice that in each case you can easily find a transitive verb synonym for the combination:

> . . . give up [relinquish] her rights.
> . . . leave out [omit] the second chapter.
> . . . put out [extinguish] the fire.
> . . . make over [alter] an old dress.
> . . . make up [invent] an excuse.*

Supplement 2

Noun reference symbols like N_x, N_y, and N_z are useful tools in distinguishing one sentence pattern from another. "John (N_x) met the senator (N_y)" is a Pattern 3 sentence: The two nouns represent separate, distinct persons. But "John (N_x) became a senator (N_x)" is Pattern 2 because the nouns refer to the same person.

These noun reference distinctions cannot be applied, however, in those occasional sentences that include a reflexive pronoun, one of the pronouns ending in *self*. Compare, for example, "John hurt the puppy" and "John hurt himself." In the second sentence, although *John* and *himself* are one and the same, the sentence is clearly Pattern 3: the verb is transitive and the action of the verb is transferred to *himself,* a direct object. This same irregularity—of noun reference, not of basic patterning—can also occur in Pattern 4 and Pattern 5 sentences:

> I bought my *son* a car. [S. — V.tr. — I.O. — D.O.]
> I bought myself a car. [S. — V.tr. — I.O. — D.O.]
>
> Laurie considers her mother a gourmet cook. [S. — V.tr. — D.O. — O.C.]
> Laurie considers herself a gourmet cook. [S. — V.tr. — D.O. — O.C.]

---

*You might try to recall as many meanings for *to make up* as you can. One modern desk dictionary gives seventeen.

Practice Sheet 4

Complements of Transitive Verbs

NAME _____ SCORE _____

Directions: Each of these sentences is a Pattern 3 sentence. In the space at the left, copy the direct object.

_____ 1. The collection agency expects your prompt response to this notice.

_____ 2. Our work in this course will cover American history up to the War of 1812.

_____ 3. The cat had knocked over one of Mother's vases.

_____ 4. Later today I'll look over your expense account.

_____ 5. According to most authorities, this popular over-the-counter remedy has little curative value.

_____ 6. Many in the audience left the room during the mayor's speech.

_____ 7. Ms. Scanlon wrote an excellent letter of recommendation for Ben.

_____ 8. I'll finish most of these chores this afternoon.

_____ 9. I've never understood the reason for these ridiculous laws.

_____ 10. The matron always turns off the dormitory lights at nine o'clock.

_____ 11. At the reunion Beth saw many of her old high school chums.

_____ 12. I'd like a piece of apple pie, please.

_____ 13. With my limited income, I could afford few luxuries.

_____ 14. Paul often inflicts his experimental desserts on his friends.

_____ 15. Among the five of us, we thought up three better endings for the movie.

_____ 16. After this concert, I will have heard all Beethoven's symphonies.

_____ 17. The angry manager pushed aside everything on the cluttered desk.

_____ 18. During those early months, the new bride attempted only the simplest meals.

_____ 19. The beautiful princess in the story rejected all of the suitors.

_____ 20. Cal finally bought the larger of the two used trucks.

Directions: The following are Pattern 3, 4, or 5 sentences. Identify the italicized complement by writing one of the following in the space at the left:

      D.O. (direct object)   I.O. (indirect object)   O.C. (objective complement)

_____   1. Sergeant Leams brought the *captain* new orders from headquarters.

_____   2. Judge Watts rarely gives a repeat *offender* another chance.

_____   3. You'll find most of these locals rather *standoffish.*

_____   4. The advance scouts found a shorter *route* over the mountain.

_____   5. My cousin found *us* a small rental cabin at Lake Stevens.

_____   6. A pinch of nutmeg will make this sauce more *flavorful.*

_____   7. A pinch of nutmeg will add more *flavor* to this sauce.

_____   8. A pinch of nutmeg will give this *sauce* added flavor.

_____   9. The salesman allowed *me* only three hundred dollars on the old car.

_____ 10. The salesman allowed me only three hundred *dollars* on the old car.

_____ 11. This new video should keep the youngsters *amused* for an hour or so.

_____ 12. For my birthday, I bought *myself* a shockingly expensive sweater.

_____ 13. The delegates elected Charley *chairperson* for the first session.

_____ 14. After only three days at camp, Clayton had acquired seven *demerits.*

_____ 15. I made two very silly *mistakes* on the first test.

_____ 16. These mistakes made me *angry* with myself.

_____ 17. For our camping trip, Grandmother made *us* five dozen cookies.

_____ 18. No one has ever called our mayor a brilliant *conversationalist.*

_____ 19. No one has ever called our *mayor* a brilliant conversationalist.

_____ 20. One of my uncles had taught me a few sleight-of-hand *tricks.*

EXERCISE 4

COMPLEMENTS

NAME _____ SCORE _____

Directions: Circle the subject and underline the verb in each of the following sentences. Identify the italicized complement by writing one of the following in the space at the left:

     S.C. [subjective complement]   D.O. [direct object]
     I.O. [indirect object]   O.C. [objective complement]

_____ 1. The city health authorities pronounced the apartment *unfit* for human habitation.

_____ 2. The teacher's comments at the end of the report proved *helpful.*

_____ 3. You customarily mail in your *payment* before the first of the month.

_____ 4. I will mail *you* each payment before the end of the month.

_____ 5. Paulson's grand-slam homer gave the *Warriors* the lead again.

_____ 6. To the family's amazement, Jerry became a really serious *student.*

_____ 7. In this good soil, we grow *dozens* of different kinds of vegetables.

_____ 8. Within ten minutes, the child had grown *bored* with the new toy.

_____ 9. At Elmwood Avenue, the police car turned off the *highway.*

_____ 10. The heavy moving van slowly turned into the *driveway.*

_____ 11. The mild-mannered librarian had apparently turned into a *monster.*

_____ 12. I'd call our review session a complete *waste* of time.

_____ 13. In six innings, Dawson allowed the *Cardinals* only two hits.

_____ 14. After a remarkably short deliberation, the jury pronounced him *guilty.*

_____ 15. These algebra problems look quite *simple* to me.

_____ 16. The storekeeper quickly washed off the offending *graffiti* from the window.

_____ 17. A major reduction in the size of the staff seems *inevitable.*

_____ 18. Gloria's resignation was a real *shock* to all of us.

_____ 19. These actions greatly lessened my *trust* in the city council.

_____ 20. Allan proudly showed the *rest* of us kids his new bike.

35

Directions: Using appropriate forms of the verbs indicated, write twenty original sentences illustrating the following patterns:

      Sentences 1–5: Pattern 2
      Sentences 6–10: Pattern 3
      Sentences 11–15: Pattern 4
      Sentences 16–20: Pattern 5

Circle every subjective complement and every direct object; underline with one line every indirect object; underline with two lines every objective complement.

1. be _____

2. appear _____

3. stay _____

4. become _____

5. feel _____

6. feel _____

7. hurt _____

8. entertain _____

9. deny _____

10. write _____

11. write _____

12. allow _____

13. bring _____

14. mail _____

15. elect _____

16. elect _____

17. pronounce _____

18. find _____

19. make _____

20. name _____

LESSON 5 ■

Forms of the Verb; Auxiliary Verbs

In this lesson we shall call attention to a few more forms and uses of verbs, including some additional auxiliary verbs. With these forms and those that you have already examined, you will be acquainted with nearly all verb forms that the average speaker and writer will ever use.

In Lesson 2 you examined a partial conjugation of three verbs, *earn, grow,* and *be.* Some of you may want to refer to that conjugation (pages 9–10) as we take note of a few more points about changes in form in verbs.

1. Remember that third-person singular verbs in the present tense end in *s* (or *es*): earn*s*, teach*es*, i*s*, ha*s*. Notice that on nouns the *s(es)* ending shows a plural form, whereas on verbs it shows a singular form.

2. The verb *be* is completely irregular. The conjugation shows you that, unlike any other verb in the language, it has three forms (*am, is,* and *are*) in the present tense and two forms (*was* and *were*) in the past tense.

3. In general, the tenses are used as follows:

- Present: Action occurring at the present moment: He *earns* a good salary.
- Past: Action occurring at a definite time before the present moment: Last year he *earned* a good salary.
- Future: Action occurring at some time beyond the present moment: Next year he *will earn* a good salary.
- Present perfect: Action continuing to the present moment: So far this year he *has earned* ten thousand dollars.
- Past perfect: Action continuing to a fixed moment in the past: Before leaving for college, he *had earned* ten thousand dollars.
- Future perfect: Action continuing to a fixed moment in the future: By next Christmas he *will have earned* ten thousand dollars.

(In Lesson 21 you will be reminded of a few usage problems involving the use of tenses.)

4. The conjugation shows you that the two verbs *earn* and *grow* differ in form in all tenses except the present tense and the future tense. *Earn* is a regular verb and *grow* is an irregular verb.

We customarily make use of three distinctive forms, called the **principal parts** of the verb, to show the difference between the two classes of verbs. The principal parts are (a) the *base* or infinitive, the "name" of the verb, used in the present tense with *(e)s* added in the third-person singular; (b) the *past,* the form used in the simple past tense; and (c) the *past participle,* the form used in the three perfect tenses.

On the basis of these three forms, we classify verbs as being regular or irregular. In all regular verbs the past and the past participle are alike, formed simply by the

37

addition of *ed* to the base form (or only *d* if the base word ends in *e*). The irregular verbs are more complicated because for nearly all of them the past tense and the participle are not spelled alike. Following are the three forms of several irregular verbs, illustrating some spelling changes and endings that are found:

Base	*Past*	*Past Participle*
be	was, were	been
become	became	become
bite	bit	bitten
break	broke	broken
catch	caught	caught
do	did	done
eat	ate	eaten
put	put	put
ring	rang	rung
run	ran	run
see	saw	seen

(You will study more principal parts of verbs and the usage problems associated with them in Lesson 21.)

Another change in form for both regular and irregular verbs—the addition of *ing* to the base form—produces the **present participle.** One of its important uses is explained in the next paragraph.

In the sample conjugation, you observed the use of *shall/will* and *have* as auxiliary verbs in the future tense and the perfect tenses. Another important auxiliary is *be,* used with the *ing* form (the present participle) of the main verb to produce what is called the **progressive** form. As an example of its use, if someone asks about the assignment in your English class, you would probably not reply, "Right now, we *review* parts of speech." Instead, you would say, "Right now, we *are reviewing* parts of speech," to show that the action is not fixed in an exact moment of time but is a continuing activity. This very useful type of verb occurs in all six tenses:

We *are reviewing.*
We *were reviewing.*
We *shall be reviewing.*
We *have been reviewing.*
We *had been reviewing.*
We *shall have been reviewing.*

Another type of auxiliary verb includes *may, might, must, can, could, would,* and *should.* These words are called **modal auxiliaries,** and they are used the way *will* and *shall* are used:

I *should study* this weekend.
I *should have studied* last weekend.

(See Supplement 1.)

Do as an auxiliary verb combines with the base form of a main verb to make a rarely used "emphatic" form (But I *did pay* that bill last month). In Lesson 6 you will examine the much more common use of the *do* auxiliary, in questions and negatives.

Here are a few other points to remember about auxiliary verbs:

1. *Have, be,* and *do* are not used exclusively as auxiliaries; they are three of our most commonly used main verbs:

I *have* a brown pen. [Main verb.]
I *have* lost my brown pen. [Auxiliary.]
He *is* a good speaker. [Main verb.]
He *is* becoming a good speaker. [Auxiliary.]
He *did* a good job for us. [Main verb.]
Yes, I *did* embellish the story somewhat. [Auxiliary.]

2. When the verb unit contains auxiliaries, there may be short adverbial modifiers separating parts of the whole verb phrase:

We *have* occasionally *been sailing.*
He *has,* of course, *been telling* the truth.

3. In a few set expressions following introductory adverbs, usually adverbs of time, we place the subject within the verb phrase between an auxiliary and the main verb:

Only lately *have I learned* to drive.
Rarely *do we turn* on the television set.

Supplement 1

Variations of some modals and "time" auxiliaries make use of *to* in the verb phrase. Here are examples of some that you use and hear regularly:

Mr. Nelson *has to retire* [= *must retire*] early.
You *ought to eat* [= *should eat*] more vegetables.
I *used to be* a secretary.
Jim *was supposed to be* here at ten o'clock.
I *am to depart* for Miami early in the morning.
I *am going to depart* for Miami early in the morning.

Practice Sheet 5

Auxiliary Verbs; Basic Sentence Patterns

NAME _____ SCORE _____

Directions: Each of these sentences contains at least one auxiliary verb. (Some have two; some have three.) Copy the auxiliary verb(s) in the first space at the left. In the second space, write 1, 2, 3, 4, or 5 to identify the sentence patterns.

_____ 1. All of you should have been taking careful notes.
_____

_____ 2. The waiting period seemed endless to the worried parents.
_____

_____ 3. Gene's being unusually stubborn on this matter.
_____

_____ 4. Recently Jason has been telling his probation officer very lit-
_____   tle about his activities.

_____ 5. Professor Jenkins usually makes his lectures very lively.

_____ 6. You're being quite unreasonable about this matter.
_____

_____ 7. The plane from Atlanta should be arriving soon.
_____

_____ 8. The possibility of a quick settlement of the strike is unlikely.
_____

_____ 9. You might find this recently published pamphlet helpful in
_____   your research.

_____ 10. By the end of the month, Glen had spent nearly all of his al-
_____   lowance.

_____ 11. Dozens of direct-mail merchants are sending me their cata-
_____   logues.

_____ 12. For the last three weeks the Joneses have been vacationing in
_____   Alaska.

_____ 13. You should have been attending classes regularly.
_____

_____ 14. We'll soon have the dormitory ready for the matron's inspec-
_____   tion.

_____ 15. Someone has been writing the mayor abusive letters.
_____

_____ 16. There might be a repeat performance of the operetta later.
_____

_____ 17. Virginia has been the office manager since 1989.
_____

_____ 18. The umpire called the next pitch a strike.
_____

_____ 19. Never again will I buy a ticket on that airline.
_____

_____ 20. This speech might well be a very important one in her bid for
_____ reelection.

_____ 21. Only a few of the youngsters seemed interested in the pro-
_____ gram.

_____ 22. One of our 1990 graduates has become a reporter for the
_____ *Globe.*

_____ 23. The absentee landlord had been paying his farmworkers
_____ below-average wages.

_____ 24. My granddaughter has named her new kitten Fluffy.
_____

_____ 25. Next Tuesday would seem the logical time for our departure.
_____

_____ 26. During the first few days new students must fill out numerous
_____ forms.

_____ 27. Oh, really; you're imagining things.
_____

_____ 28. I should give this report a second and more thorough reading.
_____

_____ 29. Within a week most of these migratory birds will have flown
_____ away.

_____ 30. You could, of course, look up the answers in your textbook.
_____

_____ 31. Myrtle might have become a better-than-average violin player.
_____

_____ 32. I'll allow you a 10 percent discount on this purchase.
_____

_____ 33. There should have been an extra guard at the railroad crossing.
_____

_____ 34. At the age of four, Bertha could skate quite well.
_____

_____ 35. We must keep this news a secret between the two of us.
_____

_____ 36. Mr. Hoagland sometimes gave us free passes to the carnival.
_____

_____ 37. The coaching staff should be feeling good about the team's
_____ recent victories.

_____ 38. Tomorrow we must turn back our clocks to standard time.
_____

_____ 39. On the other hand, the child might have made up the entire
_____ story.

_____ 40. NBC will bring you the latest reports from the flooded area.
_____

EXERCISE 5
COMPLEMENTS

NAME _____ SCORE _____

Directions: In the space at the left, write one of the following to identify the italicized word:
      S.C. [subjective complement]   I.O. [indirect object]
      D.O. [direct object]   O.C. [objective complement]

If the italicized word is *not* used as a complement, leave the space blank. Circle every auxiliary verb.

_____ 1. By midnight I had worked all except a few of the algebra *problems.*

_____ 2. Your presence tomorrow in the courtroom will not be *necessary.*

_____ 3. Among the four of us, we finally scraped up the *price* of one pizza.

_____ 4. These events made the old man quite *bitter.*

_____ 5. The old man has lately become quite *bitter.*

_____ 6. There's my *scarf* on the coffee table.

_____ 7. That's my *scarf* on the coffee table.

_____ 8. From Naples, Jean sent *me* a picture of Mount Vesuvius.

_____ 9. The apprehensive tourist finally tasted the strange-looking *morsel.*

_____ 10. To his surprise, the exotic food tasted *good.*

_____ 11. President Watt's welcoming speech to new students always seems interminably *long.*

_____ 12. President Watt should make his welcoming speech *shorter.*

_____ 13. President Watt should cut at least twenty *minutes* from his welcoming speech.

_____ 14. These instructions look rather *complicated* to me.

_____ 15. Beth is looking after two orphaned *lambs.*

_____ 16. The car owner's letter of apology gave the *family* some satisfaction.

_____ 17. There should have been five one-dollar *bills* in the envelope.

_____ 18. You can be *sure* of our support in your bid for reelection.

_____ 19. By late afternoon, the committee had read every one of the *letters.*

_____ 20. That remark was really not *worthy* of you.

_____ 21. None of us feel *good* about this recent development.

_____ 22. At the age of three, Naomi knew the letters of the *alphabet.*

_____ 23. Over the noise of the raging wind, we could barely hear the *foghorn.*

_____ 24. Later that week Mr. Long offered the *board* of supervisors his resignation.

_____ 25. Jason is *one* of the best students in my advanced writing class.

_____ 26. That hammock out there in the shade of the pear tree certainly looks *inviting.*

_____ 27. The settlers selected Reverend Tatlock as their first *governor.*

_____ 28. You must without delay write the *housekeeper* a letter of apology.

_____ 29. The college ombudsman is looking into the *matter* of Dr. West's delayed promotion.

_____ 30. Your uncle's words of encouragement were most *welcome.*

_____ 31. On her first attempt at bowling, Esther knocked over only *four* of the pins.

_____ 32. Two handwriting experts have examined this *signature.*

_____ 33. Both of the experts have pronounced the signature a *forgery.*

_____ 34. I will sell *you* this set of chessmen at a bargain price.

_____ 35. I call that verdict a *miscarriage* of justice.

_____ 36. In time you will become *accustomed* to our unpredictable weather.

_____ 37. A tall man in a floor-length overcoat walked slowly toward the *pulpit.*

_____ 38. These hateful anonymous letters caused the *family* further grief.

_____ 39. For several minutes Professor Allen mulled over Ted's *reply.*

_____ 40. At the beach, Grandfather would almost always buy *us* a bag of saltwater taffy.

LESSON 6 ■

Alterations of Basic Sentence Patterns

Any long piece of writing made up exclusively of basic sentences would be too monotonous to read. You should think of the basic sentences not as models for your writing but as elementary units, important because they are the structures from which amplified sentences develop.

In this lesson we shall look at two alterations of basic sentence patterns resulting in sentences that use passive verbs and sentences that are in the form of a question. Lessons 7 through 11 then show how basic sentences can be combined and reduced to subordinate clauses and phrases to produce varied, well-developed sentences.

Passive Voice

In Lesson 2, you examined a partial conjugation of the verb *earn*. The forms listed there are in the active voice, which means that the subject is the doer of the action. A more complete conjugation would include the passive verb forms. These make use of the auxiliary verb *be* combined with the past participle of the verb, as shown in the following illustration of the third-person singular in the six tenses:

This amount *is earned.*
This amount *was earned.*
This amount *will be earned.*
This amount *has been earned.*
This amount *had been earned.*
This amount *will have been earned.*

The present and past tenses of progressive verbs can also be shifted to the passive voice, giving us forms in which *be* is used in two auxiliary capacities in the same verb form:

These cars *are being sold* at a loss.
These cars *were being sold* at a loss.

Because only transitive verbs have passive forms, the basic patterns that can be altered to passive versions are Patterns 3, 4, and 5. When the idea of a Pattern 3 sentence is expressed with a passive verb, there is no complement in the sentence:

Active Voice: Children play games.
Passive Voice: Games are played [by children].

If the doer of the action is expressed in a sentence using a passive verb, the doer must occur as the object of the preposition *by*.

45

When a Pattern 4 sentence is altered to form a passive construction, the indirect object that followed the active verb becomes the subject of the passive verb:

Active Voice: Children give the parents pleasure.

Passive Voice: The parents are given pleasure [by children].

Here the passive verb is followed by a complement, *pleasure,* which we can continue to call a direct object in spite of the fact that it follows a passive verb.

Notice also how a Pattern 5 sentence can be given a different kind of expression by means of a passive verb, with the direct object becoming the subject:

Active Voice: The parents consider the child a genius.
                     The parents consider the child clever.

Passive Voice: The child is considered a genius [by the parents].
                     The child is considered clever [by the parents].

Here also the passive verb requires a complement (*genius, clever*), which, because it renames or describes the subject, should be called a subjective complement.

The passive voice serves a real purpose in effective communication: it should be used when the *doer* of the action is unknown or is of secondary interest in the statement. In such a situation, the writer, wishing to focus attention on the *receiver* of the action, places that unit in the emphatic subject position. The passive verb form makes this arrangement possible. Thus, instead of some vague expression such as "Somebody should wash these windows," we can say, "These windows *should be washed.*"

Some of you may have heard the passive voice called "weak." Admittedly some writers do get into the habit of using the passive form when there is little justification. In most narrative writing, the doer of the action is logically the subject of the verb. "The fullback crossed the goal line" would certainly be preferred to "The goal line was crossed by the fullback," a version that gives the same information but tends to retard the narrative flow.

The passive voice also lends itself to a kind of muddied, heavy-footed writing that produces prose like this: "It *is* now *rumored* that the Secretary of Defense *has been informed* that contingent plans *have been made* to . . . ." The writer of such a sentence, however, would find the passive voice indispensable if he or she were unable or intentionally unwilling to tell who is spreading the rumor, who has informed the Secretary of Defense, or who has made the plans.

You should practice with passive constructions so that you can use this important device when it is called for. Equally important, if a criticism of your writing mentions doubtful uses of the passive, you can hardly be expected to do much effective rewriting if you can't recognize the passive verb.

Questions

In the sentence types you examined in earlier lessons, you noted the normal positioning of the main sentence parts: the subject first, followed by the verb, followed by the complement, if any. In questions, however, other arrangements are possible. As we study these new structures, we must first recognize the fact that there are two kinds of questions: (1) questions answered by "Yes" or "No" and (2) questions answered by information.

Questions Answered by "Yes" or "No"

Notice the following paired sentences, in each case the first sentence being a statement and the second sentence a related question. By referring to these paired sentences, we can demonstrate how in present-day English the structure of a "Yes/No" question differs from that of a statement.

1. John is happy. Is John happy?
2. You were there. Were you there?

If the verb is *be* in the present or past tense, the subject and the *be* form (*am, are, is, was,* or *were*) reverse positions.

3. You see Ms. Locke often. Do you see Ms. Locke often?
4. You heard the announcement. Did you hear the announcement?

With other one-word verbs in the present or past tense, the proper form of the auxiliary *do* is used, followed by the subject and the base form of the main verb.

5. You have seen the movie. Have you seen the movie?
6. They will arrive later. Will they arrive later?
7. The house is being painted. Is the house being painted?
8. He should have been told. Should he have been told?

If the verb already has an auxiliary, the subject follows the auxiliary verb. If there are two or more auxiliaries, the subject follows the first one.

9. You have enough money. Have you enough money?
10. You have enough money. Do you have enough money?

When the verb is *have* in the present tense, two versions of the question are possible, the subject–verb reversal and the *do* auxiliary. (See Supplement 1.)

Questions Answered by Information

Some questions ask for information rather than for a "Yes" or a "No." These questions make use of words called **interrogatives,** words that stand for unknown persons, things, or descriptive qualities. The most commonly used interrogatives are these:

pronouns: *who (whom), which, what*
adjectives: *whose, which, what*
adverbs: *when, where, why, how*

The interrogative pronoun *who,* which stands for an unknown person or persons, has three forms: *who* when it is used as a subject or a subjective complement, *whose* when it is used as a possessive modifier of a noun, and *whom* when it is used as an object. (In a later lesson you will learn that these three forms of *who* have another important use in subordinate clauses. And the choice between *who* and *whom* as a problem of usage is discussed more extensively in Lesson 24.)

In questions using these interrogatives, the normal arrangement of the main sentence parts is retained only when the interrogative is the subject or a modifier of the subject. (Here again we shall use paired statements and related questions to demonstrate these structures.)

My *brother* [S.] paid the bill.
Who [S.] paid the bill?
Five cars [S.] were damaged.
How many cars [S.] were damaged?

In all other situations the subject–verb positioning is altered as it is with "Yes/No" questions, and the interrogative word, or the unit containing the interrogative word, stands at the beginning of the sentence to signal that a question, not a statement, is forthcoming:

I studied *geometry* [D.O.] last night.
What [D.O.] did you study last night?

You saw *Jim* [D.O.] at the party.
Whom [D.O.] did you see at the party?

She is Mother's *cousin* [S.C.].
Who [S.C.] is she?

You gave the note to *Sue* [O.P.].
To whom [O.P.] did you give the note?

We can use Bill's *car* [D.O.].
Whose car [D.O.] can we use?

You spent fifteen *dollars* [D.O.].
How much money [D.O.] did you spend?

You [S.] called *Bob* [D.O.] a *thief* [O.C.].
Who [S.] called Bob a thief?
Whom [D.O.] did you call a thief?
What [O.C.] did you call Bob?

When the interrogative unit is the object of a preposition, two versions of the question are often possible: the entire prepositional phrase may stand at the beginning, or the interrogative may stand at the beginning with the preposition in its usual position:

The speaker was referring *to the mayor.*
To whom was the speaker referring?
Whom was the speaker referring to?

(See Supplement 2.)

Supplement 1

The four-part classification of the verb also determines the structuring of sentences that are negative rather than positive. The positioning of the negator *not* (or its contraction *n't*) depends on the presence or absence of an auxiliary verb. Sentences using *be* or *have* must be considered special cases.

1. If the verb is *be* in the present tense or in the past tense, used either as the main verb or as an auxiliary verb, the *not* follows the *be* form:

I am *not* pleased with the report.
He was *not* [was*n't*] available.
They were *not* [were*n't*] invited.

2. With other one-word verbs in the present or past tense, the proper form of the auxiliary *do* is used, followed by the negator and the base form of the main verb:

I do *not* [do*n't*] expect a reward.
He does *not* [does*n't*] attend regularly.
We did *not* [did*n't*] respond.

3. If the verb already has an auxiliary, the negator follows the auxiliary. When there are two or more auxiliaries, the *not* follows the first one:

We could *not* [could*n't*] see very well.
I may *not* have understood him.
They will *not* [wo*n't*] refund my money.
This cake ought *not* to have been baked so long.

4. When *have* in the present tense is the main verb, two negative forms are possible:

I have *not* [have*n't*] enough time to play.

I do *not* [do*n't*] have enough time to play.

Supplement 2

At the informal language level another version—"*Who* was the speaker referring to?"—is often found, despite the traditional demand for the objective case for the object of a preposition. The formal level of both spoken and written English would call for the first version: "*To whom* was the speaker referring?"

SUMMARY OF BASIC SENTENCE PATTERNS

Pattern 1:   The child runs.

  S — V.i.

  N. — V.i.

Pattern 2:   The child is a genius.

  S. — V.lk. — S.C.

  N_x — V.lk. — N_x

  The child is clever.

  S. — V.lk. — S.C.

  N. — V.lk. — Adj.

Pattern 3:   The child plays a game.

  S. — V.tr. — D.O.

  N_x — V.tr. — N_y

Pattern 4:   The child gives the parents pleasure.

  S. — V.tr. — I.O. — D.O.

  N_x — V.tr. — N_y — N_z

Pattern 5:   The parents consider the child a genius.

  S. — V.tr. — D.O. — O.C.

  N_x — V.tr. — N_y — N_y

  The parents consider the child clever.

  S. — V.tr. — D.O. — O.C.

  N_x — V.tr. — N — Adj.

Practice Sheet 6

Alterations of Basic Sentence Patterns: Passive Verbs; Questions

NAME _____   SCORE _____

Directions: These sentences are Pattern 3, 4, or 5 sentences. In the first space at the left, write the pattern number. In the second space, write the verb form that is used when the italicized word in the sentence is made the subject.

Example:

   4

  will be sent

                  Later I will send *you* a copy of the bulletin.

_____
_____
     1. One automobile magazine called the *Thunderbolt* the best buy on the market.

_____
_____
     2. Upon receipt of the coupon, the company will send *you* the rebate.

_____
_____
     3. All of us greatly appreciate your *help*.

_____
_____
     4. Someone had already called the *police*.

_____
_____
     5. The family never did tell *Granddad* the entire story.

_____
_____
     6. All of our friends are talking about Marge's *altercation* with the music teacher.

_____
_____
     7. The used car dealer allowed *me* only two hundred dollars on the old truck.

_____
_____
     8. Jimmy usually delivers our evening *paper* before six o'clock.

_____
_____
     9. Ralph Vaughan Williams composed this *music* in 1910.

_____
_____
     10. I should have made this *path* three feet wider.

Directions: The purpose of this exercise is to contrast the structure of a question with that of a statement. In the space at the left, copy the word from the question that serves the function indicated:

S. [subject]   O.C. [objective complement]
D.O. [direct object]   O.P. [object of preposition]
S.C. [subjective complement]

The statement following the question has the same basic structure as that of the question.

_____ 1. How many pancakes did you eat?
(D.O)   I ate seven *pancakes* (D.O.).

_____ 2. How many taxis are available for our guests?
(S.)   Four *taxis* (S.) are available for our guests.

_____ 3. What are you worried about?
(O.P.)   I am worried about my *grade* (O.P.) in math class.

_____ 4. How many applicants have you interviewed?
(D.O.)   I have interviewed five *applicants* (D.O.).

_____ 5. Whose notes did you borrow?
(S.C.)   I borrowed Lucy's *notes* (S.C.).

_____ 6. Whose notes are these?
(S.C.)   These are Lucy's *notes* (S.C.).

_____ 7. How many mistakes did you make on the test?
(D.O.)   I made only two *mistakes* (D.O.) on the test.

_____ 8. Whom should we elect as presiding officer?
(D.O.)   We should elect *Will Bevin* (D.O.) as presiding officer.

_____ 9. Who will be the presiding officer?
(S.)   *Will Bevin* (S.) will be the presiding officer.

_____ 10. Who will the presiding officer be?
(S.C.)   The presiding officer will be *Will Bevin* (S.C.).

_____ 11. To whom was the letter addressed?
(O.P.)   The letter was addressed to *Dr. Stevens* (O.P.).

_____ 12. What color should I paint this door?
(O.C.)   You should paint this door *red* (O.C.).

_____ 13. Who sent Mary that comic valentine?
(S.)   *Fred* (S.) sent Mary that comic valentine.

_____ 14. What did Fred send to Mary?
(D.O.)   Fred sent Mary a comic *valentine* (D.O.).

_____ 15. To whom did Fred send a comic valentine?
(O.P.)   Fred sent a comic valentine to *Mary* (O.P.).

EXERCISE 6

ALTERATIONS OF BASIC SENTENCES: PASSIVE VERBS; QUESTIONS

NAME _____   SCORE _____

Directions: Each of the following sentences uses a passive verb. Underline the verb. Rewrite each sentence using an active form of the verb. (You will have to supply a logical subject of the active verb if the passive verb version does not provide one.) If your rewrites are correctly done, your first four sentences will be Pattern 3, your next three will be Pattern 4, and your final three will be Pattern 5.

1. The qualifying tests are taken by all transfer students.

2. This unsavory affair is being talked about by local gossips.

3. The towering flames could be seen from the highway.

4. The winner of the contest will be met at the airport by a chauffeured limousine.

5. You will later be sent an application form by our personnel officer.

6. For this boring work, we were paid a barely livable wage.

7. Their eldest daughter has been offered a job in Denmark.

8. Some residents of Fraser Valley were left homeless by the storm.

9. In a close run-off election, Ms. Sherman was elected treasurer.

10. The sad news about the president's health can no longer be kept a secret.

Directions: The italicized word in each of the following questions is a complement or the object of a preposition. In the space at the left, write one of the following to identify the italicized word:

D.O. [direct object]   O.C. [objective complement]
S.C. [subjective complement]   O.P. [object of preposition]
I.O. [indirect object]

_____ 1. *Which* of these suggested changes do you approve of?

_____ 2. Of these three candidates, which *one* do you prefer?

_____ 3. Of these three candidates, which *one* will you vote for?

_____ 4. Of these three candidates, *whom* will you vote for?

_____ 5. How *tall* has your youngest daughter grown this year?

_____ 6. Whose *keys* are these?

_____ 7. Why did you paint this door *purple*?

_____ 8. What *color* should I paint this door?

_____ 9. How *costly* will a new roof on my house be?

_____ 10. How much *rope* will you need for the children's swing?

_____ 11. How *long* should the piece of rope be?

_____ 12. *Whom* did the Republicans nominate?

_____ 13. *Who* is the Republican nominee?

_____ 14. What kind of lies has he been telling *us*?

_____ 15. What *kind* of lies has he been telling us?

_____ 16. What price did he quote *you*?

_____ 17. What *price* did he quote you?

_____ 18. *Who* will your new roommate be?

_____ 19. *What* is your new roommate's name?

_____ 20. *Whom* do you consider the best qualified applicant?

_____ 21. Whom do you consider the best qualified *applicant*?

_____ 22. *Who* is that noisy person in the row behind us?

_____ 23. What *kind* of administrator has Ms. Allen become?

_____ 24. How *long* should my next report be?

_____ 25. *Which* of these three cameras should I buy for my brother?

Clauses and Phrases
Lessons, Practice Sheets, and Exercises

LESSON **7** ■

Coordination: Compound Sentences

To begin our study of sentences that build on the simple patterns we have studied in previous lessons and exercises, let us examine this student writer's description of a snowstorm:

(1) The first really serious snowfall began at dusk and had already spread a treacherous powdering over the roads by the time the homeward-bound crowds reached their peak. (2) As the evening deepened, porch and street lights glowed in tight circles through semisolid air. (3) The snow did not fall in a mass of fat, jovial flakes; it squalled in a writhing mist of tiny particles and seemed less snow than a dense, animated fog. (4) Through the night the wind rose, worrying the trees as a puppy shakes a slipper. (5) It rushed round the corners of buildings and tumbled over roofs, from which it snatched armfuls of snow to scatter in the streets. (6) Save for the occasional grumble of a sanitation truck sullenly pushing its plow, all sound stopped. (7) Even the wind was more sensible than audible. (8) Day did not dawn. (9) The world changed from charcoal gray to lead between six and seven, but the change was one from night to lesser night. (10) The snow still whirled. (11) Drifts had altered the neat symmetry of peaked roofs into irregular mountain ranges ending in sheer cliffs four or five feet above the leeward eaves. (12) The downwind side of every solid object cast a snow shadow that tapered away from a sharp hump until it merged into the surrounding flat pallor. (13) Along the street, windshield wipers, odd bits of chrome, startling blanks of black glass, and isolated headlights decorated large white mounds. (14) Men and women shut off their alarm clocks, stretched, yawned, looked out of their windows, paused in a moment of guilt, and went back to bed. (15) Snow had taken the day for its own, and there was no point in arguing with it.

The sentences of this paragraph are made up of groups of related words: clauses and phrases. The word group that is basic to all communication is the **clause,** which contains at least one subject and one verb. (In a later lesson we shall study the **phrase,** a group of related words *not* containing a subject and verb in combination.)

The writer of the paragraph may not have consciously considered the fact, but the entire passage is based on short, simple sentences of the patterns studied in the preceding lessons. Recalling or inventing the scenes, actions, and responses associated with the event, the author projected a series of subject–verb combinations, in other words, clauses: the snowfall began, the snowfall had spread a powdering, the homeward-bound crowds reached their peak, the evening deepened, lights glowed, and so on.

The writer's problem was to combine or alter these short statements and put them into their most pleasing and effective form. Presenting all of them as basic sentences would communicate the author's ideas but in a form that, in addition to being monotonous, would not give proper emphasis to the most important ideas. Only two sentences (8 and 10) are retained as one-subject, one-verb basic sentences. Some of the sentences (3, 9, and 15) combine two basic sentences, giving each clause equal force. Some (1 and 5) join more than one verb to the same subject. Sentence 13 joins four subjects to the same verb, and Sentence 14 has two subjects joined to six verbs.

In the next several lessons we shall be examining the word groups—independent clauses, subordinate clauses, and phrases—that are the language tools allowing a writer to apply various strategies to produce effective sentences.

A sentence, as you learned in Lesson 1, is a word group containing a subject and a verb. From this definition, and from the one already given for a clause, it would seem that a sentence and a clause are identical. And this is true for one kind of clause, the **independent clause** (also called the *main clause* or *principal clause*). The independent clause can stand by itself as a sentence. Every example sentence and every exercise sentence that you have worked with thus far in this book has been made up of one independent clause. We call a sentence consisting of only one independent clause a **simple sentence.**

One means of combining or altering short statements is *compounding,* or joining grammatically equal parts so that they function together. A compound may be formed of equal parts within the independent clause of a simple sentence. All of the sentence units you have studied can be compounded; that is, a sentence may contain two or more subjects, verbs, complements, or modifiers, joined by a **coordinating conjunction.** (**Conjunctions** are words that join words, phrases, or clauses; those that join grammatically equal units are called *coordinating.*)

The three common coordinating conjunctions for this use are *and, but,* and *or;* other coordinators are *nor, for,* and *yet.* Sometimes the equal grammatical relationship is pointed out by the use of pairs of words, called **correlatives:** *not (only). . . but (also), either . . . or, neither . . . nor:*

Dad *and* I have read the notice. [Compound subjects.]

She enjoys golf *and* tennis. [Compound direct objects.]

I studied long *and* hard *but* failed the test. [Compound verbs and adverbs.]

I found the lecture *and* the discussion neither interesting *nor* instructive. [Compound direct objects and objective complements.]

I can see you either during the lunch hour *or* after 5 o'clock. [Compound prepositional phrases.]

Compounding is often used with two (sometimes more than two) independent clauses; the result is a common type of sentence called the **compound sentence.** Any of the coordinating conjunctions and any of the correlatives mentioned already can be used to join two independent clauses. In the compound sentence, the presence or absence of one of these coordinators is the basis for a decision in punctuation, a decision so important that you must be able to recognize the compound sentence and must know that it can occur in either of two patterns:

1. The two clauses are joined by a coordinating conjunction. The normal punctuation is a comma before the conjunction:

> I had reviewed the material, *but* I did poorly on the test.

It is important to distinguish this sentence from a nearly synonymous version using a compound verb:

> I had reviewed the material *but* did poorly on the test.

In this second version the sentence is not a compound sentence because there is no separate subject for the second verb. It is a simple sentence and in usual practice would be written without a comma.

2. The two independent clauses are *not* joined by a coordinating conjunction. The normal punctuation is a semicolon between the two clauses. (See Supplement 1.) Sometimes, in this kind of compound sentence, the two independent clauses stand side by side with no word tying them together:

> No one was in sight; I was alone in the huge auditorium.

Often the second clause begins with an adverbial unit that serves as a kind of tie between the clauses. This adverbial unit may be

a. A simple adverb:

> Currently we are renting an apartment; later we hope to buy a house.
> These were last year's highlights; now we must look at plans for next year.

b. A short phrase:

> I cannot comment on the whole concert; in fact, I slept through the last part of it.

c. A conjunctive adverb. The commonest conjunctive adverbs are *therefore, however, nevertheless, consequently, moreover, otherwise, besides, furthermore,* and *accordingly.* These words, often followed by a comma, should be used cautiously; they usually contribute to a heavy, formal tone. To lessen this effect, writers often place them, set off by commas, within the second clause:

> The evidences of perjury are conclusive; *therefore,* we find you guilty.
> Your arguments were well presented; *however,* we feel that the plan is too expensive.
> Your arguments were well presented; we feel, *however,* that the plan is too expensive.

Because adverbial units like *later* and *therefore* are not coordinating conjunctions, the use of a comma to join the two clauses is inappropriate. The important thing to remember is that when the independent clauses are joined by a coordinating conjunction, the use of a comma is the custom. When there is no coordinating conjunction, the comma will not suffice; the customary mark is the semicolon.

Supplement 1

The serious error that results when a writer uses a comma—or no mark at all—in a compound sentence whose clauses are not joined by a coordinating conjunction is called the **comma fault** or the **run-on sentence.**

Remember that the punctuation suggestions made in this lesson apply only to the compound sentence. At this point in your study of the English sentence, your natural fear of *under*punctuation between clauses may lead you to produce sentences like these:

> I want you to meet Jeff Lytle; with whom I often play tennis.
> Although the meetings have gone on for nearly two weeks; settlement of the strike is not expected soon.

These semicolons are inappropriate. These sentences are *not* compound sentences; in each case the sentence is made up of one independent clause and one dependent or subordinate clause. You should be able to avoid this kind of overpunctuating after your examination of dependent clauses (Lessons 8–10).

Practice Sheet 7

Coordination: Compound Sentences

NAME _____   SCORE _____

Directions: The twenty-five sentences here illustrate three types of sentences:

1. The sentence is a simple sentence with the subject having two verbs joined by a coordinating conjunction. Normal punctuation with the sentence: none.

> We worked all day on the car but could not find the trouble.

2. The sentence is a compound sentence with the two independent clauses joined by a coordinating conjunction: *and, but, or, nor, yet,* or *for.* Normal punctuation: a comma before the conjunction.

> We worked all day on the car, and now it runs well.

3. The sentence is a compound sentence without one of the coordinating conjunctions joining the independent clauses. (The second clause often begins with an adverbial unit.) Normal punctuation: a semicolon.

> We worked all day on the car; now it runs well.

In each of the following sentences, a ⌢ marks a point of coordination. If the sentence is Type 1, write 0 in the space at the left. If the sentence is Type 2, write C (for comma) in the space. If the sentence is Type 3, write S (for semicolon) in the space.

_____ 1. Major John Powell survived the Civil War ⌢ and in 1869 set out from Green River, Wyoming, to explore the Colorado River.

_____ 2. Stamps are Bill's great passion ⌢ he collects, buys, sells, and trades them with crafty devotion.

_____ 3. This gentle rain is, I admit, a relief ⌢ but what we really need is a long, hard soaking.

_____ 4. In Shakespeare's play, Lady Macbeth, tormented by her conscience, walks in her sleep ⌢ and tries to wash imaginary blood from her hands.

_____ 5. I usually don't go in for predictions ⌢ but I've a feeling our boys will make a fine showing in tonight's game.

_____ 6. "Your argument is absolutely worthless ⌢ it's nothing but name calling," said the irate lawyer.

_____ 7. "I do recall the incident vaguely ⌢ but to save my soul I can't recall the man's name," replied my uncle.

_____ 8. On these blisteringly hot days, I often think of the cool Montana mountains ⌢ and wonder why I ever left home.

_____ 9. The bemused young lady paid no attention to the remark ⌢ nor did she even seem aware of our presence.

59

_____ 10. The bemused young lady paid no attention to the remark ⌒ in fact, she didn't even seem aware of our presence.

_____ 11. The bemused young lady neither paid any attention to the remark ⌒ nor seemed even aware of our presence.

_____ 12. I scraped the sticky tar from the side of the boat ⌒ and my lazy partner sat in the shade.

_____ 13. To our amazement, the spry little old lady climbed over the fence ⌒ and separated the fighting dogs.

_____ 14. Cooley hit a towering foul over the stands at the left ⌒ and the call remained at three balls and two strikes.

_____ 15. It is not enough for the parent to provide for the child ⌒ he or she must be the child's friend and guide.

_____ 16. Measure, combine, and blend well the sugar and shortening ⌒ and then stir in the beaten eggs.

_____ 17. First, the sugar and shortening are measured and combined ⌒ when they are well blended, the beaten eggs are added.

_____ 18. Speed is not stressed in the game ⌒ therefore, the participants can become acquainted and form new friendships.

_____ 19. People's dream of an ideal world is not new ⌒ for as far back as 1516 Sir Thomas More in his *Utopia* outlined his idea of a perfect society.

_____ 20. These acts on the part of Paul's father did not solve the problem ⌒ instead, they tended to make it worse.

_____ 21. The coach called the first practice session on the first Monday of September ⌒ and nearly one hundred young athletes reported.

_____ 22. On the first Monday of September, the coach held the first practice session ⌒ and welcomed nearly one hundred young athletes.

_____ 23. To our left is a stairway leading to the basement ⌒ a little ahead and to the right is an archway to the dining room.

_____ 24. Mother put frosting on the cake ⌒ and both of the children wanted to cut the cake at once.

_____ 25. There was no response from the students ⌒ they merely sat there and stared at the new teacher.

EXERCISE *7*

COORDINATION: COMPOUND SENTENCES

NAME _____ SCORE _____

Directions: The twenty-five sentences here illustrate three types of sentences:

1. The sentence is a simple sentence with the subject having two verbs joined by a coordinating conjunction. Normal punctuation with the sentence: none.

> We worked all day on the car but could not find the trouble.

2. The sentence is a compound sentence with the two independent clauses joined by a coordinating conjunction: *and, but, or, nor, yet,* or *for.* Normal punctuation: a comma before the conjunction.

> We worked all day on the car, and now it runs well.

3. The sentence is a compound sentence without one of the coordinating conjunctions joining the independent clauses. (The second clause often begins with an adverbial unit.) Normal punctuation: a semicolon.

> We worked all day on the car; now it runs well.

In each of the following sentences, a ⌒ marks a point of coordination. If the sentence is Type 1, write 0 in the space at the left. If the sentence is Type 2, write C (for comma) in the space. If the sentence is Type 3, write S (for semicolon) in the space.

_____ 1. Sentence length is an unreliable guide to punctuation ⌒ short sentences sometimes require semicolons.

_____ 2. The new sunglasses are selling well ⌒ in fact, several retailers have exhausted their supplies.

_____ 3. Court ladies of the period often wore massive wigs ⌒ and decorated them with fruit, jewels, and even stuffed birds.

_____ 4. Estelle could answer only three of the questions ⌒ obviously she had not prepared well for the test.

_____ 5. The cashier did not answer our questions ⌒ nor did he offer to summon the manager.

_____ 6. The cashier neither answered our questions ⌒ nor offered to summon the manager.

_____ 7. The cashier did not answer our questions ⌒ moreover, he did not offer to summon the manager.

_____ 8. The members of the House will debate the amendment tomorrow ⌒ but the prospect of a compromise is remote.

_____ 9. The members of the House will debate the amendment tomorrow ⌒ the prospects of a compromise, however, are remote.

61

_____ 10. Some archeologists believe that Stonehenge was a temple for sun worshiping ⌒ others think that its use was sepulchral.

_____ 11. Desperation Shoals is well named ⌒ for many a ship has foundered there.

_____ 12. In Dad's school days, engineering students carried wooden slide rules ⌒ nowadays they appear with pocket electronic calculators.

_____ 13. At their first Thanksgiving feast, the Pilgrims not only roasted turkeys and venison ⌒ but also served steamed clams and boiled lobsters.

_____ 14. In the winter of 1776–1777, hunger, cold, and disease plagued the American army ⌒ by December, Washington had lost half of his men.

_____ 15. We tried the experiment in five different classes ⌒ and in each got nearly the same result.

_____ 16. After an early dinner, we'll still have time for some talk ⌒ Edith's flight doesn't leave until 9:20.

_____ 17. You may finance the purchase with ten monthly payments ⌒ or you will receive a 5 percent discount if you pay cash.

_____ 18. You may finance the purchase with ten monthly payments ⌒ if you pay cash, however, you will receive a 5 percent discount.

_____ 19. You may finance the purchase with ten monthly payments ⌒ or pay cash and receive a 5 percent discount.

_____ 20. Jake hastily wrote "Idaho" in the blank space ⌒ obviously he was making a wild guess at the correct answer.

_____ 21. Ms. Simpson teaches mathematics at the local community college ⌒ she is the only professional educator on the panel.

_____ 22. Some of you may be able to overlook these bits of mischief on the part of our elected officials ⌒ but I can't.

_____ 23. The folders in this stack must be mailed today ⌒ those in the other stack will be mailed next Tuesday.

_____ 24. Betsy spread the frosting on the cupcakes ⌒ and her twin sister put a small strawberry on each cake.

_____ 25. I must postpone our meeting scheduled for tomorrow ⌒ I have to drive my grandmother to her dentist's office.

LESSON **8** ■

Subordination: Adverb Clauses

To this point you have had practice with the simple sentence (one independent clause) and the compound sentence (two or more independent clauses). Basic as these sentences are to our thinking and writing, too much reliance on them can produce a deadening monotony in writing. Worse, the reader is often left to figure out what the writer has in mind but hasn't managed to express in the independent clauses.

"Rain began to fall, and we stopped our ball game" is a perfectly correct sentence. But notice these slightly altered versions:

When rain began to fall, we stopped our ball game.
After rain began to fall, we stopped our ball game.
Because rain began to fall, we stopped our ball game.

These three, in addition to lessening the singsong tone of the compound sentence, are more informative. The first two tell the time at which the game was stopped—and notice that *when* and *after* point out slightly different time elements. The third version gives a different relation between the two statements; it tells not the time of but the reason for stopping the game.

If, instead of writing the compound sentence "Rain was falling, and we continued our ball game," you write "Although rain was falling, we continued our ball game," you have refined your thinking and your expression. Your readers now interpret the sentence exactly as you want them to: They now know that the ball game was continued in spite of the fact that rain was falling.

The process by which a statement is reduced to a secondary form to show its relation to the main idea is **subordination.** The very important grammatical unit that expresses a secondary idea in relation to a main idea is the **subordinate, or dependent, clause,** which we define as a subject–verb combination that cannot stand alone as a sentence. Rather, it functions *within* a sentence as a single part of speech: an adverb, an adjective, or a noun. A sentence made up of one independent clause and at least one dependent clause is a **complex sentence.**

The **adverb clause** can be distinguished from other dependent clauses because, like the simple adverb, it describes the action or state of being by telling something about the action: the time it took place, the reason for or the result of its taking place, and so on. The most common types of adverb clauses, in fact, answer direct questions about the action: "When?" (clause of time); "Where?" (clause of place); and "Why?" (clause of cause).

The relationship between an adverb clause and the main clause is shown by the conjunction that introduces the adverb clause. Remember that the conjunction—the structural signal of subordination—is not an isolated word standing between the two clauses. It is part of the subordinate clause. In such a sentence as "We waited until the police arrived," the unit "the police arrived" could stand alone as an independent clause. But the clause is made dependent by the inclusion of *until*, which signals the dependence of the clause on something else in the sentence for its total meaning.

Various types of adverb clauses, together with their most common conjunctions, are listed for you here, with examples:

Time *(when, whenever, before, after, since, while, until, as, as soon as)*

> The baby cried *when the telephone rang.*
> The cat ran out *before Lou could shut the door.*
> *After the bell rings,* no one can enter.
> I've known Palmer *since he was in high school.*
> You should not whisper *while Dr. Fuller is lecturing.*
> You may leave *as soon as your replacement arrives.*

Place *(where, wherever)*

> We parted *where the paths separated.*
> I shall meet you *wherever you want me to.*

Cause (or **Reason**) *(because, since, as, in order that)*

> I walk to work every day *because I need the exercise.*
> *Since she could not pay the fine,* she could not drive the car.
> *As you are the senior member,* you should lead the procession.
> They came to America *in order that they might have freedom.*

Purpose *(so that, that)*

> We left early *so that we could catch the last bus.*
> They died *that their nation might live.*

Manner *(as, as if, as though)*

> Stan acted *as if the party was boring him.*
> Please do the work *as you have been instructed.*

Result *(so . . . that, such . . . that)*

> Jerry arrived so late *that he missed the concert.*
> The workmen made such a racket *that I got a headache.*

Condition *(if, unless, provided that, on condition that).* This kind of adverb clause gives a condition under which the main clause is true:

> Sit down and chat *if you are not in a hurry.*
> He will not give his talk *unless we pay his expenses.*
> She will sign the contract *provided that we pay her a bonus.*
> *If I were you,* I would accept the offer.
> *If you had told me earlier,* I could have helped.

Certain kinds of conditional clauses can occur in an alternate arrangement. The *if* is not used; instead, a subject–verb inversion signals the subordination. Sentences like the last two preceding examples sometimes take this form:

Were I you, I would accept the offer.
Had you told me earlier, I could have helped.

Concession *(although, though, even if, even though).* This clause concedes or admits a fact in spite of which the main idea is true:

Although she is only nine years old, she plays chess.
Our car is dependable *even though it is old.*

Comparison *(than, as).* Two distinctive characteristics of the adverb clause of comparison should be noted: (1) Part or all of the verb, although it is needed grammatically, is usually not expressed; and (2) when an action verb is not expressed in the subordinate clause, the appropriate form of the auxiliary *do* is often used even though the *do* does not occur in the main clause:

Gold is heavier *than iron [is].*
Your computer is not as new *as mine [is].*
Her theme was better *than any other student's in the class [was].*
Ellen earned more bonus points *than her brother did.*

Your attention was directed in the preceding discussion to the omission of parts of the adverb clause of comparison. **Ellipsis** is the term used for this omission, and a clause that leaves some parts understood or unexpressed is called an **elliptical clause.** (See Supplement 1.) In addition to clauses of comparison, other kinds of adverb clauses may be elliptical. You should be aware of them; although they are structures that can lend variety to your writing, some of them must be used with caution if you are to avoid an awkward error (the dangling modifier) that you will study in a later lesson.

In the following examples, brackets enclose the parts of the clauses that may be unexpressed:

While [I was] walking home, I met Mr. Jones.
When [he is] in Cleveland, he stays with us.
Call your office *as soon as [it is] possible.*
Adjustments will be made *whenever [they are] necessary.*
Mary, *although [she is] a talented girl,* is quite lazy.
If [you are] delayed, call my secretary.
Your ticket, *unless [it is] stamped,* is invalid.

Adverb clauses may modify adjectives and adverbs:

We are sorry *that you must leave early.* [Modifies the adjective *sorry.*]
I am sure *(that) he meant no harm.* [In this type of clause, the conjunction *that* is sometimes unexpressed.]
The car is running better *than it did last week.* [Modifies the adverb *better.*]

A Note on Sentence Variety

Although some adverb clauses—those of comparison, for instance—have a fixed position within the sentence, many adverb clauses may be placed before, inside, or following the main clause. The beginning writer should practice various arrangements to relieve the monotony that comes from reliance on too many "main-subject-plus-main-verb" sentences:

When they deal with the unknown, Greek myths are usually somber.
Greek myths, *when they deal with the unknown,* are usually somber.
Greek myths are usually somber *when they deal with the unknown.*
[NOTE: Usually a comma is not needed when the adverbial clause is the final element of the sentence.]
Although he did not have authority from Congress, President Theodore Roosevelt ordered construction of the Panama Canal.
President Theodore Roosevelt, *although he did not have authority from Congress,* ordered construction of the Panama Canal.
President Theodore Roosevelt ordered construction of the Panama Canal *although he did not have authority from Congress.*

Supplement 1

Occasionally an elliptical adverb clause of comparison must be recast because the exact meaning is unclear when parts of the clause are unexpressed. Here are two sentences that are ambiguous in the shortened forms of the clauses:

	Mr. Alton will pay you more *than Stan.*
Probable Meaning:	Mr. Alton will pay you more than [he will pay] Stan.
Possible Meaning:	Mr. Alton will pay you more than Stan [will pay you].

	Parents dislike homework as much *as their offspring.*
Probable Meaning:	Parents dislike homework as much as their offspring [dislike homework].
Possible Meaning:	Parents dislike homework as much as [they dislike] their offspring.

SUMMARY OF ADVERB CLAUSES

1. Function: to modify a verb, an adjective, or an adverb.
2. Position: fixed for some types (She sold more tickets *than I did*); others may be at the beginning, in the interior, or at the end of main clause.
3. Subordinators: conjunctions, most of which show adverbial relationships such as time *(when, since, while),* cause *(because, as),* and so on.
4. Special structures:
   a. A clause modifying an adjective subjective complement and subordinated by *that* is sometimes unexpressed: I'm sure *(that) you are wrong.*
   b. Elliptical clauses: Mary is older *than I (am old). If (you are) unable to attend,* call me. *While (she was) preparing lunch,* Mary cut her finger.

Practice Sheet 8
Adverb Clauses

NAME _____ SCORE _____

Directions: Identify each of the italicized clauses by writing one of the following numbers in the space at the left:

1. Time	4. Purpose	7. Condition	10. Modifying an
2. Place	5. Manner	8. Concession	adjective
3. Cause	6. Result	9. Comparison	

_____ 1. *Before your bus leaves,* I'll give you my new address.

_____ 2. The family would stop off *wherever the men could find work.*

_____ 3. Laura left the beach *because the sun was too hot for her.*

_____ 4. John worked on the family farm *so that his older brother could attend college.*

_____ 5. Copy this chart *exactly as it appears in the textbook.*

_____ 6. Derwood drank so much strong coffee *that he slept poorly that night.*

_____ 7. You'll win the prize *if you answer this last question correctly.*

_____ 8. *Although the office is small,* three teachers have their desks in it.

_____ 9. This year's graduating class is slightly smaller *than last year's.*

_____ 10. All of us are happy *that you have returned to Centerville.*

_____ 11. Only two students received higher grades *than you did.*

_____ 12. *Though Cheri had not seen me in ten years,* she remembered my name.

_____ 13. *If you were I,* would you apply again next year?

_____ 14. The child reads so slowly *that he is usually behind in his assignments.*

15. The referee is walking *as if his left foot hurts him.*

_____ 16. My grandfather customarily smoked a smelly cigar *after he finished his dinner.*

_____ 17. I have always lived *where I can look out and see mountains.*

_____ 18. *Since he had no choice in the matter,* Mr. Trent paid the fine.

67

_____ 19. These heroes gave their lives *that we might enjoy freedom.*

_____ 20. I am now sure *that the investment was not a wise one.*

_____ 21. *As the plane gained altitude,* my ears hurt slightly.

_____ 22. The faithful old dog waited patiently *where he had last seen his master.*

_____ 23. Russ studies at home *because his Walkman is not allowed in the college library.*

_____ 24. Cut the logs into eighteen-inch lengths *so that the pieces will fit in the fireplace.*

_____ 25. Address the envelopes *as Miss Lambert told you to.*

_____ 26. The explosion made such a loud noise *that the windows rattled.*

_____ 27. We will cancel your reservation *unless we are notified otherwise.*

_____ 28. Bob's resume, *though quite lengthy,* did not impress the committee.

_____ 29. Are you as old *as Susie?*

_____ 30. The authorities are reasonably certain *that the man is an impostor.*

_____ 31. I'm afraid *you're wrong.*

_____ 32. At the age of twenty, Larry is earning more money *than his father ever earned.*

_____ 33. The car is dependable *even though it is fifteen years old.*

_____ 34. *Unless we get some rain soon,* my garden will suffer.

_____ 35. Ned's guardian made such bad investments *that he soon used up the money.*

_____ 36. Children rarely behave in public *as their parents hope they will.*

_____ 37. I am cutting out most sweets *so that I can lose weight.*

_____ 38. *As I had plenty of free time,* I enrolled in a ballet class.

_____ 39. *Where there is this much smoke and haze,* there must be a forest fire.

_____ 40. I have heard nothing from Clark *since he moved to Atlanta.*

EXERCISE 8
ADVERB CLAUSES

NAME _____ SCORE _____

Directions: Each sentence contains one adverb clause. Underline each adverb clause. In the space at the left, write one of the following numbers to identify the type of clause:

1. Time	4. Purpose	7. Condition	10. Modifying an
2. Place	5. Manner	8. Concession	adjective
3. Cause	6. Result	9. Comparison	

_____ 1. He screamed as if he had seen a ghost.

_____ 2. The child stood on a stool so that she could see the parade better.

_____ 3. Because the storm had cut off our electricity, we ate dinner by candlelight.

_____ 4. The family would stop wherever harvest hands were being hired.

_____ 5. I'll pay the rest of the amount after my February check arrives.

_____ 6. The team had such a bad season last year that the coaching staff resigned.

_____ 7. If you don't claim your ticket by ten o'clock, it will be sold to someone else.

_____ 8. Although we have been friends for years, he would not lend me the necessary funds.

_____ 9. Jenny gets better grades in math than her older brother does.

_____ 10. I'm sure that I'm right.

_____ 11. I can run faster than you can.

_____ 12. The house, although old, is in excellent condition.

_____ 13. Your account, if not paid by June 1, will be turned over to a collection agency.

_____ 14. The departing guests made such a clatter that the neighbors were awakened.

_____ 15. One publisher will publish my novel on condition that I change the title.

_____ 16. Although I followed the recipe exactly, the dessert was a failure.

_____ 17. In spite of his gray hair, Laswell is younger than you.

_____ 18. Our entire family is delighted that you will visit us soon.

_____ 19. The mechanic did not do the repair work as he had been ordered to.

_____ 20. Please step aside so that I may enter the auditorium.

_____ 21. As I had much free time that year, I accepted the part-time job.

_____ 22. Wherever he goes, the candidate is greeted by enthusiastic crowds.

_____ 23. We should withhold our applause until the last prizewinner has been introduced.

_____ 24. How can you concentrate where there is so much noise and confusion?

_____ 25. Since no overnight accommodations were available at Compton, we drove on to Pleasantville.

_____ 26. Betsy got extra babysitting jobs so that she could pay for her tennis lessons.

_____ 27. Unfortunately, some of the children giggled while Mrs. Jackman was reciting her poem.

_____ 28. The prisoner had apparently escaped from the compound where the barbed wire had been cut.

_____ 29. Bud wears a gold stud in his earlobe because it annoys his father.

_____ 30. Get to the stadium early so that you can get a good seat for the game.

_____ 31. This has been a happier office since the assistant manager resigned.

_____ 32. The bank guard usually stands where he can see both entrances.

_____ 33. Because I missed the final three class meetings, I must take an extra test.

_____ 34. Grip the golf club exactly as the instructor demonstrated.

_____ 35. Our candidate received so many votes that a run-off election was not necessary.

_____ 36. I certainly would have attended had I been invited.

_____ 37. Beth's son, although still in grade school, is an excellent chess player.

_____ 38. This year's sales figures are slightly better than last year's.

_____ 39. The first witness was certain that the accused man had carried a gun.

_____ 40. We grew so many tomatoes last year that we kept all of our neighbors well supplied.

LESSON 9 ■

Subordination: Adjective Clauses

An **adjective clause** modifies a noun or a pronoun by giving information that points out, identifies, describes, or limits the meaning of the noun or the pronoun. The normal position of an adjective clause is immediately following the noun or the pronoun that it modifies.

Nearly all of the adjective clauses you read, write, or speak use *that, which, who(m), whose, when,* or *where* to tie the adjective clause to the noun or the pronoun it modifies. These subordinators are called **relatives.** Unlike the simple conjunctions that introduce adverb clauses, the relatives function *within* the adjective clause as pronouns (used as subjects, direct objects, or objects of prepositions), adjectives, or adverbs.

It is helpful to think of an adjective clause as a reduced simple sentence that is incorporated within another sentence. This combining is possible when the second clause repeats, directly or by reference, a noun or a pronoun in the first clause. The relative word, by substituting for the repeated noun or pronoun, refers ("relates") directly to the word being modified. Notice that the relative, because it is the word signaling the subordination, always begins the adjective clause.

The following paired units illustrate this process. Every "A" unit has two simple sentences, the second of which repeats a noun in the first. The "B" sentence shows how the second idea has been reduced to a subordinate clause and has become part of the first sentence:

A. This is a well-built truck. *The truck* will save you money.

B. This is a well-built truck *that* will save you money. [The clause modifies *truck. That,* the relative pronoun, is the subject in the adjective clause.]

A. Alice has a new boyfriend. *The new boyfriend* [or *He*] sings in a rock group.

B. Alice has a new boyfriend *who* sings in a rock group. [*Who* is the subject in the clause that modifies *boyfriend.*]

A. Here is the book. I borrowed *the book* [or *it*] yesterday.

B. Here is the book *that* I borrowed yesterday. [*That* is the direct object in the adjective clause.]

A. The firm hired Chet Brown. The boss had known *Chet Brown* [or *him*] in Omaha.

B. The firm hired Chet Brown, *whom* the boss had known in Omaha. [*Whom* is the direct object in the adjective clause.

A. May I introduce Dick Hart? I went to college with *Dick Hart* [or *him*].

B. May I introduce Dick Hart, with *whom* I went to college? [The clause modifies *Dick Hart.* Notice that the preposition *with* stands at the beginning of the clause with its object *whom.* At the informal level of language usage, the preposition in this structure is sometimes found at the end of the clause. See also Supplement 2 of Lesson 6 on page 49.]

A. She is a young artist. I admire the *young artist's* [or *her*] work.

B. She is a young artist *whose* work I admire. [*Work* is in this position because, although it is the direct object of *admire,* it cannot be separated from its modifier, the relative adjective *whose,* which must be placed at the beginning of the adjective clause.]

The relative adverbs *when* and *where* introduce adjective clauses in combinations meaning "time when" and "place where." The following examples show that the subordinator is really the equivalent of an adverbial prepositional phrase. (The "B" sentences are complex sentences combining the material of the two "A" sentences.)

A. Beth and I recalled the time. We considered ourselves rebels *at that time.*

B. Beth and I recalled the time *when* we considered ourselves rebels.

A. This is the spot. The explorers came ashore *at this spot.*

B. This is the spot *where* the explorers came ashore.

These clauses are logically considered adjective clauses because they immediately follow nouns that require identification, and the clauses give the identifying material. If you remember the "time-when" and "place-where" combinations, you will not confuse this type of adjective clause with other subordinate clauses that may use the same subordinators.

NOTE: In certain adjective clauses the relative word is often unexpressed; the meaning is instantly clear without it: the food *(that) we eat,* the house *(that) he lived in,* the man *(whom) you saw,* the time *(when) you fell down,* and so on.

Restrictive and Nonrestrictive Adjective Clauses

An adjective clause is either restrictive or nonrestrictive, and, as you will learn in Lesson 18, an important use of the comma requires that you understand the difference between the two types.

The restrictive adjective clause, the kind that is not set off by commas, *is essential to the identification of the word being modified:*

The grade *that I received on my report* pleased me.
Anyone *who saw the accident* should call the police.

You can see that without the modifying clauses ("The grade pleased me"; "Anyone should call the police") the nouns are not identified. What grade and what anyone are we talking about? But when we add the modifiers, we identify the *particular* grade and the *particular* anyone. In other words, this kind of clause restricts the meaning of a general noun to one specific member of its class.

The nonrestrictive adjective clause, which does require commas, supplies additional or incidental information about the word that it modifies, *but the information is not needed for identifying purposes.* Don't, however, get into the habit of thinking that a nonrestrictive clause is unimportant; unless it has some importance to the meaning of the sentence, it has no right to be in the sentence. If the noun being modified does not require identification, the modifier following it is nonrestrictive and requires commas. It follows, then, that nonrestrictive modifiers are found following proper nouns *(Mount Everest, Philadelphia, Mr. Frank Lockwood);* nouns already identified (the oldest *boy* in her class, her only *grandchild*); and one-of-a-kind nouns (Alice's *mother,* the *provost* of the college, the *writer* of the editorial).

The following examples contrast restrictive and nonrestrictive adjective clauses. (See Supplement 1.)

I visited an old and close friend *who is retiring soon.* [Restrictive.]
I visited my oldest and closest friend, *who is retiring soon.* [Nonrestrictive.]

The man *whose car had been wrecked* asked us for a ride. [Restrictive.]
Mr. Ash, *whose car had been wrecked,* asked us for a ride. [Nonrestrictive.]

A small stream *that flows through the property* supplies an occasional trout. [Restrictive.]
Caldwell Creek, *which flows through the property,* supplies an occasional trout. [Nonrestrictive.]

She wants to retire to a place *where freezing weather is unknown.* [Restrictive.]
She wants to retire to Panama City, *where freezing weather is unknown.* [Nonrestrictive.]

Supplement 1

A few distinctions in the use of *who, which,* and *that* in adjective clauses are generally observed. *Which* refers only to things; *who* refers to people; and *that* refers to things or people. *That* is used only in restrictive clauses; in other words, a "that" adjective clause is not set off by commas. Because *which* is the relative pronoun that must be used in a nonrestrictive clause modifying a thing, a convention that *which* should not introduce a restrictive adjective clause is generally, but by no means always, observed.

SUMMARY OF ADJECTIVE CLAUSES

1. Function: to modify a noun or a pronoun.
2. Position: follows the noun or pronoun that it modifies.
3. Subordinators:
   a. relative pronouns *(who, whom, which, that),* which function within the adjective clause as subjects, direct objects, or objects of prepositions
   b. relative adjectives *(whose, which)*
   c. relative adverbs *(when, where)*
4. Special problem: Adjective clauses that are vital to the identification of the nouns being modified are restrictive and do not require commas. Clauses not necessary for identification are nonrestrictive and are set off by commas.

Practice Sheet 9

Adjective Clauses

NAME _____ SCORE _____

Directions: Each italicized unit is an adjective clause. (Some of the sentences contain adverb clauses also.) In the space at the left, copy the noun or pronoun that the adjective clause modifies. Be sure you can explain why the following sentences contain nonrestrictive clauses and thus require commas: 2, 5, 8, 11, 12, 15, 25, 28, 31, 32, 35, 37, 38, 40. Here is some information to guide you in the examination of the sentences:

    1. In these sentences the italicized clause occurs *within* an adverb clause: 1, 3, 5, 13, 17, 21, 22, 33, 35, 39.

    2. In these sentences an adverb clause occurs *within* the italicized adjective clause: 2, 9, 16, 19, 24, 29.

_____ 1. Our history teacher will be satisfied only if we read both the books *that she assigned to us.*

_____ 2. Joyce took her cousin to see the local high school, *where she had played volleyball when she was a senior.*

_____ 3. Jim changed his plans because the flight *on which he had reservations* was canceled.

_____ 4. Andy still carries the watch *his grandfather gave him when he graduated from high school.*

_____ 5. I have never trusted Dick Lee, *who probably gave the story to the reporters.*

_____ 6. Since the road *we usually took to the farm* was closed, we had to take a long detour.

_____ 7. The police are certain that they will find someone *who witnessed the altercation.*

_____ 8. Jerry spent his vacation in Dallas, *where his cousin manages a theater.*

_____ 9. Last week I read a mystery *which was better than anything I read last summer.*

_____ 10. If you can find the spot *where the money is hidden,* you'll be a very rich person.

_____ 11. When I was a girl, I always envied Julie Ross, *whose hair was longer and silkier than mine.*

_____ 12. Ms. Treadwell looked at Tim's theme, *one page of which was stained with grease and ketchup.*

_____ 13. If the report *the sergeant gave us* is true, heads will roll.

_____ 14. I revisited the house *where I roomed when I was in college.*

_____ 15. This trip took place in 1938, *when rural roads were not maintained as well as they are today.*

_____ 16. The usher stopped a woman *who was trying to slip into her seat after the performance started.*

_____ 17. When the fellow *whose car I had borrowed* reappeared, I was mightily embarrassed.

75

_____ 18. I am sure that those *who arrive late* will not be seated until intermission.

_____ 19. Our new neighbor had a dog *that barks whenever anyone walks down the street.*

_____ 20. Lou is the only one of my close friends *who is older than I.*

_____ 21. Janice's car alarm went off so often last weekend that the man *who lives downstairs* called the police.

_____ 22. The dean is still angry because he cannot identify the person *who wrote that funny satire on college life.*

_____ 23. My advisor enrolled me in Speech 301, *which is not a required course.*

_____ 24. After George pitched the no-hitter, he heard from scouts *who hadn't called him since he was in the tenth grade.*

_____ 25. Although Grandma's sofa, *where I was lying,* was so short that I could not stretch out, I soon fell asleep anyway.

_____ 26. I reminded Terry of the time *our boat ran out of gas in the middle of the lake.*

_____ 27. Nearly everything *Dad read in the paper this morning* upset him.

_____ 28. James, *whose car was parked next to mine,* had left his lights on.

_____ 29. Robert probably left that book on the table *where he was sitting when he ate his lunch.*

_____ 30. Beth was upset because the term paper subject *she was assigned* seemed very dull.

_____ 31. Martin grew up in Guthrie Center, *where most public activities cease as soon as the sun goes down.*

_____ 32. I'll send this article to my father-in-law, *whose hobby is numismatics.*

_____ 33. I would take a nap if I could find a place *where I could not hear all those children playing.*

_____ 34. Ben was late for the meeting because the bus *he usually takes at 7:15* was involved in an accident.

_____ 35. When Joan's old van, *which was carrying the children,* skidded off the road, everyone remained remarkably calm.

_____ 36. Phil is always distressed if his special pickles, *which he enters every year at the fair,* don't win a prize.

_____ 37. I'll help you with the dishes as soon as I finish Mark's article, *which I just started.*

_____ 38. The test covered five of Shakespeare's plays, *only two of which I had read.*

_____ 39. Roy left the library after he was told the name of the person *who runs the Periodicals Department.*

_____ 40. The guard was standing where he could see Jane's fall, *which happened in the hallway.*

EXERCISE 9

Adjective Clauses

NAME _____ SCORE _____

Directions: Each of these sentences contains an adjective clause. None of the clauses are set off by commas. Put parentheses around each adjective clause. (NOTE: In some sentences, an adverb clause that relates to the adjective clause should be included within the parentheses.) In the first space at the left, write the word that the clause modifies. In the second space, write R (restrictive) or N (nonrestrictive). Put commas where needed to set off the nonrestrictive clauses.

_____ 1. The freezing wind was so strong that the road crew who usu-
_____   ally work until five o'clock went home at noon.

_____ 2. Although the restaurant you recommended was crowded, the
_____   food and the service were good.

_____ 3. After dinner our host showed us pictures he had taken while
_____   he was traveling in Chile.

_____ 4. Mr. Starbuck is one of those people who are generous to a
_____   fault.

_____ 5. Mr. Starbuck is the only one of my neighbors who owns a
_____   pickup truck.

_____ 6. We neighbors, I'm afraid, take advantage of generous Mr.
_____   Starbuck who owns a pickup truck.

_____ 7. Jane's last appearance with the marching band was at the 1991
_____   owa-Wisconsin game where rain poured down during the en-
                               tire game.

_____ 8. Mother kept every one of the letters Mark wrote her when he
_____   was in Africa.

_____ 9. He worked on the docks at a time when stevedores were
_____   poorly organized.

_____ 10. We'll discuss this matter on Easter Sunday when the entire
_____   family will be assembled at Aunt Mary's house,

_____ 11. The manager introduced me to an assistant who would handle
_____   my account.

_____ 12. The manager introduced me to Edith Tate who would handle
_____   my account.

_____ 13. The new regulation does not apply to transfer students who
_____   took basic math courses before they came to Ohio State.

_____ 14. I have never met the person who will teach my classes while
_____   I am on leave.

—————————————— 15. Yesterday, I met Bonnie Stewart who will teach my classes
—————   while I am on leave.

—————————————— 16. The battered package contained fresh oranges from Florida
—————   only a few of which were still edible.

—————————————— 17. The central figure of the movie is a young boy whose parents
—————   are unaware that he has real musical talent.

—————————————— 18. Although the apartment is in an undesirable part of town, it
—————   was the only one we could find when we moved to the city.

—————————————— 19. The sonnet is a poetic form that contains fourteen lines of five-
—————   foot iambic verse.

—————————————— 20. You might receive a term grade of Incomplete if your record
—————   hows many absences for which you have no acceptable
    excuse.

—————————————— 21. Jake's father had bought one hundred shares of the stock at a
—————   time when prices were depressed.

—————————————— 22. Jake's father had bought one hundred shares of the stock in
—————   1951 when prices were depressed.

—————————————— 23. Anne was wearing one of the scarves she had bought when she
—————   was in Rome last year.

—————————————— 24. Anne was wearing her favorite scarf which she had bought
—————   when she was in Rome last year.

—————————————— 25. The family next moved to Mobile where rents were much
—————   cheaper than those in New York.

—————————————— 26. Beth found a term paper she had written when she was an
—————   undergraduate.

—————————————— 27. The twins were born on January 15 which is also the birthday
—————   of Martin Luther King, Jr.

—————————————— 28. If you take the bus that leaves Chicago at 9:30, you should
—————   arrive in plenty of time.

—————————————— 29. Mr. Layton generally seems quite self-conscious when he is
—————   with people who are much younger than he is.

—————————————— 30. Jenny sent the old letters to her mother-in-law who is keeping
—————   all of the family records.

LESSON 10 ■

Subordination: Noun Clauses

The noun clause contains, of course, a subject–verb combination and some kind of subordinator that keeps the clause from being an independent clause. The noun clause, unlike most adverb and adjective clauses, is not an appendage detachable from the main clause. Rather, it functions *within* the main clause in one of the noun "slots": subject, direct object, renaming subjective complement, object of preposition, or appositive.

You will better understand the use of the noun clause if you think of it as a clause equivalent of a "something" or a "someone" in one of these noun slots:

Someone told a lie.   } [Single-word subjects.]
The *witness* told a lie.   }

Whoever repeated that story told a lie.   [Noun clause as subject.]

Mr. Allen announced *something.*   } [Single-word direct objects.]
Mr. Allen announced *his resignation.*   }
Mr. Allen announced *that he would resign.*   [Noun clause as direct object.]

Give the package to *someone.*   } [Single-word objects of preposition.]
Give the package to *the janitor.*   }
Give the package to *whoever opens the door.*   [Noun clause as object of preposition.]

His *story* is very convincing.
What he told us is very convincing.   [Noun clause as subject.]

This is his *story.*
This is *what he told us.*   [Noun clause as subjective complement.]

Can you tell me your *time* of arrival?
Can you tell me *when you will arrive?*   [Noun clause as direct object.]

Most of the noun clauses that you read and write will be in the above-mentioned positions: subject, direct object (the commonest use), subjective complement, or object of preposition. Two other rather special uses should be noted, the "delayed" noun clause and the appositive noun clause.

One common use of a noun clause is as a delayed subject. The signal for this construction is the word *it* standing in subject position, with the meaningful subject being a noun clause following the verb:

It is unfortunate *that you were delayed.* [Although the clause follows the verb, it is the real subject and therefore is a noun clause. The meaning of the sentence is "That you were delayed is unfortunate."]

A related noun clause use puts *it* in the direct object slot with a noun clause following an objective complement. This use, which is encountered less frequently than the delayed subject, gives us a clause that we can call a delayed direct object:

> We think it unlikely *that Jones will be reelected.*

To understand the other special noun clause, we must know what an appositive is. The **appositive** is a noun unit inserted into a sentence to *rename* another noun that usually immediately precedes the appositive. A simple example occurs in the following sentence:

> Senator Jones, *a dedicated environmentalist,* objected.

Because any noun unit can be used as an appositive, noun clauses sometimes function in this position. Some noun clause appositives are separated from the first noun by at least a comma, sometimes by a heavier mark:

> There still remains one mystery: *how the thief knew your name.* [The noun clause renames the preceding noun, *mystery.*]

A rather special type of noun appositive clause, subordinated by *that* and following such nouns as *fact, belief, hope, statement, news,* and *argument,* is usually not set off by any mark of punctuation:

> You cannot deny the fact *that you lied under oath.*
> Your statement *that the boss is stupid* was undiplomatic.

(See Supplement 1.)
   The subordinating words that serve to introduce noun clauses are conjunctions *(that, if, whether);* pronouns *(who, whom, what, which, whoever, whatever, whichever);* adjectives *(whose, which, what);* and adverbs *(when, where, why, how).* Remember that the subordinating word is part of the clause and always stands at or near the beginning of the clause. Remember also that in noun clauses used as direct objects the conjunction *that* is often unexpressed because the meaning is usually clear without it.

> I know *that you will be happy here.* [Noun clause subordinated by the conjunction *that.*]
> Jill now wonders *if her answer was the correct one.* [Noun clause subordinated by the conjunction *if.*]
> All of us hope *you'll return soon.* [Noun clause subordinated by the understood conjunction *that.*]
> I do not know *who he is.* [Noun clause subordinated by the pronoun *who* used as the subjective complement within the clause.]
> I know *what I would do with the extra money.* [Noun clause subordinated by the pronoun *what* used as the direct object within the clause.]
> Tell me *whom Mary is feuding with now.* [Noun clause subordinated by the pronoun *whom* used as the object of the preposition *with.*]
> You must decide *which car you will use today.* [Noun clause subordinated by the adjective *which* modifying the direct object *car.*]
> *Why Morton left school* still puzzles his friends. [Noun clause subordinated by the adverb *why.*]

(See Supplement 2.)

Supplement 1

Because an appositive is a renamer, it represents a reduced form of a Pattern 2 sentence in which a subject and a noun subjective complement are joined by a form of *be.* The writer of the sentence "Senator Jones, a dedicated environmentalist, objected" could have written two simple sentences, the second one repeating a noun used in the first:

Senator Jones objected.
Senator Jones [*or* He] is a dedicated environmentalist.

The adjective clause offers the writer one device for compressing this information into one sentence:

Senator Jones, *who is a dedicated environmentalist,* objected.

The appositive represents a further compression:

Senator Jones, *a dedicated environmentalist,* objected.

If you think of the appositive as a renamer of the preceding noun (the two nouns could be joined by a form of *be*), you have a handy test to help you recognize any noun appositive use:

There still remains one mystery: *how the thief knew your name.* [Test: The mystery *is* how the thief knew your name.]
You can't deny the fact *that she has real talent.* [Test: The fact *is* that she has real talent.]
Your contention *that the witness lied* has some merit. [Test: The contention *is* that the witness lied.]

If you remember a few points about the form, the function, and the positioning of adjective clauses and noun clauses, you should have little difficulty in distinguishing between them. Although certain kinds of noun clauses in apposition may, at first glance, look like adjective clauses, a few simple tests clearly show the difference:

The news *that you brought us* is welcome. [Adjective clause.]
The news *that Bob has recovered* is welcome. [Noun clause.]

If you remember that an adjective clause is a *describer* and that an appositive noun clause is a *renamer,* you can see that in the first sentence the clause describes—in fact, identifies—the noun *news,* but it does not actually tell us what the news is. In the second sentence the clause does more: It tells us what the news is. Remember the *be* test. "The news is *that you brought us . . .*" does not make sense, but "The news is *that Bob has recovered . . .*" does; therefore the second clause is a noun clause in apposition. Another test that can be applied to these two types of sentences is based on the fact that in adjective clauses, but not in noun clauses, *which* can be substituted for *that.* "The news *which* you brought us . . ." is acceptable English; the clause, in this case, is an adjective clause. But because we can't say "The news *which* Bob has recovered . . .," this time the clause is a noun clause; it cannot be an adjective clause.

Supplement 2

You have probably already noticed that the pronouns, adjectives, and adverbs that subordinate noun clauses are essentially the same words that are used in questions (Lesson 6). The two uses are alike in the important respect that they always stand at the beginning of the clause. The two uses differ in that as interrogatives the words bring about the subject–verb inversion, whereas in noun clauses the subject–verb positioning is the normal one:

> *Whom* will the mayor appoint? [This sentence is a direct question; it calls for an answer. *Whom* is the direct object of the main verb.]
> *I wonder whom* the mayor will appoint. [This sentence is a statement, not a direct question. Notice that a question mark is not required. *Whom* is the direct object within the noun clause.]

SUMMARY NOUN CLAUSES

1. Function: to fill a noun "slot" within the main clause.
2. Positions: subject (or delayed subject), renaming subjective complement, direct object (or delayed direct object), object of preposition, or appositive.
3. Subordinators:
   a. conjunctions *(that, if, whether)*
   b. pronouns *(who, whom, which, what,* and . . . *ever* forms, standing for unknown persons or things
   c. adjectives *(whose, which, what)*
   d. adverbs *(when, where, why, how)*
4. Special problem: Some noun appositive clauses closely resemble adjective clauses. But they differ in that, in addition to *describing* the noun, the appositive clause *renames* the noun:
   The remark *that Jim made* (adjective clause) was unwise.
   The remark *that Mr. Smith cannot be trusted* (noun clause) was unwise.

Practice Sheet 10
Noun Clauses

NAME _____ SCORE _____

Directions: Identify the use of each italicized noun clause by writing one of the following abbreviations in the space at the left:

    S. [subject or delayed subject]   S.C. [subjective complement]
    D.O. [direct or delayed direct object]   O.P. [object of preposition]
                                     Ap. [appositive]

_____ 1. And that is *why I have always disliked parsnips.*

_____ 2. *Whoever did this* must have had a key to the office.

_____ 3. Can you explain to me *how I might improve my golf swing?*

_____ 4. I hope *you'll feel better soon.*

_____ 5. It's a foregone conclusion *that our football coach will be replaced soon.*

_____ 6. *How he became a skilled photographer* is a long story.

_____ 7. We were amazed at *how cheerful Uncle Norm was.*

_____ 8. Thatcher's main objection to the lease is *that the rent on the warehouse is too high.*

_____ 9. It's a pity *that the lecture series did not receive more publicity.*

_____ 10. It really distresses me *that you doubt my story.*

_____ 11. Do you think it possible *that Schaeffer might be elected?*

_____ 12. The belief *that milk sours during a severe thunderstorm* was once popular.

_____ 13. Your statement *that the legislators are a bunch of crooks* will earn you few votes.

_____ 14. Your advisor will tell you *where your first class meets.*

_____ 15. I agree with your contention *that the bankruptcy laws should be simplified.*

_____ 16. I sometimes wonder *if this rain will ever cease.*

_____ 17. Have the police revealed *whose fingerprints were found on the knife?*

_____ 18. I think *I'm ready for the exam.*

_____ 19. This spot is *where the first settlers from Norway landed.*

_____ 20. Why have the newspapers printed nothing about *what really happened?*

83

Directions: Each of the following sentences contains a noun clause. Put parentheses around each noun clause and identify its use by writing one of the following in the space at the left:

    S. [subject or delayed subject]   S.C. [subjective complement]
    D.O. [direct object or delayed direct object]   O.P. [object of preposition]
                                        Ap. [appositive]

NOTE: In the following sentences the noun clause is within another subordinate clause: 1, 3, 6, 11, 20.

In the following sentences the noun clause contains within it another subordinate clause: 2, 5, 10, 13, 14, 16.

1. Martha chuckled softly while Jim tried to remember where he had left his keys.

2. Jack's contention was that the price we had paid was too high.

3. Although the old man could not tell me where the county courthouse is, we had an interesting conversation.

4. Her friends think it unlikely that Fran will every marry again.

5. Part of Dennis's problem is that he resists those who try to help him.

6. Since the item that was delivered to my apartment was not what I had purchased at the store, I returned it the next day.

7. It's true that I should have studied harder for the exam.

8. I must admit that I should have studied harder for the exam.

9. My admission that I should have studied harder for the exam surprised my roommates.

10. I suspect that voters who live in farming areas will defeat the referendum.

11. Why didn't you object if you knew that you were being overcharged?

12. The truth of the matter is that Jackson could not pay the initiation fee.

13. Whoever owns the Buick that is blocking my driveway should be arrested.

14. It is quite possible that the report you got the figures from is out of date.

15. Don't you ever worry about how you will pay for these luxuries?

16. Why Mary Ellen still works when she could retire with a good pension puzzles some of us.

17. I know that the receptionist was surprised by the request I made.

18. Right-thinking citizens think it a crime that the school levy was defeated.

19. One reporter asked the candidate if he had any inherited wealth.

20. Frankly, I was shocked when Al admitted he had never voted.

EXERCISE 10
NOUN CLAUSES

NAME _____ SCORE _____

Directions: Each of the following sentences contains one noun clause. Put parentheses ( ) around each noun clause. In the space at the left, write one of the following to identify the use of the noun clause:

    S. [Subject or delayed subject]   S.C. [subjective complement]
    D.O. [direct object or delayed direct object]   O.P. [object of preposition]
                                           Ap. [appositive]

_____ 1. If what you say is true, the authorities should be notified.

_____ 2. Ellie asked Professor Twiggs if she could leave as soon as she finished her exam.

_____ 3. It is understandable that Marcia was surprised by the remark.

_____ 4. Whoever wrote the anonymous letter was probably someone who once worked for Mr. Sumner.

_____ 5. I'm sure that the office staff will work cooperatively with whoever replaces Ms. Benson.

_____ 6. The new directive emphasizes the fact that, whenever possible, local people will be hired.

_____ 7. This is where I was standing when the sirens sounded.

_____ 8. When she was told she had won first prize, Maxine burst into tears.

_____ 9. Local soccer fans are wondering why the coach is keeping Landers on the bench.

_____ 10. Some fans think it odd that Landers has had little playing time in the last three games.

_____ 11. One rumor that is circulating is that Landers will soon lose his job.

_____ 12. My neighbor asked me how I liked my new typewriter.

_____ 13. It's unlikely that we'll ever learn much about Christopher Columbus's origins.

_____ 14. The underlying theme of the book is that there are hundreds of tasty recipes that dieters can safely use.

_____ 15. I'll never forget how pleased Lynn's father was when he was told about her promotion.

_____ 16. The police would like statements from whoever was in the vicinity when the blast occurred.

_____ 17. Because it has been serviced well, no one would suspect the car has been driven nearly 200,000 miles.

_____ 18. The police think it quite possible that Brisbane has already fled to Mexico.

_____ 19. Some pundits believe that war between the two countries is inevitable.

_____ 20. The belief that war between the two countries is inevitable is held by some pundits.

_____ 21. The belief that is held by some pundits is that war between the two countries is inevitable.

_____ 22. I'm sure that you can rely on whatever Ms. Lawson tells you.

_____ 23. The students are not told why the school requires the information that is asked for on the questionnaire.

_____ 24. Did you see the announcement in the bulletin that the lecture has been postponed?

_____ 25. One problem that worries local sportsmen is that Lake Elkins is becoming dangerously polluted.

_____ 26. Local sportsmen worry about the fact that Lake Elkins is becoming dangerously polluted.

_____ 27. It's possible, of course, that you picked up someone else's notebook.

_____ 28. Can you explain why a service charge was added to the bill I received this month?

_____ 29. This service is available to whoever needs counseling.

_____ 30. Will what you have just heard have any effect on the way that you vote?

_____ 31. Jackie soon realized that the purchases she had made at the mall were unwise.

_____ 32. Everyone in the main office is curious about who Marcie's replacement will be.

_____ 33. The reporter's version was quite different from what the candidate really said.

_____ 34. Pack nothing except what you will need while you are on the cruise.

_____ 35. It has recently been revealed that Lambert was once an agent for the FBI.

_____ 36. Ned's excuse was that he had stayed home because of illness.

_____ 37. Do you believe Ned's excuse that he stayed home because of illness?

_____ 38. Have you learned when the new city manager will assume office?

_____ 39. I'm afraid that few people will find much merit in what you propose.

_____ 40. Don't you find it amusing that Freddie has become an ultra-conservative voter?

EXERCISE 10A

SUBORDINATE CLAUSES

NAME _____   SCORE _____

Directions: The italicized material in each of these sentences is a subordinate clause. In the first space at the left, write Adv., Adj., or N. to identify the clause. Within the italicized clause, the word printed in boldface type is a complement. Identify it by writing in the second space at the left one of the following:

      S.C. [subjective complement]   I.O. [indirect object]
      D.O. [direct object]   O.C. [objective complement]

_____   1. The handwriting expert explained carefully to the court *why he considered*
_____   *the signature a **forgery**.*

_____   2. Shortly after she was inaugurated, the governor appointed as her assistant
_____   a man *who had once been her business **partner**.*

_____   3. Uncle Bart will vote for anyone *who promises him lower **taxes**.*
_____

_____   4. Uncle Bart will vote for *whoever promises **him** lower taxes.*
_____

_____   5. The first bird *that visited our new feeding **station*** was an ugly crow.
_____

_____   6. "We'll release you *as soon as you tell **us** the name of the driver of the car*,"
_____   said the detective.

_____   7. Was Anderson's reply to your question ***what** you expected?*
_____

_____   8. The crowd of alumni, *although **smaller** than we had anticipated*, had a
_____   good time.

_____   9. Annabelle is always pleased when anyone tells her *she looks **younger** than*
_____   *her brother.*

_____ 10. When the crowded bus unloaded, the detective momentarily lost sight of
_____   the man ***whom** he was keeping under surveillance.*

_____ 11. "And now you know *why most experts call this statue a **masterpiece**,*" he
_____   answered.

_____ 12. The crowd moved indoors *because the weather had turned quite **chilly**.*
_____

_____ 13. "It shouldn't surprise you," said the doctor, "*that you lack the* **energy** *you*
_____ *had fifteen years ago.*"

_____ 14. The loan officer insisted *that I tell* **her** *what my annual salary is.*
_____

_____ 15. At summer camp Elaine shared with her tentmates some family events *that*
_____ *should have been kept* **secret.**

_____ 16. In a corner of the main library reading room, I finally found a quiet spot
_____ *where I could review my* **notes.**

_____ 17. I'll sell my old jalopy to the person *who makes* **me** *the best offer.*
_____

_____ 18. I'll sell my old jalopy to *whoever makes me the best* **offer.**
_____

_____ 19. Mark's financial situation this month shows some improvement, *although*
_____ *a few old bills still remain* **unpaid.**

_____ 20. *While attending a national PTA* **convention** *in Atlanta,* Mrs. Loomis lost
_____ a purse that contained all of her credit cards.

_____ 21. By this time tomorrow, we'll know **who** *the two finalists will be.*
_____

_____ 22. Grandma Thorpe produced some old comic books *that kept the two young-*
_____ *sters* **amused** *for nearly an hour.*

_____ 23. "Do you think the neighbors will be unhappy *if we paint our fence* **pur-**
_____ **ple**?" asked Ben.

_____ 24. "Do you think *the neighbors will be* **unhappy** if we paint our fence pur-
_____ ple?" asked Ben.

_____ 25. The meal *she served the hungry* **boys** was simple but tasty.
_____

LESSON 11 ■

Subordination: Gerund Phrases; Infinitive Phrases

A phrase is a group of related words that does *not* contain a subject and a verb in combination. Like the subordinate clause, the phrase is used in the sentence as a single part of speech.

Many of the sentences that you have studied thus far have shown the common modifying uses of the **prepositional phrase,** which consists of a preposition (see Lesson 2), a noun or a pronoun used as its object, and any modifiers of the object. Most prepositional phrases are used as adjectives or adverbs:

> Most *of my friends* live *in the East.* [The first phrase is used as an adjective to modify the pronoun *most;* the second is used as an adverb to modify *live.*]

Much less commonly, a prepositional phrase is used as a noun:

> *Before lunch* is the best time for the meeting. [The phrase is the subject of the verb *is.*]
> She waved to us from *inside the phone booth.* [The phrase is the object of the preposition *from.*]

Another very important kind of phrase makes use of a verbal. A **verbal** is a word formed from a verb but used as a different part of speech. There are three kinds of verbals: the gerund, the participle, and the infinitive.

A **gerund** is recognized by the ending *ing,* either on the simple form *(studying)* or on an auxiliary *(having studied, being studied, having been studied).* As was suggested about noun clauses, you might think of the gerund phrase as the equivalent of a "something" that fills one of the noun slots in the sentence: subject, direct object, renaming subjective complement, object of preposition, or (rarely) appositive.

> *Studying* demands most of my time. [Subject.]
> I usually enjoy *studying.* [Direct object.]
> My main activity is *studying.* [Renaming subjective complement.]
> You won't pass the course without *studying.* [Object of preposition.]
> Might I suggest to you another activity: *studying?* [Appositive.]

These single-word gerund uses are uncomplicated. "He enjoys *studying*" and "He enjoys *football*" are alike in their structure; the only difference is that in one the direct object is a word formed from a verb and in the other it is a regular noun. But verbals have a quality that nouns do not have: they can take adverbial modifiers and they can take complements. As in basic sentences, the kind of complement in a verbal phrase is determined by the kind of verb from which the verbal is derived. Thus the verbal form

89

of a transitive verb must be followed by a direct object (sometimes used with an indirect object or an objective complement), and the verbal form of a linking verb must be followed by a subjective complement. The following examples will help to clarify this important point. In each of the sentences the phrase is a **gerund phrase** because it is used as the direct object of the main verb.

> He enjoys *walking in the snow.* [The gerund has no complement. Compare "He walks in the snow."]
>
> She enjoys *building model airplanes.* [*Airplanes* is the direct object of the gerund *building.* Compare "She builds model airplanes."]
>
> He enjoys *being helpful.* He enjoyed *being elected treasurer.* [*Helpful* is the subjective complement of the gerund *being; treasurer* is the subjective complement of the passive gerund *being elected.* Compare "He is helpful" and "He was elected treasurer."]
>
> She enjoyed *telling us the good news.* [*Us* is the indirect object and *news* the direct object of the gerund *telling.* Compare "She told us the good news."]
>
> He enjoyed *making our vacation pleasant.* [*Vacation* is the direct object and *pleasant* the objective complement of *vacation.* Compare "He made our vacation pleasant."]

An **infinitive** is a verbal consisting of the simple stem of the verb, generally preceded by *to* (*to* is called the sign of the infinitive). The infinitive uses auxiliaries to show tense and voice: *to study, to have studied, to be studying, to have been studying, to be studied, to have been studied.*

An **infinitive phrase** consists of an infinitive plus its modifiers and/or complements. Infinitive units are used as nouns, as adjectives, and as adverbs:

> *To attend the party without an invitation* would be tactless. [The infinitive phrase is used as the subject of the sentence. Within the phrase, *party* is the direct object.]
>
> It would be tactless *to attend the party without an invitation.* [In this pattern the infinitive phrase is called a delayed subject; hence it serves a noun use. The signal word is *it;* although it stands in subject position, the infinitive phrase is the meaningful subject. Sometimes the *it* is in the direct object slot with the delayed infinitive phrase following an objective complement: I would consider it tactless *to attend the party without an invitation.* Compare a similar noun clause use in Lesson 10.]
>
> I wanted *to give Chalmers another chance.* [The infinitive phrase is the direct object of *wanted.* Within the phrase, *Chalmers* is the indirect object and *chance* the direct object of the infinitive. Compare "I gave Chalmers another chance."]
>
> My plan is *to become an active precinct worker.* [The infinitive phrase is used as a noun; it is a subjective complement that renames the subject *plan.* Within the phrase, *worker* is the subjective complement of the infinitive. Compare "I became an active precinct worker."]
>
> The test *to be taken next Friday* is an important one. [The infinitive phrase is used as an adjective modifying *test.*]
>
> I am happy *to make your acquaintance.* [The infinitive phrase is used as an adverb modifying the adjective *happy.*]
>
> *To be sure of a good seat,* you should arrive early. [The infinitive phrase is used as an adverb modifying *should arrive.*]

(See Supplement 1.)

Infinitive phrases sometimes include their own subjects. (Notice that a pronoun used as the subject of an infinitive is in the objective case.) And in a rather common sentence type, the subject of an infinitive is preceded by *for,* which in this use is considered part of the phrase.

We wanted *her to resign.*
We know *him to be a good referee.*
For us to leave now would be impolite.
It's silly *for you to feel neglected.*

The infinitive without the *to* may form a phrase that is used as the direct object of such verbs as *let, help, make, see, hear,* and *watch:*

The teacher let *us leave early.*
Martha watched *her son score the winning touchdown.*

The infinitive without *to* is also sometimes used as the object of a preposition, such as *except, but,* or *besides:*

He could do nothing except *resign gracefully.*

SUMMARY OF GERUND PHRASES; INFINITIVE PHRASES

GERUND PHRASES

1. Forms: *studying, having studied, being studied, having been studied.*
2. Function: used as a noun within the larger unit.
3. Positions: subject, renaming subjective complement, direct object, object of preposition, and (rarely) appositive.

INFINITIVE PHRASES

1. Forms: *to study, to have studied, to be studying, to have been studying, to be studied, to have been studied.* Some infinitive phrases have subjects (We wanted *her to run for office*).
2. Function: may be used as adjective (Here are the letters *to be mailed today*) as adverb (I am happy *to meet you*), or as noun (*To leave* now would be unwise).
3. Positions: subject (or delayed subject), direct object (or delayed direct object), renaming subjective complement, and (rarely) object of preposition.
4. Special structures:
   a. "For" sometimes introduces a phrase that has a subject (*For you to criticize his work* would be presumptuous).
   b. A phrase with a subject but without the marker "to" is often used as a direct object following one of these verbs: *let, help, make, see, hear, watch:*

      Mother let *us mix the cookie dough.*

      Ms. Jones heard *the man threaten the cashier.*

Supplement 1

In Lesson 6 you learned that in a direct question an interrogative unit stands at the beginning of the sentence. Notice how this positioning can affect the internal makeup of a gerund phrase or an infinitive phrase:

How many natives did the missionaries succeed in *converting?* [*Converting* is the gerund form of a transitive verb and therefore requires a direct object, in this case *natives.*]
Which car did you finally decide *to buy?* [*Car* is the direct object of the infinitive *to buy.*]

Practice Sheet 11

Gerund Phrases; Infinitive Phrases

NAME _____ SCORE _____

Directions: In the space at the left, write one of the following numbers to identify the use of the italicized gerund phrase:
   1. Subject   3. Subjective Complement
   2. Direct Object   4. Object of Preposition

_____ 1. Pat thinks we should consider *hiking the Appalachian Trail.*

_____ 2. Harold tried to find his lost ring by *using a metal detector.*

_____ 3. In class yesterday, we practiced *drawing small circles.*

_____ 4. Is *keeping the dog free of fleas* the hardest part of the dog owner's job?

_____ 5. After *finishing that novel,* you should read her first book, which is far better than anything else she has written.

_____ 6. The least interesting part of that job was *filing the letters written in response to customers' complaints.*

_____ 7. Max insisted on *opening the mail first thing in the morning.*

_____ 8. When did she stop *writing those mushy love letters to Albert?*

_____ 9. Has *studying for the bar exam* proved to be a tedious piece of work?

_____ 10. The toughest job for any politician is *finding volunteers who are willing to raise campaign funds.*

_____ 11. After *leaving the campus,* I drove to the lake for the class picnic.

_____ 12. Everyone in the family wishes that you would stop *bringing those strange friends of yours home for dinner.*

_____ 13. I never thought that *studying for exams* would be this difficult.

_____ 14. A friend of mine has made a great deal of money by *collecting and trading baseball cards.*

_____ 15. Aunt Lois's chief ambition these days is *learning to drive race cars.*

_____ 16. Because my first class is very early, I never get to read the morning paper before *leaving for the campus.*

_____ 17. For my next diet I think I will try *skipping every other meal.*

_____ 18. My job in the mail room is *sorting the mail addressed to the sixth floor.*

_____ 19. Jonathan was very proud of himself for *serving as drum major in the marching band.*

_____ 20. Upon *reaching the bottom of the hill,* every skier let out a loud whoop of triumph.

Directions: In the space at the left, write one of the following abbreviations to identify the use within the sentence of the italicized infinitive phrase:

N. [subject, delayed subject, direct object, subjective complement, object of preposition]

Adj. [adjective]
Adv. [adverb]

_____ 1. *To be sure of a good seat at the concert,* you must buy your tickets early.

_____ 2. The frustrated student could do nothing except *select another topic for the research project.*

_____ 3. It is always easy *to be nice to a person as sweet as Margaret.*

_____ 4. The coach very much wants *Helen to run on the cross-country team this year.*

_____ 5. His drive *to become the next class president* made Taft a very unpleasant person.

_____ 6. Mark forgot to tell us *when to take the pie out of the oven.*

_____ 7. I was very unhappy this morning *to find my car had a flat tire.*

_____ 8. This new term will give several of us a chance *to make a new start academically.*

_____ 9. That extra hour will let *Al finish the test without any pressure.*

_____ 10. Is there anyone sufficiently interested in that project *to take on the leadership?*

_____ 11. Those two students were chosen *to represent the school at the national convention.*

_____ 12. "Can someone help *me set up this display?*" asked Sam.

_____ 13. Barbara was in the library trying *to find another source for her speech.*

_____ 14. It seems impossible *for them to control those children.*

_____ 15. "*To set up your schedule by phone,* you should call any of the numbers listed on the bulletin," said the clerk.

_____ 16. They hope that we will try our very best *to come to their wedding in November.*

_____ 17. Our fumble gave the other team the opportunity *to score and win the game.*

_____ 18. Jane moved near the Columbia River *to be close to the boardsailing center of North America.*

_____ 19. The fraternity's plan was *to steal their mascot during the thunderstorm.*

_____ 20. Most undergraduates would be glad for a chance *to evaluate their teachers.*

EXERCISE **11**

GERUND PHRASES; INFINITIVE PHRASES

NAME _____ SCORE _____

Directions: Each sentence contains one gerund phrase. Underline the gerund phrase. In the space at the left, write one of the following numbers to show the use of the gerund phrase:
  1. Subject   3. Direct object
  2. Subjective complement   4. Object of preposition

_____ 1. Every member of our class agrees to work toward building better relations with the other classes.

_____ 2. Discussing that amendment at some length might have prevented the current misunderstanding.

_____ 3. For a brief period Amanda considered becoming an interior designer.

_____ 4. Before joining our partnership, Robinson was an associate in a major law firm in Chicago.

_____ 5. Both senators from our state voted against increasing the tax on gasoline.

_____ 6. Her biggest break was getting to play against the state champs in her first season.

_____ 7. As soon as she smelled smoke, Melissa began dialing the fire department.

_____ 8. Missing that turn in Manderville cost us about three hours of time on a very bad road.

_____ 9. One of my most pleasant summer memories concerns picking blueberries on the mountain behind the cabin.

_____ 10. Would using the wood from that old barn as paneling for the kitchen be a completely impossible idea?

_____ 11. Terry said he would enjoy fishing for northern pike on one of the lakes near town.

_____ 12. "Do you remember being told that your appointment was for 5:00 P. M. yesterday?" asked Mr. Waters.

_____ 13. This article states that we can all improve our health significantly by drinking mineral water instead of tap water.

_____ 14. The dean has certainly never been accused of having a well-developed sense of humor.

_____ 15. "I think I can explain the workings of that computerized ignition system without becoming too technical," said the engineer.

_____ 16. "I hate being told what kind of day I ought to have," said the grumpy secretary.

_____ 17. Since having those mild chest pains, my father has been very careful about his health.

_____ 18. Loaning the boat to your cousin was a very kind thing to do.

_____ 19. "I'd like to conclude my speech by expressing my deepest gratitude to those of you who donated to my campaign," said the politician.

_____ 20. Figuring out how to assemble my little brother's swing set last Christmas was a major intellectual achievement.

95

Directions: Each sentence contains one infinitive phrase (some with subjects). Underline each infinitive phrase. In the space at the left, write N. [noun], Adj. [adjective], or Adv. [adverb] to show the use of the infinitive phrase.

_____ 1. My little sister was only too eager to tell everyone about my attempts at horseback riding.

_____ 2. "I don't think it will be possible to get those books to you before tomorrow," said Laura.

_____ 3. Sometimes I wish you would let someone else select the restaurant when we go out for dinner.

_____ 4. To be assured of a good supply of paper, buy several packs at the store tomorrow.

_____ 5. Can anyone show me the proper way to carve the turkey?

_____ 6. During your tour of the hospital, you will have a chance to witness an actual operation.

_____ 7. I like to arrange the papers from my classes in alphabetical order.

_____ 8. After they had walked almost all day, the girls were much too tired to go to the art gallery.

_____ 9. In another month we will take a vacation from school to help harvest the wheat.

_____ 10. It's hard to decide how I should invest the profits from the sale of the house.

_____ 11. In the first class the instructor distributed a list of books to be read for the course.

_____ 12. The thief found that it was a simple task to remove one pane of glass and open the window.

_____ 13. The thief found that it was simple to remove one pane of glass and open the window.

_____ 14. Marcia's accountant was unable to reduce her tax bill for last year.

_____ 15. With all that evidence against her, the embezzler couldn't do anything but plead guilty.

_____ 16. Two of the younger kids helped James wash and wax his car.

_____ 17. The storm came up so suddenly that we had no chance to run for cover.

_____ 18. To speed up the registration process, the college has provided advisors in every department.

_____ 19. Marcella learned how to make patchwork quilts last summer.

_____ 20. Reading this one book will tell you everything you need to know about bargaining with an automobile salesman.

LESSON 12 ■

Subordination: Participial Phrases; Absolute Phrases

The **participle** is identical in form with the four gerund forms; in addition, there are the past participle *(studied)* and a progressive form *(having been studying)*. The difference between the participle and the gerund is one of use. Whereas the gerund is used as a noun, most commonly as a subject, a direct object, an object of a preposition, or a renaming subjective complement, the participle is used as an adjectival modifier:

> The *injured* bird clung to the *swaying* branch. [The past participle *injured* modifies the noun *bird;* the present participle *swaying* modifies the noun *branch.*]

A **participial phrase** consists of a participle plus its modifiers and/or complements. As with the gerund phrase and the infinitive phrase, the kind of complement(s), if any, is determined by the kind of verb from which the participle is derived:

> *Handing me the receipt,* the manager thanked me. [The participial phrase modifies the noun *manager.* Within the phrase, *me* is an indirect object and *receipt* is a direct object.]
> The taxi driver, *being a war veteran,* signed the petition. [The participial phrase modifies the noun *taxi driver.* Within the phrase, *veteran* is a subjective complement.]
> *Calling the bomb threat a hoax,* the authorities did nothing. [The participial phrase modifies the noun *authorities.* Within the phrase, *threat* is a direct object and *hoax* is an objective complement.]

The similarity between an adjective clause and a participial phrase is obvious:

> A man grabbed the microphone. The man [*or* He] was wearing a black mask. [Two independent clauses.]
> A man *who was wearing a black mask* grabbed the microphone. [Adjective clause. *Mask* is a direct object of the verb.]
> A man *wearing a black mask* grabbed the microphone. [Participial phrase. *Mask* is a direct object of the participle.]
> Jo's parents left the concert early. They found the music uncomfortably loud. [Two independent clauses.]
> Jo's parents, *who found the music uncomfortably loud,* left the concert early. [Adjective clause. *Music* is a direct object and *loud* an objective complement of the verb.]
> Jo's parents, *finding the music uncomfortably loud,* left the concert early. [Participial phrase. *Music* is a direct object and *loud* an objective complement of the participle.]

These two examples point out another similarity: Like the adjective clause, the participial phrase is either restrictive or nonrestrictive. The phrase in the first example is an identifier; it is restrictive and is not set off by commas. The phrase in the second example is not needed for identifying purposes. It requires commas because it is nonrestrictive.

The structural similarity between the adjective clause and the participial phrase carries another implication concerning sentence variety. The adjective clause has little freedom of movement within the sentence. It follows as closely as possible the word it modifies; even a few words intervening between the two units might confuse the reader. And the restrictive (identifying) participial phrase normally follows the noun it modifies (as in the "man carrying a gun . . ." sentence).

But the nonrestrictive participial phrase, unlike the nonrestrictive adjective clause it closely resembles, need not always follow immediately the word it modifies. Here we have an important device for achieving variety in sentence structure: Skilled writers often place a nonrestrictive participial phrase *before* the noun, to begin the sentence. Some phrases of this type also lend themselves effectively to placement at the end of the clause:

> Steve, *having passed the test with flying colors,* decided to celebrate.
> *Having passed the test with flying colors,* Steve decided to celebrate.
> Steve decided to celebrate, *having passed the test with flying colors.*

Because the participial phrase, in addition to its value as a describing unit, shows its verb origin by naming an activity, it offers a possible substitute for a string of monotonous independent clauses:

> Pam wanted desperately to hear the rock concert, but she was temporarily short of funds, and she knew that her cousin Alice had an extra ticket, and so she decided to call her. [Four independent clauses.]
> Wanting desperately to hear the rock concert but being temporarily short of funds, Pam decided to call her cousin Alice, knowing that she had an extra ticket. [One independent clause and three participial phrases.]
>
> Jensen stood at home plate. He waggled his bat. He eyed the pitcher malevolently. He took a mighty swing at the first pitch. He hit the ball out of the park. [Five independent clauses.]
> Standing at home plate, waggling his bat and eyeing the pitcher malevolently, Jensen took a mighty swing at the first pitch, hitting the ball out of the park. [One independent clause and four participial phrases.]

The **absolute phrase** is a special kind of phrase, different from the standard participial phrase in both form and function. Within the absolute phrase, the participle follows a noun or a pronoun that is part of the phrase. The phrase adds to the meaning of the whole sentence, but it does not directly modify any noun or pronoun in the sentence. The absolute phrase is a versatile structure capable of many variations and widely used in modern prose writing to point out subtle relationships underlying the ideas within a sentence:

> *All things being equal,* Mary should easily win the race.
> *The storm having passed,* the ball game resumed.
> The police recovered eight of the paintings, *three of them badly damaged.*
> The mob reached the palace gates, *the leader (being) a burly, redhaired sailor.* [Occasionally an absolute phrase having a noun plus a renamer or describer appears with the participle *being* unexpressed.]

A special kind of phrase using *with* to introduce one of these absolute phrases can add subtle modifying and narrative coloring to a sentence:

With the band playing and the crowd applauding furiously, Jim Kinman was obviously uncomfortable.

They held the funeral on the second day, *with the town coming to look at Miss Emily beneath a mass of bought flowers, with the crayon face of her father musing profoundly above the bier....*(W. Faulkner)

But we can't possibly have a garden party *with a dead man just outside the front gate.* (K. Mansfield)

The face was a curious mixture of sensibility, *with some elements very hard and others very pretty*—perhaps it was in the mouth. (K. A. Porter)

Notice that the *with* in this construction is quite unlike *with* in its common prepositional use:

The acquitted woman left the courtroom *with her lawyer.*
The acquitted woman left the courtroom *with her head held high.*

SUMMARY OF PARTICIPIAL PHRASES; ABSOLUTE PHRASES

PARTICIPIAL PHRASES

1. Forms: *studying* (present), *studied* (past), *having studied, being studied, having been studied, having been studying.*
2. Function: to modify a noun or pronoun. Those that *identify* the noun or pronoun are restrictive and require no punctuation; others are nonrestrictive and are set off by commas.
3. Position: If restrictive, the phrase always follows the word it modifies. Nonrestrictive phrases may stand after the noun, at the beginning of the sentence, and occasionally at the end of the sentence.

ABSOLUTE PHRASES

1. Form: a noun or pronoun followed by a participle (*The crops having failed,* Grandfather sold the farm).
2. Function: does not modify a word or fill a noun "slot."
3. Position: at the beginning, in the interior, or at the end of the larger unit; it is always set off by commas.
4. Special structures:
   a. The phrase sometimes begins with the word *with* (*With its supply of ammunition exhausted,* the garrison surrendered).
   b. The participle *being* is sometimes unexpressed (*Its chairman (being) a retired military person,* the committee is well disciplined).

Practice Sheet 12

Participial Phrases; Absolute Phrases

NAME _____   SCORE _____

Directions: The italicized unit in each sentence is either a participial phrase or an absolute phrase. If the unit is a participial phrase, copy in the space at the left the noun or pronoun that the phrase modifies. If the unit is an absolute phrase, leave the space blank. Be prepared to discuss in class the complements, if any, within the phrases.

NOTE: Study also the other verbal phrases. Of the following sentences, five contain gerund phrases and seven contain infinitive phrases.

_____ 1. The candidate's advertising campaign relied heavily on television commercials *attacking the incumbent.*

_____ 2. Only those *wearing red or white jackets* will be admitted to the special cheering section.

_____ 3. *The noise of the sirens having shattered the quiet,* the campers all raced to safety up the side of the hill.

_____ 4. My sister has a serious case of lateral epichondylitis, *commonly known as tennis elbow.*

_____ 5. Forrest definitely needs a tutor, *the instructor having criticized him for making several errors in math.*

_____ 6. *Sensing that there was only one chance for escape,* John left the classroom before his name was called.

_____ 7. *The only other strong runner having dropped out of the race,* Alexis moved easily into the lead.

_____ 8. Without turning another page, she closed the book and walked away, *leaving the book on the table where it lay.*

_____ 9. My previous boss had carefully retained every memo and note *written to him by anyone in the company.*

_____ 10. *Having left his heavy coat back in the dorm,* Harry shivered as he walked to his first class.

_____ 11. *The evening news being exceptionally bleak,* we turned off the television and listened to music during dinner.

_____ 12. My brother, *being an avid baseball card collector,* pushed his way to the front of every autograph line.

_____ 13. Tell me why you, *knowing that such food is bad for your health,* continue to eat eggs and pork chops.

_____ 14. *My keys being locked inside my car,* I'm afraid I won't be on time for class this morning.

_____ 15. Anyone *having seen that precious little brown dog* is asked to call me as soon as possible.

_____ 16. "Any merchandise *left here for thirty days* will be sold for charity," said the sign in the shoe repair shop.

_____ 17. Freshmen students *passing the comprehensive math test* are exempt from taking additional math courses.

101

_____ 18. Emily did not work during the school year, *her uncle having established a trust fund for her education.*

_____ 19. A number of those books will be discarded, *most of them having simply worn out through constant use.*

_____ 20. Martha James, *once thought of as an up-and-coming defense attorney,* has taken a job as a prosecutor.

_____ 21. While running, Marie listens to a personal stereo, *with the strains of Beethoven wafting gently around her.*

_____ 22. *Looking enormously happy,* the monkey ate the banana he stole from his neighbor.

_____ 23. Anita, *no longer struggling with quantitative analysis,* seems very much at peace with the world.

_____ 24. Three police officers, *the tallest one scarcely able to fit through the door,* were standing in the hotel lobby.

_____ 25. By noon, *with the smoke still rising slowly from the ashes,* the investigators were hard at work.

_____ 26. A woman *covered with tattoos* began calling people into the carnival tent.

_____ 27. *Observed from a distance,* the prison looks like a college campus.

_____ 28. *Observing the prison from a distance,* one notices that it looks very much like a college campus.

_____ 29. The cleanup crew found several old pizza boxes, *two of them dating from last semester.*

_____ 30. The view down the valley is a little foggy, *the waterfall in the distance showering the area with mist.*

_____ 31. *Talking with the engineer for the first time,* I was impressed by his ability to simplify technical matters.

_____ 32. After searching for several hours, the soldiers found a second road *leading into the valley.*

_____ 33. Martha selected a second topic, *the teacher having told everyone to select one with ample source material.*

_____ 34. *Wanting desperately to play ball for the college,* Tom chose to report for practice a week ahead of time.

_____ 35. *Standing vigilantly by the stable,* the guard kept watch over the valuable stakes winner.

_____ 36. *Left quite weak by her bout with pneumonia,* Angela built up her stamina by running on a treadmill.

_____ 37. In the garden was a tomato plant *covered with small brown bugs.*

_____ 38. My little sister has become famous in her elementary school, *her rock collection having won a science prize.*

_____ 39. *Having paid his ticket and the towing fee,* Jim was able to retrieve his car from the impound area.

_____ 40. Helen is still a regular spectator at high school games, *having once played soccer in college.*

EXERCISE **12**

PARTICIPIAL PHRASES; ABSOLUTE PHRASES

NAME _____ SCORE _____

Directions: The italicized unit in each sentence is either a participial phrase or an absolute phrase. If the unit is a participial phrase, copy in the space at the left the noun or pronoun that the phrase modifies. If the phrase is an absolute phrase, leave the space blank. Be prepared to discuss in class the complements, if any, within the phrases.

NOTE: Study also the other verbal phrases. Of the following sentences, eight contain gerund phrases and five contain infinitive phrases.

_____ 1. Reporters *issued press credentials last week* must exchange them for new credentials today.

_____ 2. Elizabeth, *suddenly realizing that her books were missing,* ran quickly from the room.

_____ 3. Our trip west could continue, *the car having finally been repaired.*

_____ 4. My Uncle Jack let me borrow his power saw, *mine having burned up its motor last week.*

_____ 5. A few dingy photographs *taken by former staff members* sat forlornly in the files.

_____ 6. *Finding few people in the office,* Martin and Jim made the time count by organizing reports from the staff.

_____ 7. *Being the only one in the group who had taken astronomy,* Elaine was chosen to learn celestial navigation.

_____ 8. Rock climbers come in droves to Yosemite, *the rock faces in the park being some of the best in the country.*

_____ 9. *Its runners having already broken several state records,* Southern Tech is favored at the state track meet.

_____ 10. *Having very few strong runners,* Northwest's task of defending its state title seems almost impossible.

_____ 11. The noise *drifting in through the open windows* kept me from sleeping.

_____ 12. *Having finished running the day's experiments,* the astronauts were free to go to sleep.

_____ 13. *With one of its axles broken,* Karen's car is in no shape to be driven anywhere.

_____ 14. In simpler times a person *needing a meal* could earn one by working for a local farmer.

_____ 15. *Having read a favorable review of the new movie,* Martin bought tickets for the late show.

_____ 16. *His date having read a favorable review of the new movie,* Martin bought tickets for the late show.

_____ 17. *Having received a phone call earlier in the evening,* Helene was prepared for the arrival of her parents.

_____ 18. We spent most of the day in a vain attempt to clean up the rocks and sand *left by the flood.*

_____ 19. A reporter *carrying a notebook* questioned everyone at the scene of the accident.

_____ 20. Harvey finally returned my ax last night, *the blade badly nicked from hitting rocks.*

_____ 21. *Being thoroughly prepped on the new techniques,* Beth felt confident about taking the next test.

_____ 22. That light plane *flying so low over these houses* ought to be reported to the FAA.

_____ 23. Mitchell returned his book at the end of the day, *having completed the last three chapters.*

_____ 24. Barbara arrived quite early, *the traffic on the streets having been surprisingly light for that time of day.*

_____ 25. Barbara arrived quite early, *having found the traffic on the streets surprisingly light for that time of day.*

_____ 26. The child laughed and pointed at the clowns *running and jumping in the center ring of the circus.*

_____ 27. I've misplaced the map *giving directions for hiking to that special pool on the trout stream.*

_____ 28. The teacher, *having been shown the grade on my paper,* entered it in his grade book.

_____ 29. The little girl jumped eagerly into the pool, *never doubting that her mother would catch her.*

_____ 30. The little girl jumped eagerly into the pool, *there being no doubt that her mother would catch her.*

_____ 31. The freshman team played with renewed dedication, *their new captain a recent transfer from a junior college.*

_____ 32. My new jacket, *having been left out in the rain,* needed to be cleaned and pressed.

_____ 33. My sister lives on Ridgeland Avenue, *sometimes called State Road 44.*

_____ 34. *Dressed in a factory worker's uniform,* the manager could move about without detection by the workers.

_____ 35. *That motion having been tabled,* I believe we can entertain a motion for adjournment.

_____ 36. The band earned money for uniforms by collecting aluminum cans *scattered along the roadsides.*

_____ 37. The company will be closed tomorrow, *that being the anniversary of the move from Scranton.*

_____ 38. The applicant's only experience in show business was a bit part in a play *satirizing Truman's presidency.*

_____ 39. The young surfer, *recognizing that she was literally in over her head,* called loudly for help.

_____ 40. Meg moved slowly and fearfully to the end of the diving board, *the drop to the water being well over forty feet.*

VERBAL PHRASES; COMPLEMENTS IN PHRASES

NAME _____   SCORE _____

Directions: In the first space at the left, write one of the following letters to identify the italicized verbal phrase:

    G. [gerund phrase]   I. [infinitive phrase]
    P. [participial phrase]   A. [absolute phrase]

In the second space, write one of the following abbreviations to identify the complement printed in boldfaced type within the phrase:

    S. C. [subjective complement]   I. O. [indirect object]
    D. O. [direct object]   O. C. [objective complement]

_____ 1. The efficiency expert warned *against leaving the walkways* **unpainted.**
_____

_____ 2. *Having recently been appointed* **Ambassador** *to the Philippines,* James
_____   Bentley is preparing to move his family to Manila.

_____ 3. The servers, *by singing* **"Happy Birthday"** *very loudly,* embarrassed shy,
_____   retiring Uncle Walter immensely.

_____ 4. *Having no way to contact her* **brother** *for a ride,* Emily was forced to take
_____   the bus home yesterday.

_____ 5. *To get an* **idea** *of the difficulties involved in running a small business,* you
_____   might spend a day at a local restaurant.

_____ 6. It is clear that no officials in the bank suspected Jane Fellows *of being an*
_____   **embezzler.**

_____ 7. Arline was grateful to her brother *for helping* **her** *to select a new car.*
_____

_____ 8. We decided to go to a different restaurant, *the line for a table being*
_____   *extremely* **long.**

_____ 9. *After handing* **me** *the gift,* my grandmother waited patiently for me to
_____   open it.

_____ 10. Barbara filled her time last summer by *playing* **softball.**
_____

_____ 11. I certainly didn't mean *to appear* **angry.**
_____

_____ 12. Jim had to park his car on the street, *the cars of visiting relatives completely filling his **driveway.***
_____

_____ 13. *Being the best math **student** in the family,* Joan tutored the rest of us in
_____ math.

_____ 14. *The weather being very **stormy,*** soccer practice for this afternoon has been
_____ canceled.

_____ 15. The radio announcer advised us *to leave all our windows **closed.***
_____

_____ 16. Most people believe that Carla wants *to be appointed **captain*** *of the*
_____ *debate team.*

_____ 17. *How many **people*** did you manage *to recruit?*
_____

_____ 18. We probably should have made one major change—*starting the **meeting***
_____ *promptly at nine o'clock.*

_____ 19. I wish the manager would let us *give the **people** a refund.*
_____

_____ 20. The loud complaints from the staff succeeded only in *making the **manager***
_____ *more angry.*

_____ 21. *Having won a **scholarship** for next semester,* Wanda will be able to con-
_____ tinue her education.

_____ 22. The people were able to leave the building on time, *the technicians hav-*
_____ *ing repaired the **elevator.***

_____ 24. *Sending **Rouse** a copy of that paper* seemed to be the only way to satisfy
_____ his curiosity.

_____ 25. *The project having been deemed a **failure,*** all of us team members were
_____ given new work assignments.

Sentence Building
Lessons, Practice Sheets, and Exercises

LESSON **13** ■
Completeness

A complete sentence contains a subject and a verb as its core. Without a subject and a verb, there is no complete sentence. A sentence, moreover, must be able to stand alone as an independent unit of communication. Therefore a clause introduced by a subordinating word cannot be a complete sentence even though it contains a subject and a verb, as all clauses must. The subordinating word makes it dependent instead of independent.

A group of words punctuated like a sentence but lacking subject, verb, or independence is an incomplete sentence, or **sentence fragment.** The mistake of punctuation that creates a sentence fragment is called a **period fault.** When they appear in writing, sentence fragments are usually considered serious errors.

The undesirable sentence fragments that inexperienced writers sometimes construct are almost always of the three following types:

1. A subordinate clause standing as a sentence. (But remember that *and, but, for, or,* and *nor* do not subordinate. A clause introduced by one of these words may stand as a sentence.)

Fragments: The clerk finally let us see the contract. *Although she clearly hated to reveal its contents.*
Bob tried to start the old lawn mower. *Which always seemed to malfunction for him.*

2. A verbal phrase punctuated as a sentence:

Fragments: The delegates agreed on a compromise wage scale. *Realizing that the strike could not go on indefinitely.*
Nell had ordered her tickets a month ago. *To be sure of getting good seats.*

3. A noun followed by a phrase or a subordinate clause but lacking a verb to go with it:

Fragments: The committee should include Ms. Tartar. *A tireless worker with many constructive ideas.*
The mayor asked Bentley to take the job. *Bentley being the only available person with field experience.*

> The coach thinks our prospects are good. *A chance, perhaps, to win back the league championship.*
>
> Junior will require a special kind of tutor. *Someone who will realize how sensitive the child really is.*

You can avoid sentence fragments if you have a working knowledge of the grammatical makeup of the sentence and if you practice reasonable care in your writing. If you have repeatedly had fragments called to your attention, try this technique: When you reread and revise what you have written, read the sentences in a paragraph in reverse order. Start with your last sentence and work back to your first. This process, by breaking the tie between a fragment and the sentence that it depends on, makes any grammatically incomplete sentence reveal itself prominently.

Then, when you have discovered a fragment in your writing, any one of several possible corrections is easy to make. Sometimes you can attach the fragment to the preceding sentence by doing away with the fragment's capital letter and supplying the right punctuation. Or you can change the fragment to a subordinate clause and attach it to the appropriate main clause by means of the right connective. Or you can change the fragment to an independent clause by supplying a subject or a verb or both.

Corrected: The clerk finally let us see the contract, *although she clearly hated to reveal its contents.*

Bob tried to start the old lawn mower, *which always seemed to malfunction for him.*

The delegates agreed on a compromise wage scale *because they realized that the strike could not go on indefinitely.*

To be sure of getting good seats, Nell had ordered her tickets a month ago.

The committee should include Ms. Tartar, *a tireless worker with many constructive ideas.*

The mayor asked Bentley to take the job, *Bentley being the only available person with field experience.*

The coach thinks our prospects are good; *we have a chance, perhaps, to win back the league championship.*

Junior will require a special kind of tutor. *He or she must be someone who will realize how sensitive the child really is.*

A few types of word groups, although lacking a complete subject—verb combination, are not objectionable fragments. They are accepted as legitimate language patterns. These are

1. Commands, in which the subject *you* is understood:

Please be seated. Put your name on a slip of paper. Pass the papers to the left aisle.

2. Exclamations:

What excitement! Only two minutes to go! Good Heavens, not a fumble? How terrible!

3. Bits of dialogue:

"New car?" she asked. "Had it long?"
"Picked it up last week," he replied.

4. Occasional transitions between units of thought:

On with the story.
And now to conclude.

You have very likely observed in your reading that experienced writers sometimes use sentence fragments, especially in narrative and descriptive writing. But they are skilled workers who know how to use fragments to achieve particular stylistic effects. You, as a beginning writer, must first master the fundamental forms of the sentence. Once you have learned to write clear, correct sentences without faltering, there will be plenty of time for experimenting.

PRACTICE SHEET 13
COMPLETENESS

NAME _____   SCORE _____

Directions: Study these word groups for completeness. In the space at the left, write S if the word group is a grammatically complete sentence. Write F (for Fragment) if it is not a grammatically complete sentence.

_____ 1. A student who always puts forth her best effort and always seems to add insightful comments to the discussions.

_____ 2. And that's why I can't even look at green beans, no matter how they are fixed.

_____ 3. A difficult problem, but not a reason for any kind of panic.

_____ 4. Let me see your driver's license, please.

_____ 5. Because it is not true that everyone who can play a game can also teach others how to play.

_____ 6. And she never again came to class unprepared.

_____ 7. Although tempted to eat a second piece of cake, Jan nevertheless turned away from the dessert table.

_____ 8. A consideration that has, apparently, never crossed the minds of our leaders.

_____ 9. None of those possibilities did he consider for even a moment.

_____ 10. Sleeping late, drowsing in the sun, wandering down pleasant back roads—those were the attractions of his summer vacation.

_____ 11. Heart pounding, lungs about to burst, straining every fiber of his being toward the finish line.

_____ 12. Not unless we know when John will arrive from Columbus.

_____ 13. The last week I spent just wandering around, chatting with old friends and taking a few snapshots.

_____ 14. Give me your undivided attention.

_____ 15. Then, when it seemed almost too late, the sound of a bugle and a cavalry charge just in time to save the settlers.

_____ 16. Then, when it seemed almost too late, a bugle sounds and the cavalry charges just in time to save the settlers.

111

_____ 17. But a woman with little money can hardly afford to shop at such a store.

_____ 18. The reason for the change in plans being that the highway department could not maintain a highway in such high mountains.

_____ 19. Furthermore, the skills I develop this summer will almost certainly be useful after graduation.

_____ 20. Oh, to be in Paris in the springtime.

_____ 21. Let's move this chair over into that corner.

_____ 22. The referee's whistle, a shrill call to action that focused everyone's attention on the center of the court.

_____ 23. But Jim did not feel ready to take the test.

_____ 24. Although Jim did not feel ready to take the test.

_____ 25. Therefore Jim did not feel ready to take the test.

_____ 26. To run or not to run: that is the question every politician must ask.

_____ 27. Definitely the only teacher on this campus with enough imagination to make that subject interesting.

_____ 28. Either of whom could have provided us with the information.

_____ 29. With those questions answered, I could vote for that proposal.

_____ 30. Assuming, of course, that the materials for the fireplace have been delivered.

_____ 31. Standing tall in the middle of the cornfield was a scarecrow wearing what was left of Uncle Al's tuxedo.

_____ 32. Coming across the last hill, which we flew over so fast that my stomach leaped into my throat and my life flashed before my eyes.

_____ 33. Few are the musicians who display sufficient skill to gain the approval of our Dr. Steincross.

_____ 34. Onion peels, apple cores, moldy crusts of bread, and, alas, the chef's favorite paring knife, all swept into the garbage bag.

_____ 35. There appeared at the end of the campaign a growing consensus that neither of the candidates was adequately prepared for the office.

EXERCISE 13
COMPLETENESS

Directions: Each numbered unit consists of a sentence followed by a fragment. In the space provided, rewrite enough of the material to show how you would correct the error, by either attaching the fragment to the sentence or recasting the fragment into a complete sentence. In either case, use correct punctuation and be prepared to discuss in class the structuring of the fragments.

1. Jim's new car occupies a great deal of his free time. Forcing him to work extra hours to make the payments.

2. The results of the election were quite surprising. Because, I assume, most people had believed the predictions of the political polls.

3. My grade on that test was very good. Good study habits and hard work finally paying off for me.

4. Rumors rarely turn out to be true. Most stories changing many times as they pass from person to person.

5. Several people have applied for the job as night clerk. A job that does not require much work and allows time for studying.

6. Mary has become a specialist in the history of Moscow. After living for several years in the Soviet Union.

7. Marlene has decided to retire as a marathon runner. Her knees having been severely damaged over the years.

8. Wanda, who works in sales, wants to become a manager. A position which will offer her a more stable income.

9. Morris is losing weight steadily these days. First, by dieting carefully, and second, by exercising more than usual.

10.   Winning at baseball requires three strengths. One being good hitting, the second, good pitching, and the third, good defense.

11.   All of my friends are looking for the ideal job. One offering inside work with no heavy lifting.

12.   My sister is shopping for a new car. Her old car being no longer safe to drive.

13.   We are in need of a new fax machine. An easily used model that is fairly inexpensive.

14.   My little brother does not like his new book on penguins. The sort of book that tells him too many facts at one time.

15.   Mr. Payson is a terrific copywriter. But, sad to say, a man not abundantly blessed with common sense.

16.   The literal meaning of the names of certain cars is often amusing. *Prelude,* for example, which means an introductory effort or unit.

17.   The savings and loan president had the bank pay for his boat. Thinking, probably, that his money and the bank's money were one and the same.

18.   Tom turned off the alarm about thirty seconds too late. The call to the police department having gone out almost immediately.

19.   Tom Wolfe writes about people's never-ending search for status among their peers. *The Bonfire of the Vanities* being his most recent book.

20.   The new "no-fat" desserts promise to be a boon to dieters. Limiting fat being a good way to reduce calories.

EXERCISE 13A
COMPLETENESS

NAME _____ SCORE _____

Directions: Each numbered unit consists of a sentence followed by a fragment. Be prepared to discuss in class the structure of the fragments. In the space provided, rewrite enough of the material to show how you would correct the error, by either attaching the fragment, properly punctuated, to the sentence or recasting the fragment so that it becomes a complete sentence.

1. Selecting a new house was an extremely difficult task. Finally provoking a series of arguments between the man and the woman.

2. The explanation of the electronic circuit baffled the new students. Although an experienced student could have understood it easily.

3. The concert was extremely well received. The combination of comedy routines and good music offering something for everyone.

4. After the first course, the program splits in two directions. One emphasizing programming, the other business applications.

5. The wily politician tried to induce the special interest groups to vote for him. By offering programs tailored to meet their needs.

6. Last summer we found several arrowheads on the riverbank. One of which is a nearly perfect specimen.

7. The new fund-raiser has increased donations considerably this year. Many donations from new donors.

8. The new salesperson came up against the most difficult type of prospect. A person who is extremely knowledgeable about the product.

9. The new teacher went home exhausted at the end of the day. After dealing all day with bored, talkative students.

10. My friend Alfred has opened a high-priced restaurant. A venture that has little chance of success.

11. Every nursing student passed the state board tests this year. Causing great pride in the nursing department.

12. My brother just bought a car that will travel over one hundred miles an hour. Even though the speed limit is still fifty-five miles an hour.

13. The school's volleyball team won last night by one point. The opposing team having had a very bad night.

14. My uncle, who just turned forty, has returned to school this term. Planning to earn a degree in nursing and work in emergency rooms.

15. Polly has become very excited about training to run a marathon. A recent television movie about a woman marathoner having inspired her.

16. Mary is saving all her money for a trip to Colorado. A dream that developed when she became interested in the environmental movement.

17. We are eagerly awaiting the publication of Dr. Marcus's new book. The first definitive work by an American on gene splicing.

18. Harold recently dug up a large part of his yard. Supposedly to grow tomatoes and cucumbers.

19. The bright purple and orange walls in Myrtle's apartment almost blinded me. A color scheme she developed on her own.

20. The new office manager came to us from a major real estate sales firm. The firm having only recently gone bankrupt.

Misplaced Modifiers;
Dangling Modifiers

Proper arrangement of the parts of your sentence will help make your meaning clear. Ordinarily the main parts—the subjects, the verbs, the complements—cause no problems. Here we shall consider five possible trouble spots in the placing of modifiers.

1. Although usage sanctions a rather loose placing of some common adverbs, such as *only, nearly, almost,* and *hardly,* sentences of precise meaning result only when such adverbs are placed close to the words they modify:

Loose: This will *only* take five minutes.
Jill *nearly* saw ninety movies last year.

Better: This will take *only* five minutes.
Jill saw *nearly* ninety movies last year.

2. Words and phrases that attach themselves to the wrong word can confuse the reader:

Poor: I wish every person in this class could know the man I'm going to talk about *personally.*
It was reported that the Italian premier had died *on the eight-o'clock newscast.*
The police department will be notified of all reported obscene phone calls *by the telephone company.*

Better: I wish every person in this class could know *personally* the man I'm going to talk about.
On the eight-o'clock newscast, it was reported that the Italian premier had died.
The police department will be notified *by the telephone company* of all reported obscene phone calls.

3. The squinting modifier is one that is placed between two units, either of which it could modify:

Poor: Students who can already type *normally* are put into an advanced class.
He said *after the dinner* some color slides would be shown.

Better: Students who can already type are *normally* put into an advanced class.
He said some color slides would be shown *after the dinner.*

4. The split infinitive results from the placing of an adverbial modifier between the *to* and the root verb of an infinitive. Although greatly overemphasized by some as an error, the split infinitive, particularly with a modifier consisting of more than one word, is usually avoided by careful writers:

Poor: Dad likes to *once in a while* plan and cook a dinner.

Better: *Once in a while*, Dad likes to plan and cook a dinner.

5. The correlatives *both ... and, not only ... but also, either ... or,* and *neither ... nor* are used in pairs and should be placed immediately before the parallel units that they connect:

Poor: We sent invitations *both* to Webster *and* Jenkins.
This woman *not only* can get along with young people *but also* with their parents.
You must *either* promise me that you will come *or* send a substitute.

Better: We sent invitations to *both* Webster *and* Jenkins. [The parallel words are *Webster* and *Jenkins.*]
This woman can get along *not only* with young people *but also* with their parents.
You must promise me that you will *either* come *or* send a substitute.

Dangling Modifiers

In a well-constructed sentence, any modifying phrase containing a participle, a gerund, or an infinitive (see Lessons 11, 12) is attached to the word that it logically modifies. By this we mean that the noun or pronoun being modified could be a logical subject of the verb from which the verbal is derived:

Being alone in the house, Ginny was apprehensive. [Test: Ginny was alone in the house.]
After *studying all afternoon,* Mary had a headache. [Test: Mary studied all afternoon.]
To qualify for the job, an applicant must be able to type. [Test: An applicant qualifies for the job.]

If the modifying unit attaches itself to a noun or a pronoun that does not produce this logical subject–verb relationship, we say that the phrase dangles:

After *studying all afternoon,* Mary's head ached. [Test: Mary's head studied all afternoon.]

Although danglers are occasionally detected in the writings of very good authors, a dangler is undesirable if it calls attention to itself, if it causes even momentary confusion, or if it gives a ludicrous meaning that the writer did not intend.

The easiest way to correct a dangler is to supply the word that the phrase should modify and to place the phrase next to that word. Another way is to change the dangling phrase to a subordinate clause with a subject and verb expressed.

1. The most common type of dangler is the participial phrase beginning a sentence:

Dangler: *Stepping into the boat,* my camera dropped into the water. [Was the camera stepping into the boat? Of course not. The trouble here is that the word that the phrase should modify is not expressed in the sentence.]
Burned to a cinder, I could not eat the toast. [The sentence sounds as if *I* were burned to a cinder. The word that the dangler should modify is *toast,* but this word is too far from the phrase to be immediately associated with it.]

Better: Stepping into the boat, I dropped my camera into the water.
As I was stepping into the boat, my camera dropped into the water.
Burned to a cinder, the toast could not be eaten.
I could not eat the toast because it was burned to a cinder.

2. Another type of dangler is the gerund that follows a preposition. The phrase that contains the verbal must have a word to refer to, and that word must be close enough to the phrase so that the reader does not associate the phrase with the wrong word:

Dangler: Before *making a final decision,* other cars should be driven. [Are the other cars making a final decision? That is not what is meant, and yet that is what the sentence states.]
On *graduating from high school,* my father let me work in his office. [The sentence says that your father let you work in his office when *he,* not *you,* graduated from high school.]
Since *breaking my leg,* my neighbors have helped with my farm chores. [A logical sentence only if the neighbors broke your leg.]

Better: Before making a final decision, drive other cars.
Before you make a final decision, you should drive other cars.
On graduating from high school, I was given a chance to work in my father's office.
After I had graduated from high school, my father let me work in his office.
Since breaking my leg, I have been helped with my farm chores by my neighbors.
My neighbors have helped with my farm chores since I broke my leg.

3. One type of introductory elliptical clause (see Lesson 8) that must be used carefully is a "time" clause, usually introduced by *when* or *while.* The clause becomes a dangler if the understood subject of the adverb clause is different from the subject of the main clause. The reader wrongly assumes that both clauses have the same subject, and the result can be a ridiculous meaning that the writer never intended:

Dangler: *When ten years old,* my father sold the farm and moved to Dallas.
While weeding my vegetable garden, a garter snake startled me.

Better: When ten years old, I moved to Dallas after my father sold the farm.
When I was ten years old, my father sold the farm and we moved to Dallas.
While weeding my vegetable garden, I was startled by a garter snake.
While I was weeding my vegetable garden, a garter snake startled me.

4. You may occasionally have trouble with an introductory infinitive phrase. If the infinitive names a specific action, be sure that the word that the phrase attaches to names the logical doer of that action.

Dangler: *To enter the contest,* a box top must be sent with your slogan.

Better: To enter the contest, you must send a box top with your slogan.
If you want to enter the contest, a box top must be sent with your slogan.
When you enter the contest, send a box top with your slogan.

PRACTICE SHEET 14

MISPLACED MODIFIERS

NAME _____ SCORE _____

Directions: From each of the following pairs of sentences select the one that is clearer and write its letter in the space at the left. Be prepared to justify your choice.

_____ 1. A. Studying for an exam often is more tiring than taking one.
B. Studying for an exam is often more tiring than taking one.

_____ 2. A. Max had only been gone for a few minutes when the fire broke out.
B. Max had been gone for only a few minutes when the fire broke out.

_____ 3. A. The students in the junior high school were not all interested in listening to a symphony.
B. Not all the students in the junior high school were interested in listening to a symphony.

_____ 4. A. For months Jack's favorite pastime has been watching old movies.
B. Jack's favorite pastime has been watching old movies for months.

_____ 5. A. We must either return the car now or rent it for another day.
B. Either we must return the car now or rent it for another day.

_____ 6. A. Ms. Winslow's lecture yesterday was not only long but also boring.
B. Ms. Winslow's lecture yesterday not only was long but also boring.

_____ 7. A. When Dad looked the other way, my little brother picked up a donut and downed it in one bite.
B. My little brother picked up a donut when Dad looked the other way and downed it in one bite.

_____ 8. A. Last summer my two cousins almost found a thousand dollars in an old box buried in the barn.
B. Last summer my two cousins found almost a thousand dollars in an old box buried in the barn.

_____ 9. A. James said that he would either send the book over today or bring it with him tomorrow.
_____ B. James either said that he would send the book over today or bring it with him tomorrow.

_____ 10. A. Did you realize that you have nearly a hundred pages left to read?
B. Did you realize that you nearly have a hundred pages left to read?

121

Directions: In the space at the left, write either A or B to indicate the logical placing of the italicized modifier.

_____ 1. (*when she had the time*) **A** Ms. Jenkins told how she used to drive the combine on her family's farm **B**.

_____ 2. (*not all*) Marsha soon saw that **A** the members of the office staff were **B** amused by her practical jokes.

_____ 3. (*by the metropolitan police*) Last year it was reported **A** that 1000 homes were broken into every night **B**.

_____ 4. (*frequently*) Laughing at other people's mistakes **A** is **B** a symptom of deep personal insecurity.

_____ 5. (*nearly*) Yesterday on his way to school, Tommy **A** found **B** forty dollars.

_____ 6. (*running into the building*) **A** Nancy raced up the stairs to the second floor to meet Adele and Barbara **B**.

_____ 7. (*only*) Ralph selected a lab partner who **A** had been in school **B** three days.

_____ 8. (*on Saturday mornings*) Years ago my father and Uncle Hal used to **A** fish off Cape Reliance **B**.

_____ 9. (*regularly*) Freshmen who cannot swim **A** are **B** placed in a special beginning swimming class.

_____ 10. (*not only*) "My grandmother," said Yolanda, "**A** takes a nap **B** in the morning but also in the afternoon."

_____ 11. (*in some confusion*) **A** The boys left the other students **B** before the end of the assembly.

_____ 12. (*almost*) On Tuesday the dog **A** destroyed **B** all of Mom's roses by digging in the garden.

_____ 13. (*with joy*) The grandparents **A** greeted their newest grandchild **B**.

_____ 14. (*every morning*) "When I was a kid, "said Uncle Jim, "I had to **A** get up and milk the cows **B**.

_____ 15. (*either*) To take scuba diving, one must **A** be able **B** to swim 100 yards under water or to tread water for twenty minutes.

EXERCISE 14
MISPLACED MODIFIERS

NAME _____ SCORE _____

Directions: In each of the following sentences, there is a poorly positioned word or phrase. Rewrite each sentence.

1. John works in a company that translates textbooks for Japanese students located in Montana.

2. Albert used to always send his mother flowers on her birthday.

3. Most biologists either specialize in fieldwork or in laboratory work.

4. The contestant on the quiz show said that he had only worked as a carpenter for the past few years.

5. The famous singer kept one copy all of the songs she had written in her closet.

6. The person who had seen the crime clearly called the police.

7. While the rest of us worked, Mary almost slept for two hours.

8. All the club members were urged to call the university president and complain at the meeting.

9. Everyone who can work these math problems easily can succeed in advanced calculus.

10. Jordan checked out two books of poetry composed by Whitman with the encouragement of his mother.

Directions: In the space at the left, write A or B to indicate the logical placing of the italicized modifier within the parentheses.

_____ 1. (*almost*) "In looking for the perfect breakfast, I've **A** tried **B** thirty brands of cereal," said Manny.

_____ 2. (*neither*) Your proposed solution **A** has **B** the logic nor the technical quality to succeed.

_____ 3. (*only*) Marcie is a musical snob; she **A** listens **B** to a limited number of heavy metal bands.

_____ 4. (*quickly*) We will need an expert to **A** assess this problem **B**.

_____ 5. (*with their advisors*) All students should discuss their situations **A** before entering the testing program **B**.

_____ 6. (*at two-thirty*) My uncle made a doctor's appointment **A** to discuss his coughing and wheezing **B**.

_____ 7. (*at least once every da*y) My cousin Ralph promises **A** to go on a diet **B**.

_____ 8. (*not*) **A** Everyone in our office can **B** agree with the new no-smoking policy.

_____ 9. (*not only*) The job offer made to Helen **A** contains **B** an expense account but also a company car.

_____ 10. (*usually*) Students who **A** enjoy computer games **B** respond positively to computerized instruction.

_____ 11. (*in the trash behind the restaurant*) **A** Detectives found evidence of Latham's money laundering activities **B**.

_____ 12. (*either*) For your exercise session this morning **A** you may **B** ride a stationary bike or walk on the track.

_____ 13. (*almost*) Morton **A** found **B** 500 dollars on the sidewalk this morning.

_____ 14. (*in even the worst circumstances*) An optimist is usually able to **A** find a silver lining behind the clouds **B**.

_____ 15. (*using a crosscut saw this morning*) **A** Art and William cut down a tall pine tree **B**.

DANGLING MODIFIERS

NAME _____ SCORE _____

Directions: One sentence of each pair contains a dangling modifier. Underline the dangler. In the space at the left, write the letter that identifies the correct sentence.

_____ 1. A. Climbing to a height of 4000 feet, my ears began to hurt.
           B. Climbing to a height of 4000 feet, I felt my ears begin to hurt.

_____ 2. A. Before varnishing that desktop, you should sand it thoroughly.
           B. Before varnishing that desktop, it should be sanded thoroughly.

_____ 3. A. Having reached a temperature of 450 degrees, the cake is ready for the oven.
           B. Having reached a temperature of 450 degrees, the oven is ready for the cake.

_____ 4. A. Having twisted my ankle quite badly, my doctor gave me crutches.
           B. Having twisted my ankle quite badly, I was given crutches by my doctor.

_____ 5. A. When looked at by the naked eye, most people don't realize that a TV picture is made up of many small dots.
           B. When looked at by the naked eye, the small dots that make up a TV picture are not recognized by most people.

_____ 6. A. If you protect the paint of your new car with our product, fading and chipping will not mar the car's finish.
           B. Protecting the paint of your new car with our product, fading and chipping will not mar the car's finish.

_____ 7. A. When looking for new sources, consult *Books in Print.*
           B. When looking for new sources, *Books in Print* should be consulted.

_____ 8. A. Carefully protected by a polyurethane coating, nothing can damage the top of that desk.
           B. Carefully protected by a polyurethane coating, the top of that desk is impossible to damage.

_____ 9. A. Quite pleased with his quick reply, Frank's smile lit up the room.
           B. Quite pleased with his quick reply, Frank lit up the room with his smile.

_____ 10. A. While preparing my resume, my grandmother brought me tea and cookies.
B. While I was preparing my resume, my grandmother brought me tea and cookies.

_____ 11. A. While working on that committee project, Jim's secretary called him to the phone.
B. While working on that committee project, Jim was called to the phone by his secretary.

_____ 12. A. When I bumped into an old friend at the shopping mall, I completely forget her name for a moment.
B. Bumping into an old friend at the shopping mall, her name completely slipped my mind for a moment.

_____ 13. A. Watched from a distance, the soaring hawk was a beautiful sight.
B. Watching from a distance, the soaring hawk was a beautiful sight.

_____ 14. A. To call me at the office, you must punch in my extension number.
B. To call me at the office, my telephone extension number must be punched in.

_____ 15. A. Library patrons may obtain a new card by submitting a written request.
B. A new library card may be obtained by submitting a written request.

_____ 16. A. Having moved to the edge of the cliff, a beautiful valley spread out below me.
B. Having moved to the edge of the cliff, I saw a beautiful valley below me.

_____ 17. A. Following the old river road, there should be no difficulty in finding the new marina.
B. Following the old river road, you should have no difficulty in finding the new marina.

_____ 18. A. Badly damaged in the accident, Mark's car was towed to the body shop by the wrecker.
B. Badly damaged in the accident, Mark had his car towed to the body shop by the wrecker.

_____ 19. A. Being early in the term, my average in this class is still fairly high.
B. This being early in the term, my average in this class is still fairly high.

_____ 20. A. While sitting on the deck late in the afternoon, two squirrels amused us with their antics.
B. While sitting on the deck late in the afternoon, we were amused by the antics of two squirrels.

EXERCISE 14A

DANGLING MODIFIERS

NAME _____ SCORE _____

Directions: One sentence of each pair contains a dangling modifier. Underline the dangler. In the space at the left, write the letter that identifies the correct sentence.

_____ 1. A. Opening the front door of Aunt Martha's house, the smell of fresh-baked bread fills the air.
B. When you open the front door of Aunt Martha's house, the smell of fresh-baked bread fills the air.

_____ 2. A. After opening your umbrella, you can go outside without getting wet.
B. After opening your umbrella, the rain outside will not get you wet.

_____ 3. A. When spending a quiet week at Sleepy Hollow Ranch, it is best to bring along several books.
B. When spending a quiet week at Sleepy Hollow Ranch, you should bring along several books.

_____ 4. A. When opened up suddenly, the popcorn often spills out of the package onto the floor.
B. When opening the package suddenly, you often spill the popcorn out of the package onto the floor.

_____ 5. A. To make a proper selection, several options ought to be considered.
B. To make a proper selection, you ought to consider several options.

_____ 6. A. Full of cracks and leaking badly, Dad filled the swimming pool with dirt and grew tomatoes in it.
B. Because the swimming pool was full of cracks and leaking badly, Dad filled it with dirt and grew tomatoes in it.

_____ 7. A. Getting into the elevator together, John and Roberta rode to the penthouse restaurant.
B. Getting into the elevator together, John rode to the penthouse restaurant with Roberta.

_____ 8. A. Yesterday, while enjoying a brief afternoon nap, a bolt of lightning struck the corner of the house.
B. Yesterday, while I enjoyed a brief afternoon nap, a bolt of lightning struck the corner of the house.

_____ 9. A. Trying desperately to find a position acceptable to both sides, the committee members offered several compromises.
B. Trying desperately to find a position acceptable to both sides, several compromises were offered by the committee.

_____ 10. A. Consistently undervalued in the auction market, the auto broker highly recommended a carefully restored 1936 Ford.
   B. Consistently undervalued in the auction market, a carefully restored 1936 Ford was highly recommended by the auto broker.

_____ 11. A. The penguin surprises people, once in the water, with its tremendous grace as a swimmer.
   B. Once in the water, the penguin surprises people with its tremendous grace as a swimmer.

_____ 12. A. Situated in a quiet residential section, the home buyer will appreciate the beautiful design of this house.
   B. The home buyer will appreciate the beautiful design of this house, which is situated in a quiet residential section.

_____ 13. A. By buying that player's rookie card, your baseball card collection will have its value enhanced considerably.
   B. By buying this player's rookie card, you will enhance the value of your baseball card collection considerably.

_____ 14. A. To be accepted into the honor society, you must maintain a 3.0 average.
   B. To be accepted into the honor society, a 3.0 average must be maintained.

_____ 15. A. After I found two new sources, the quality of my research paper went up quite a bit.
   B. After finding two new sources, the quality of my term paper went up quite a bit.

_____ 16. A. Being a television announcer, Alice is supposed to pronounce every word correctly.
   B. Being a television announcer, it is expected that Alice will pronounce every word correctly.

_____ 17. A. After wrecking my car, two of my neighbors offered me rides to work.
   B. After I wrecked my car, two of my neighbors offered me rides to work.

_____ 18. A. To paint the trim on that door, you need a small brush and a steady hand.
   B. To paint the trim on that door, a small brush and a steady hand are necessities.

_____ 19. A. Having recently returned from the Far East, Mack Adams spoke last night about his stay in Thailand.
   B. Mack Adams spoke last night about his stay in Thailand, having recently returned from the Far East.

_____ 20. A. Obviously pleased by our arrival, the big dog wagged his tail rapidly.
   B. Obviously pleased by our arrival, the big dog's tail wagged rapidly.

Exercise 14B
DANGLING MODIFIERS

NAME _____   SCORE _____

Directions: Rewrite each of the following sentences twice:
    a. Change the dangler to a complete clause with subject and verb.
    b. Retain the phrase but begin the main clause with a word that it can logically modify.

1. While pulling and hauling on the anchor rope, John's foot slipped and he went headfirst into the bay.
    a.

    b.

2. To run a large company such as this one, great business sense and ability to work with people are essential.
    a.

    b.

3. Thrilled by our arrival at the summit, the challenge of the next peak was welcomed by all of us climbers.
    a.

    b.

4. After seeing his grade, Charlie's shoulders slumped and his smile faded.
    a.

    b.

5. Carrying on in spite of her problems, Marlene's unquenchable spirit inspired the rest of the team.
    a.

    b.

Directions: Reduce the italicized material to a verbal phrase (a participial phrase or a gerund phrase) or an elliptical clause. Write the verbal phrase or the elliptical clause on the line provided. Then, in the space at the left, write A or B to designate the independent clause that the phrase or clause can logically modify.

Example:

__B__   *While I was jogging this morning,* (A) A vicious dog chased me. (B) I was chased by a vicious dog.

   (While) jogging this morning _____

_____ 1. *After she had submitted her application,* (A) Maria's confidence soared. (B) Maria felt her confidence soar.

_____

_____ 2. *You are extremely tired from your workout.* (A) SportAid's quick energy will revive you. (B) You will be revived by SportAid's quick energy.

_____

_____ 3. *He has several years experience in engineering.* (A) Jim has ample background for this project. (B) Jim's background for this project is ample.

_____

_____ 4. *Before you buy a health club membership,* (A) check the fine print in the contract. (B) the fine print in the contract should be checked.

_____

_____ 5. *As you look up Front Street,* (A) the renovation of the old church is plainly visible. (B) you can plainly see the renovation of the old church.

_____

_____ 6. *She was a senior.* (A) Jane registered easily for the new semester. (B) Registration for the new semester was easy for Jane.

_____

_____ 7. *When it becomes dark and dirty,* (A) you need to change the oil. (B) the oil needs to be changed.

_____

_____ 8. *While she was sweeping the walkway,* (A) Fay broke the broom handle. (B) the broom handle broke.

_____

_____ 9. *I called my sister in New York.* (A) she asked me to come visit her. (B) I was asked to come visit her.

_____

_____ 10. *Since Jim read that book on herpetology,* (A) Arthur has become interested in snakes. (B) snakes have become quite interesting to Arthur.

_____

LESSON 15 ▪
Subordination

Two common faults among beginning writers are the habit of stringing short sentences together and the habit of tying clauses together by *and, but, so,* and *and so,* connectives that do not show that one idea is subordinate to another.

Poor: Sally usually attends each concert. She missed this one. She went to the airport to meet her cousin Ellen. Ellen was arriving from Atlanta.

I tramped around town for three days but I couldn't find quarters and then I located this apartment and so I am comfortable.

If you determine the exact relationships between the parts of the sentences, your expression will be more mature, more economical, and more meaningful:

Improved: Although Sally usually attends each concert, she missed this one because she went to the airport to meet her cousin Ellen, who was arriving from Atlanta.

After tramping around town unsuccessfully for three days, I located this apartment, where I am comfortable.

Get in the habit of trying out the various methods of subordinating material. Notice in the following sentences how an idea can be expressed in diminishing degrees of emphasis:

Two Sentences:	The small car was inexpensive to drive. It had only four cylinders.
Compound Sentence:	The small car was inexpensive to drive, for it had only four cylinders.
Compound Verb:	The small car had only four cylinders and was inexpensive to drive.
Absolute Phrase:	The small car having only four cyclinders, it was inexpensive to drive.
Adverbial Clause:	Because the small car had only four cylinders, it was inexpensive to drive.
Adjective Clause:	The small car, which had only four cylinders, was inexpensive to drive.
Participial Phrase:	The small car, having only four cylinders, was inexpensive to drive. Having only four cylinders, the small car was inexpensive to drive. The small car was inexpensive to drive, having only four cylinders.
Prepositional Phrase:	The small car with only four cylinders was inexpensive to drive.
Appositive:	The small car, a four-cylinder model, was inexpensive to drive.
Adjective Modifier:	The small four-cylinder car was inexpensive to drive.

Note that the use of subordination produces more than a pleasing surface texture in writing. It also makes a crucial contribution to meaning by eliminating uncertainty about what is most important in a message.

> The management and union representatives announced an agreement. A strike had been threatened but was averted. The employees of Grantex Company reported for work today. They were relieved.

In this string of simple sentences there is no way of knowing which fact is most significant: The agreement? The avoidance of a strike? The workers' reporting for work? Their relief? Rewritten with proper subordination, the news reveals the writer's sense of significance:

> The relieved employees of Grantex Company reported for work today after the management and union representatives announced an agreement that averted a threatened strike.

The only independent clause in the sentence concerns the workers' return to work. That is the important message. A writer more interested in strikes and their effect on the general economy might report the event thus:

> The threatened strike was averted at Grantex Company when the management and union representatives announced an agreement, after which the relieved employees reported for work today.

A Note on Sentence Variety

Preceding lessons have demonstrated how subordinate clauses and phrases, by compressing material, help the writer avoid tiresome strings of independent clauses. You have also seen that certain subordinate units—adverbial clauses and participial phrases in particular—permit a variety of placements within the sentence and thus help prevent monotony of sentence structure.

Another unit useful for achieving compression and variety is the appositive. (See Lesson 10.) As noun renamers, appositives closely resemble—they might be called the final reduction of—Pattern 2 clause and phrase modifiers of nouns:

> Ted could explain the trick to us. Ted [or He] is an amateur magician. [Two independent clauses.]
>
> Ted, *who is an amateur magician,* could explain the trick to us. [Adjective clause.]
>
> Ted, *being an amateur magician,* could explain the trick to us. [Participial phrase.]
>
> Ted, *an amateur magician,* could explain the trick to us. [Appositive.]

Although the usual position of appositives is immediately following the nouns they rename, many of them, like many nonrestrictive participial phrases, can precede the main noun (in which case we call them *pre-positional appositives*); sometimes they are effectively placed at the end of the clause:

> Lawyer Somers, *a master of wit and guile,* cajoles and browbeats in the courtroom.
>
> *A master of wit and guile,* Lawyer Somers cajoles and browbeats in the courtroom.
>
> Lawyer Somers cajoles and browbeats in the courtroom, *a master of wit and guile.*

As a final example of language tools for renaming and modifying nouns, study this effective, compact sentence:

One of the five largest towns in Roman England, home of King Arthur's legendary Round Table, seat of Alfred the Great, whose statue looks down its main street, early capital of England, and victim of Cromwell's destructive forces, Winchester is an enchanting cathedral city in which layer after layer of history is visibly present.

Elisabeth Lambert Ortiz
"Exploring Winchester," *Gourmet,*
March 1978, p. 21

This sentence is made up of one independent clause, which includes an adjective clause, and five pre-positional appositives, the third of which contains an adjective clause. The statements underlying this sentence might be charted thus:

Winchester is an enchanting cathedral city.

In [this city] which layer after layer of history is visibly present.
Winchester was one of the five largest towns in Roman England.
Winchester was the home of King Arthur's legendary Round Table.
Winchester was the seat of Alfred the Great.

[Alfred the Great's] whose statue looks down its main street.
Winchester was the early capital of England.
Winchester was the victim of Cromwell's destructive forces.

We see here that eight statements—enough to make up a paragraph of clear but unrelieved simple sentences—have been shortened into one complex sentence, the layering of appositives and adjective clauses producing compression, sentence variety, and proper emphasis.

Practice Sheet 15

Subordination

NAME _____ SCORE _____

Directions: The purpose of this practice sheet is to demonstrate some of the commonest ways to subordinate material, to show how an independent clause can be reduced to a subordinate unit that is then attached to or incorporated within the main clause of the sentence.

Each of the following numbered units consists of two independent clauses in the form of a compound sentence or two short sentences. The sentences used for this demonstration are purposely simple so that you can easily see the process followed. One of the independent clauses is italicized. Following this is a single rewritten sentence, one italicized unit of which gives in subordinate form the material of the italicized independent clause. In the space at the left of each numbered unit, write one of the following numbers to identify the italicized subordinate unit in the rewritten sentence:

1. Adverb clause	4. Gerund phrase	7. Infinitive phrase
2. Adjective clause	5. Absolute phrase	
3. Participial phrase	6. Appositive	

_____ 1. *My grandfather has owned that car for twelve years,* but it still runs quite well.
Although my grandfather has owned that car for twelve years, it still runs quite well.

_____ 2. Pay for your subscription before April 10, *and you will receive a free video.*
Pay for your subscription before April 10 *to receive a free video.*

_____ 3. Pay for your subscription before April 10, *and you will receive a free video.*
By paying for your subscription before April 10, you will receive a free video.

_____ 4. Charlene Walsh has been appointed manager for the softball team. *She is a very popular student.*
Charlene Walsh, *who is a very popular student,* has been appointed manager for the softball team.

_____ 5. Charlene Walsh has been appointed manager for the softball team. *She is a very popular student.*
Charlene Walsh, *being a very popular student,* has been appointed manager for the softball team.

_____ 6. Charlene Walsh has been appointed manager for the softball team. *She is a very popular student.*
Charlene Walsh, *a very popular student,* has been appointed manager for the softball team.

_____ 7. Ron Starnes is on vacation this week. *He usually runs the milling machine.*
Ron Starnes, *who usually runs the milling machine,* is on vacation this week.

_____ 8. *Ron Starnes is on vacation this week,* and so Stu Alexander is running the milling machine.
Because Ron Starnes is on vacation this week, Stu Alexander is running the milling machine.

_____ 9. *Ron Starnes is on vacation this week,* and so Stu Alexander is running the milling machine.
Ron Starnes being on vacation this week, Stu Alexander is running the milling machine.

_____ 10. *Study a few minutes a day for the next Spanish test.* You will avoid a last minute panic.
If you study a few minutes a day for the next Spanish test, you will avoid a last minute panic.

135

_____ 11. *Study a few minutes a day for the next Spanish test.* You will avoid a last minute panic.
By studying a few minutes a day for the next Spanish test, you will avoid a last minute panic.

_____ 12. School is closed today. *Most students are preparing for final exams.*
School is closed today *because most students are preparing for final exams.*

_____ 13. As the new volleyball coach, the college has hired Janet Bancroft. *She was the junior varsity coach last year.*
As the new volleyball coach, the college has hired Janet Bancroft, *who was the junior varsity coach last year.*

_____ 14. As the new volleyball coach, the college has hired Janet Bancroft. *She was the junior varsity coach last year.*
As the new volleyball coach, the college has hired Janet Bancroft, *the junior varsity coach last year.*

_____ 15. *The new contract was ratified.* The players went to spring training.
After the new contract was ratified, the players went to spring training.

_____ 16. *The new contract was ratified.* The players went to spring training.
The new contract having been ratified, the players went to spring training.

_____ 17. *Change the oil every 3000 miles.* You will prevent problems later in the life of the car.
If you change the oil every 3000 miles, you will prevent problems later in the life of the car.

_____ 18. *Change the oil every 3000 miles.* You will prevent problems later in the life of the car.
Changing the oil every 3000 miles will prevent problems later in the life of the car.

_____ 19. Change the oil every 3000 miles. *You will prevent problems later in the life of the car.*
Change the oil every 3000 miles *to prevent problems later in the life of the car.*

_____ 20. *We must clean up the banquet hall thoroughly after the dinner,* or the company will assess a $200 cleanup charge.
Unless we clean up the banquet hall thoroughly after the dinner, the company will assess a $200 cleanup charge.

_____ 21. We should probably confer with Norm Reynolds. *He traveled widely in Australia last year.*
We should probably confer with Norm Reynolds, *who traveled widely in Australia last year.*

_____ 22. We should probably confer with Norm Reynolds. *He traveled widely in Australia last year.*
We should probably confer with Norm Reynolds *because he traveled widely in Australia last year.*

_____ 23. Betsy Crawford called you yesterday afternoon for advice about computers. *You met her last Saturday at Marcia's house.*
Betsy Crawford, *whom you met last Saturday at Marcia's house,* called you yesterday afternoon for advice about computers.

_____ 24. *You need to walk carefully on that icy walkway,* or you will fall and hurt yourself.
If you do not walk carefully on that icy walkway, you will fall and hurt yourself.

_____ 25. Billy stayed home from work all last week. *He sprained his ankle in a touch football game last Sunday.*
Having sprained his ankle in a touch football game last Sunday, Billy stayed home from work all last week.

EXERCISE 15
SUBORDINATION

NAME _____ SCORE _____

Directions: Reduce the italicized sentence to the grammatical structure indicated in the parentheses and rewrite each numbered unit as one sentence.

1. *The hard disk on Maria's computer crashed yesterday.* She spent the whole day restoring data to the disk. (adverbial clause of reason)

2. *The hard disk on Maria's computer crashed yesterday.* She spent the whole day restoring data to the disk. (absolute phrase)

3. *The teleconference ended at 2:00 P.M.* We discussed two important problems and left for the day. (adverbial clause of time)

4. *Tammy spent three months training for the triathlon.* She felt confident that she would perform well. (participial phrase)

5. *The two carpenters finished the last door frame.* They moved on to the next house. (preposition plus gerund phrase)

6. *I added two long paragraphs to my psychology paper.* It was still 750 words too short. (adverb clause of concession)

7. *Leave the roses in the plastic shield until you get home.* This will protect them from damage. (gerund phrase)

8. Leave the roses in the plastic shield until you get home. *This will protect them from damage.* (infinitive phrase)

9. I am amazed at the skills of Martha Morrisey. *She is my computer teacher.* (appositive)

10. I am amazed at the skills of Martha Morrisey. *She is my computer teacher.* (adjective clause)

Directions: Rewrite each sentence by removing the coordinating conjunction (and, but, or) and changing the italicized material to the kind of unit indicated in the parentheses.

1. Changing channels, we watched two men, and *they were building a model bridge out of toothpicks.* (adjective clause)

2. *My little brother has become intensely interested in dinosaurs,* and he often goes to the museum to study them. (adverb clause of reason or cause)

3. *Take your raincoat with you this morning,* or you will probably get wet. (adverb clause of condition)

4. *The bell rang,* and all the sixth-graders raced out to the playground. (absolute phrase)

5. *I took a history class with Walt,* but I do not know him very well at all. (adverb clause of concession)

6. *Annie went fishing about five o'clock this morning,* and she caught three fine trout. (participial phrase)

7. *Annie went fishing about five o'clock this morning,* and she caught three fine trout. (adverb clause of time)

8. *Try to get away early,* and I'll drive with you as far as Albany. (adverb clause of condition)

9. I saw a police officer, and *she was directing traffic past the disabled truck.* (participial phrase)

10. I saw a police officer, and *she was directing traffic past the disabled truck.* (adjective clause)

EXERCISE 15A
SUBORDINATION

NAME _____   SCORE _____

Directions: Preceding lessons have demonstrated various types of noun modification. When two sentences employ the same noun or pronoun, one sentence may be incorporated into the other by being reduced to an adjective clause, a participial phrase, or (in some cases) an appositive. In the following pairs of sentences, the word printed in bold type in the first sentence is the noun or pronoun to be modified. Combine the sentences by reducing the second sentence to the kind of unit indicated by the following letters:
   A. Adjective clause
   B. Participial phrase following the noun
   C. Participial phrase preceding the noun
   D. Appositive
(You need not write the entire sentence; copy enough to show how the combining is done.)

1. Ms. Lucas recently took on a new **assignment.** It involves development of new marketing plans.

   A. _____

   B. _____

   D. _____

2. Jill wants to go to work for her older **sister.** She is the owner of a small security company.

   A. _____

   D. _____

3. In Industrial Relations class last Tuesday we heard **Allen Marcus.** He is a well-known authority on union contracts.

   A. _____

   D. _____

4. There is a picture of **Elaine.** She is standing beside her new car.

   A. _____

   B. _____

5. The **senator** threw out the first pitch at the World Series. He was wearing a baggy baseball uniform.

   A. _____

   B. _____

6. **Jane** walked slowly through the door. She looked at the guests with surprise in her eyes.

   A. _____

   B. _____

   C. _____

7. **Mrs. Ramsay** was very popular in our neighborhood. She often baked delicious apple pies for us kids.

   A. _____

   B. _____

   C. _____

8. **Jack Wallace** made a detailed assessment of the team's chances in the tournament. He played professional basketball for six years.

   A. _____

   B. _____

   C. _____

   D. _____

9. Rhoda's **Uncle Bob** has access to the latest in computers and electronic gadgets. He owns an electronics company.

   A. _____

   B. _____

   C. _____

10. The two **boys** finally found the lost dog. They had been searching for hours.

    A. _____

    B. _____

    C. _____

EXERCISE 15B
SUBORDINATION

NAME _____   SCORE _____

Directions: Rewrite each of the following numbered sections as one sentence. In each case use the italicized subject and verb for the main clause. Use a variety of the subordinating units listed in Lesson 15.

1. *Jim Johnson* is the new baseball coach. He knows everything about the game. He is also a hard worker. He *will develop* a successful program.

2. *My boss* seems to love a new challenge. He seems to love good causes. He is leaving the company. He *will head* a new recycling company in Canada.

3. This morning *the sales people* all *came* to the office before lunch. They completed their paperwork early. They are going to a football game.

4. *Melissa* plans to work in Central America this summer. She *will work* on an archaeological dig.

5. *Joanne Cassidy* has never done any painting before. She is studying painting now. This summer she *will paint* her uncle's house.

6. At first we were impressed by Jim Claxton. He keeps busy. He turns out reams of memos. But recently *we recognized* something. Jim never finishes anything important.

7. At first *Jimmy* loved football. He loved to run. He loved to catch the ball. He got tackled by a huge guy. He *is* not sure he loves football.

8. *Tom* knew nothing about computers. He didn't want to know anything about computers. He met a girl. She is a programmer. He *is* now very interested in computers.

9. *Laura Lawson* writes a column for the campus paper. The column deals with the problems of lovelorn students.

10. *Alice* has never understood football. It is too complicated. She *can understand* chess. She is interested in chess.

11. Mr. Lindsay's barn was damaged by lightning. The lightning occurred during a recent storm. *Mr. Lindsay was* glad the damage was minor.

12. *Jason* is my little brother. He recently *surprised* me. He became the news anchor at the local television station.

13. *The shopper* was amazed by the quality of the car. The car was not very expensive. She *bought* the car immediately.

14. As a young girl, Laura never liked to read. Now she is a successful editor of popular fiction. *I was amused* to learn this.

15. *Jack Andrews* has written a new computer program. The new program allows fax copy to be read directly into a computer. He *is* about to become wealthy.

16. *Billy* once weighed less than 150 pounds. He has been working out at a gym. He *can bench–press* 250 pounds.

17. *Patricia* learned cross-stitching by reading an instruction manual and has now begun to teach other people and *has opened* her own crafts company.

18. *Lucille* was interested in woodworking in high school, and now she *owns* her own cabinet shop and the shop produces beautiful pieces of furniture.

19. *Robert and his mother will both graduate* from college this June. His mother left college after her freshman year twenty years ago.

20. *Marilyn Atkins operates* the town's only garage. The garage was established by her father many years ago. She runs the garage very successfully.

LESSON 16 ■
Parallel Structure; Comparisons

Our examination of the construction of effective sentences should deal with two other situations where underlying logic demands careful selection of sentence units.

Parallel Structure

When two or more parts of a sentence are similar in function, they should normally be expressed in the same grammatical construction; in other words, they should be made parallel. The principle of parallelism implies that, in a series, nouns should be balanced with nouns, adjectives with adjectives, prepositional phrases with prepositional phrases, clauses with clauses, and so forth. The following sentence owes much of its clarity and effectiveness to the careful parallel arrangement: Two adjective clauses are joined with *and,* two adverbs with *but,* and three noun direct objects with *and.*

Anyone ‖ who studies world affairs *and*
     ‖ who remembers our last three wars will realize ‖ sadly *but*
                                                        ‖ inevitably,
    that another conflict will endanger ‖ the economic strength of our nation,
                                            the complacency of our political institutions,
                                            and the moral fiber of our people.

Here we shall deal with two types of errors, the false series and the *and who* construction, both of which use a coordinator to join unlike grammatical units.
   1. The false or shifted series:

Weak: Most people play golf for exercise, pleasure, and so they can meet others. [The *and* ties an adverb clause to two nouns.]

Better: Most people play golf for exercise, for pleasure, and for social contacts.

Weak: Our new teacher was young, tall, slender, and with red hair. [The *and* suggests that it will be followed by a fourth adjective, not a prepositional phrase.]

Better: Our new teacher was young, tall, slender, and red-haired.

Weak: Mr. Little's speech was tiresome, inaccurate, and should have been omitted.

Better: Mr. Little's speech was tiresome, inaccurate, and unnecessary.

   2. The *and who* or *and which* construction:

Weak: Their son is an athlete with great talent *and who* will soon be well known.

Better: Their son is an athlete who has great talent and who will soon be well known.
                Their son is a greatly talented athlete who will soon be well known. [Here the unbalanced modification is avoided.]

Weak: I am taking Physics 388, a difficult course *and which* demands much time.

Better: I am taking Physics 388, which is a difficult course and which demands much time.
I am taking Physics 388, which is difficult and demands much time.

COMPARISONS

A common type of sentence is one in which a comparison or a contrast is made. This kind of sentence offers a few difficulties that you should be aware of.

1. Be sure that you compare only those things that are capable of being compared:

Faulty: The storage capacity of this computer is much greater than our old one. [What is wrong with this sentence is that two unlike things, *capacity* and *one* (meaning *computer*) are being compared.]
The influence of the political leader is more ephemeral than the artist.

Improved: The storage capacity of this computer is much greater than *the capacity of* our old one.
The storage capacity of this computer is much greater than *that of* our old one.
The influence of the political leader is more ephemeral than *the influence of* the artist.
The influence of the political leader is more ephemeral than *that of* the artist.
The political leader's influence is more ephemeral than *the artist's.*

2. When you are using the comparative form in a comparison, use *any other* when it is necessary to exclude the subject of the comparison from the group:

Faulty: Wilson, the first-string center, is heavier than *any* man on the team. [In this version the writer is comparing Wilson to a group that *includes* Wilson.]

Improved: Wilson, the first-string center, is heavier than *any other* man on the team.

3. When your sentence contains a double comparison, you should include all the words necessary to make the idiom complete:

He is now as tall *as,* if not taller *than,* his mother.
He is now as tall as his mother, if not taller.
She is one of the best *runners,* if not the best *runner,* in the club.
She is one of the best runners in the club, if not the best.

(See Supplement 1.)

Supplement 1

In addition to requiring the structural units already mentioned, comparison–contrast sentences place a few constraints on the *form* of the adjective or adverb.

When your comparison is limited to two things, use the comparative degree. Use the superlative for more than two things:

Both Jane and Edwina sing well, but Jane has the *better* voice.
Which takes *more* time, your studies or your job?
January is the *worst* month of the year.

You learned in Lesson 2 that there are two ways of forming the comparative and superlative degrees. In general, *er* and *est* are used with short words, and *more* and *most* with longer words.

> When I was *younger,* I was *more apprehensive* about thunder and lightning.
> This encyclopedia is the *newest* and the *most comprehensive.*
> Maria works *faster* than I and also *more accurately.*

Remember that in present-day standard English we don't combine *er* or *est* with *more* or *most* in the same word. We don't say, for example, *more pleasanter, most loveliest,* or *more faster.*

Practice Sheet 16

Parallel Structure; Comparisons

NAME _____   SCORE _____

Directions: In the space at the left of each pair of sentences, copy the letter identifying the sentence that is logically structured. Be prepared to point out in class the faulty parallelism in the sentence you rejected.

_____ 1. A. James read that book not simply for information but for the pleasure in the reading.
          B. James read that book not simply for information but because he took pleasure in the reading.

_____ 2. A. My family decided to stay home during vacation rather than going off on an expensive trip.
          B. My family decided to stay home during vacation rather than go off on an expensive trip.

_____ 3. A. The new math professor is a person who has great energy and with a keen interest in students.
          B. The new math professor is a person who has great energy and possesses a keen interest in students.

_____ 4. A. Last week's geography test was very complex, highly difficult, and almost impossible to finish within the time limit.
          B. Last week's geography test was very complex, the difficulty was high, and almost impossible to finish within the time limit.

_____ 5. A. Martin Keene is a stockbroker whose nose for great buys is terrific and has a fine sense of timing.
          B. Martin Keene is a stockbroker who has a terrific nose for great buys and a fine sense of timing.

_____ 6. A. As a veteran crusader on ecological issues, Bill Waters is disliked by politicians and feared by developers.
          B. As a veteran crusader on ecological issues, Bill Waters is disliked by politicians and bringing fear to developers' hearts.

_____ 7. A. In the spring our backyard will need to be seeded and a good dose of fertilizer.
          B. In the spring our backyard will need to be seeded and thoroughly fertilized.

_____ 8. A. I will improve my basketball by careful practice and studying tactics diligently.
          B. I will improve my basketball by practicing carefully and studying tactics diligently.

_____ 9. A. Watch Mark, staring at his notes and pretending to study for the test.
          B. Watch Mark, staring at his notes and pretends to study for the test.

_____ 10. A. Some outside consultants offer stale solutions rather than thinking constructively about problems.
          B. Some outside consultants offer stale solutions rather than constructive thinking about problems.

Directions: From each of the following pairs of sentences, select the one you prefer and write the letter in the space at the left. Be prepared to justify your choice.

_____ 1. A. The mountains of the eastern United States are far older than the western United States.
       B. The mountains of the eastern United States are far older than those in the western United States.

_____ 2. A. Which car is longest, the coupe or the station wagon?
       B. Which car is longer, the coupe or the station wagon?

_____ 3. A. The Montreal Expos are as good a baseball team, if not a better team, than any other in this decade.
       B. The Montreal Expos are as good a baseball team as any other in this decade, if not a better team.

_____ 4. A. My sister has a better jump shot than any kid in her ninth-grade class.
       B. My sister has a better jump shot than any other kid in her ninth-grade class.

_____ 5. A. This new spark plug lasted longer than the other company's.
       B. This new spark plug lasted longer than the other company.

_____ 6. A. Because she has been teaching for several years, Marge's knowledge of geography is greater than the average person.
       B. Because she has been teaching for several years, Marge's knowledge of geography is greater than the average person's.

_____ 7. A. He is very grim looking, with a thick neck and a face like a bulldog.
       B. He is very grim looking, with a thick neck and a face like a bulldog's.

_____ 8. A. The girls on this team are not much different from those on any other team.
       B. The girls on this team are not much different from any other team.

_____ 9. A. June has a better curve ball than any member of this team.
       B. June has a better curve ball than any other member of this team.

_____ 10. A. In general, roads in Britain are much more narrow than the United States.
       B. In general, roads in Britain are much more narrow than roads in the United States.

EXERCISE 16
PARALLEL STRUCTURE; COMPARISONS

NAME _____ SCORE _____

Directions: Rewrite each sentence to correct the faulty parallelism.

1. I always thought of Camp Wellmore more as a resort than as if it were a place where I could work.

2. Jim is looking for an affordable car but which was still able to look good at the country club.

3. That new novel has an interesting story, colorfully written, and the characters are people I identify with.

4. We looked for a leader who will take a stand on important issues and with great courage.

5. To be a good golfer, Marsha needs to groove her swing, hit through the ball, and with great concentration.

6. John Ormond is one man whose power of persuasion is great and has widely known ability as an organizer.

7. This company needs people who think innovatively and always working to develop new products.

8. Our job here as ushers is the safety of the crowd and to protect the rock stars from autograph seekers.

9. My problem with that test came more from lacking time than from the fact that I did not understand the material.

10. The president of that toy company looks like a typical teenager wearing old jeans and with hair down in her eyes.

Directions: Rewrite each sentence so that the comparison in it is logical.

1. I did not know that the work here was so much harder than college.

2. My sister is the smartest of any girl in her school.

3. That movie is one of the dullest, if not the dullest movie, I've seen in years.

4. Who is tallest, you or Martha?

5. The goalie is short and stocky with legs like a gorilla.

6. Sam likes rock music just as much as his mother.

7. Yesterday's temperature was much lower here than the interior of the state.

8. The local bicycle shop has a better mechanic than any shop in this area.

9. Using a computer to balance your checkbook is as complicated, if not more complicated, than a calculator.

10. Her accuracy record is equal, and in many cases better than, the other secretaries.

Punctuation
Lessons, Practice Sheets, and Exercises

PART IV

LESSON 17 ■
Commas to Separate

Commas are used to separate certain parts of the sentence so that written communication will be clear and direct. Commas to separate are used in the following situations:

1. Before *and, but, for, or, nor,* and *yet* when they join the clauses of a compound sentence:

> I placed the typed sheet on his desk, and he picked it up and read it slowly. His face turned red, but he did not say a word. I knew he was angry, for he rose and stomped out of the room. [Note that no comma is used before the conjunction in a compound predicate.]

At this point you might reread Lesson 7. There you will find a detailed explanation, with examples, of this rule. Remember that a semicolon rather than a comma is usually required in a compound sentence when no coordinating conjunction is present.

2. Between the items of a series. A series is composed of three or more words, phrases, or clauses of equal grammatical rank. A series usually takes the form of *a, b, and c;* sometimes it may be *a, b, or c.* In journalistic writing the comma is omitted before *and* or *or;* in more formal writing it is generally not omitted. The beginning writer will do well to follow formal practice:

> The land looked brown, parched, lifeless, and ominous. [Four adjectives.]
> Volunteers included high schoolers, office workers, housewives, and retirees. [Four nouns.]
> The dog charged through the door, down the steps, and into the garage. [Three phrases.]
> He understands what he must do, when he must do it, and why it must be done. [Three subordinate clauses.]
> Larry fetched the water, Mort built the fire, and I opened the cans. [Independent clauses.]

Notice the last example. Three or more short independent clauses arranged in the form of a series may be separated by commas. But long clauses—independent clauses especially, but sometimes dependent clauses also—are better separated by semicolons, particularly if there is other punctuation within the clauses. The following sentences

151

illustrate the punctuation between and within the long clauses. Although you would probably hesitate to attempt such sentences, you will encounter them in your reading:

> The first week of the tour called for long hops and little free time; the second week, with longer rest periods in Amsterdam and Antwerp, was less exhausting; but the third week, which took us to four countries in seven days, left us numb and bewildered. [Three lengthy independent clauses in series, with internal punctuation.]

> These dark days will be worth all they have cost if they show us that happiness is not a matter of money; if they force upon us the joy of achievement, the thrill of creative effort; if they teach us that our true destiny is to serve, to the best of our ability, our fellows. [Three lengthy adverbial clauses in series, with internal punctuation.]

3. Between coordinate adjectives preceding a noun. A comma separating two adjectives signifies that the two adjectives are equal in their modifying force. A comma is not used when the modifier closer to the noun has more importance as an identifier of the noun. Thus we use a comma with "a difficult, unfair examination" but not with "a difficult midterm examination." Another explanation is that in the first example *difficult* and *unfair* modify *examination* with equal force, whereas in the second example *difficult* really modifies the unit *midterm examination.*

The problem here is to determine when adjectives are coordinate, that is, equal in modifying force. Two tests may prove helpful.

a. If the insertion of *and* between the modifiers produces a reading that still makes sense, the adjectives are equal and a comma should be used. "A difficult *and* unfair examination" would sound correct to most native speakers of English, but "a difficult *and* midterm examination" would not.

b. If the adjectives sound natural in reversed position, they are equal and should be separated by a comma. Thus we could say "an unfair, difficult examination" but not "a midterm difficult examination" without meaning something quite different from a difficult midterm examination.

When you use a noun preceded by more than two adjectives, you should test the adjectives by pairs, the first with the second, the second with the third, and so on. It may help you to know that we usually do not use commas before adjectives denoting size or age. And you must remember that we never use a comma between the last adjective and the noun.

Observe how use of the above-mentioned tests determines punctuation like the following:

a tall, dark, and handsome gentleman
the dark, cold, drafty classroom
a heavy, soiled leather ball
a mean old local gossip

a tall, dark, handsome gentleman
a neat, courteous little boy
her funny little upturned nose

4. After most introductory modifiers, especially if they are long and not obviously restrictive. In this situation modern usage varies considerably. You must depend on your own good sense and judgment. The following explanations will provide a general guide.

a. Put commas after introductory adverbial clauses except those that are short or in no need of special emphasis. No hard-and-fast rule governs this situation. The inexperienced writer would probably do well to use commas after all introductory adverbial clauses except very short clauses denoting time:

Unless the flood water recedes soon, we're in trouble.
If we can prove that the signature was forged, we will win the case.
Before sophomores will be admitted to courses numbered 300 or above, they must have official permission.
Before I answer you I want to ask another question.
When he arrived he seemed distraught.

b. Put commas after introductory verbal-phrase modifiers:

Having climbed the steep trail up Cougar Mountain, Bob decided to take some pictures. To get the best view of the valley, he walked to the edge of the cliff. After opening his rucksack, he searched for his new telephoto lens.

c. Put a comma after an introductory absolute element, such as a phrase, an adverb modifying the whole sentence, a mild exclamation, and *yes* and *no*:

In fact, there was no way to keep the front door closed.
Certainly, I'll be glad to help you.
Well, what are we to do now?
No, we are not in danger.

d. Ordinarily, do not put a comma after a prepositional phrase that precedes a main clause unless the phrase is long or unless a comma is needed to add special emphasis or to prevent a misreading:

After a heavy dinner we usually went for a short walk.
In early summer many birds nested there.
In spite of the very heavy wind and the pelting hailstones, the third race was completed.
Never at a loss for words, he answered with a joke.
After school, teachers were expected to find time for grading papers and preparing lessons.

5. Between any two words that might be mistakenly read together:

Before, he had been industrious and sober. [Not *before he had been.*]
Once inside, the dog scampered all over the furniture. [Not *inside the dog.*]
While we were eating, the table collapsed. [Not *eating the table.*]
After we had washed, Mother prepared breakfast. [Not *washed Mother.*]
Ever since, he has been afraid of deep water. [Not *ever since he has been.*]
Shortly after ten, thirty new recruits appeared. [Not *shortly after ten thirty.*]

PRACTICE SHEET 17
COMMAS TO SEPARATE

NAME _____ SCORE _____

Directions: Each of the following sentences has two commas missing. Add the commas where they are necessary. Then in the spaces at the left, write the numbers of the rules that apply to the commas you have added:

    1. Before a coordinate conjunction   3. Between coordinate adjectives
       in a compound sentence   4. After an introductory modifier
    2. In a series   5. To prevent misreading

_____
_____   1. After losing her way Jill wished that she had read the map carefully before she turned onto the tricky twisting dirt road.

_____
_____   2. We saw Mary, Alice and Marie in town but they had to study and could not go to the movies with us.

_____
_____   3. The four friends went to the dock, untied the boat and went quickly out to the small secret cove where the fish were biting hungrily.

_____
_____   4. After the dogs ran off the little boy wandered sadly around the yard for hours and he called their names over and over.

_____
_____   5. Because they had already seen that sad boring movie June and Marge decided to go shopping instead.

_____
_____   6. We have the boat, the ropes and the skis but we'll have to borrow three more life jackets from Charles.

_____
_____   7. Frightened by the car's headlights the deer jumped the fence and then she leaped across the creek in one long jump.

_____
_____   8. When I changed my car's oil last week I made a sticky gooey mess and decided that I would never try to do that sort of thing again.

_____
_____   9. In his schedule this term Rick is taking a CAD/CAM course ROTC, and a higher level math course that sounds very difficult.

_____
_____ 10. Looking extremely tired Alicia walked slowly into class and then she fell asleep almost as soon as she sat down.

155

_____ 11. The boys found a shovel, a hoe and a rake but they want me to bring a
_____   wheelbarrow when I go up to the cabin.

_____ 12. After the mail came John remembered that he had intended to mail some
_____   bills a letter, and a thank-you note to his Uncle Doug.

_____ 13. Because the study group met every night last week most of the members
_____   passed the long detailed midterm exam with ease.

_____ 14. Adjournment of the meeting was postponed for fifteen minutes and the
_____   committee heard an angry frustrated member give a report.

_____ 15. The cafeteria serves hamburgers, spaghetti and meatballs and meat loaf,
_____   but some people would prefer more healthful low-fat choices.

_____ 16. Walking slowly into the library Mary Lou spent a pleasant restful hour
_____   browsing through some magazines.

_____ 17. Jeremy took math, physics and chemistry last term but this term he is
_____   working as an intern at a television station.

_____ 18. Since Jamie began training for the marathon last year she has been lifting
_____   weights, doing yoga and running fifty miles a week.

_____ 19. A few bored uninterested students slept in the back of the room but most
_____   found the video on time management very interesting.

_____ 20. Mario worked for a week as a political pollster; after that finding a job in
_____   politics became his secret compelling goal.

EXERCISE 17
COMMAS TO SEPARATE

NAME _____ SCORE _____

Directions: Each of the following sentences has two commas missing. Add the commmas where they are necessary. Then in the spaces at the left, write the numbers of the rules that apply to the commas you have added:

1. Before a coordinating conjunction   3. Between coordinate adjectives
    in a compound sentence   4. After an introductory element
2. In a series   5. To prevent misreading

_____   1. As the boys were leaving the crowd cheered wildly and the band played
_____   the school fight song.

_____   2. If we can find a new route down the coast the long tedious trip to the fish-
_____   ing camp might seem more interesting.

_____   3. Having worked hard during her summer internship Racquel had increased
_____   her skills in accounting sales, and broadcasting.

_____   4. Smiling only briefly Maria turned away from the computer and removed
_____   the short carefully worded memo from the printer.

_____   5. Shortly after three ten tired, sweaty Boy Scouts walked up on the porch
_____   and Ben gave them some cold water and directions to the road.

_____   6. Excited by their discovery the three students picked up the fossil carried
_____   it to the campus, and gave it to their professor.

_____   7. The clerk brought out fifteen pairs of shoes but neither Laura Annie, nor
_____   Alice bought anything.

_____   8. Working very quickly the three men packed the boxes, loaded the truck
_____   and drove off to the warehouse.

_____   9. After the smoke cleared the room filled with firefighters and their captain
_____   ordered them to carry the furniture into the yard.

_____   10. Since we had come to early registration the lines were short and the se-
_____   lection of classes was still good.

157

Directions: Under each rule, write two sentences of your own composition to illustrate the punctuation to be used. Bring your paper to class for discussion. The purpose of this exercise is to help you recognize punctuation situations in your own writing.

1. Comma used before a coordinating conjunction in a compound sentence.
    a.

    b.

2. Commas used in a series (one a series of single words and one a series of phrases).
    a.

    b.

3. Commas used after an introductory modifier (one adverbial clause and one verbal phrase).
    a.

    b.

4. Comma used between coordinate adjectives.
    a.

    b.

5. Comma used to prevent misreading.
    a.

    b.

EXERCISE 17A
COMMAS AND SEMICOLONS TO SEPARATE

NAME _____ SCORE _____

Directions: The following sentences contain numbered spots where punctuation might be needed. In the correspondingly numbered spaces at the left, write C where a comma is needed, S for a semicolon, and 0 where no punctuation is needed.

1. _____   (1) After spending a long day in committee meetings Senator Gorham

2. _____   left her office and went to the gym for a workout.

3. _____   (2) I believe that Morton will be happy in the new company he's

4. _____   interested in accounting, computers and stereos.

5. _____   (3) The two students spent hours in the library but they didn't find

6. _____   much useful material on their research projects.

7. _____   (4) In every closet of the office there were hidden old books newspapers,

8. _____   and file folders.

9. _____   (5) Nearby the police chief and her assistants met in her office they were

10. _____   discussing assignments for the homecoming parade.

11. _____   (6) The tall brawny football players left the library, walked to their

12. _____   car and drove slowly to the gym.

13. _____   (7) Stopping the car in the hotel driveway the parking attendant opened

14. _____   the door and held out her hand for a tip.

15. _____   (8) The low quiet hum of the car's engine put the baby to sleep the

16. _____   screech of brakes woke him up suddenly.

17. _____   (9) Yesterday the delivery service brought seven large boxes we must

18. _____   open them and set up the computers today.

19. _____   (10) Jan usually prefers to type her own letters for special work however,

20. _____   she always uses a typing service.

21. _____   (11) After leaving the office staff members went to the nearby deli for

22. _____   delicious hot pastrami sandwiches.

23. _____ (12) After they had worked for about three hours the two men walked to
24. _____ the store and bought coffee and pastries.

25. _____ (13) Because Marge had closed the windows, locked the doors and set the
26. _____ burglar alarm she felt secure in the house by herself.

27. _____ (14) My uncle sent me a small check on November 20 the money helped
28. _____ me to pay a few small bills that were past due.

29. _____ (15) Whenever you pass an anthill take a moment and watch one of
30. _____ nature's great organizations at work.

31. _____ (16) At the zoo the delighted little boy petted the goat, rode in the horse
32. _____ cart and watched a blue jay building a nest.

33. _____ (17) Although that road is quite rocky the kids love to ride their bikes
34. _____ there the long, steep hills are very exciting.

35. _____ (18) Plowing through the rough seas the small boat finally made the
36. _____ harbor the women on board were glad to tie up safely.

37. _____ (19) The rare juicy hamburger tasted great but the french fries were cold
38. _____ and soggy.

39. _____ (20) After the car broke down the wrecker towed it to a small auto repair
40. _____ shop, and we spent the afternoon in a shopping mall.

LESSON 18 ■

Commas to Enclose

Commas are used to set off words, phrases, or clauses that break into the normal word order of a sentence. Notice that these interrupters are *set off* by commas. This means that although interrupters that begin or end a sentence have only one comma, any such unit that comes in the interior of the sentence has *two* commas, one before it and one after it.

The following are the most common types of interrupters:

1. Nonrestrictive adjective clauses and phrases. To understand this comma use, you should now reread pages 71–73 of Lesson 9 for an explanation of the difference between restrictive and nonrestrictive adjective clauses.

Other modifiers of nouns—participial phrases especially and, less frequently, prepositional phrases—must be set off by commas when they are nonrestrictive, that is, when they are not necessary for the *identification* of the noun modified. (The same distinction applies also to a few appositives, as noted in the next item of this lesson.)

Examine these additional examples contrasting restrictive and nonrestrictive modifiers of nouns. Notice in the last pair of sentences how the writer, by using or not using commas with the adjective clause, gives important information to the reader:

> The speech *that the coach made at the awards banquet* was one of her best. [Restrictive adjective clause.]
> The coach's awards banquet speech, *which was one of her best,* should be printed. [Nonrestrictive adjective clause.]
> Anyone *holding a winning ticket* should come to the desk. [Restrictive participial phrase.]
> Jan's mother, *holding a winning ticket,* went to the desk. [Nonrestrictive participial phrase.]
> A woman *at the far end of the head table* summoned a waiter. [Restrictive prepositional phrase.]
> Professor Angela Cheney, *at the far end of the head table,* summoned a waiter. [Nonrestrictive prepositional phrase.]
> My brother-in-law *who lives in Akron* is a chemist. [The writer has more than one brother-in-law. The restrictive clause is needed to distinguish this brother-in-law from other brothers-in-law.]
> My brother-in-law, *who lives in Akron,* is a chemist. [Identification is not explicit, so the writer is telling us that he has only one brother-in-law.]

2. Most appositives. As you learned in Lesson 10, the most common type of appositive immediately follows the noun or pronoun that it renames:

> One comedian, *the one with the lisp,* was booed.
> The major, *a veteran of three wars,* accepted the award.
> Mr. Tate, *our head counselor,* will speak.
> Our head counselor, *Mr. Tate,* will speak.

Appositives like these are called *loose* or *nonrestrictive* appositives and are set off. But an appositive may sometimes function the same way that a restrictive adjective clause

161

functions; that is, it may identify a preceding noun that, without the appositive, could refer to any member of a class. An appositive of this sort is not set off:

my brother Jack, the poet Keats, the apostle Paul, the preposition *to,* Henry IV.

3. Absolute phrases. An absolute phrase, which consists of a noun or a pronoun plus a verbal (see p. 98, Lesson 12), modifies the sentence as a whole, not any special part of it:

Today being a holiday, I plan to loaf and relax.
Her replacement having arrived early, Bea had time to shop.
He sat there in silence, *his left cheek twitching as usual.*
He stood in the doorway, *his wet cloak dripping water on the rug,* and waited for some sign of recognition.

4. Parenthetical expressions. These are words, phrases, or clauses that break into the sentence to explain, to emphasize, to qualify, or to point the direction of the thought:

The text, *moreover,* had not been carefully proofread.
You will find, *for example,* that the format is not attractive.
The meal, *to tell the truth,* was quite unappetizing.
His appearance, *I must admit,* would startle anyone.

5. Words used in direct address:

"Remember, *Jimmy,* that we like your work," he said.
"Henry," said the teacher, "you must remain after school."
"I believe, *sir,* that you have been misinformed," she replied.
"And now, *dear friends and neighbors,* let us eat," announced Father Jamison.

6. Expressions designating the speaker in direct quotations:

"With your permission," *he replied,* "there's nothing I'd rather do."
"That must do," *he said,* "until we think of something better."

Other marks may be used instead of the comma if the sentence justifies their use:

"How shall I tell him?" *asked Mary timidly.* [Question mark after question.]
"Silence!" *he shouted.* "Get to work at once!" [Exclamation point.]
"Two of the buildings are firetraps," *replied the comptroller;* "moreover, the library needs a new roof." [Semicolon required to avoid a comma fault between independent clauses.]

7. Negative insertions used for emphasis, units out of their position, and "tag" questions (short interrogative clauses combined with statements):

Our plane was an old propeller model, *not the 747 we had expected.*
Tired and footsore, the hikers finally reached camp.
The hikers finally reached camp, *tired and footsore.*
[*But*] The tired and footsore hikers finally reached camp.
Her answer was a good one, *don't you think?*
You remember, *don't you,* Dr. Wade's eloquent eulogy?

8. Degrees, titles, and the like when they follow names:

Helen Lyle, *Ph.D.,* gave the opening address.
The new ambassador is Peter Jones, *Esq.*

9. In dates and addresses:

On July 14, *1904,* in a little cottage at 316 High Street, *Mayville, Illinois,* the wedding took place. [Journalistic practice usually omits the comma *after* the year and the state.]

When a year follows a month, rather than a day of the month, it is usually not set off. And a comma is not needed before a zip code:

As of March 1985 his mailing address was 1675 East Union Street, Seattle, Washington 98122.

Practice Sheet 18
Commas to Enclose

NAME _____ SCORE _____

Directions: Insert commas where they are necessary in the following sentences. Then, before each sentence, write one of the following numbers to indicate the rule that governs the punctuation of the sentence. Commas are used to enclose

1. a nonrestrictive clause or phrase
2. an appositive
3. a noun in direct address
4. a parenthetical element
5. the speaker in dialogue
6. an absolute phrase

_____ 1. The wild ponies live on Assateague Island an island off Virginia and Maryland.

_____ 2. That package in my opinion should have been wrapped more carefully.

_____ 3. The blizzard having arrived earlier than expected we were all trapped in the gymnasium for two days.

_____ 4. "I need to pay some bills today" said Mike.

_____ 5. Jim March easily the best athlete in the school broke his ankle yesterday in a skiing accident.

_____ 6. Yolanda her interest in playing bridge having died dropped out of the neighborhood bridge club.

_____ 7. Take the other children Mary to see the puppies in the barn.

_____ 8. Alma looking very tired from the drive arrived about midnight last night.

_____ 9. Ms. Marshal the most experienced teacher in the department is also very popular with the students.

_____ 10. I heard the news from Mel who always seems to know what's going on in the office.

_____ 11. My last class for today economic geography was canceled.

_____ 12. My sister left for Seattle yesterday her car loaded with luggage and her collection of teddy bears.

_____ 13. Richard who usually works with great accuracy made three errors on that last set of problems.

_____ 14. My cousin recently moved to New York City where he hopes to find a job in the television industry.

_____ 15. My brother's children who watched "Sesame Street" learned to count at an early age.

_____ 16. "I wonder" said Carl "if anyone can tell me where to find a book on microsurgery."

_____ 17. Friday being a holiday most people left campus Thursday afternoon.

_____ 18. Our teacher concerned about our performance on the final exam began review sessions last week.

_____ 19. The river swollen by a week of heavy rains washed away the bridges on the highway out of town.

_____ 20. "Well Martha tell us your answer to the first problem" said the instructor.

165

Directions: Each of the following sentences contains either an adjective clause or a participial phrase in italics. Insert commas where they are needed. In the space at the left of each sentence write:

R if the clause or phrase is restrictive
N if the clause or phrase is nonrestrictive

_____ 1. Every student *who buys at least fifty dollars worth of books* will receive a free backpack from the bookstore.

_____ 2. That baseball glove *faded and worn from years of use* is still my brother's prize possession.

_____ 3. Students in the Lofton Building *where the air conditioning is being replaced* will find the heat very difficult to bear.

_____ 4. John Johnson *desperately trying to finish an overdue paper* was the last student out of the library today.

_____ 5. Some students *desperately trying to finish overdue papers* worked late in the library last night.

_____ 6. The new long-lasting paint *which was developed in our university's laboratories* will surely revolutionize building maintenance.

_____ 7. June wants to buy a word processing program *that can correct her grammatical mistakes.*

_____ 8. Bob's cousin Rhoda *who recently moved here from Texas* is studying hotel management.

_____ 9. Dr. Lamont's first article *which was published five years ago* is still considered a definitive study on diabetes.

_____ 10. In fact, all the articles *that Dr. Lamont has written* have made major contributions in that area.

_____ 11. A family friend *who is an accountant* does my income tax for me every year.

_____ 12. Jim Travers *who is an accountant* does my income tax for me every year.

_____ 13. Students *already enrolled in the aviation program* need not attend tomorrow's meeting.

_____ 14. Marsha *who is already enrolled in the aviation program* does not need to attend tomorrow's meeting.

_____ 15. Everyone *needing a student ID card* should report to the dean's office on Tuesday morning.

_____ 16. Unfortunately, the article *that you gave me* provided almost no information on politics in New York City prior to 1925.

_____ 17. I think that I will read that novel next April *when I'll be out of class for the spring break.*

_____ 18. Don Carlson *who is trying to change his major* spent three hours looking for an advisor this morning.

_____ 19. Wilson needs to buy a computer *that has enough RAM to run a graphics program.*

_____ 20. Wilson intends to buy an Omega 1486T *which has 10 megabytes of RAM.*

EXERCISE 18
COMMAS TO ENCLOSE

NAME _____ SCORE _____

Directions: Recognizing typical punctuation situations in your own writing is a very important skill. In the spaces provided, write two sentences to illustrate each of the rules indicated. Be sure to include all necessary punctuation.

1. Two sentences with nonrestrictive adjective clauses.
   a.

   b.

2. Two sentences with nonrestrictive participial phrases.
   a.

   b.

3. Two sentences with appositives.
   a.

   b.

4. Two sentences with nouns used in direct address.
   a.

   b.

5. Two sentences with parenthetical elements.
   a.

   b.

6. Two sentences with absolute phrases.
   a.

   b.

Directions: Each of the following sentences contains one adjective clause or one participial phrase. Underline the phrase or clause. Insert commas where they are needed. In the space at the left of each sentence write:

R if the clause or phrase is restrictive
N if the clause or phrase is nonrestrictive

_____ 1. James is one of those people who never lose their optimistic outlook on life.

_____ 2. How long is that plank lying on the workbench?

_____ 3. Janice Moore who attended college here last year has gone to England to study.

_____ 4. Our apartment complex needs to hire someone who can do minor repairs in the apartments.

_____ 5. Our apartment complex hired Ron Jones who can do minor repairs in the apartments.

_____ 6. The girl standing at the end of the front row in that picture is my brother's daughter.

_____ 7. Marlene running down the street missed the bus by about thirty seconds.

_____ 8. The new junior class treasurer is a girl who is majoring in anthropology.

_____ 9. The new junior class treasurer is Arline Rollins who is majoring in anthropology.

_____ 10. Two students standing in the back of the room left class before the end of the lecture.

_____ 11. How old is that child standing at the end of the line?

_____ 12. My old jacket which Dad gave me for my sixteenth birthday has finally gotten too torn to wear.

_____ 13. A man wearing a gray coat and old, scuffed boots walked up the path.

_____ 14. My grandfather wearing a gray coat and old, scuffed boots walked up the path.

_____ 15. My little brother is one of those people who will always need extra tutoring in math.

_____ 16. Marsha Richmond who graduated from law school last year has joined the FBI.

_____ 17. A woman who graduated from the law school last year joined the FBI.

_____ 18. I always enjoy movies that are set in the old west.

_____ 19. My father loves *Stagecoach* which is set in the old west.

_____ 20. Rosie standing on a chair to reach a book on a high shelf fell and hurt her ankle.

EXERCISE 18A
COMMAS AND SEMICOLONS: ALL USES

NAME _____ SCORE _____

Directions: The following sentences contain fifty numbered spots, some with punctuation and some with no punctuation. In the correspondingly numbered spaces at the left, write C if the punctuation is correct and W if the punctuation is wrong.

1. _____   (1) When the team left$_1$ about 1500 avid,$_2$ football fans stood beside the

2. _____   road and cheered.

3. _____   (2) Ed Lindsay left Nebraska on April 20,$_3$ 1991,$_4$ he arrived in Seattle two

4. _____   days later.

5. _____   (3) I had a wonderful day yesterday;$_5$ I slept late, went out for a delicious

6. _____   breakfast$_6$ and spent the day watching football.

7. _____   (4) After Joan left$_7$ the meeting was adjourned, and all the new,$_8$ club

8. _____   members went to lunch together.

9. _____   (5) That old building$_9$ once a restaurant, has been purchased by a

10. _____   company$_{10}$ that wants to put a bank in it.

11. _____   (6) The race course was long, hilly$_{11}$ and extremely steep$_{12}$ but Maria ran

12. _____   her best time for the season.

13. _____   (7) The computers were down for the whole weekend,$_{13}$ no accounts, I

14. _____   guess,$_{14}$ were updated or corrected.

15. _____   (8) Arnold Russel, who moved here from upstate has$_{15}$ opened a shop,$_{16}$ that

16. _____   specializes in repairing old musical instruments.

17. _____   (9) The ski trip$_{17}$ we scheduled for next week has been postponed,$_{18}$ the

18. _____   weather has been unseasonably warm for three weeks.

19. _____   (10) The easiest way to Ruston is to drive up Highway 18,$_{19}$ turn north onto

20. _____   Rutledge Road$_{20}$ and then take Weston Lane into town.

21. _____   (11) The test was difficult,$_{21}$ but I'm certain$_{22}$ that a take-home test would

22. _____   have been far more difficult.

169

23. _____   (12) After that grouchy, older man moved next door; we kids never could

24. _____   play ball in the street again.

25. _____   (13) When the lightning struck the old water tower toppled into the city

26. _____   square.

27. _____   (14) Cynthia did not know that we had left the room, she was drowsing

28. _____   peacefully on the couch.

29. _____   (15) The lecture having ended we wearily closed our notebooks and

30. _____   walked out of the room.

31. _____   (16) Wilma's favorite food is pasta, she tries to go to a different Italian

32. _____   restaurant every weekend.

33. _____   (17) The biggest house on Main Street, the old Spencer house, has been

34. _____   sold; the new owner is an architect.

35. _____   (18) "For most of you in the room rent is a major item in your budget,"

36. _____   said the speaker.

37. _____   (19) In this morning's mail I received a large envelope containing a copy

38. _____   of an article about a friend of mine.

39. _____   (20) Since Al is the person who holds the school record for the 100-meter

40. _____   dash he is expected to do well at every track meet.

41. _____   (21) After Tom left, the two dogs at the kennel he went home and sprayed

42. _____   the yard for fleas.

43. _____   (22) You already told me, didn't you, that your birth date is July 5, 1965?

44. _____

45. _____   (23) Jim Ralston, an expert on the history of Spain also speaks Spanish

46. _____   quite fluently.

47. _____   (24) One person who speaks Spanish fluently, is Jim Ralston, who lived

48. _____   in Spain for several years.

49. _____   (25) "Joan you will be starting as catcher in Friday's game," said the

50. _____   coach.

LESSON 19 ■

Apostrophes, Colons, Dashes, Hyphens, and Quotation Marks

1. The apostrophe (') has three uses: (a) to form the possessive case of nouns and indefinite pronouns; (b) to mark the omitted material in contractions; and (c) to form certain plurals, such as those of letters and abbreviations.

a. Any noun, whether singular or plural, that does not end in *s* forms its possessive by adding an apostrophe and *s:*

a boy's hat, the horse's tail, Carol's car, men's shoes, children's toys

All plural nouns that end in *s* form the possessive by adding an apostrophe after the *s:*

boys' hats, horses' tails, the Smiths' home, ladies' dresses

In singular nouns ending in *s* or *z,* an apostrophe following the *s* or *z* is the usual way to form the possessive:

the countess' castle, Frances' reply, Archimedes' law, Mr. Gomez' report

However, modern-day usage is divided. Some dictionaries and style manuals sanction the *'s* spelling also if the possessive form can be easily pronounced with an extra syllable and if the following word does not begin with an *s:*

the boss' [*or* boss's] answer, Mr. Jones' [*or* Jones's] house, the witness' [*or* witness's] testimony [*but*] the witness' story

The indefinite pronouns, but not the personal pronouns, form the possessive with the aid of the apostrophe:

somebody's sweater, anyone's opinion, anybody's game [But note the possessive forms of these pronouns: his, hers, its, theirs, ours, yours, whose.]

b. The apostrophe is used to stand for the omitted material in contractions:

doesn't [does not], won't [will not], she's [she is, she has], o'clock [of the clock]

rock 'n' roll [rock and roll]

You must learn to distinguish carefully between the following pairs of contractions and possessives:

it's [it is, it has]	its	who's [who is, who has]	whose
there's [there is, there has]	theirs	you're [you are]	your
they're [they are]	their		

c. The apostrophe with *s* is customarily used to form the plural of letters and sometimes to form the plural of abbreviations:

the three R's, mind your p's and q's, several OK's, studying for M.A.'s and Ph.D.'s

In the past the apostrophe was quite regularly used to form the plural of numbers, letters, symbols, words treated as words (too many *and's*), etc. In such matters usage today is noticeably divided.* Fortunately, the situation arises so rarely in the writing of the average college student that the matter should cause little concern. But many beginning writers need to be reminded regularly of an important related fact: An apostrophe is never used in forming the plural of either a common or a proper noun.

2. The colon (:) is a formal mark announcing a list, an explanation, or a quotation to follow. (Notice, for example, its use in the first rule on the preceding page.)

My fellow Americans: My speech tonight will examine . . .
All hikers must bring the following: a flashlight, a small ax, and a waterproof tarpaulin.

Do not use a colon to separate a verb from its complement or a preposition from its object:

Faulty: All hikers must bring: a flashlight, a small ax, and a waterproof tarpaulin.

Faulty: The things a hiker must bring are: a flashlight, a small ax, and a waterproof tarpaulin.

Faulty: The hiker's equipment should consist of: a flashlight, a small ax, and a waterproof tarpaulin.

3. The dash (—) is used to show an abrupt change in thought in the sentence. It must be used sparingly and never as a substitute for other marks:

Superior students—notice that I said *superior*—will not have to take the test. New surroundings, new friends, a challenging new job—all these helped Eugene overcome his grief.

4. The hyphen (-) is used to divide a word at the end of a line and to join words to form various types of compounds.
a. Divide a word only between syllables. With words having a prefix or a suffix, divide the word after the prefix and before the suffix. Avoid dividing a word so that

---

*The trend, however, is well stated in *Webster's Dictionary of English Usage* (1989): "The use of -*'s* to form the plurals of numerals, abbreviations and symbols is not now as common as pluralization with simple -*s;* 1970s, CPUs, &s are more likely to be found than their apostrophized counterparts." (p. 109)

a single letter ends or begins a line. (Consult your dictionary for problems of syllabic division.)

mathe-matics [not] mathem-atics
inter-collegiate [not] intercol-legiate
govern-ess [not] gov-erness
enough [not] e-nough
many [not] man-y

b. Use hyphens to join the parts of compound modifiers preceding nouns:

Observe his well-kept lawn. His lawn is well kept.
We deplore your devil-may-care attitude.

This use of a hyphen sometimes determines an exact meaning:

a roll of twenty-dollar bills; a roll of twenty dollar bills
all-American boys; all American boys

c. Use hyphens with compound numbers from twenty-one to ninety-nine and with fractions:

Twenty-two people claimed the one-third share of the reward money but received only one-eighth.

d. Use hyphens, particularly with prefixes and suffixes, to avoid awkward combinations of letters or to distinguish between two meanings of a word:

anti-intellectual
pre-Aztec
her doll-like face
re-cover a couch [recover the money]

5. Quotation marks (" ") are used to enclose quoted material and words used in some special way.
a. Use double quotation marks (" ") to enclose the exact words of a quoted speech.
Quotation marks always come in pairs. The marks show the beginning and the end of a speech, whether it is part of a sentence, one sentence, or several sentences. If a speech is interrupted by material showing who said it, quotation marks set off the quoted material from the explanatory material. Use quotation marks where the directly quoted material begins and where it ends or is interrupted.
Indirect quotations are *not* set off by quotation marks:

"I admit," said Ralph, "that I was mistaken." [Note that the explanatory material is set off from the direct quotation.]
Peg answered, "I didn't attend. I wasn't in town." [More than one sentence.]
Peg answered that she hadn't attended because she hadn't been in town. [This is an indirect quotation. Words not directly quoted do not need quotation marks.]

b. Use double quotation marks to set off the subdivisions of books, names of songs, and titles of units of less than book length, such as short stories, short poems, essays, and articles:

> The second chapter of *Moby Dick* is entitled "The Carpet-Bag."
> Nanki-Poo sings "A Wandering Minstrel I" early in Act I of *The Mikado.*
> Our anthology includes "Threes," a poem from Sandburg's *Smoke and Steel.*
> The first article I read for my research paper was John Lear's "How Hurricanes Are Born" in the *Saturday Review.*

NOTE: In printed copy, titles of books, magazines, long poems, newspapers, motion pictures, and radio and television series are set in italic type. (Other special uses of italics are for foreign words and phrases and for names of ships, planes, and spacecraft.) In handwritten or typewritten papers, underlining (<u>typescript like this</u>) is the equivalent of italics in printed material *(type like this).*

c. Use double quotation marks to set off slang words used in serious writing. Quotation marks are also sometimes used to set off words when they are referred to as words:

> The witness had only recently been released from the "slammer."
> Words like "seize" and "siege" are often misspelled.

Usage is divided on these uses of quotation marks. In printed material the two words in the second example would almost certainly appear in italics. Student writers of handwritten or typed material should underline such words or set them off by quotation marks, the first method being the more common practice.

d. Follow this usage in the placing of quotation marks in relation to other marks: (1) commas and periods always inside quotes; (2) semicolons and colons always outside quotes; (3) question marks and exclamation points inside if they belong to the quoted part, outside if they do not:

> "Come in," said my uncle, "and take off your coats." [Comma and period.]
> Mr. Lowe said, "I heartily endorse this candidate"; unfortunately most of the audience thought he said *hardly* instead of *heartily.* [Semicolon outside.]
> "Heavens!" he exclaimed. "Is this the best you can do?" [Exclamation point and question mark.]
> Mother asked, "Where were you last night?" [No double punctuation.]
> Did she say, "I came home early"? [Question mark belongs to the whole sentence, not to the quoted part.]
> Did Mother ask, "Where were you last night?" [Note that there is only one question mark after a double question like this.]

e. Use single quotation marks to enclose a speech within a speech:

> "I wonder what he meant," said Betty, "when he said, 'There are wheels within wheels.' " [You may not write many sentences like this one, but just the same, you should note that when you have quotes within quotes, the period comes inside both single and double quotes.]

Apostrophes, Colons, Dashes, Hyphens, and Quotation Marks

NAME _____ SCORE _____

Directions: In the spaces at the left, write C if the punctuation is correct or W if it is incorrect. Within the incorrect sentences, correct the faulty punctuation by adding, removing, or changing marks.

_____ 1. Three hundred-dollar bills were found hidden in the lining of my grandmother's overcoat.

_____ 2. Three hundred dollars will cover your share of the party, but it won't pay for my share and her's too.

_____ 3. There is a very loud radio playing near my house: I wish I could find out who's it is.

_____ 4. "Did you hear June when she said, 'I can't find my house key'?" asked Jim.

_____ 5. "Somebody's in the yard," said Tom: I can see a shadow against the back fence."

_____ 6. Tell me whose book is on the seat of my car; your's is still in the house, isn't it?

_____ 7. Thats a great movie: I liked it better than the book.

_____ 8. Let me tell you about the test—oh, wait a minute, the phone's ringing.

_____ 9. If youll give Jim and Bob your report, they will let you read their's.

_____ 10. The police report failed to list several stolen items: a stereo, a microwave oven, and three boxes of compact disks.

_____ 11. That's no good—its always a bad practice to turn papers in late.

_____ 12. "I left home quite early," said Luci, "but I got caught in the eight o'clock traffic on Maple Street."

_____ 13. My uncle is a collector of pre-Columbian pottery, which he re-covered from an old temple many years ago.

_____ 14. "My scores—two sixty-fives and a seventy—don't average out to a passing grade," said Mark.

_____ 15. Mr. Ramirez letter describing the childrens need for medical care moved the members to donate several hundred dollars to the clinic.

Directions: Sentences 1–5 are indirect quotations. In the space provided, rewrite each sentence as a direct quotation. Sentences 6–10 are direct quotations. Rewrite each as an indirect quotation. You will have to alter some verb forms and some pronoun forms as well as the punctuation.

1. The caller told us that the owner's manual for the new car is not very clear.

2. Marian says that she intends to look for a new job unless she gets a raise.

3. Julia said that she had worked for weeks on the report and she was disappointed by the boss' lack of enthusiasm for it.

4. Jim said that he was leaving for his vacation in two days and would not be back for four weeks.

5. Do the instructions say that we are supposed to leave that valve open 24 hours a day?

6. The announcement said, "The airport will be closed to departures after midnight tonight until the weather clears."

7. Randolph said, "I need a ride home from class tomorrow afternoon."

8. The child asked, "When can I go back to the zoo to see the tigers?"

9. Mr. Watson complained, "The mysteries I have read lately are too gory and their plots are too simple."

10. Did you hear Professor Lopez say, "There will be a test on the first two chapters in the text next Tuesday?"

EXERCISE 19

APOSTROPHES, COLONS, DASHES, HYPHENS, AND QUOTATION MARKS

NAME _____ SCORE _____

Directions: In the spaces at the left, write C if the punctuation is correct or W if it is incorrect. Within the incorrect sentences, correct the faulty punctuation by adding, removing, or changing marks.

_____ 1. My replacement—he signed a contract yesterday—has experience thats sure to be valuable in the coming months.

_____ 2. I have always admired George Washington's response to his father: Yes, I cut down your cherry tree.

_____ 3. Yesterday my roommate got a package filled with: cookies, popcorn, and several cans of macadamia nuts.

_____ 4. Is this your racket? Mines at home, and I need to use your's during PE class.

_____ 5. "How will we know who's supposed to bring the donuts for the study session tonight?" asked Al.

_____ 6. Last nights practice session was canceled: the drama teacher was out of town.

_____ 7. Thats a difficult job, but we can do it. All it takes is time—hours and hours of time.

_____ 8. Its not clear to me why our cars time in the quarter mile is so much slower than all the others times.

_____ 9. My grandmother had an interesting definition of "luck": hard work and preparation meeting an opportunity for achievement.

_____ 10. "I was amazed," said Ramona; "I had never seen thirty one hundred dollar bills before."

_____ 11. "I read Irwin Shaw's short story, 'The Eighty-Yard Run,' and I found it just a little depressing," said Shane.

_____ 12. "I always misspell the word 'independent,' " said Marcie; I put an 'A' in the last syllable instead of an 'E.' "

_____ 13. My list for the canoe trip includes: duct tape, candles, and waterproof matches. What's on your's?

_____ 14. The Jones' left for town early this morning: they needed to drop Mrs. Jones' car at the repair shop.

_____ 15. Its too bad that the spelling checker in my computer cannot make distinctions among words such as "to," "two," and "too."

Directions: Sentences 1–5 are indirect quotations. In the space provided, rewrite each sentence as a direct quotation. Sentences 6–10 are direct quotations. Rewrite each as an indirect quotation. You will have to alter some verb forms and some pronoun forms as well as the punctuation.

1. Tom said that he had just opened his book and started to read when the fire alarm rang.

2. The teacher said she would cover the answers to those questions in the next class.

3. The boss reminded Harry that he had agreed to work on Saturday night for the next four weeks.

4. Fifteen minutes after we began to work, June asked when we would stop for lunch.

5. Art told Shelly that he wanted to read her paper after she had finished typing it.

6. The technician said, "I think I will check the fuses before I do anything else."

7. When the bell rang, Rick told Tom, "We should get lunch before we go to our next class."

8. Wilma said, "I won't be home until after eight o'clock tonight."

9. The students asked, "Can we have another day to study for the test?"

10. As soon as the plane took off, the small children next to me asked, "Will you read us a story?"

LESSON 20 ■
End Marks; Summary of Punctuation Rules

The **period** is used after a complete declarative sentence and after ordinary abbreviations. Its use as end punctuation after sentences needs no examples. Its use after abbreviations is a little more complicated.

A few abbreviations are proper in the ordinary sort of writing, such as *Mr., Mrs., Ms., Messrs., Mmes.,* and *Dr.,* before names; *Jr., Sr., Esq., D.D., Ph.D.,* and so forth, after names. Miss does not require a period. *Ms.,* used instead of *Miss* or *Mrs.* when marital state is not indicated, is usually considered an abbreviation and uses a period, although some modern dictionaries have entries for it either with or without a period.

The following, correct in footnotes, bibliographies, and tabulations, should be written out in ordinary writing: *e.g. (for example), etc. (and so forth), i.e. (that is), p., pp. (page, pages),* and *vol. (volume).*

A.D., B.C., A.M., and *P.M.* (usually set in small caps in printed material) are used only with figures and where necessary for clearness.

The following are acceptable in addresses but should be spelled out in ordinary writing: *St. (Street), Ave. (Avenue), Blvd. (Boulevard), Dr. (Drive), Rd. (Road), Co. (Company),* and *Inc. (Incorporated).* Conventionally, periods have been used with abbreviations of the states *(Mass., Minn., Tex., W. Va.).* However, the two-letter capitalized symbols authorized by the U.S. Postal Service *(MA, MN, TX, WV)* do not require periods.

Poor: Last Mon. P.M. I met my two older bros., who live in N.Y. Chas. works for a mfg. co. there. Thos. attends NYU, preparing himself for a gov't. job. He's coming home for Xmas.

Better: Last Monday afternoon I met my two older brothers, who live in New York. Charles works for a manufacturing company there. Thomas attends New York University, preparing himself for a government job. He's coming home for Christmas.

In modern usage, the "alphabet" name forms, or acronyms, of various governmental or intergovernmental agencies, social or professional organizations, and units of measurement used in scientific contexts are usually not followed by periods: *ACLU, CARE, CBS, CEEB, CIA, ICBM, NCAA, NATO, SEC, UNESCO, Btu, mpg, mph, rpm.* New acronyms and abbreviated forms spring into existence nowadays with regularity. The following examples contain some that have gained common acceptance fairly recently: *AIDS* (acquired immune deficiency syndrome), *CAT scan* (computerized axial tomography), *CATV* (community antenna television), *CD* (certificate of deposit), *CEO* (chief executive officer), *COLA* (cost-of-living adjustment), *CPR* (cardiopulmonary resuscitation), *DWI* (driving while intoxicated), *IRA* (individual retirement account), *MIA* (missing in action), *MRI* (magnetic resonance imaging), *OPEC* (Organization of Petroleum-Exporting Countries), *PC* (personal computer), *STOL* (short takeoff and landing), *VCR* (videocassette recorder). Refer to your dictionary when in doubt about the meaning of an abbreviated form or the possibility of using periods. Be prepared to find apparent inconsistencies and divided usage.

The **question mark** is used after a direct question, which is an utterance that calls for an answer. (See Lesson 6.) But we do not use a question mark after an indirect question, which is a *statement* giving the substance of a question but not the words that would be used in a direct question.

> **Direct:** Who goes there? Is that you? When do we eat? How much do I owe you? "Who goes there?" he demanded. [In dialogue.]
>
> **Indirect:** She asked me how old I was. I wondered why she would ask such a question. [Note that periods are used. These are statements, not direct questions.]

The **exclamation point** is used sparingly in modern writing and should be reserved for statements of strong feeling. Mild exclamations, such as *oh, goodness, well, yes,* and *no,* are followed by commas, not exclamation points. Be sure to place the exclamation mark after the exclamation itself.

> "Help! I'm slipping!" he shouted. [Note period after *shouted.*]
> "Stop that!" she screamed. [Do not put the exclamation point after *screamed.*]
> Well, it was exciting, wasn't it? Oh, I had a pleasant time.

Summary of Punctuation Rules

Punctuation is not complex, nor are the rules many and involved; they can be learned quickly. In this review we shall simplify them still more by listing only the important ones that you use constantly in your everyday writing. You can see how few of them there actually are. Colons, dashes, parentheses, hyphens, and even question marks and exclamation points do have other uses for special occasions or effects; but these occasional applications rarely cause problems for most writers.

The important thing for you to do now is to study these really indispensable rules until you are perfectly at home with them. And then, of course, if all of this is to do you any good, you must use your knowledge in everything you write, whether it is "for English," or in a letter to a friend, or in a notebook for a course in biology.

COMMAS TO SEPARATE: FIVE RULES

1. Coordinate clauses
2. Items in a series
3. Coordinate adjectives
4. Introductory modifiers
5. Words that may be misread together

COMMAS TO ENCLOSE: EIGHT RULES

1. Nonrestrictive clauses and phrases
2. Appositives
3. Absolute phrases
4. Parenthetical expressions
5. Words in direct address
6. The speaker in dialogue
7. Negative insertions
8. Dates, addresses, degrees, and titles

SEMICOLON: ONE RULE

1. In compound sentences without conjunction

APOSTROPHE: TWO RULES

1. With possessives
2. With contractions

QUOTATION MARKS: THREE RULES

1. About direct quotations
2. About titles
3. About words used in some special way

PERIOD: TWO RULES

1. After declarative sentences
2. After most abbreviations

QUESTION MARK: ONE RULE

1. After direct questions

Practice Sheet 20
Review of Punctuation

NAME _____ SCORE _____

Directions: The following sentences contain fifty numbered spaces between words or beneath words. (The number is beneath the word when the problem involves the use of an apostrophe in that word.) In the correspondingly numbered spaces at the left, write C if the punctuation is correct or W if it is incorrect.

1. _____ (1) The most useful tools for college students are: a computer, a good

2. _____   dictionary and the ability to stay awake.

3. _____ (2) Maria, who recently graduated from nursing school, said, "I worked

4. _____   at two jobs when I was in school."

5. _____ (3) "Can you tell me the name of the architect who designed the Empire

6. _____   State Building?" asked Miss. Marcus.

7. _____ (4) I have read several good mysteries lately, there are several highly

8. _____   skilled new writers on the market.

9. _____ (5) The map says the town is five miles away, if we don't reach it in a

10. _____   few minutes, we must be lost.

11. _____ (6) Whenever my little brother goes away to camp, he complains about

12. _____   the horrible tasteless food served in the cafeteria.

13. _____ (7) I went to the bookstore yesterday, I tried to find a book pack exactly

14. _____   like your's.

15. _____ (8) "When will you be ready to leave?" asked Robert, who was standing

16. _____   impatiently in the doorway.

17. _____ (9) Her books, her stereo, two pairs of new jeans—all were in her car

18. _____   when it was stolen.

19. _____ (10) The smiling mischievous little boys pushed the two pretty girls into

20. _____   the sloppy mud puddle.

21. _____ (11) "Have you ever read 'The Pit and the Pendulum'," asked Donna, who

22. _____   is a fan of Edgar Allan Poe?

23. _____ (12) We finished eating the cats got the scraps, and we cleared the table

24. _____   and washed the dishes.

183

· 25. _____ (13) The room was painted a deep blue; the only light came from a large

26. _____ window, that overlooked a parking lot.

27. _____ (14) The young law students all want one thing; to get a job with a big

28. _____ firm in a large city.

29. _____ (15) "After all my friends," said the president, "we've just begun to

30. _____ evaluate the impact of those changes on operating costs."

31. _____ (16) Al doesnt think he will leave tomorrow, his car needs some work

32. _____ before he can go.

33. _____ (17) A stack of twenty dollar bills sat in front of the teller and he handed

34. _____ ten to a customer needing two hundred dollars.

35. _____ (18) Tony asked Cary why she had not returned the librarys copy of the

36. _____ new sports magazine?

37. _____ (19) The staff needs some special equipment for the new project; a

38. _____ microscope, two new computers and an optical scanner.

39. _____ (20) If properly maintained tents can be used for many camping seasons,

40. _____ without any problems.

41. _____ (21) Alice said, "I wonder if I can hire an assistant who can type, operate

42. _____ a CD-ROM, and locate sources in a library?"

43. _____ (22) "I lost my biology text," said Millie. "Do you suppose that Andrea

44. _____ thought it was her's and took it?"

45. _____ (23) Although that room holds three hundred fifty people had to move to

46. _____ a second room and watch the lecture on television.

47. _____ (24) Everybodys opinion in this case is important, please feel free to speak

48. _____ up whenever you wish.

49. _____ (25) "Why aren't you finished with the painting yet," asked Mark, who

50. _____ had been waiting for his car for three days.

EXERCISE 20

END MARKS; REVIEW OF PUNCTUATION

NAME _____ SCORE _____

Directions: In the following sentences, if the punctuation is wrong, write W in the space before the sentence and draw a circle around each error in punctuation. If the punctuation is correct, write C in the space.

_____ 1. Did you hear that Mr Johnson and Ms. Roberts will be here at 10.30 A.M. on Tuesday.

_____ 2. Please send my new subscription to my home address, 1050 Willow Lane, Ascot, IN 87105.

_____ 3. The history of the US in the 18th. century is extremely exciting.

_____ 4. "Here we are in Hollywood," said my little sister; I wonder if we will see any movie stars?"

_____ 5. Now that she has completed her PhD in physics, Janice hopes to work for N.A.S.A.

_____ 6. "How many Btus does your new air conditioner produce," asked Miles?

_____ 7. Pens and pencils, scraps of paper, a few rubber bands, etc tumbled out of my briefcase when it fell open.

_____ 8. Johnson and Associates, Inc has hired a new CEO, Nathan Wilder.

_____ 9. "Did Art say, 'I think I'll leave early today'?" asked Mona.

_____ 10. Alice asked me why I had to work so late last night?

_____ 11. Roberta plans to work on an MBA as soon as she finishes her B.A. degree next spring.

_____ 12. The note card read: These statistics come from pp 24–30, Vol XI, No. 5, Oct. 17, 1989.

_____ 13. "Watch out!" screamed Javier; "that car isn't going to stop."

_____ 14. My clock stopped at 3:47 A.M., exactly the time when NOAA says the storm struck the city.

_____ 15. Blanca's new car has a CAFE rating of 22.5 mpg.

_____ 16. "What famous American admiral said, 'I have not yet begun to fight'? asked Mr Lucas, our history teacher.

_____ 17. We can't possibly, it appears, finish our work by the deadline, 5;00 PM on June 25, 1995.

_____ 18. Ms Randolph recently joined the law firm of Hernandez, Goldburg, and Jones PA. as an associate.

_____ 19. NASA and the US Air Force worked together to launch that new spy satellite.

_____ 20. Lt. Colonel James Warner heads the recruiting office at 175 Riverside Dr., Brockton, Mass., doesn't he?

185

Directions: In the following sentences correct every error in punctuation. Then in the column of figures at the left circle every number that represents an error in that sentence. Use these numbers:

1. Comma omitted
2. Apostrophe omitted or misused

3. Comma misused for semicolon
4. Semicolon misused for comma

1 2 3 4   (1) Working around the clock the crew members exhausted themselves, the heat, the humidity and the pressure to finish made matters very difficult.

1 2 3 4   (2) Although Ike followed Ralph's directions exactly; he still got lost and wandered around for two hours in the dark.

1 2 3 4   (3) "Here's an article, I think you'll enjoy," said Dr. Cummings, its called "Grammar for Fun and Profit."

1 2 3 4   (4) Those plans you know, were made by the committee, the people who will actually do the work were not consulted.

1 2 3 4   (5) A dozen people had gathered to watch Alices presentation, however the projector broke; and she could not even begin.

1 2 3 4   (6) On Wednesday, April 29 we turned in our project; all the important questions on the topic having been answered.

1 2 3 4   (7) About twenty people signed up for the tour, among them a plumber, two doctors and three businesswomen.

1 2 3 4   (8) The Davis house is being remodeled, they are adding a porch and thinking about converting the garage to a workshop.

1 2 3 4   (9) After we had left the office manager turned out the lights, locked the doors and set the buildings burglar alarm.

1 2 3 4   (10) The Randolphs left for Santa Fe at three oclock yesterday, the Randolphs two children will fly out tomorrow.

EXERCISE 20A
REVIEW OF PUNCTUATION

NAME _____ SCORE _____

Directions: The following sentences contain fifty numbered spaces between words or beneath words. (The number is beneath the word when the problem involves the use of an apostrophe in that word.) In the correspondingly numbered spaces at the left, write C if the punctuation is correct or W if it is incorrect.

1. _____   (1) "I think its time for lunch," said Yolanda, "but Barb hasn't come—
         $_1$ $_2$

2. _____   ah, there she is now."

3. _____   (2) The nursery sold us three small oak trees, a red maple tree, and
                                                   $_3$

4. _____   several small shrubs planted in fancy pots.
                                       $_4$

5. _____   (3) As we started to walk down the trail came three laughing kids on
                                          $_5$

6. _____   fancy mountain bikes.
              $_6$

7. _____   (4) Ms. Jacksons novel is extremely exciting and seems destined to make
                        $_7$ $_8$

8. _____   the best-seller list very soon.

9. _____   (5) Marcia Wilson, our most experienced player came in to pinch-hit in
                                                   $_9$

10. _____   the ninth inning; unfortunately, she struck out.
                           $_{10}$

11. _____   (6) Since Saturday was a cold damp day; we could not paint the trim on
                                       $_{11}$ $_{12}$

12. _____   the outside of the house.

13. _____   (7) Janice Thompson, our sales manager, joined the company on May 17,
                                               $_{13}$

14. _____   1992, sales have increased dramatically since then.
              $_{14}$

15. _____   (8) The book I just finished has all the important qualities; suspense, a
                                              $_{15}$

16. _____   little comedy, and a fast-paced tricky climax.
                                  $_{16}$

17. _____   (9) The shoes I found in my locker in the gym are not mine; I wonder

18. _____   who's they are?
            $_{17}$ $_{18}$

19. _____   (10) "My life," said Harold, "has only three parts to it: going to class,
                                                   $_{19}$

20. _____   studying, and going to work.
                 $_{20}$

21. _____   (11) After Alma gave her speech about student government; the usually
                                                     $_{21}$

22. _____   sullen drowsy class gave her a round of applause.
               $_{22}$

23. _____   (12) The two children, while rummaging in the basement, discovered an
                                                     $_{23}$

24. _____   old sword, a pair of boots and a couple of medals.
                               $_{24}$

25. _____ (13) "Anyone who is interested in a tour of the local planetarium should
25

26. _____ pick up a ticket from my office," said Professor Hall.
26

27. _____ (14) The parts are all stored in this box, to begin the assembly, check the
27   28

28. _____ parts list to be sure they're all there.

29. _____ (15) Uncle Will's tractor, which is his pride and joy, seems to be perfectly-
29   30

30. _____ maintained.

31. _____ (16) Almost as soon as I stopped the policeman signaled me to get out of
31

32. _____ the car and walk toward him.
32

33. _____ (17) Janice left on vacation yesterday, taking with her: two novels, a
33   34

34. _____ supply of sunscreen, and a big umbrella.

35. _____ (18) We decided not to go fishing this morning, the water being disturbed
35

36. _____ and cloudy because of the storm.
36

37. _____ (19) A beautiful horse, a palomino, I believe, ran across the pasture with
37

38. _____ its golden mane shimmering in the sunlight.
38

39. _____ (20) In the opinion of some researchers tend to concentrate too much on
39

40. _____ basic research and not enough on practical matters.
40

41. _____ (21) When Charles was sick last week, he lost two days pay; he had
41   42

42. _____ already used his sick leave for the year.

43. _____ (22) When he opened his locker on Monday morning, Jed found the two
43

44. _____ books that he thought he had lost.
44

45. _____ (23) "I need to add a little hot pepper to the meat loaf," said Marge, "it
45   46

46. _____ needs a little more tang."

47. _____ (24) Before I leave on my trip tomorrow; I need to buy: a warm jacket, a
47   48

48. _____ pair of gloves, and some thermal underwear.

49. _____ (25) Ms Roberts left for London yesterday; she plans to visit relatives
49   50

50. _____ whom she has never met before.

LESSON 21 ▪

Using Verbs Correctly: Principal Parts; Tense

In Lesson 2 you learned that verbs are either regular or irregular and that the principal parts of the two classes are formed in different ways. We shall now examine certain trouble spots where incorrect forms sometimes appear because of confusion in the use of the principal parts. (See Supplement 1.)

To gain assurance in your use of verbs, you must remember how the past tense and the past participle are used:

The **past tense** is always a single-word verb; it is never used with an auxiliary:

I *ate* my lunch. [*Not* I *have ate* my lunch.]

The **past participle** is never a single-word verb; it is used with the auxiliary *have* (to form the perfect tenses) or the auxiliary *be* (to form the passive voice):

I *have done* the work. The work *was done*. [*Not* I *done* the work.]

(The past participle is, of course, used as a single word when it is a modifier of a noun: the *broken* toy, the *worried* parents, some *known* criminals.)

Four groups of verbs that often cause confusion are illustrated in this lesson, each group containing verbs that have similar trouble spots. The basic solution for the problem in each group is to master the principal parts of the verbs; they are the ones that account for most of the verb form errors found in writing. The principal parts are listed in the customary order: base form, past tense, and past participle.

1. The error in the form of the verb results from a confusion of the past tense and the past participle:

Later they *became* [not *become*] more friendly.	become	became	become
They *began* [not *begun*] to laugh at us.	begin	began	begun
He had never *broken* [not *broke*] the law.	break	broke	broken
I should have *chosen* [not *chose*] a larger car.	choose	chose	chosen
Yesterday the child *came* [not *come*] home.	come	came	come
I *did* [not *done*] what she told me to do.	do	did	done

He *drank* [not *drunk*] some water.	drink	drank	drunk
I had *driven* [not *drove*] all day.	drive	drove	driven
The lamp had *fallen* [not *fell*] over.	fall	fell	fallen
The bird has *flown* [not *flew*] away.	fly	flew	flown
Small puddles have *frozen* [not *froze*] on the sidewalks.	freeze	froze	frozen
Dad has *given* [not *gave*] me a car.	give	gave	given
Theresa has *gone* [not *went*] to school.	go	went	gone
I've never *ridden* [not *rode*] a horse.	ride	rode	ridden
We ran out when the fire alarm *rang* [not *rung*].	ring	rang	rung
Lenny has *run* [not *ran*] in two marathons.	run	ran	run
I *saw* [not *seen*] your nephew yesterday.	see	saw	seen
It must have *sunk* [not *sank*] in deep water.	sink	sank	sunk
She should have *spoken* [not *spoke*] louder.	speak	spoke	spoken
The car had been *stolen* [not *stole*].	steal	stole	stolen
The witness was *sworn* [not *swore*] in.	swear	swore	sworn
John has *swum* [not *swam*] across the lake.	swim	swam	swum
Someone had *torn* [not *tore*] the dollar bill.	tear	tore	torn
You should have *worn* [not *wore*] a hat.	wear	wore	worn
I have already *written* [not *wrote*] my essay.	write	wrote	written

2. The error results from a confusion of regular and irregular verb forms:

The wind *blew* [not *blowed*] steadily all day.	blow	blew	blown
John *brought* [not *bringed*] Mary some flowers.	bring	brought	brought
This house was *built* [not *builded*] in 1795.	build	built	built
Barbara *caught* [not *catched*] two trout.	catch	caught	caught
Slowly they *crept* [not *creeped*] up the stairs.	creep	crept	crept
He *dealt* [not *dealed*] me a good hand.	deal	dealt	dealt
The men quickly *dug* [not *digged*] a pit.	dig	dug	dug
She *drew* [not *drawed*] a caricature of me.	draw	drew	drawn
All the men *grew* [not *growed*] long beards.	grow	grew	grown
Ben *hung* [not *hanged*] his cap on the hook.	hang	hung	hung
I *knew* [not *knowed*] him at college.	know	knew	known
I have never *lent* [not *lended*] him money.	lend	lent	lent
We *sought* [not *seeked*] shelter from the rain.	seek	sought	sought
The sun *shone* [not *shined*] all day yesterday.	shine	shone	shone
The prince *slew* [not *slayed*] the fierce dragon.	slay	slew	slain
I soon *spent* [not *spended*] the money.	spend	spent	spent
Ms. Andrews *taught* [not *teached*] us algebra.	teach	taught	taught
Lou *threw* [not *throwed*] the receipt away.	throw	threw	thrown
The old man *wept* [not *weeped*] piteously.	weep	wept	wept

3. The error results from the use of an obsolete or dialectal form of the verb, a form not considered standard now:

I *am* [not *be*] working regularly.	be*	was, were	been
I *have been* [not *been*] working regularly.			
The child *burst* [not *busted*] out crying.	burst	burst	burst
I've *bought* [not *boughten*] a car.	buy	bought	bought
I *climbed* [not *clumb*] a tree for a better view.	climb	climbed	climbed

*As you learned in Lesson 2, the irregular verb *be* has three forms *(am, are, is)* in the present tense and two forms *(was, were)* in the past tense.

The women *clung* [not *clang*] to the raft. | cling | clung | clung
The dog *dragged* [not *drug*] the old shoe home. | drag | dragged | dragged
The boy was nearly *drowned* [not *drownded*]. | drown | drowned | drowned
At the picnic I *ate* [not *et*] too many hot dogs. | eat | ate | eaten
Betty *flung* [not *flang*] the stick away. | fling | flung | flung
You *paid* [not *payed*] too much for it. | pay | paid | paid
It had been *shaken* [not *shooken*] to pieces. | shake | shook | shaken
He had never *skinned* [not *skun*] a cat. | skin | skinned | skinned
A bee *stung* [not *stang*] me as I stood there. | sting | stung | stung
The girl *swung* [not *swang*] at the ball. | swing | swung | swung
I wonder who could have *taken* [not *tooken*] it. | take | took | taken

4. The error results from a confusion of forms of certain verbs that look or sound almost alike but are actually quite different in meaning, such as *lie, lay; sit, set;* and *rise, raise.* Note that three of these troublesome verbs—*lay, set,* and *raise*—in their ordinary uses take an object. The other three—*lie, sit, rise*—do not take an object.

Please *lay* your books [D.O.] on the table.
Mary *laid* several logs [D.O.] on the fire.
The men have *laid* some boards [D.O.] over the puddle. | lay | laid | laid
Our cat often *lies* [not *lays*] on the couch.
Yesterday our cat *lay* [not *laid*] on the couch.
Our cat has *lain* [not *laid*] on the couch all morning. | lie | lay | lain
She *sets* the plate [D.O.] in front of me.
An hour ago Tom *set* out some food [D.O.] for the birds.
I had *set* the camera [D.O.] at a full second. | set | set | set
I usually *sit* in that chair.
Yesterday he *sat* in my chair.
I have *sat* at my desk all morning. | sit | sat | sat
At her command they *raise* the flag [D.O.].
The boy quickly *raised* his hand [D.O.].
He had *raised* the price [D.O.] of his old car. | raise | raised | raised
He *rises* when we enter the room.
Everyone *rose* as the speaker entered the room.
The water has *risen* a foot since midnight. | rise | rose | risen

The rules and illustrations given here will serve as a guide in most situations. They show the importance of knowing the principal parts of these verbs. Note, however, that there are a few exceptions, such as the intransitive uses of *set:*

A *setting* [not *sitting*] hen *sets* [that is, *broods;* of course, a hen, like a rooster or any other appropriate entity, may be said to *sit* when that is what is meant].
The sun *sets* in the west.
Cement or a dye *sets.*
A jacket *sets (fits)* well.

With a few verbs special meanings demand different principal parts. For example, the past tense and the past participle of *shine,* when the verb is used as a transitive verb, are *shined:*

This morning I *shined* [not *shone*] my shoes.

The verb *hang* with the meaning "to execute by suspending by the neck until dead" uses *hanged,* not *hung,* for the past tense and the past participle. When in doubt, always refer to your dictionary.

Sequence of Tenses

In Lesson 2 you studied a partial conjugation showing the forms of three sample verbs as they occur in six tenses. And in Lesson 5 you were told the basic uses of the six tenses. Although most student writers usually have little difficulty in establishing and maintaining logical time relationships in their sentences, we should note a few situations that sometimes cause confusion.

1. The tense in a subordinate clause is normally the same as that in the main clause unless a different time for the subordinate statement is clearly indicated.

We suspect that Jim *cheats* on his tax return.
We suspect that Jim *cheated* on his tax return last year.
We suspect that Jim *will cheat* on his tax return next year.
We suspect that Jim *has* often *cheated* on his tax returns.
We suspect that Jim *had cheated* on his tax return before he finally was arrested.

2. The present tense is used for a statement that is universally true.

The dietitian reminded us that whipped cream *is* (not *was*) fattening.
I wonder who first discovered that oysters *are* (not *were*) edible.

3. In narrative writing a shift from past tense to present tense, a device sometimes used effectively by skilled writers, should be used cautiously.

The library *was* silent except for an occasional whisper, when suddenly a side door *opened* (not *opens*) and a disheveled young man *dashed* (not *dashes*) in and *started* (not *starts*) yelling "Man the lifeboats!" After the librarians *had managed* to restore order . . .

4. The perfect form of an infinitive should not be used when the controlling verb is in the present perfect tense.

Correct: I would like to have seen that performance.

Correct: I would have liked to see that performance.

Incorrect: I would have liked to have seen that performance.

Supplement 1

Mention should be made here of another slight change in verb form that is possible. The partial conjugation given in Lesson 2 showed only the **indicative mood** (or **mode**), the forms that are used in nearly all statements and questions that you read or write. A second mood, the **imperative,** causes no complications: It is merely the base form of the verb when used to give a command or a request, with the subject *you* generally not expressed:

Be here by noon.
Please *come* to my office.

A third mood, the **subjunctive,** is sometimes shown by a change in the form of the verb. In this change *be* is used instead of *am, is,* or *are; were* is used instead of *was;* and, rarely, a third-person singular verb is used without the *s,* for instance, "he *leave*" instead of "he *leaves.*"

There is really only one situation in modern English in which the subjunctive form *were* is regularly used instead of *was,* and that is in an *if* clause making a statement that is clearly and unmistakably contrary to fact. The most obvious example is the everyday expression "If I *were* you, I'd. . . ." Remember the "If-I-were-you" set pattern to remind you of other "contrary-to-fact" clauses in which the subjunctive *were* would be expected in serious writing and speaking:

> If I *were* able to fly . . .*Were* I president of this country . . . If she *were* thirty years younger . . .

Divided usage prevails in a few other remnants of earlier subjunctive uses, especially in formal writing, for example, in "wish" clauses (reflecting also a contrary-to-fact situation):

> On frigid days like this, I wish I *were* in Tahiti.

The subjunctive is also found in certain set patterns of resolutions and demands:

> I move that Mr. Shaw *be* appointed.
> The chairman demanded that the reporter *leave* the room.
> It is imperative that you *be* here by ten o'clock.

In many of these and similar sentence situations in which older English insisted on subjunctive forms, modern speakers and writers often choose either an indicative form or one of the modal auxiliaries, such as *should, may,* or *might.*

Practice Sheet 21

Using Verbs Correctly: Principal Parts; Tense

NAME _____ SCORE _____

Directions: In the space at the left, write the correct form of the verb shown within the parentheses. Do not use any *ing* forms.

_____ 1. Everyone in the stadium (rise) when the color guard (raise) the
_____   flag at the beginning of the game.
_____ 2. Yesterday the men (begin) work on the house; they (dig) a
_____   huge hole for the basement.
_____ 3. I have not (withdraw) any money from my savings account;
_____   with interest, the balance has (grow) quite quickly.
_____ 4. Police (seek) the fugitive for several weeks and finally (set) a
_____   trap for her last week.
_____ 5. After we had (swim) for an hour, I (lie) down on the raft to
_____   rest.
_____ 6. The county (build) that building in 1974; since then, the
_____   county has not (spend) much money on repairs.
_____ 7. Ellen (swing) at the ball, and her bat (fly) all the way to third
_____   base.
_____ 8. The snow (fall) for three days, and the pond (freeze) solid
_____   from one side to the other.
_____ 9. The children (creep) down the stairs and (spend) the evening
_____   waiting for Santa Claus.
_____ 10. After Jane (set) the plate on the table, she (lay) the napkin be-
_____   side it.
_____ 11. Professor Landrum has (speak) quite highly of Ralph, but he
_____   (write) a rather negative recommendation for him.
_____ 12. Last week someone (draw) cartoons in my textbook, and so I
_____   (throw) it in the trash.
_____ 13. "Last month I (lend) Anne fifty dollars, and she has not (pay)
_____   it back yet," said Terry.
_____ 14. The men have already (begin) the class, but they have not yet
_____   (break) up into their groups yet.
_____ 15. A man nearly (drown) at the beach earlier today, but a life
_____   guard (drag) him from the water just in time.
_____ 16. Barb was (sting) by a wasp this morning, but she (take) an an-
_____   tihistamine to counteract the effects of the sting.
_____ 17. I should have (wear) a heavier jacket today; the sun has not
_____   (shine) all day long.
_____ 18. Mr. Brown (give) Cal his tickets yesterday, but Cal said they
_____   were (steal) last night.
_____ 19. Denice has not (see) that movie, but she (go) to a concert last
_____   night.
_____ 20. Ms. Thomas has (teach) that seminar twice, and she has (for-
_____   get) to ask for an evaluation both times.

Directions: Each sentence contains two italicized verb units. If the principal part or tense of the verb is the proper form for serious writing, write C in the corresponding space at the left. If the verb is incorrect, write the correct form in the space.

1. If I *was* you, I would not have *drove* so late last night in that fog.

2. From her answer we should have *known* that she had not *rode* a bike for years.

3. "Although I *been* working at this stadium for years, I never *seen* a bigger crowd," said Warren.

4. The book was *laying* on the floor; it had *fell* from the table during the storm.

5. Mary *wrote* three pages of the test, but she could not finish before the bell *rung*.

6. Jane *been* flying for this airline for three years, but she *has* not learned all the procedures yet.

7. Soon Jose *became* very interested in the project and was quite happy that he had *chose* that topic.

8. "My tomato plants *growed* about six inches last week, but they have not *set* any blossoms yet," said Marge.

9. Wanda *lended* Jill her lecture notes last week, and Jill has *forgot* to return them.

10. Ralph *knowed* that the sun *shined* brightly all day yesterday.

11. The boy *throwed* the baseball through the window, but he *sweared* that he did not do it.

12. We *bringed* some sandwiches from the kitchen and *et* very quickly before leaving for town.

13. "We nearly *drownded* in that rainstorm," laughed Tina, "but fortunately we *runned* home before it was too late."

14. The pond was almost *froze* over, but those silly people *swum* in it for a few minutes anyway.

15. The meeting *drug* on for hours, and Yolanda realized that she should have *tooken* the day off.

16. The woman *clang* desperately to the ladder as it *shaked* wildly in the wind.

17. Yesterday I *sat* in front of my computer all morning, but I *spended* all afternoon on the lake.

18. Mr. Ransom *teached* me how to find that book, but someone had *tore* several pages out of it earlier.

19. If I *had* been able to run faster, I would not have *bursted* into the room so long after the lecture began.

20. Alice *skun* her knee quite badly when she *swung* down from the roof of the garage.

EXERCISE 21

USING VERBS CORRECTLY: PRINCIPAL PARTS; TENSE

NAME _____ SCORE _____

Directions: In the space at the left, write the correct form of the verb shown within parentheses. Do not use any *ing* forms.

_____ 1. The fishing rod (sink) quickly to the bottom and (lie) there
_____   among the rocks and fallen trees.
_____ 2. "I (lay) aside my books about three o'clock this morning; I
_____   had finally (took) enough notes," said Jan.
_____ 3. Yesterday Tom (wear) his new running shoes to class; he
_____   should have (choose) to wear socks also.
_____ 4. We have not (eat) lunch, but we had (drink) two cups of cof-
_____   fee earlier in the day.
_____ 5. The class had not (begin) to work, but Jim (raise) his hand to
_____   ask for help from the teacher.
_____ 6. The audience (rise) to applaud the band, and the singer (burst)
_____   into tears of joy.
_____ 7. I have (speak) to the boss, but she has not (give) me an answer
_____   to my question.
_____ 8. Alice had (fall) on the walk where the rain had (freeze) into
_____   icy patches.
_____ 9. Mother has not (see) the place where the cat had (tore) the cur-
_____   tain.
_____ 10. Melissa has not (do) any of the problems in the text, but she
_____   has (write) the essay already.
_____ 11. Barbara has (buy) a new car and (drive) it to work for the last
_____   three days.
_____ 12. Ms. Martin has not (deal) with that type of problem before; so
_____   she has (bring) in a consultant to help her.
_____ 13. Sam's parrot has (fly) out of the cage and has (go) up to the
_____   roof of the garage.
_____ 14. Adam has already (run) out of food this week, and he has also
_____   (spend) all his money for the week.
_____ 15. I (pay) my tuition last month, and I (buy) my textbooks for
_____   next semester.
_____ 16. The playful puppy (drag) the towel out into the yard and
_____   (shake) it wildly.
_____ 17. The woman (hang) up the phone and (weep) softly for a few
_____   moments.
_____ 18. The sun has (shine) brightly all day long, but now it has (set)
_____   in the west.
_____ 19. The little boy had (climb) high into the tree and (sit) down on
_____   a large branch.
_____ 20. Tom said, "I have (buy) some shoe polish and (shine) my
_____   shoes for tomorrow's interview."

197

Directions: Each sentence has two italicized verb forms. If the principal part or the tense of the verb is the proper form in serious writing, write C in the corresponding space at the left. If the verb is incorrect, write the correct form in the space.

_____ _____	1. The man *rose* slowly and walked out of the room after the bell *rung*.
_____ _____	2. The instructor *lay* aside her notes and *teached* us a few tricks for taking tests.
_____ _____	3. That money has *lain* on the table for two days, and so far no one has *took* it.
_____ _____	4. The water-filled balloon *busted* when the boy *throwed* it out the window.
_____ _____	5. I should have *wore* a hat because the sun *shone* so brightly this morning.
_____ _____	6. Jack's uncle has *lended* him enough money to buy a car; the one he has *drove* for three years no longer runs.
_____ _____	7. "I would have liked to *have* run in last week's marathon," said Rhoda, "but I had not *done* enough training."
_____ _____	8. The bill for the repairs *come* in the mail today; I wish now that I had *boughten* a new tape player instead.
_____ _____	9. "I *been* awfully tired lately," said Betsy; "maybe I should have *payed* someone to do this typing for me."
_____ _____	10. The thick fog *creeped* down the valley and *hung* over the road like a thick curtain.
_____ _____	11. Joan has already *drank* two cups of coffee this morning, but I haven't *saw* her do any work at all.
_____ _____	12. We almost *froze* on the road last night because the temperature never *clumb* above five degrees.
_____ _____	13. Dad never *gave* the girls any idea that he had *spoke* to the teacher about their progress in the class.
_____ _____	14. Yesterday Paul *went* to a concert; he had never *gone* to a live musical performance before.
_____ _____	15. Two boys *raised* their hands when the group leader asked if anyone had ever *rode* a Ferris wheel before.
_____ _____	16. "We have *drug* out this discussion far too long," said Kim; "I have *set* in this chair for almost two hours."
_____ _____	17. The wind has *blown* at about thirty knots for three days, and we *spended* the whole weekend working on the boats.
_____ _____	18. Has Carmen *seeked* legal counsel after the other driver *brought* suit against her?
_____ _____	19. After Lisa *swang* the stick at their nest, the hornets *stinged* her three times.
_____ _____	20. After we had *digged* our way out of the snowbank, we *run* quickly back to the lodge.

LESSON 22 ∎

Using Verbs Correctly: Subject–Verb Agreement

I earn	We earn
You earn	You earn
He, She, It earns	They earn

Observe that in the present tense the third-person singular form *(He, She, It earns)* differs from the third-person plural *(They earn)*. This change we call a change in number: **Singular number** means that only one thing is talked about; **plural number** means that more than one thing is talked about. Notice how verbs and nouns differ in this respect: The *s* ending on nouns is a plural marker, but on verbs it designates the singular form.

The following examples show how the number of the subject (one or more than one) affects the form of the verb. The verbs *have, do,* and *be* are important because they have auxiliary uses as well as main-verb uses. *Be* is an exceptional verb; it changes form in the past tense as well as in the present tense.

Singular	*Plural*
She *walks* slowly.	They *walk* slowly.
Mother *seems* pleased.	My parents *seem* pleased.
Mary *has* a new dress.	All of the girls *have* new dresses.
He *has traveled* widely.	They *have traveled* widely.
She *does* her work easily.	They *do* their work easily.
Does he *have* enough time?	*Do* they *have* enough time?
He *is* a friend of mine.	They *are* friends of mine.
My brother *is coming* home.	My brothers *are coming* home.
His camera *was taken* from him.	Their cameras *were taken* from them.

The relation of verb form to subject follows an important principle of usage: **The verb always agrees in number with its subject.** Although the principle is simple, some of the situations in which it applies are not. You will avoid some common writing errors if you keep in mind the following seven extensions of the principle. The first is probably the most necessary.

1. The number of the verb is not affected by material that comes between the verb and the subject. Determine the *real* subject of the verb; watch out for intervening words that might mislead you. Remember that the number of the verb is not altered when other nouns are attached to the subject by means of prepositions such as *in addition to, together with, as well as, with, along with.* Remember also that indefinite pronoun subjects like *either, neither, each, one, everyone, no one, somebody* take singular verbs:

Immediate *settlement* of these problems *is* [not *are*] vital. [The subject is *settlement. Problems,* being here the object of the preposition *of,* cannot also be a subject.]

199

The cost of replacing the asbestos shingles with cedar shakes *was* [not *were*] considerable.
Tact, as well as patience, *is* [not *are*] required.
Mr. Sheldon, together with several other division heads, *has* [not *have*] left.
Each of the plans *has* [not *have*] its good points.
Is [not *Are*] *either* of the contestants ready?

None may take either a singular or a plural verb, depending on whether the writer wishes to emphasize "not one" or "no members" of the group:

None of us *is* [or *are*] perfect.

(See Supplement 1.)

2. A verb agrees with its subject even when the subject follows the verb. Be especially careful to find the real subject in sentences starting with *there* or *here:*

On the wall *hangs* a *portrait* of his father. [*Portrait hangs.*]
On the wall *hang portraits* of his parents. [*Portraits hang.*]
He handed us a piece of paper on which *was* scribbled a *warning.* [*Warning was* scribbled.]
There *was* barely enough *time* remaining.
There *were* only ten *minutes* remaining.
There *seems* to be one *problem* remaining.
There *seem* to be a few *problems* remaining.
Here *is* a free *ticket* to the game.
Here *are* some free *tickets* to the game.

3. Compound subjects joined by *and* take a plural verb:

A little *boy* and his *dog were* playing in the yard.
On the platform *were* a *table* and four *chairs.*

But the verb should be singular if the subjects joined by *and* are thought of as a single thing, or if the subjects are considered separately, as when they are modified by *every* or *each:*

Plain *vinegar* and *oil is* all the dressing my salad needs. [One thing.]
Every *man* and every *woman is* asked to help. [Considered separately.]

4. Singular subjects joined by *or* or *nor* take singular verbs:

Either a *check* or a money *order is* required.
Neither the *manager* nor his *assistant has* arrived yet.
Was Mr. Phelps or his *son* put on the committee?

In some sentences of this pattern, especially in questions like the last example, a plural verb is sometimes used, both in casual conversation and in writing. In serious and formal writing, the singular verb is considered appropriate.

If the subjects joined by *or* or *nor* differ in number, the verb agrees with the subject nearer to it:

Neither the *mother* nor the two *boys were* able to identify him.
Either the *players* or the *coach is* responsible for the defeat.

5. Plural nouns of amount, distance, and so on, when they are used as singular units of measurement, take singular verbs:

A hundred *dollars was* once paid for a single tulip bulb.
Thirty *miles seems* like a long walk to me.
Seven *years* in prison *was* the penalty that he had to pay.

6. A collective noun is considered singular when the group is regarded as a unit; it is plural when the individuals of the group are referred to. Similarly, words like *number, all, rest, part, some, more, most, half* are singular or plural, depending on the meaning intended. A word of this type is often accompanied by a modifier or referred to by a pronoun, either of which gives a clue to the number intended. When the word *number* is a subject, it is considered singular if it is preceded by *the* and plural if it is preceded by *a:*

The *audience is* very enthusiastic tonight.
The *audience are* returning to their seats. [Notice pronoun *their.*]
The *band is* playing a rousing march.
Now the *band are* putting away their instruments. [Again note *their.*]
Most of the book *is* blatant propaganda.
Most of her novels *are* now out of print.
The *rest* of the fortune *was* soon gone.
The *rest* of his debts *were* left unpaid.
The *number* of bank failures *is* increasing.
A *number* of these bank failures *are* being investigated.

7. When the subject is a relative pronoun, the antecedent of the pronoun determines the number (and person) of the verb:

He told a joke *that was* pointless. [*Joke was.*]
He told several jokes *that were* pointless. [*Jokes were.*]
I paid the expenses of the trip, *which were* minimal. [*Expenses were.*]
Jack is one of those boys *who enjoy* fierce competition. [*Boys enjoy.*]

The last example, sometimes called the "one of those . . . who" sentence, is particularly troublesome. Generally we find a plural verb used. If we recast the sentence to read "Of those boys who enjoy fierce competition, Jack is one," it becomes clear that the logical antecedent of *who* is the plural noun *boys.* However, usage is divided. And notice that a singular verb must be used when the pattern is altered slightly:

Jack is the only *one* of my friends *who enjoys* fierce competition.

Because a relative pronoun subject nearly always has an antecedent that is third-person singular or third-person plural, we are accustomed to pronoun–verb combinations like these:

A boy *who is* . . .
Boys *who are* . . .
A woman *who knows* . . .
Women *who know* . . .

But in those occasional sentences in which a relative pronoun subject has an antecedent that is in the first or second person, meticulously correct usage calls for subject–verb combinations like the following:

I, *who am* in charge here, should pay the bill. [*I . . . am.*]
They should ask me, *who know* all the answers. [*I . . . know.*]

You, *who are* in charge here, should pay the bill. [*You . . . are.*]
They should ask you, *who know* all the answers. [*You . . . know.*]

Supplement 1

One particular error of subject–verb agreement warrants special attention. The third-person singular present tense form of the verb *do* is *does*. The plural form is *do*. The misuse of the negative contraction *don't* (instead of *doesn't*) with a third-person singular subject is quite often encountered in spoken English. Many people, justly or unjustly, look on the "it-don't" misuse as an important marker of grossly substandard English.

Such forms as the following should be avoided in all spoken and written English:

My father *don't* like broccoli.
It really *don't* matter.
Jack Johnson *don't* live here now.
One of her teachers *don't* like her.
This fudge tastes good, *don't* it?
The fact that the bill is overdue *don't* bother him.

SUMMARY OF CORRECT VERB USE

1. The principal parts of a verb are the present, the past, and the past participle. Avoid confusing principal parts of irregular verbs *(run, ran, run; eat, ate, eaten; fly, flew, flown)* with those of regular verbs *(study, studied, studied)*. Be especially careful with the often confused principal part of *lie* and *lay, sit* and *set.*
2. Singular verbs are used with singular subjects; plural verbs are used with plural subjects.
   a. Nouns intervening between the subject and the verb do not determine the number of the verb. (Resistance to the actions of these government agencies *is* [not *are*] growing.)
   b. Singular subjects joined by *and* normally take plural verbs. Singular subjects joined by *or* or *nor* normally take singular verbs.
   c. Some nouns and pronouns (collective nouns, and words like *number, all, half,* etc.) are singular in some meanings, plural in others.

Practice Sheet 22

Using Verbs Correctly: Subject–Verb Agreement

NAME _____ SCORE _____

Directions: These sentences are examples of structures that often lead to errors in subject–verb agreement. In the space at the left, copy the correct verb in parentheses. In each sentence the subject of the verb is printed in bold type.

_____ 1. The **number** of books missing from the shelves last semester (was, were) quite high.

_____ 2. In my front yard this morning when I walked outside (was, were) three cute little **puppies.**

_____ 3. **Mark and James** (do, does) not want to work for their father this summer.

_____ 4. The boss found several people **who** (was, were) willing to work on the holiday.

_____ 5. Thirty **miles** (seem, seems) like a long drive just to eat at a particular restaurant.

_____ 6. The host should ask you, **who** (know, knows) almost everyone in the room, to help with introductions.

_____ 7. Neither **Alice** nor **Javier** (has, have) attended any sessions of the special lab.

_____ 8. **Patience,** as well as a sense of humor, (is, are) necessary for anyone who works as Dr. Porter's assistant.

_____ 9. Every **student** and every **teacher** (has, have) been asked to contribute to the library's building fund.

_____ 10. Fifty **dollars** (was, were) all we had allotted for food for the trip home.

_____ 11. Jane is the only one of my friends **who** (plays, play) the piano competently.

_____ 12. Of all my friends, only **Al** (gocs, go) to thc gym regularly.

_____ 13. When we finally got to the campus, there (was, were) a **car** parked in every single spot in the parking lot.

_____ 14. Either **Jim** or **Mary** (was, were) told about the schedule change yesterday.

_____ 15. The new **group** of students (is, are) supposed to arrive on the next bus.

Directions: If you find an error in subject–verb agreement, underline the incorrect verb and write the correct form in the space at the left. Circle the subject of every verb you change. Some of the sentences may be correct.

_____ 1. "Sixteen weeks are not enough time to develop control of American history," said Larry, a history major.

_____ 2. My father used to believe that constant repetition of instructions were the only way to teach me anything.

_____ 3. "There is," the guide said, "three routes to the camp across the lake, but all three are difficult."

_____ 4. Neither the manager nor her secretary are able to tell me when the meeting will occur.

_____ 5. The one thing that you forgot to tell me to bring on the trip is my binoculars.

_____ 6. Ms. Maxwell is one of the few programmers who has been able to make that program work successfully.

_____ 7. There is few injuries more difficult to rehabilitate than a sprained ankle.

_____ 8. A few hours a week spent working in the computer lab have helped Jacob to master word processing successfully.

_____ 9. "Pancakes, bacon and eggs is my favorite breakfast," said Lila.

_____ 10. In my order from the office supply store is legal pads, pencils, and a box of computer paper.

_____ 11. "I see that neither Ralph nor Joan have signed up for a lab," said the lab instructor.

_____ 12. Jim's earlier efforts to write a clear paper was not successful.

_____ 13. Stored in that trunk, in addition to my boots and gloves, was the rest of my baseball card collection.

_____ 14. The cost of replacing those worn tires have left my bank balance quite low.

_____ 15. Have either Mark or Nancy made any preparations for finding a summer job?

EXERCISE 22

USING VERBS CORRECTLY: SUBJECT–VERB AGREEMENT

NAME _____ SCORE _____

Directions: If you find an error in subject–verb agreement, underline the incorrect verb and write the correct form in the space at the left. Circle the subject of every verb you change. Some of the sentences may be correct.

_____ 1. "Three days seem to me to be enough time for us to build that deck," said Walt.

_____ 2. The box with three computers and a laser printer inside have been taken to the loading dock.

_____ 3. In addition to the small rowboat, there is three fine wooden canoes in the boathouse.

_____ 4. Usually a list of your expenses and a folder containing your receipts are included with your monthly report.

_____ 5. When you begin to teach, the first day's meetings with the new students is going to be unforgettable.

_____ 6. Monday afternoon's discussion of all the errors from the previous two games are extremely dreary.

_____ 7. The lecturer told several stories that were quite funny, and the laughter helped the audience to relax.

_____ 8. My friend Jerry is one of those people who seems to be naturally talented in music.

_____ 9. A large number of the books in our library is old and should be replaced.

_____ 10. Were either Jim or Yolanda in that group that left on the first bus?

_____ 11. Immediate solutions to the large number of problems plaguing our computer network are vital.

_____ 12. The twins and their sister Amy are arriving tonight on the ten o'clock plane.

_____ 13. Ten thousand dollars were paid as a reward for information leading to the capture of that embezzler.

_____ 14. A large part of the student body don't know who the student government president is.

_____ 15. The baseball team is picking up their bats and gloves and walking slowly to the clubhouse.

_____ 16. There is a billiard table and a bowling alley in the basement of the student union.

_____ 17. We received a letter in which there was directions to the hotel and a picture of its entrance.

_____ 18. Ms. Rogers, along with all the division directors, is taking the plane to Charlotte tonight.

_____ 19. All the division directors and Ms. Rogers is taking the plane to Charlotte tonight.

_____ 20. Everyone who read that book has been asked to give some kind of opinion of it to the class.

_____ 21. Neither of the two children were able to find an article on dog training.

_____ 22. In that one picture is an All-American and three all-conference players.

_____ 23. Each manager and each assistant director was asked for an opinion on the new vacation policy.

_____ 24. Neither the two sisters nor their mother were able to attend the first meeting of the fund-raising committee.

_____ 25. Most of the people asked about the reform program know very little about its details.

_____ 26. Most of the information on those programs are very confusing.

_____ 27. Lance is the only member of that group who enjoy horror movies as much as I do.

_____ 28. Mark London, along with several co-workers, are organizing a trip to the Orient.

_____ 29. One of the first things Jon did when he started the project were to interview the police chief.

_____ 30. The chance to win a small fortune and a good deal of fame lead many to play the lottery.

LESSON 23 ■

Using Pronouns Correctly: Reference and Agreement

A pronoun is a word that substitutes for a noun or another pronoun. The word for which a pronoun stands is called its **antecedent:**

> I called *Harry,* but *he* didn't answer. [*He* substitutes for *Harry. Harry* is the antecedent of *he.*]
> *My cap and scarf* were where I had left *them.* [The antecedent of *them* is the plural unit *cap and scarf.*]
> *I* will wash *my* car tomorrow.
> *One* of my friends is painting *his* house.
> *Three* of my friends are painting *their* houses.

To use pronouns effectively and without confusing your reader, you must follow two basic principles:

1. You must establish a clear, easily identified relationship between a pronoun and its antecedent.

2. You must make the pronoun and its antecedent agree in person, number, and gender.

Let us examine these requirements more fully.

1. Personal pronouns should have definite antecedents and should be placed as near their antecedents as possible. Your readers should know exactly what a pronoun stands for. They should not be made to look through several sentences for its antecedent, nor should they be asked to manufacture an antecedent for it. When you discover in your writing a pronoun with no clear and unmistakable antecedent, your revision, as many of the following examples demonstrate, will often require rewriting to remove the faulty pronoun from your sentence:

> **Faulty:** A strange car followed us closely, and *he* kept blinking his lights at us.
>
> **Improved:** A strange car followed us closely, and the driver kept blinking his lights at us.
>
> **Faulty:** Although Jenny was a real sports fan, her brother never became interested in *them.*
>
> **Improved:** Although Jenny really liked sports, her brother never became interested in them.
>
> **Faulty:** Mike is an excellent typist, although he never took a course in *it.*
>
> **Improved:** Mike is an excellent typist, although he never took a course in typing.

The indefinite *you* or *they* is quite common in speech and in chatty, informal writing, but one should avoid using either in serious writing:

> **Faulty:** In Alaska *they* catch huge king crabs.

Improved: In Alaska huge king crabs are caught. [Often the best way to correct an indefinite *they* or *you* sentence is to use a passive verb.]

Faulty: Before the reform measures were passed, *you* had few rights.

Improved: Before the reform measures were passed, people had few rights.
Before the reform measures were passed, one had few rights.

Faulty: At the employment office *they* gave me an application form.

Improved: A clerk at the employment office gave me an application form.
At the employment office I was given an application form.

A pronoun should not appear to refer equally well to either of two antecedents:

Faulty: Frank told Bill that *he* needed a haircut. [Which one needed a haircut?]

Improved: "You need a haircut," said Frank to Bill. [In sentences of this type, the direct quotation is sometimes the only possible correction.]

The "it says" introduction to statements, although common in informal language, is objectionable in serious writing:

Faulty: *It* says in the directions that the powder will dissolve in hot water.

Improved: The directions say that the powder will dissolve in hot water.

Faulty: *It* said on the morning news program that a bad storm is coming.

Improved: According to the morning news program, a bad storm is coming.

(See Supplement 1.)
Avoid vague or ambiguous reference of relative and demonstrative pronouns:

Faulty: Only twenty people attended the lecture, *which* was due to poor publicity.

Improved: Because of poor publicity, only twenty people attended the lecture.

Faulty: Good writers usually have large vocabularies, and *this* is why I get poor grades on my themes.

Improved: Good writers usually have large vocabularies, so I get poor grades because my vocabulary is inadequate.

A special situation relates to the antecedent of the pronouns *which, this,* and *that*. In a sentence such as "The children giggled, *which* annoyed the teacher" or "The children giggled, and *this* annoyed the teacher," the thing that annoyed the teacher is not the *children* but "the giggling of the children" or "the fact that the children giggled." This kind of reference to a preceding idea rather than to an expressed noun is unobjectionable provided that the meaning is instantly and unmistakably clear. But you should avoid sentences like the following. In the first one readers would be hard pressed to discover exactly what the *which* means, and in the second they must decide whether the antecedent is the preceding idea or the noun immediately preceding the *which:*

Faulty: Hathaway's application was rejected because he spells poorly, *which* is very important in an application letter.

Improved: Hathaway's application was rejected because he spells poorly; correct spelling is very important in an application letter.

Faulty: The defense attorney did not object to the judge's concluding remark, *which* surprised me.

Improved: I was surprised that the defense attorney did not object to the judge's concluding remark.

2. Pronouns should agree with their antecedents in person, number, and gender. The following chart classifies for you the three forms of each personal pronoun on the basis of person, number, and gender:

	Singular	*Plural*
1st person	[the person speaking] *I, my, me*	[the persons speaking] *we, our, us*
2nd person	[the person spoken to] *you, your, you*	[the persons spoken to] *you, your, you*
3rd person	[the person or thing spoken of] *he, his, him* *she, her, her* *it, its, it*	[the persons or things spoken of] *they, their, them*

A singular antecedent is referred to by a singular pronoun; a plural antecedent is referred to by a plural pronoun.

Dad says that *he* is sure that *his* new friend will visit *him* soon.
Dad and Mother say that *they* are sure that *their* new friend will visit *them* soon.

This principle of logical pronoun agreement is not as simple as these two examples might suggest. Recent language practices have given rise to two situations for which "rules" that apply in every instance cannot possibly be made. Student writers must, first of all, be aware of certain changing ideas about pronoun usage; then they must prepare themselves to make decisions among the choices available.

The first of these two troublesome situations relates to some of the indefinite pronouns: *one, everyone, someone, no one, anyone, anybody, everybody, somebody, nobody, each, either,* and *neither.* These words have generally been felt to be singular; hence pronouns referring to them have customarily been singular and, unless the antecedent specifies otherwise, masculine. Singular pronouns have also been used in formal writing and speaking to refer to noun antecedents modified by singular qualifiers such as *each* and *every.* The four following examples illustrate the traditional, formal practice:

Everybody has *his* faults and *his* virtues.
Each of the sons is doing what *he* thinks is best.
England expects every man to do *his* duty.
No one succeeds in this firm if Dobbins doesn't like *him.*

The principal difficulty with this usage is that these indefinites, although regarded by strict grammarians as singular in form, carry with them a group or plural sense, with the result that people are often unsure whether pronouns referring to them should be singular or plural. Despite traditional pronouncements, every day we hear sentences of the "Everyone-will-do-*their*-best" type. Beginning writers, however, would do well to follow the established practice until they feel relatively secure about recognizing the occasional sentence in which a singular pronoun referring to an indefinite produces a strained or unnatural effect even though it does agree in form with its antecedent.

Closely related to this troublesome matter of pronoun agreement is a second problem, this one dealing with gender. The problem is this: What reference words should be used to refer to such a word as *student*? Obviously there are female students and there are male students. With plural nouns there is no problem; *they, their,* and *them* refer to both masculine and feminine. But for singular nouns the language provides *she, hers, her* and *he, his, him* but not a pronoun to refer to third-person singular words that contain both male and female members.

Here again, as with the reference to third-person singular indefinites, the traditional practice has been to use masculine singular pronouns. Eighty or so years ago Henry James wrote the following sentence: "We must grant the artist his subject, his idea, his *donné;* our criticism is applied only to what he makes of it." In James's day that sentence was undoubtedly looked upon as unexceptionable; the pronouns followed what was then standard practice. But attitudes have changed. In the 1990s, if that sentence got past the eyes of an editor and appeared on the printed page, its implication that artists are exclusively male would make the sentence unacceptably discriminatory to many readers.

Reliance on the *he-or-she* pronoun forms is an increasingly popular solution to some of these worrisome problems of pronoun reference. The *he-or-she* forms agree in number with the third-person singular indefinites. And the use of these forms obviates any possible charge of gender preference. However, a piling up of *he-or-she*'s, *his-or-her*'s, and *him-or-her*'s is undesirable. (Notice the cumbersome result, for instance, if a *he-or-she* form is substituted for all four of the third-person singular masculine pronouns in the Henry James sentence.)

Here is a very important point for you to remember: When you are worried about a third-person singular masculine pronoun you have written, either because its reference to an indefinite antecedent sounds not quite right to you or because it shows an undesirable gender preference, you can remove the awkwardness, in nearly every instance that arises, by changing the antecedent to a plural noun, to which you then refer by using *they, their,* and *them.*

By way of summary, study these four versions of a sentence as they relate to the two problems just discussed:

Every member of the graduating class, if *he* wishes, may have *his* diploma mailed to *him* after August 15. [This usage reflects traditional practice that is still quite widely followed. The objection to it is that the reference words are exclusively masculine.]

Every member of the graduating class, if *he or she* wishes, may have *his or her* diploma mailed to *him or her* after August 15. [The singular reference is satisfactory, but the avoidance of masculine reference has resulted in clumsy wordiness.]

Every member of the graduating class, if *they* wish, may have *their* diplomas mailed to *them* after August 15. [This version, particularly if used in spoken English, would probably not offend many people, but the lack of proper number agreement between the pronouns and the antecedent would rule out its appearance in edited material.]

Members of the graduating class, if *they* wish, may have *their* diplomas mailed to *them* after August 15. [In this version the pronouns are logical and correct in both number and gender.]

A few other matters of pronoun reference, mercifully quite uncomplicated, should be called to your attention. If a pronoun refers to a compound unit or to a noun that may be either singular or plural, the pronoun agrees in number with the antecedent. (See Lesson 22.)

> Wilson and his wife arrived in *their* new car.
> Neither Jill nor Martha has finished *her* term paper.
> The rest of the lecture had somehow lost *its* point.
> The rest of the workers will receive *their* money soon.
> The eight-o'clock class has *its* test tomorrow.
> The ten-o'clock class finished writing *their* themes.

An antecedent in the third person should not be referred to by *you.* This misuse develops when writers, forgetting that they have established the third person in the sentence, shift the structure and begin to talk directly to the reader:

Faulty: In a large university a *freshman* can feel lost if *you* have grown up in a small town.

   If *a person* really wants to become an expert golfer, *you* must practice everyday.

Improved: In a large university a freshman can feel lost if *he or she* has grown up in a small town.

   If a person really wants to become an expert golfer, *she or he* must practice every day.

Supplement 1

At this point you should be reminded that *it* without an antecedent has some uses that are completely acceptable in both formal and informal English. One of these is in the delayed subject or object pattern. (See Lesson 10.) Another is its use as a kind of filler word in expressions having to do with weather, time, distance, and so forth.

> *It* is fortunate that you had a spare tire.
> I find *it* difficult to believe Ted's story.
> *It* is cold today; *it* snowed last night.
> *It* is twelve o'clock; *it* is almost time for lunch.
> How far is *it* to Phoenix?

Practice Sheet 23

Using Pronouns Correctly: Reference and Agreement

NAME _____ SCORE _____

Directions: One sentence in each of the following pairs is correct, and the other contains at least one reference word that is poorly used. In the space at the left, write the letter that identifies the correct sentence. In the other sentence, circle the pronoun or pronouns that have vague or incorrect reference.

_____ 1. A. Many people dream of winning a vast fortune, but for most it's only a dream that can never come true.
   B. Many people dream of winning a vast fortune, but for most such a fortune is only a dream that can never come true.

_____ 2. A. All those who want to play in the slow-pitch softball league should pay their fees before Tuesday night's practice.
   B. Everyone who wants to play in the slow-pitch softball league should pay their fees before Tuesday night's practice.

_____ 3. A. The company president told Maurine that she was going to be assigned to the new committee on relocation.
   B. The company president told Maurine, "You are going to be assigned to the new committee on relocation."

_____ 4. A. "I don't think anyone could pass that course without working himself half to death," said Marvin.
   B. "I don't think anyone could pass that course without working themself half to death," said Marvin.

_____ 5. A. It said over the loudspeaker that those who have reserved seats would be admitted to the stadium first.
   B. Over the loudspeaker the announcer said that those who have reserved seats would be admitted to the stadium first.

_____ 6. A. As a kid Marlene always wanted to study acting, but in college she decided not to become one.
   B. As a kid Marlene always wanted to study drama, but in college she decided not to become a drama major.

_____ 7. A. According to the registrar's office, all applicants for the freshman class must complete their applications before June 1.
   B. According to the registrar's office, everyone applying for the freshman class must complete their applications before June 1.

_____ 8. A. The note in the catalog suggests that you should take typing before you take a computer course.
   B. The note in the catalog suggests that students should take typing before they take a computer course.

_____ 9. A. When the students finished with the tools, not any of them were returned to the toolbox.
   B. When the students finished with the tools, they did not return any of the tools to the toolbox.

213

_____ 10. A. Martha said to Anna, "I need to find a new tennis partner because Robert has sprained his ankle severely."

B. Martha told Anna that she needed to find a new tennis partner because Robert has sprained his ankle severely.

_____ 11. A. As a student registered for chemistry, you need to get some tutoring if you start to fall behind.

B. A student registered for chemistry needs to get some tutoring if you start to fall behind.

_____ 12. A. The FBI sent out a brochure advertising openings for jobs in their organization.

B. The FBI sent out a brochure advertising openings for jobs in its organization.

_____ 13. A. All the members of the Brain Bowl team received new blue blazers, and they gave the old blazers to Goodwill.

B. Every member of the Brain Bowl team received a new blue blazer, and they gave the old blazers to Goodwill.

_____ 14. A. The newscaster reported that the local school board will soon hold elections by districts for the first time.

B. It said on the news that the local school board will soon hold elections by districts for the first time.

_____ 15. A. The board of directors announced that they will soon offer its stock for sale to the public.

B. The board of directors announced that it will soon offer the company's stock for sale to the public.

_____ 16. A. A recorded voice on the telephone said, "The customer you have called might have left their phone unattended."

B. A recorded voice on the telephone said, "The customer you have called might have left his or her phone unattended."

_____ 17. A. "I'm looking for a good mystery novel; those stories are a great diversion after all this studying," said Pam.

B. "I'm looking for a good mystery novel; they are a great diversion after all this studying," said Pam.

_____ 18. A. That book told Amy that when you prepare for a test you should rewrite your lecture notes in an organized form.

B. That book told Amy that when students prepare for a test they should rewrite their lecture notes in an organized form.

_____ 19. A. In that article it said that the Alps are now showing the effects of global warming.

B. In that article scientists reported that the Alps are now showing the effects of global warming.

_____ 20. A. "Whoever took my history textbook by mistake should get his act together and give it back to me," said Tom.

B. "Whoever took my history textbook by mistake should get their act together and give it back to me," said Tom.

EXERCISE 23

USING PRONOUNS CORRECTLY: REFERENCE AND AGREEMENT

NAME _____ SCORE _____

Directions: In the space at the left, copy the correct pronoun or pronoun–verb combination given in parentheses. Circle the antecedent of the pronoun.

_____ 1. Not one of the older employees feels that (he or she owes, they owe) any loyalty to the new managers.

_____ 2. Has Jane's group finished (its, it's, their) part of the project yet?

_____ 3. By the time the average student graduates, (he or she, they) should have spent many hours learning computers.

_____ 4. Before students can enroll for a scuba diving course, (he or she, you, they) must swim 100 yards under water.

_____ 5. The citizens of our county registered (its, their) opinion of county government by electing a new mayor.

_____ 6. Anyone who buys an older car must prepare (himself, themselves) for some expensive repairs.

_____ 7. Out of the students surveyed, only a few knew (his or her, their) exact GPA.

_____ 8. People who intend to take that cruise will want to get (his or her, their) immunization shots early.

_____ 9. Did you know that each of those clubs has (its, their) own representative on the Interclub Council?

_____ 10. The members of the clubs elect (its, their) representatives annually.

_____ 11. Neither Jim nor Walt has worked very much on (his, their) speech for next week's election.

_____ 12. Barbara, Marge, and Roberta will each bring in (her, their) report on Monday.

_____ 13. My brothers, Jim, Rob, and Harry, intend to show (his, their) old Ford at the next classic car show.

_____ 14. Some seniors find it difficult to remember how strange college was when (he or she was, they were) freshmen.

_____ 15. The local bookstore is holding a sale; all (its, their) book prices have been reduced by 25 percent.

215

Directions: Each sentence contains at least one reference word that is poorly used. In the space at the left, copy the pronoun or pronouns that have vague or incorrect references. In the space below each sentence, rewrite enough of the sentence to make the meaning clear.

_____ 1. When someone tries to call that phone number, they usually get two of the digits reversed.

_____ 2. After Max had waited in line for an hour, they told him that the class he wanted was already closed.

_____ 3. My dad told George that he needed to invest a little money from each paycheck to pay for his retirement.

_____ 4. The announcer said that anyone who is not completely happy with a purchase can get their money back.

_____ 5. The ten o'clock class will have their test tomorrow, and they must turn in their projects on Friday.

_____ 6. In the town of Wilder, they enforce the speed limits strictly, and you can get a ticket if you speed.

_____ 7. Connie wants to be an artist although you have a hard time getting started and most don't make much money.

_____ 8. If anyone enjoys hard work, they might consider studying accounting.

_____ 9. Sue does not enjoy tennis because she does not serve well, which is a basic requirement of the game.

_____ 10. On my birthday each one of my relatives sent me a card they thought I might enjoy.

LESSON 24 ▪

Using Pronouns Correctly: Case

In Lesson 23 a chart classifies the forms of the personal pronouns on the basis of person, number, and gender. For each pronoun the three forms that are listed—first-person singular, *I, my, me;* third-person plural, *they, their, them;* and so on—illustrate the three case forms. *I* and *they* are nominative, *my* and *their* are possessive, and *me* and *them* are objective, for example.

The way you use these pronouns in everyday language, in sentences such as "Two of *my* books have disappeared; *they* cost *me* twenty dollars, and *I* must find *them*," shows you that the case form you choose depends on how the word is used within the sentence. In this lesson we shall examine some spots where the wrong choice of pronoun form is possible.

The only words in modern English that retain distinctions between nominative and objective case forms are a few pronouns. These two forms are identical in nouns, and the correct use of the distinctive form, the possessive, requires essentially only a knowledge of how the apostrophe is used. (See Lesson 19.)

Here are the pronouns arranged according to their case forms. The first eight are the personal pronouns; notice that the only distinctive form of *you* and *it* is the possessive. The last three pronouns, which we shall examine separately from the personal pronouns, are used only in questions and in subordinate clauses.

Nominative	*Possessive*	*Objective*
I	my, mine	me
you	your, yours	you
he	his, his	him
she	her, hers	her
it	its, its	it
we	our, ours	us
you	your, yours	you
they	their, theirs	them
which	—	which
who	whose	whom
whoever	whosever	whomever

The **possessive case** is used to show possession. Three possible trouble spots should be noted.

1. The preceding chart shows two possessive forms for the personal pronouns. The first form for each pronoun is used as a *modifier* of a noun. The second form is used

as a nominal; in other words, it fills a noun slot, such as the subject, the complement, or the object of a preposition:

> This is *your* seat; *mine* is in the next row.
> Jane preferred *my* cookies; some of *hers* were burned.
> *Their* product is good, but the public prefers *ours*.

2. The indefinite pronouns use an apostrophe to form the possessive case: *everybody's* duty, *one's* lifetime, *everyone's* hopes, someone *else's* car. But the personal pronouns do not:

> These seats are *ours* [not *our's*]. *Yours* [not *Your's*] are in the next row.

Learn to distinguish carefully between the following possessives and contractions that are pronounced alike; *its* (possessive), *it's* (it is, it has); *theirs* (possessive), *there's* (there is, there has); *their* (possessive), *they're* (they are); *whose* (possessive), *who's* (who is, who has); *your* (possessive), *you're* (you are):

> *It's* obvious that the car has outworn *its* usefulness.
> *There's* new evidence that *they're* changing *their* tactics.

3. Formal usage prefers the possessive form of pronouns (occasionally of nouns also) preceding gerunds in constructions like the following:

> He was unhappy about *my* [not *me*] voting for the bill.
> Her report led to *our* [not *us*] buying additional stock.
> Chad boasted about his *son's* [not *son*] having won the scholarship.

The rules governing the uses of the other two cases are very simple. A pronoun is in the **nominative case** when it is used:

1. As a subject: *They* suspected that *he* was lying.
2. As a subjective complement: This is *she* speaking.
3. As an appositive of a nominative noun: *We* truck drivers help stranded motorists.

A pronoun is in the **objective case** when it is used:

1. As an object of a verb or verbal: Ted told *her* the news. We enjoyed meeting *them*.
2. As an object of a preposition: Everyone except *me* had left the room.
3. As the subject of an infinitive: The police officer ordered *me* to halt.
4. As an appositive of an objective noun: Three of *us* truck drivers stopped to help.

We need not examine in detail every one of these applications. As one becomes more adept at using the English language, he or she learns that such usages as "*Them* arrived late" and "I spoke to *she*" do not conform to the system of the language. Instead, we should examine the trouble spots where confusion may arise. When we use the personal pronouns, we must exercise care in the following situations:

1. When the pronoun follows *and* (sometimes *or*) as part of a compound unit, determine its use in the sentence and choose the appropriate case form. The temptation

here is usually to use the nominative, although the last example in the following list shows a trouble spot where the objective case is sometimes misused. Test these troublesome constructions by using the pronoun by itself, and you will probably discover which form is the correct one:

> The man gave Sue and *me* some candy. [Not Sue and *I*. Both words are indirect objects. Apply the test. Notice how strange "The man gave . . . *I* some candy" sounds.]
>
> Send your check to either my lawyer or *me*. [Not "to . . . *I*."]
>
> Have you seen Bob or *her* lately? [Direct objects require the objective case.]
>
> Just between you and *me*, the lecture was a bore. [Never say "between you and *I*." Both pronouns are objects of the preposition *between*. If this set phrase is a problem for you, find the correct form by reversing the pronouns: You would never say "between I and you."]
>
> Ms. Estes took *him* and *me* to school. [Not *he* and *I* or *him* and *I*. Both pronouns are direct objects.]
>
> Will my sister and *I* be invited? [Not *me*. The subject is *sister* and *I*.]

2. In comparisons after *as* and *than,* when the pronoun is the subject of an understood verb, use the nominative form:

> He is taller than *I* [*am*]. I am older than *he* [*is*].
>
> Can you talk as fast as *she* [*can talk*]? No one knew more about art than *he* [*did*].

Sentences like these nearly always call for nominative case subjects. Occasionally the meaning of a sentence may demand an objective pronoun. Both of the following sentences are correct; notice the difference in meaning:

> You apparently trust Mr. Alton more than *I*. [The meaning is ". . . more than I (trust Mr. Alton")].
>
> You apparently trust Mr. Alton more than *me*. [The meaning here is ". . . more than (you trust) me."]

3. Ordinarily use the nominative form for the subjective complement. The specific problem here concerns such expressions as *It's me* or *It is I, It was they* or *It was them.* Many people say *It's me,* but they would hesitate to say *It was her, It was him,* or *It was them,* instead of *It was she, It was he,* or *It was they.* However, this is a problem that does not arise often in the writing of students. The following are examples of correct formal usage:

> It is *I*.
>
> It could have been *he*.
>
> Was it *she*?
>
> Was it *they* who called?

4. See that the appositive is in the same case as the word that it refers to. Notice particularly the first three examples that follow. This usage employing *we* and *us* as an appositive modifier preceding a noun is a real trouble spot:

> *We* boys were hired. [The unit *We boys* is the subject and requires the nominative.]
>
> Two of *us* boys were hired. [The object of a preposition requires the objective case.]

Mr. Elder hired *us* boys. [Not *we boys* for a direct object.]
Two boys—you and *I*—will be hired. [In apposition with the subject.]
Mr. Elder will hire two boys—you and *me*. [In apposition with the object.]

The only other pronouns in standard modern English that have distinctive nominative, possessive, and objective forms are *who/whose/whom* and *whoever/whosever/whomever*. (See Supplement 1.) The rules that apply to the personal pronouns apply to these words as well: In the subject position *who/whoever* should be used; in the direct object position *whom/whomever* should be used; and so forth. (These pronouns, it should be noted, are never used as appositives.)

The special problem in the application of the case rules to these words comes from their special use as interrogatives and as subordinating words. As you learned in Lessons 6, 9, and 10, these words, because they serve as signal words, always stand at the beginning of their clauses. To locate the grammatical function of the pronoun within its clause, you must examine the clause to determine the normal subject–verb–complement positioning.

1. In formal usage, *whom* is required when it is a direct object or the object of a preposition, even though it stands ahead of its subject and verb:

Whom did Mr. Long hire? [If you are troubled by this sort of construction, try substituting a personal pronoun and placing it after the verb, where it normally comes: "Did Mr. Long hire *him*?" You would never say "Did Mr. Long hire *he*?" The transitive verb *hire* requires a direct object pronoun in the objective case.]
He is a boy *whom* everyone can like. [*Whom* is the object of *can like*.]
Wilson was the man *whom* everybody trusted. [Everybody trusted *whom*.]
She is the girl *whom* Mother wants me to marry. [Object of the verbal *to marry*.]
Whom was she speaking to just then? [To *whom* was she speaking?]

2. When *who(m)* or *who(m)ever* begins a subordinate clause that follows a verb or a preposition, the use of the pronoun *within its own clause* determines its case form:

We do not know *who* broke the window. [*Who* is the subject of *broke*, not the direct object of *do know*.]
No one knows *who* the intruder was. [*Who* is the subjective complement in the noun clause.]
We do not know *whom* the police have arrested. [The objective form *whom* is used because it is the direct object of *have arrested*. The direct object of *do know* is the whole noun clause.]
I will sell the car to *whoever* offers the best price. [The whole clause, *whoever offers the best price*, is the object of the preposition *to*. A subject of a verb must be in the nominative case.]

3. When the pronoun subject is followed by a parenthetical insertion like *do you think, I suspect, everyone believes*, or *we know*, the nominative case form must be used:

Who do you think *has* the best chance of winning? [*Who* is the subject of *has*. The *do you think* is a parenthetical insertion.]
Jenkins is the one *who* I suspect *will make* the best impression. [Determine the verb that goes with the pronoun. If you are puzzled by this type of sentence, try reading it this way: "Jenkins is the one *who will make* the best impression—I suspect."]

But if the pronoun is not the subject of the verb, the objective form should be used:

He is an achiever *whom* I suspect you will eventually envy. [*Whom* is the direct object of *will envy.*]

Supplement 1

The chart on page 217 shows that the pronoun *which* has no possessive case form, a situation that brings about a minor problem of word choice. As you learned when you studied the adjective clause, *who(m)* normally refers to persons and *which* to things. But *whose* may be used in an adjective clause as the possessive form of *which* to refer to a nonhuman antecedent:

It is a disease *whose* long-term effects are minor.

If *whose* is not used in such a sentence, the "of-which" form must be used, producing a perfectly correct but cumbersome sentence:

It is a disease the long-term effects *of which* are minor.

SUMMARY OF CORRECT PRONOUN USE

1. A pronoun should have a clearly identified antecedent, with which it agrees in person, number, and gender.
2. Be aware of the special problem of pronoun reference to third-person singular antecedents that include both masculine and feminine members—pronouns like *everybody* and *someone* and nouns like *person, student, employee,* and so on. NOTE: Using a plural rather than a singular antecedent is one obvious way of avoiding this problem.
3. Use nominative forms of pronouns used as subjects, subjective complements, and appositives that rename nominative nouns. Use objective forms of pronouns used as objects of verbs or prepositions, subjects of infinitives, and appositives that rename objective nouns.
4. Be aware of a particular pronoun problem when a personal pronoun is tied to a noun or another pronoun by *and* or *or:*

   Mickey and I [not *Mickey and me*] were sent to the principal's office.
   Mr. Case sent *Mickey and me* [not *Mickey and I*] to the principal's office.
   And so, neighbors, please vote for *Ms. Stone and me* [not *Ms. Stone and I*].

5. Remember that the case of *who* is determined by its use in its own clause. It may be a direct object that precedes the subject [*Whom* has your wife invited?] or a subject immediately following a verb or a preposition [We wonder *who* will win. Our dog is friendly with *whoever* pets it.]

Practice Sheet 24

Using Pronouns Correctly: Case

NAME _____ SCORE _____

Directions: Each italicized pronoun in these sentences is correctly used. In the space at the left, write one of the following numbers to identify the use of the pronoun:

1. Subject   4. Direct or indirect object
2. Subjective complement   5. Object of preposition
3. Appositive modifier of nominative noun   6. Appositive modifier of objective noun

_____ 1. Yesterday Professor Jones asked both Tom and *me* to make a speech next week.

_____ 2. *We* players don't resent hard work because it helps us to improve our performance.

_____ 3. None of *us* employees received that memorandum.

_____ 4. Do you think that Marge is a better speaker than *I*?

_____ 5. That letter should be sent to *whoever* is responsible for handling such insurance claims.

_____ 6. I'd like to keep this information a secret between you and *me*.

_____ 7. That candidate is a woman *who,* according to her biography, has no prior experience in politics.

_____ 8. The clerk handed Jane and *me* new registration packets.

_____ 9. Martin seems puzzled; it could have been *he* who was outside when the instructions were read.

_____ 10. *Whom* do you think we should appoint as Arthur's replacement?

_____ 11. *Who* do you think should be Arthur's replacement?

_____ 12. Every one of *us* programmers can do that simple work.

_____ 13. Maria asked *who* the coach was in 1987.

_____ 14. Diligent students like you and *me* can always be counted on to take thorough notes.

_____ 15. The letter writer, *whoever* she is, failed to do any significant research on that problem.

_____ 16. The new officers are Ray, Alice, and *I*.

_____ 17. The list of new officers includes Ray, Alice, and *me*.

_____ 18. Roger thought the assignment was for Barbara, Jack, and *him*.

_____ 19. The girls didn't know *whom* the garage was sending to pick up the car.

_____ 20. The girls didn't know *who* was being sent to pick up the car.

223

Directions: In the space at the left, copy the correct pronoun from within the parentheses.

_____ 1. (Who, Whom) do you think the department will send as its representative at the conference in London?

_____ 2. Will you tell me (who, whom) your assistant was on that project last year?

_____ 3. The men's basketball coach recruited three of (us, we) tallest intramural players for the varsity.

_____ 4. Every worker on that shift, including James and (I, me), worked overtime last night.

_____ 5. When Marie was in elementary school, the three best spellers were Alex, Tammie, and (her, she).

_____ 6. Are you sure that the black umbrella is (yours, your's) and not Nancy's?

_____ 7. The general public needs to be informed about politicians as corrupt as (he, him) and his colleagues.

_____ 8. The business students will support (whoever, whomever) the Business Council selects.

_____ 9. The business students will vote for (whoever, whomever) gets the approval of the Business Council.

_____ 10. Most people say that only good math students like you and (her, she) should take that course in the summer.

_____ 11. "I don't think making coffee in the morning is actually (anybodies, anybody's) job," said Edwina.

_____ 12. "A few of (us, we) players would like to practice Saturday morning," said Wanda.

_____ 13. The manager (whose, who's) in charge of that new project is in town today.

_____ 14. Those who work as slowly as Rick and (I, me) don't belong in this advanced class.

_____ 15. Annabelle is a person (who, whom) creates a very good first impression on people she meets.

_____ 16. "I can predict (who, whom) the coach will choose as captain in the fall," said Alan.

_____ 17. Almost everyone, except, of course, for Robin and (I, me), was on time this morning.

_____ 18. If you can't type that paper for me, (who, whom) do you think can do it?

_____ 19. When we went to San Francisco, my aunt took my sister and (I, me) to a very famous restaurant.

_____ 20. The prize goes to (whoever, whomever) solves that problem first.

EXERCISE 24

USING PRONOUNS CORRECTLY: CASE

NAME _____ SCORE _____

Directions: If you find an incorrectly used pronoun, underline it and write the correct form in the space at the left. If a sentence is correct, leave the space blank.

_____ 1. I told Marta that, if I were she, I would study for tomorrow's test.

_____ 2. Except for she and Ellen, all the women on the committee voted to meet tomorrow night at eight o'clock.

_____ 3. Would you please send all of we members of the nominating committee a list of your previous elected offices.

_____ 4. Does the coach know about my leaving practice early yesterday?

_____ 5. How do the detectives find who the thief is?

_____ 6. I think the detectives should look for whomever they think has the missing file folders.

_____ 7. "That plan was proposed by the class president, but it was not accepted by us," said Bob.

_____ 8. Joanna bought a new car last week; it's stereo system includes a compact disk changer.

_____ 9. John and Tom are back for the summer; it could have been they whom you saw in the mall today.

_____ 10. Standing all together at the front of the room were the president, the treasurer, and us department heads.

_____ 11. Betsy said, "Keep this news between you and I, but I heard that next Tuesday is going to be a holiday."

_____ 12. The receptionist answered the phone and asked, "And whom may I say is calling?"

_____ 13. Who is the president expecting to call on today?

_____ 14. Someone else's application arrived earlier than those submitted by Joyce and I.

_____ 15. Janice wants to call her sister, whom she thinks will want to join us for dinner.

_____ 16. I think Paul might need help; a beginner like he might have trouble installing that program.

_____ 17. Everyone except us new workers will be covered by the new benefits package.

_____ 18. "Whose going to tell the boss that the hard disk crashed last night?" asked Raymond.

225

_____ 19. "And can you guess whose job it will be to restore the data to that disk?" groaned Meryl.

_____ 20. Every rookie, whoever he is, has to endure practical jokes played by the veterans.

_____ 21. The office manager promised to give my brother and I good references for our work this past summer.

_____ 22. Who do you think we should choose as our advisor for next semester?

_____ 23. Dr. Magnusen is one man who's opinion I value.

_____ 24. I'd like to use your computer; our's is in the repair shop.

_____ 25. Roberta just hired a new secretary who, she learned, cannot operate a computer.

_____ 26. The argument between he and Jim lasted almost three hours.

_____ 27. Those selected to take the special accounting course were Larry, Liz, and we two accounting majors.

_____ 28. The editor of the newspaper didn't realize who the writer of the letter was.

_____ 29. "I hope you don't mind me using your textbook," said Barb; "mine seems to have disappeared."

_____ 30. "Before I select the winner, Janice, I need to listen to all the speeches, not just your's," said the teacher.

_____ 31. I wish I knew whom I should call to repair my television.

_____ 32. The station manager wants to meet with all five of we announcers on Saturday morning.

_____ 33. All we accounting students wish that the library opened earlier in the morning.

_____ 34. The other team has three players who are much more experienced than us.

_____ 35. Who would you guess owns that beautiful black car with it's fancy stereo system?

_____ 36. There was enough time for Paul to speak, but not for my friends and I.

_____ 37. Phil spends his time talking sports with anyone whom he can corner.

_____ 38. Most of us don't mind him talking sports, but we wish he'd listen to someone else's opinion occasionally.

_____ 39. I'd defy you to show me anyone who has worked harder than me on this course.

_____ 40. Marcy wants whoever left this mess to clean it up instead of leaving it for her to take care of.

EXERCISE 24A

USING PRONOUNS CORRECTLY:
REFERENCE AND CASE

NAME _____ SCORE _____

Directions: Whenever you find an incorrectly used pronoun, copy it in the space at the left. Then in the space below the sentence, write enough of the sentence to show how you would make the sentence clear and correct. No sentence contains more than two poorly used pronouns; some sentences may be correct.

_____ 1. The director told we students that they've decided not to use
_____   any students as extras in the movie.

_____ 2. Ask Jenny if that book on the back seat of my car is hers; it's
_____   not mine or yours.

_____ 3. The clerk told Ed that you have to have your registration form
_____   signed by someone in the dean's office.

_____ 4. Give this note to whoever you can find downstairs and tell
_____   them to take it to the coach's office, please.

_____ 5. Mary asked Sue if her sister had brought back her clean laun-
_____   dry when she came for the weekend.

_____ 6. It says in the handbook that March first is the last day you can
_____   withdraw from a course.

_____ 7. "You can select whoever you wish for a partner; its your
_____   choice," said the teacher.

_____ 8. The boss called earlier; she wants to know who we've hired
_____   and how we located them.

_____ 9. Uncle Walt, who is a scuba diver, says he can teach us to dive
_____   if we are interested in it.

_____ 10. Each student should have their own computer and they should
_____   give each one individual instructions.

_____ 11. Jane Roberts, whom most of us think should be the next man-
_____   ager, has better credentials for it than anyone else.

_____ 12. I lost yesterday's lecture notes, but John and Anne, who sit
_____   next to me, will lend me their's.

_____ 13. On the television last night they announced that people who use well water should boil it before drinking it.
_____

_____ 14. Every entering freshman must take orientation before they can sign up for their courses.
_____

_____ 15. My parents, who both attended a local college, allowed my sister and I to choose an out-of-state school.
_____

_____ 16. The guides gave each hiker a picnic lunch, but they had eaten everything well before noon.
_____

_____ 17. "The climax of that movie was so frightening it made you forget how funny you thought the opening was," said Tom.
_____

_____ 18. I wonder if our leaving the party early angered anyone who was there.
_____

_____ 19. Everyone who my father employed last summer has returned to college to pursue their degree.
_____

_____ 20. Please send copies of the schedule to all we freshmen so we can pick out our classes early.
_____

_____ 21. I will give my set of keys to whoever Mr. Andrews chooses as my replacement.
_____

_____ 22. I will give my set of keys to whoever is chosen as my replacement by Mr. Andrews.
_____

_____ 23. Who do you think us volunteers should ask to lead our group on the cleanup campaign?
_____

_____ 24. Who do you think would be the best person for us to ask to lead our group in the cleanup campaign?
_____

_____ 25. "Whom may I say is calling?" asked the receptionist when I asked to speak to whoever was in charge of new employees.
_____

LESSON 25 ■

Using Modifiers and Prepositions Correctly

In Lesson 2 you learned that an adjective is a word that describes or limits a noun or a pronoun. An adverb modifies a verb, an adjective, or another adverb. Many adverbs end in *ly*, such as *happily, beautifully,* and *extremely*. (But some adjectives—*lovely, likely, deadly, neighborly,* and *homely,* for instance—also end in *ly.*). Some adverbs do not end in *ly,* and these happen to be among the most frequently used words in speech and writing: *after, always, before, far, forever, here, not, now, often, quite, rather, soon, then, there, too, very.*

Some words can be used either as adjectives or as adverbs, as the following examples show:

Adverbs	*Adjectives*
He came *close.*	That was a *close* call.
She talks too *fast.*	She's a *fast* thinker.
Hit it *hard.*	That was a *hard* blow.
She usually arrives *late.*	She arrived at a *late* hour.
He went *straight* to bed.	I can't draw a *straight* line.

Some adverbs have two forms, one without and one with the *ly: cheap, cheaply; close, closely; deep, deeply; hard, hardly; high, highly; late, lately; loud, loudly; quick, quickly; right, rightly; slow, slowly.* In some of these pairs the words are interchangeable; in most they are not. The idiomatic use of adverbs is a rather complex matter; no rules can be made that govern every situation. We can, however, make a few generalizations that reflect present-day practice:

1. The shorter form of a few of these—*late, hard,* and *near,* for example—fills most adverbial functions because the corresponding *ly* forms have acquired special meanings:

We must not stay *late.*	I have not seen him *lately* [recently].
I studied *hard* last night.	I *hardly* [scarcely] know him.
Winter is drawing *near.*	I *nearly* [almost] missed the last flight.

2. The *ly* form tends toward the formal, with the short form lending itself to more casual, informal speech and writing:

It fell *close* to the target.	You must watch him *closely.*
They ate *high* off the hog.	She was *highly* respected.
Drive *slow!*	Please drive more *slowly.*
Must you sing so *loud?*	He *loudly* denied the charges.
We searched *far* and *wide.*	She is *widely* known as an artist.

229

3. Because the short form seems more direct and forceful, it is often used in imperative sentences:

Hold *firm* to this railing.
"Come *quick*," yelled the officer.

4. The short form is often the one used when combined with an adjective to make a compound modifier preceding a noun:

a *wide*-ranging species	The species ranges *widely*.
a *slow*-moving truck	The truck moved *slowly*.

For the sake of simplifying the problem of the right use of adverbs and adjectives, we may say that there are three main trouble spots:

1. Misusing an adjective for an adverb. A word is an adverb if it modifies a verb, an adjective, or another adverb. The words that usually cause trouble here are *good, bad, well; sure, surely; real, really; most, almost; awful, awfully;* and *some, somewhat:*

Chip played *well* [not *good*] in the last game. [Modifies the verb *played*.]
This paint adheres *well* [not *good*] to concrete. [Modifies the verb *adheres*.]
Almost [not *Most*] every student has a job. [Modifies the adjective *every*.]
Today my shoulder is *really* [or *very*—not *real*] sore. [Modifies the adjective *sore*.]
He was driving *really* [or *very*—not *real*] fast. [Modifies the adverb *fast*.]
This rain has been falling *steadily* [not *steady*] for a week.
The champion should win his first match *easily* [not *easy*].
You'll improve if you practice *regularly* [not *regular*].
She wants that prize very *badly* [not *bad*].

2. Misusing an adverb for an adjective in the subjective complement. The most common verb to take the subjective complement is *be;* fortunately mistakes with this verb are nearly impossible. A few other verbs—like *seem, become, appear, prove, grow, go, turn, stay,* and *remain,* when they are used in a sense very close to that of *be*—take subjective complements. This complement must be an adjective, not an adverb.

The house *seems empty*. [House *is* empty.]
Their plans *became apparent*. [Plans *were* apparent.]
The work *proved very hard*. [Work *was* hard.]

The adjective subjective complement is also used with another group of verbs, the so-called verbs of the senses. These are *feel, look, smell, sound,* and *taste:*

You shouldn't feel *bad* about this. [Not *badly*.]
His cough sounds *bad* this morning. [Not *badly*.]
At first our prospects looked *bad*. [Not *badly*.]
Doesn't the air smell *sweet* today? [Not *sweetly*.]

The verb *feel* is involved in two special problems. In the first place, it is often used with both *good* and *well*. These two words have different meanings; one is not a substitute for the other. When used with the verb *feel, well* is an adjective meaning "in good health." The adjective *good*, when used with *feel*, means "filled with a sense of vigor and excitement." Of course, both *well* and *good* have other meanings when used with other verbs. In the second place, the expression "I feel badly" has been used so widely, especially in spoken English, that it can hardly be considered an error in usage. Many careful writers, however, prefer the adjective here, with the result that "feel bad" is usually found in written English.

3. Misusing a comparative or a superlative form of a modifier. (For a discussion of the comparison of adjectives, see Lesson 2.) Most adverbs are compared in the same way as adjectives. Some common adverbs cannot be compared, such as *here, now, then, when,* and *before.* As you learned in Lesson 16, we use the comparative degree *(taller, better, more intelligent, more rapidly)* in a comparison limited to two things. We use the superlative degree *(tallest, best, most intelligent, most rapidly)* for more than two things. Two other problems, both of minor importance, are involved in comparisons. First, we do not combine the two forms *(more + er, most + est)* in forming the comparative and superlative degrees:

Later the landlord became *friendlier* [not *more friendlier*].
Please drive *slower* [not *more slower*].
Please drive *more slowly* [not *more slower*].

Second, some purists object to the comparison of the so-called absolute qualities, such as *unique* ("being the only one"), *perfect, round, exact,* and so forth. They argue that, instead of such uses as *most perfect, straighter, more unique,* the intended meaning is *most nearly perfect, more nearly straight, more nearly unique.* General usage, however, has pretty well established both forms.

Three reminders should be made about the use of prepositions. One problem is the selection of the exact preposition for the meaning intended:

1. Many words, especially verbs and adjectives, give their full meaning only when modified by a prepositional phrase. In most cases the meaning of the preposition dictates a logical idiom: to sit *on* a couch, to walk *with* a friend, to lean *against* a fence, and so on. For some more abstract concepts, however, the acceptable preposition may seem to have been selected arbitrarily. Here are a few examples of different meanings of different prepositions:

agree *to* a proposal, *with* a person, *on* a price, *in* principle
argue *about* a matter, *with* a person, *for* or *against* a proposition
compare *to* to show likenesses, *with* to show differences [sometimes similarities]
correspond *to* a thing, *with* a person
differ *from* an unlike thing, *with* a person
live *at* an address, *in* a house or city, *on* a street, *with* other people

NOTE: Any good modern dictionary will provide information about and examples of the correct usage of prepositions.

2. Although at colloquial levels of language we sometimes find unnecessary prepositions used, examples like the following are improved in serious contexts if written without the words in brackets:

I met [up with] your uncle yesterday.
We keep our dog inside [of] the house.
Our cat, however, sleeps outside [of] the house.
The package fell off [of] the speeding truck.
The garage is [in] back of the cottage.

Avoid especially the needless preposition at the end of a sentence or the repeated preposition in adjective clauses and in direct or indirect questions:

Where is your older brother *at*?
He is one of the few people *to* whom I usually feel superior *to*. [Use one or the other, but not both.]
To what do you attribute your luck at poker *to*?

3. When two words of a compound unit require the same preposition to be idiomatically correct, the preposition need not be stated with the first unit:

Correct: We were both *repelled* and *fascinated by* the snake charmer's act.

But when the two units require different prepositions, both must be expressed:

Incomplete: The child shows an *interest* and a *talent for* music. [interest . . .*for* (?)]

Correct: The child shows an *interest in* and a *talent for* music.

Incomplete: I am sure that Ms. Lewis would both *contribute* and *gain from* a summer workshop.

Correct: I am sure that Ms. Lewis would both *contribute to* and *gain from* a summer workshop.

Practice Sheet 25
Using Modifiers Correctly

NAME _____ SCORE _____

Directions: In the first space at the left, write the word or words that the italicized word modifies. In the second space write Adj. if the italicized word is an adjective or Adv. if it is an adverb.

_____ 1. Jim looked *happy* because he made an A on the test.
_____

_____ 2. Tim was *certain* that Jim had arrived yesterday.
_____

_____ 3. Arthur *certainly* thought that you had his textbook.
_____

_____ 4. On the map, that mountainous road looks *straight*.
_____

_____ 5. We watched *closely* as the band went through its morning practice.
_____

_____ 6. Jan did not feel *good* about her performance in last night's game.
_____

_____ 7. Alan went *outside* to watch the meteor shower.
_____

_____ 8. "We have only an *outside* chance of finding Racquel in this huge crowd," said Lois.
_____

_____ 9. The distribution of that political pamphlet was quite *wide*.
_____

_____ 10. The candidate's staff distributed that political pamphlet quite *widely*.
_____

_____ 11. The recent debate was one of the *most* exciting times in the political campaign.
_____

_____ 12. *Most* debaters got their training in high school.
_____

_____ 13. After the treatment on his ankle, Bart did not feel *well* for about three hours.
_____

_____ 14. Bart did feel, however, that he got *good* results from the treatment.
_____

_____ 15. The treatment is highly sophisticated and usually works quite *well*.
_____

_____ 16. "I'm exhausted," whined Harry; "can we walk *slower*?"
_____

_____ 17. The *slower* pace allowed Harry to recover his energy.
_____

_____ 18. Kelly is very *interested* in political developments in Central Europe.
_____

_____ 19. Janice ran a *better* time in the last marathon than she did in the earlier one.
_____

_____ 20. My room looks *better* since I painted it.
_____

Directions: In the space at the left, copy the correct form given in the parentheses.

_____ 1. That computer screen does not work (good, well) in a brightly lit room.

_____ 2. The (bright, brightly) lights obscure the images.

_____ 3. Cynthia's GPA has improved (considerable, considerably) in the past two semesters.

_____ 4. The color of the walls in that room is not a (true, truly) blue.

_____ 5. To improve your putting stroke, hold your putter a little more (loose, loosely).

_____ 6. Because my addition was not done (correct, correctly), my checkbook is out of balance.

_____ 7. Jill had not practiced her serve for weeks; in the match serving was (harder, more harder) than anything else.

_____ 8. Although Ronnie was not actually sick, he really looked (bad, badly).

_____ 9. "I look at that decision (different, differently) now that I know the background," said Angelo.

_____ 10. The beautiful red leaves fell (gentle, gently) to the ground when the breeze blew.

_____ 11. "I chose to read *Heart of Darkness* because it was the (shorter, shortest) book on the required list," said Jo.

_____ 12. Theresa does not feel (good, well); she thinks she is catching a cold.

_____ 13. Only one of the stocks chosen by our investment club has performed (poor, poorly).

_____ 14. "You didn't stir that paint (good, well) enough," said James; "it looks all streaky on the wall."

_____ 15. Babs is certainly smiling and happy this morning; she must feel (good, well) about the world.

_____ 16. (Sure, Surely) we can find something more exciting to do than going to that mall again.

_____ 17. Doing the research (proper, properly) did not take a great deal of time.

_____ 18. Ask Terry to come in early; she seems to think (better, more better) at that time of day.

_____ 19. The cake baking in the oven smells (wonderful, wonderfully).

_____ 20. (Almost, most) every student will take that test tomorrow morning.

USING MODIFIERS AND PREPOSITIONS CORRECTLY

NAME _____   SCORE _____

Directions: Study these sentences for misused adjectives, adverbs, and prepositions. If you find a misused modifier, underline it and write the correct form in the space at the left. If you find a superfluous preposition, circle it and write *omit* in the space at the left. If you find a spot that requires a preposition, write the preposition in the space at the left and use a caret (^) to show where it should be inserted in the sentence. Some sentences are correct as they stand; in these cases leave the spaces blank.

_____   1. The students' reaction to that announcement was negative; they have been talking angry for several moments now.

_____   2. Richard started work early this morning and has now completed most all of the research for his paper.

_____   3. My cup slid off of the table and spattered coffee in a wide pattern on the carpet.

_____   4. Rick said, "I stayed up late last night studying, and this morning I don't feel well at all."

_____   5. The boys polished the car real well, but the paint still doesn't look very good.

_____   6. Can you tell me where I can buy one of those special mechanical pencils at?

_____   7. "We need to try more harder," said Angela; "we haven't really accomplished much yet."

_____   8. I was intrigued and frightened by that new mystery novel about the serial killer.

_____   9. "Please work more quietly in the back of the room," said Mrs. White quite loud.

_____   10. Rose worked very diligent, but her efforts did not prove to be very fruitful.

_____   11. Walden is a really small college; it's the kind of place in which I don't feel comfortable in.

_____   12. The yard certainly looks differently now that we have carefully trimmed the shrubs.

_____ 13. "My time in the race was not very good," said Martha; "I wanted to run a little more faster."

_____ 14. Mr. Ramsey told June that she had not itemized her hours on the timecard specific enough.

_____ 15. Jaime was sure happy that he had gotten a good grade on that extremely difficult test.

_____ 16. The rain fell intermittently, but the wind blew continuously all afternoon.

_____ 17. We were all amazed at Jeremy's interest and efforts for his sister's T-ball team.

_____ 18. Loretta's brilliant performance on the balance beam seemed almost effortless.

_____ 19. No matter how effortlessly her performance seemed, we all knew it was an exhausting routine.

_____ 20. My confidence and respect for Mr. Tate has diminished considerably since he first came to work here.

_____ 21. Pull that rope more tighter; I don't want the flag to slip down from the top of the pole.

_____ 22. "Do you remember clearly where we parked the car at when we drove into the parking lot?" asked Meredith.

_____ 23. The steps were icy but we walked very careful and did not slip.

_____ 24. The human resources department selected you because you will contribute and benefit from the conference.

_____ 25. The pitching at last night's game was excellent, but our fielders played very badly all night long.

LESSON 26 ■
A Glossary of Usage

In many of the entries in the following list, the other forms suggested are those usually preferred in standard formal English—the English appropriate to your term papers, theses, term reports, examination papers in all your courses, and most of the serious papers written for your English classes. Many of the words or expressions in brackets, marked *not,* are appropriate enough in informal conversation and in some informal papers.

Some of the entries are labeled *colloquial,* a term you should not think of as referring to slang, to forms used only in certain localities, or to "bad" English. The term applies to usages that are appropriate to informal and casual *spoken* English rather than to formal written English. However, the expressions marked *substandard* should be avoided at all times.

A, an. Use *a* when the word immediately following it is sounded as a consonant; use *an* when the next sound is a vowel sound: *a, e, i, o,* or *u* (*a* friend, *an* enemy). Remember that it is the consonantal or vowel *sound,* not the actual letter, that determines the choice of the correct form of the indefinite article: *a* sharp curve, *an* S-curve; *a* eulogy, *an* empty house; *a* hospital, *an* honest person; *a* united people, *an* uneven contest.

Ad. Clipped forms of many words are used informally, such as *ad (advertisement), doc (doctor), exam (examination), gent (gentleman), gym (gymnasium), lab (laboratory), math (mathematics),* and *prof (professor).* Formal usage requires the long forms.

Aggravate. In standard formal English the word means "make more severe," "make worse." Colloquially it means "annoy," "irritate," "exasperate."

> Walking on your sprained ankle will aggravate the hurt. [*Informal:* All criticism aggravates him.]

Ain't. Substandard for *am not, are not, is not, have not.*

> Am I not [not *Ain't I*] a good citizen?
> The command hasn't [not *hain't* or *ain't*] been given yet.
> They are not [not *ain't*] going either.

All the farther, all the faster, and the like. Generally regarded as colloquial equivalents of *as far as, as fast as,* and the like.

> This is as far as [not *all the farther*] I care to go.
> That was as fast as [not *all the faster*] he could run.

A lot of. See *Lots of.*

Alright. This spelling, like *all-right* or *allright,* although often used in advertising, is generally regarded as very informal usage. The preferred form is *all right.* In strictly formal usage, *satisfactory* or *very well* is preferred to *all right.*

> Very well [not *Alright*], you may ride in our car.
> The members agreed that the allocation of funds was satisfactory [not *all right*].

Among, between. *Among* is used with three or more persons or things, as in "Galileo was among the most talented people of his age," or "The estate was divided among his three sons." *Be-*

tween usually refers to two things, as in "between you and me," "between two points," "between dawn and sunset."

Amount, number. Use *number,* not *amount,* in reference to units that can actually be counted:

> the *amount* of indebtedness, the *number* of debts.

And etc. Because *etc. (et cetera)* means "and so forth," *and etc.* would mean "and and so forth." You should not use *etc.* to replace some exact, specific word, but if you do use it, be sure not to spell it *ect.* And remember that *etc.* requires a period after it.

Anywheres. Colloquial for *anywhere.* Similar colloquial forms are *anyways* for *anyway* or *anyhow, everywheres* for *everywhere, nowheres* for *nowhere, somewheres* for *somewhere.*

> I looked for my books everywhere. They must be hidden somewhere.

As, like. See *Like.*

As to whether. *Whether* is usually enough.

Awful, awfully. Like *aggravate,* these words have two distinct uses. In formal contexts, they mean "awe-inspiring" or "terrifying." Often in conversation and sometimes in writing of a serious nature, *awful* and *awfully* are mild intensifiers, meaning "very."

Because. See *Reason is because.*

Because of. See *Due to.*

Being that, being as how. Substandard for *because, as,* or *since.*

Beside, besides. These two prepositions are clearly distinguished by their meanings. *Beside* means "at the side of" and *besides* means "in addition to."

> Lucy sits beside me in class.
> Did anyone besides you see the accident?

Between. See *Among.*

But what, but that. Colloquial for *that.*

> Both sides had no doubt that [not *but what*] their cause was just.

Can, may. *Can* suggests ability to do something. *May* is the preferred form when permission is involved.

> Little Junior can already count to ten.
> May [not *Can*] I borrow your pencil?

Can't hardly, couldn't hardly, can't scarcely, couldn't scarcely. Substandard for *can hardly, could hardly, can scarcely, could scarcely.* These are sometimes referred to as double negatives.

> I can hardly [not *can't hardly*] believe that story.
> We could scarcely [not *couldn't scarcely*] hear the foghorn.

Caused by. See *Due to.*

Complected. Dialectal or colloquial for *complexioned.*

> Being light-complexioned [not *light-complected*], Sue must avoid prolonged exposure to sunlight.

Contact. Used as a verb meaning "to get in touch with," this word, probably because of its association with sales-promotion writing, annoys enough people to warrant caution in its use in serious writing.

Continual, continuous. A fine distinction in meaning can be made if you remember that *continual* means "repeated regularly and frequently" and that *continuous* means "occurring without interruption," "unbroken."

Could(n't) care less. This worn-out set phrase indicating total indifference is a colloquialism. A continuing marvel of language behavior is the large number of people who insist on saying "I could care less" when they obviously mean the opposite.

Could of, would of, might of, ought to of, and so on. Substandard for *could have, would have,* and so on.

Couple. Colloquial in the sense of *a few, several.*

> The senator desired to have a few [not *a couple*] changes made in the bill.

A couple of is standard English.

Criteria. The singular noun is *criterion;* the plural is *criteria* or *criterions.* Such combinations as *"a criteria," "one criteria"* and *"these criterias"* are incorrect.

Data. Originally the plural form of the rarely used Latin singular *datum, data* has taken on a collective meaning so that it is often treated as a singular noun. "This data has been published" and "These data have been published" are both correct, the latter being the use customarily found in scientific or technical writing.

Different from, different than. *Different from* is generally correct. Many people object to *different than,* but others use it, especially when a clause follows, as in "Life in the Marines was different than he had expected it to be."

> Their customs are different from [not *different than*] ours.
> Life in the Marines was different from what he had expected it to be.

Different to, a form sometimes used by British speakers and writers, is rarely used in the United States.

Disinterested, uninterested. Many users of precise English deplore the tendency to treat these words as loose synonyms, keeping a helpful distinction between *disinterested* ("impartial," "free from bias or self-interest") and *uninterested* ("lacking in interest," "unconcerned"). Thus we would hope that a referee would be disinterested but not uninterested.

Due to, caused by, because of, owing to. *Due to* and *caused by* are used correctly after the verb *to be:*

> His illness was caused by a virus.
> The flood was due to the heavy spring rains.

Many people object to the use of *due to* and *caused by* adverbially at the beginning of a sentence, as in "Due to the heavy rains, the streams flooded," and "Caused by the storm, the roads were damaged." It is better to use *because of*

in similar situations. *Due to* is also used correctly as an adjective modifier immediately following a noun:

> Accidents due to excessive speed are increasing in number.

Note in the examples what variations are possible:

> The streams flooded because of the heavy rains.
> The flooding of the streams was due to the heavy rains.
> The floods were caused by the rapid melting of the snow.

Emigrate, immigrate. To *emigrate* is to *leave* one region to settle in another; to *immigrate* is to *enter* a region from another one.

Enthuse. Colloquial or substandard (depending on the degree of a person's aversion to this word) for *be enthusiastic, show enthusiasm.*

> The director was enthusiastic [not *enthused*] about her new program.

Everywheres. See *Anywheres.*

Farther, further. Careful writers observe a distinction between these two words, reserving *farther* for distances that can actually be measured.

> Tony can hit a golf ball farther than I can.
> We must pursue this matter further.

Fewer, less. *Fewer* refers to numbers, *less* to quantity, extent, or degree.

> Fewer [not *Less*] students are taking courses in literature this year.
> Food costs less, but we have less money to spend.

Figure. Colloquial for *consider, think, believe, suppose.*

> He must have thought [not *figured*] that nobody would see him enter the bank.

Fine. Colloquial, very widely used, for *well, very well.*

> The boys played well [not *just fine*].

Graffiti. The singular form is *graffito.* In serious writing *graffiti* takes a plural verb. Avoid combinations such as "a graffiti," "this graffiti," etc.

Had(n't) ought. *Ought* does not take an auxiliary.

> You ought [not *had ought*] to apply for a scholarship.
> You ought not [not *hadn't ought*] to miss the lecture.

Hardly. See *Can't hardly.*

Healthy, healthful. *Healthy* means "having health," and *healthful* means "giving health." Thus a person or an animal is healthy; a climate, a food, or an activity is healthful.

Immigrate. See *Emigrate.*

Imply, infer. Despite the increasing tendency to use these words more or less interchangeably, it is good to preserve the distinction: *Imply* means "to say something indirectly," "to hint or suggest," and *infer* means "to draw a conclusion," "to deduce." Thus you *imply* something in what you say and *infer* something from what you hear.

Incredible, incredulous. An unbelievable *thing* is incredible; a disbelieving *person* is incredulous.

In regards to. The correct forms are *in regard to* or *as regards.*

Inside of. *Inside* or *within* is preferred in formal writing.

> We stayed inside [not *inside of*] the barn during the storm.
> The plane should arrive within [not *inside of*] an hour.

Invite. Slang for *invitation.*

> They will be sent an invitation [not *invite*] to join us in a peace conference.

Irregardless. Substandard or humorous for *regardless.*

> The planes bombed the area regardless [not *irregardless*] of consequences.

Is when, is where. The *is-when, is-where* pattern in definitions is clumsy and should be avoided. Write, for example, "An embolism is an obstruction, such as a blood clot, in the bloodstream," instead of "An embolism is where an obstruction forms in the bloodstream."

Kind, sort. These words are singular and therefore should be modified by singular modifiers. Do not write *these kind, these sort, those kind, those sort.*

> Those kinds [not *those kind*] of videos sell very well.
> Who could believe that sort [not *those sort*] of arguments?

Kinda, sorta, kind of a, sort of a. Undesirable forms.

Kind of, sort of. Colloquial for *somewhat, in some degree, almost, rather.*

> They felt somewhat [not *sort of*] depressed.

Learn, teach. *Learn* means "to acquire knowledge"; *teach* means "to give or impart knowledge."

> Ms. Brown taught [not *learned*] me Spanish.

Leave. Not to be used for *let.*

> Let [not *Leave*] me carry your books for you.

Less. See *Fewer.*

Let. See *Leave.*

Let's us. The *us* is superfluous, because *let's* means "let us."

Like, as, as if. The use of *like* as a conjunction (in other words, to introduce a clause) is colloquial. It should be avoided in serious writing.

> As [not *Like*] you were told earlier, there is a small entry fee.
> She acts as if [not *like*] she distrusts us.
> Do as [not *like*] I tell you.

Line. Often vague and redundant, as in "What do you read *in the line of books*?" "Don't you enjoy fishing and other sports *along that line*?" It is better to say, more directly,

> What kind of books do you read?
> Don't you enjoy fishing and sports like that?

Lots of, a lot of. Colloquial in the sense of *many, much.*

> Many [not *Lots of*] families vacation here every summer.
> The storms caused us much [not *lots of*] trouble that spring.
> All of us owe you much [not *a lot* or *alot*].

Mad. Colloquially *mad* is often used to mean "angry." In formal English, it means "insane."

> Marge was angry [not *mad*] because I was late.

May. See *Can.*

Media. A plural noun, currently in vogue to refer to all mass communicative agencies. The singular is *medium.* Careful writers and speakers avoid the use of *media* as a singular noun, as in "Television is an influential media." Even more objectionable is the use of *medias* as a plural.

Might of. See *Could of.*

Most. This word is the superlative form of *much* and *many* (much, more, most; many, more, most). Its use as a clipped form of *almost* is colloquial.

> Almost [not *Most*] all of my friends work during the summer.

Nauseated, nauseous. Despite the increasingly wide use of these words as synonyms, there are still speakers and writers of precise English who insist that *nauseated* should be used to mean "suffering from or experiencing nausea" and that *nauseous* should be used only to mean "causing nausea."

Nohow. This emphatic negative is substandard.

Not all that. A basically meaningless substitute for *not very* or *not really;* it can easily become a habit.

> The movie was not very [not *not all that*] amusing.

Nowheres. See *Anywheres.*

Number. See *Amount.*

Of. See *Could of.*

Off of. Dialectal or colloquial for *off.*

> She asked me to get off [not *off of*] my high horse.

OK. This form calls attention to itself in serious writing. It is appropriate only to business communications and casual speech or writing. Modern dictionaries offer several permissible forms: *OK, O.K.,* and *okay* for the singular noun; *OKs, O.K.s,* and *okays* for the plural noun; and *OK'd, OK'ing, O.K.'d, O.K.'ing, okayed,* and *okaying* for verb forms.

Ought. See *Had(n't) ought.*

Ought to of. See *Could of.*

Owing to. See *Due to.*

Party. Colloquial in the sense of *man, woman, person.*

> Dr. Tartar, a man [not *party*] is waiting for you in your office.

Plenty. Colloquial for *very, extremely, fully. Plenty* is a noun, not an adjective or an adverb.

> Filmore's defensive work in the second half was very [not *plenty*] effective.

Plenty of is standard English.

Quote, unquote. Although these words may be needed in the oral presentation of quoted material, they have no use in written material, in which quotation marks or indentation sets off the quoted material from the text proper.

Real, really. The use of *real,* which is an adjective, to modify another adjective or an adverb is colloquial. In formal contexts *really* or *very* should be used.

> We had a really [not *real*] enjoyable visit.
> The motorcycle rounded the corner very [not *real*] fast.

Reason is because, reason is due to, reason is on account of. In serious writing, a *reason is* clause is usually completed with *that,* not with *because, due to,* or *on account of.*

> The reason they surrendered is that [not *because*] they were starving.

The reason for my low grades is that I have poor eyesight [not *is on account of my poor eyesight*].

Same. The use of *same* as a pronoun, often found in legal or business writing, is inappropriate in most other types of writing.

I received your report and look forward to reading it [not *the same*].

Scarcely. See *Can't hardly.*

So, such. These words, when used as exclamatory intensifiers, are not appropriate in a formal context. Sentences like the following belong in informal talk: "I am *so* tired," "She is *so* pretty," or "They are having *such* a good time."

Some. Colloquial for *somewhat, a little.*

The situation at the border is said to be somewhat [not *some*] improved today.

Somewheres. See *Anywheres.*

Sort. See *Kind.*

Such. See *So.*

Suppose to. See *Use to.*

Sure. *Sure* is correctly used as an adjective:

We are not sure about her plans.
He made several sure investments.

Sure is colloquial when used as an adverbial substitute for *surely, extremely, certainly, indeed, very, very much.*

The examination was surely [not *sure*] difficult.
The lawyer's plea certainly [not *sure*] impressed the jury.

Sure and. See *Try and.*

Suspicion. *Suspicion* is a noun; it is not to be used as a verb in place of *suspect.*

No one suspected [not *suspicioned*] the victim's widow.

Swell. Not to be used as a general term of approval meaning *good, excellent, attractive, desirable,* and so on.

Teach. See *Learn.*

That there, this here, those there, these here. Substandard for *that, this, those, these.*

Them. Substandard when used as an adjective.

How can you eat those [not *them*] parsnips?

Try and, sure and. *Try to, sure to* are the preferred forms in serious writing.

We shall try to [not *try and*] make your visit a pleasant one.
Be sure to [not *sure and*] arrive on time.

Type. Colloquial when used as a modifier of a noun. Use *type of* or *kind of.*

I usually don't enjoy that type of [not *type*] movie.

Uninterested. See *Disinterested.*

Use to, suppose to. Although these incorrect forms are difficult to detect in spoken English, remember that the correct written forms are *used to, supposed to.*

Want in, want off, want out. Colloquial and dialectical forms for *want to come in, want to get off, want to go out.* Inappropriate in serious writing.

Ways. Colloquial for *way,* in such expressions as

It is just a short distance [not *ways*] up the canyon.
We do not have a long way [not *ways*] to go.

What. Substandard when used for *who, which,* or *that* as a relative pronoun in an adjective clause.

His raucous laugh is the thing that [not *what*] annoys me most.

When, where clauses. See *Is when.*

Where . . . at. The *at* is unnecessary. Undesirable in both speech and writing.

Where [not *Where at*] will you be at noon?
Where is your car? [Not *Where is your car at?*]

-wise. The legitimate function of this suffix to form adverbs like *clockwise* does not carry with it the license to concoct such jargon as "Entertainmentwise this town is a dud" or "This investment is very attractive long-term-capital-gains-wise."

Without. Not to be used as a conjunction instead of *unless.*

He won't lend me his car unless [not *without*] I fill the gas tank.

Worst way. Not acceptable for *greatly, very much, exceedingly,* and similar words.

Della wanted very much [not *in the worst way*] to become a vocalist with a rock group.

Would of. See *Could of.*

Practice Sheet 26

Appropriate Use

NAME _____ SCORE _____

Directions: In the space at the left, write the number of the expression given in parentheses that you consider the more appropriate form to use in serious writing.

_____ 1. Martin thought we (1. had ought, 2. ought) to (1. learn, 2. teach) the of-
_____   fice staff how to operate the paper shredder.

_____ 2. (1. That, 2. Those) kind of remark ordinarily makes a police officer ex-
_____   tremely (1. angry, 2. mad).

_____ 3. (1. Lots of, 2. Many) of the questions from the audience seemed (1. kind
_____   of, 2. rather) hostile, didn't they?

_____ 4. I didn't (1. figure, 2. think) that more than a (1. couple, 2. couple of)
_____   people would attend the award ceremony.

_____ 5. (1. Because of, 2. Due to) the size of the prize, a vast (1. amount,
_____   2. number) of people are buying lottery tickets.

_____ 6. Ken stared (1. incredibly, 2. incredulously) as Karl told a story (1. imply-
_____   ing, 2. inferring) that he had seen a UFO.

_____ 7. A student applying to our graduate school must meet several (1. real,
_____   2. very) strict (1. criteria, 2. criterion).

_____ 8. The (1. continual, 2. continuous) rush of water over the falls seemed to
_____   (1. aggravate, 2. irritate) Richard's nervous state.

_____ 9. (1. Being that, 2. Because) spring is almost here, we (1. should have,
_____   2. should of) already repaired the tractor.

_____ 10. The reason we are so tired this morning is (1. because, 2. that) the weather
_____   yesterday was (1. awfully, 2. extremely) hot.

_____ 11. "There are (1. fewer, 2. less) people here today than I (1. would have,
_____   2. would of) expected," said Jackson.

_____ 12. People are (1. real, 2. really) (1. enthused, 2. enthusiastic) about that new
_____   CD–ROM in the library.

_____ 13. "Do you have any doubt (1. but that, 2. that) (1. among, 2. between) the
_____   two of us we can solve that silly riddle?" asked Josh.

_____ 14. (1. Irregardless, 2. Regardless) of Ms. Jones's opinion, I think we should
_____   (1. try and, 2. try to) finish that report soon.

_____ 15. (1. Can, 2. May) we find a (1. disinterested, 2. uninterested) person to re-
_____   solve that dispute?

_____ 16. Marge said, "I (1. ain't, 2. am not) tired, but another mile is (1. all the far-
_____   ther, 2. as far as) I can go today."

_____ 17. Morris's work is usually (1. all right, 2. satisfactory), but today he seems
_____   (1. nowhere, 2. nowheres) near his usual standard.

_____ 18. The climate here is not very (1. healthful, 2. healthy); we should consider
_____   moving (1. farther, 2. further) into the mountains.

_____ 19. (1. Beside, 2. Besides) Jim, did anyone else (1. call, 2. contact) the radio
_____   station about running our announcement?

_____ 20. These new (1. data, 2. datum) suggest that fewer people have (1. emi-
_____   grated, 2. immigrated) from the United States in the last six months.

Directions: Each sentence contains two italicized words or expressions. If you think that the word or expression is inappropriate in serious writing, write an acceptable form in the space at the left. If an expression is correct, write C in the space.

_____
_____
1. We *should of* known that Yolanda would act *like* she didn't want to go to the movies.

_____
_____
2. Shelly badly wanted to get *off of* that program because she is not very *enthusiastic* about the subject matter.

_____
_____
3. *Most* all of the people assigned to that project work *real* well together.

_____
_____
4. The reason that we left early is *because* class was dismissed *due to* a power failure.

_____
_____
5. Mr. Sweeney *wants out* of that deal because he *suspicions* that one partner is dishonest.

_____
_____
6. Four of *them* fine snow tires would *sure* make driving safer this winter.

_____
_____
7. *Lots of* people do not believe that *those data,* taken from opinion polls, reflect the opinions of all citizens.

_____
_____
8. Alicia spent a *couple* thousand dollars on that stereo, but that amount is *less* money than she planned to spend.

_____
_____
9. Our proposal is different *than* theirs in ways that are *not all that* important.

_____
_____
10. "Our candidate has nothing *in the line of* a response *in regards* to that accusation," said the press secretary.

_____
_____
11. If the reporters look *farther,* I have no doubt *that* they will discover some problems.

_____
_____
12. Melanie ought to *of* dropped that course because she was so *uninterested* in the subject matter.

_____
_____
13. *Can* you tell me where the trail to Abrams Falls begins *at*?

_____
_____
14. *Let's us* ask for directions; the map Jim gave us is *awfully* faded.

_____
_____
15. *Beside* Martha, Alex *use* to be the only person who knew the passwords to the office computer files.

_____
_____
16. "*Being that* I lost all my note cards, I'm a long *ways* from finishing my research project," groaned Terry.

_____
_____
17. *A large amount* of people in the class *inferred* from the teacher's remarks that the test had been postponed.

_____
_____
18. *These kind* of clumsy procedures *aggravate* people who are trying to get a library card.

_____
_____
19. We should try *and* find some new *criteria* for selecting candidates for public office.

_____
_____
20. *Being that* voter turnout was heavy, the lines at the polls were *kind of* long.

EXERCISE 26

APPROPRIATE USE

NAME _____ SCORE _____

Directions: In the space at the left, write the number of the expression given in parentheses that you consider the more appropriate form to use in serious writing.

_____ 1. "I would like to (1. contact, 2. talk to) the (1. party, 2. person) who banged
_____ into my car," said Lisa.

_____ 2. The lab technicians (1. should have, 2. should of) called me when they saw
_____ changes in all the (1. data, 2. datum) in that experiment.

_____ 3. (1. Being as how, 2. Since) we were (1. suppose, 2. supposed) to leave yes-
_____ terday and didn't, we called to change our reservations.

_____ 4. (1. Irregardless, 2. Regardless) of your financial condition, you must pay
_____ (1. almost all, 2. most all) of your tuition by Friday.

_____ 5. Jill became (1. nauseated, 2. nauseous) (1. because of, 2. due to) the ex-
_____ tremely sharp curves on that mountain road.

_____ 6. Jack says that he is not (1. all that, 2. very) (1. enthusiastic, 2. enthused)
_____ about that midwinter camping trip.

_____ 7. The reason June was selected for the program is (1. because, 2. that) she
_____ had an (1. incredible, 2. incredulous) story to tell.

_____ 8. "We've seen (1. fewer, 2. less) (1. real, 2. really) close baseball games this
_____ season," said the announcer.

_____ 9. The instructor's statement seemed to (1. imply, 2. infer) that this diet is
_____ not (1. healthful, 2. healthy).

_____ 10. In our early history people (1. use, 2. used) to employ shells or beads as
_____ a (1. media, 2. medium) of exchange.

_____ 11. (1. Beside, 2. Besides) Andrew, there is no (1. disinterested, 2. uninter-
_____ ested) person available to referee the match.

_____ 12. "The new sewage treatment plant works (1. just fine, 2. quite well)," said
_____ the engineer, "but the cost was (1. awfully, 2. very) high."

_____ 13. Our route didn't take us (1. anywhere, 2. anywheres) near the park, but we
_____ were not (1. all that, 2. at all) interested in seeing it.

_____ 14. The president (1. could have, 2. could of) hired a consultant, but she
_____ wanted the staff to (1. try and, 2. try to) find a solution.

_____ 15. (1. Due to, 2. Because of) a heavy influx of tourists, we (1. could hardly,
_____ 2. couldn't hardly) find a hotel room for Mac.

_____ 16. We didn't drive much (1. farther, 2. further) because we had lost track of
_____ the (1. amount, 2. number) of miles we had traveled.

_____ 17. "Just (1. among, 2. between) us three," said Morris, "I thought that was
_____ the most (1. aggravating, 2. irritating) memorandum ever."

_____ 18. Tom is different (1. from, 2. than) Robert; Tom (1. figures, 2. thinks) that
_____ he can be successful in school.

_____ 19. (1. Unless, 2. Without) we find that lost file, we've gone (1. all the farther,
_____ 2. as far as) we can go on this project.

_____ 20. I (1. certainly, 2. sure) would like to find that report and read (1. it, 2. the
_____ same).

Directions: Each sentence contains two italicized words or expressions. If you think that a word or expression is inappropriate in serious writing, write an acceptable form in the space at the left. If you think the expression is correct, write C in the space.

1. "We *might of* gone *farther* in our discussion," said Reggie, "but the baseball game came on television."

2. *Plenty of* people believe that it is *okay* to leave before the end of a concert or a play.

3. Meryl acts *like* she is not too *enthused* about going on that three-day camping trip.

4. We left the campus *some* early today; the reason is *because* we wanted to get to the restaurant before the crowd.

5. Jim *inferred* from my comments that I do not want a large *amount* of people to come to the picnic.

6. "That test was no different *than* the others; I think I did *just fine*," said Will.

7. The men decided that they *should of* brought an axe, a good lantern, an ice chest, and *etc.* to the work site.

8. "I *can't hardly* go out in the sun," said Alex, "because I am so *light-complected.*"

9. The *continual* drip of the leaky faucet was *kinda* annoying to the students in the classroom.

10. Those *kind* of problems with computers are not *real* easily solved.

11. *Most* all the work of the committee is completed; we *hadn't ought to* need to work this Saturday.

12. "Will the *party* that left the red car in the driveway please move it *somewheres* else?" asked the announcer.

13. *Lots* of people want to *immigrate* from that strife-torn country.

14. June felt *somewhat nauseous* when the smell of leaking gas filled the room.

15. Little Jimmy hid himself *inside of* the closet because his big brother was *mad at* him.

16. No one in the college got an *invite* to the president's dinner, but our students could *care less* about that affair.

17. A *couple* items in my checkbook look like *graffiti* written on a wall; I can't read them at all.

18. "We sat *besides* Sylvester Stallone in the restaurant because there was *nowheres* else to sit," said Marge.

19. The various news *medias* sent people to cover that story even though the city seems *uninterested* in it.

20. *Due to* lack of enrollment, *them* dance classes have been cancelled.

PART VI Spelling and Capitalization

Lessons, Practice Sheets, and Exercises

LESSON 27 ■

Spelling Rules; Words Similar in Sound

Rule 1: A word ending in silent *e* generally drops the *e* before a suffix beginning with a vowel and retains the *e* before a suffix beginning with a consonant.

After *c* or *g*, if the suffix begins with *a* or *o*, the *e* is retained to preserve the soft sound of the *c* or *g*.

Drop E before a Vowel

become	+ ing	—becoming	hope	+ ing	—hoping
bride	+ al	—bridal	imagine	+ ary	—imaginary
conceive	+ able	—conceivable	noise	+ y	—noisy
desire	+ able	—desirable	remove	+ able	—removable
fame	+ ous	—famous	white	+ ish	—whitish
force	+ ible	—forcible	write	+ ing	—writing

Retain E before a Consonant

excite	+ ment	—excitement	life	+ like	—lifelike
force	+ ful	—forceful	pale	+ ness	—paleness
hope	+ less	—hopeless	sincere	+ ly	—sincerely

Retain E after C or G if the Suffix Begins with A or O

advantage	+ ous	—advantageous	notice	+ able	—noticeable
change	+ able	—changeable	outrage	+ ous	—outrageous
manage	+ able	—manageable	service	+ able	—serviceable

(See Supplement 1.)

249

Rule 2: In words with *ie* or *ei* when the sound is long *ee*, use *i* before *e* except after *c*.

Use **I** *before* **E**

apiece	frontier	priest
belief	grieve	reprieve
fiend	niece	shriek
fierce	pierce	thievery

Except after **C**

ceiling	conceive	perceive
conceited	deceit	receipt

The common exceptions to this rule may be easily remembered if you memorize the following sentence: Neither financier seized either species of weird leisure.

Rule 3: In words of one syllable and words accented on the last syllable, ending in a single consonant preceded by a single vowel, double the final consonant before a suffix beginning with a vowel.

Words of One Syllable—Suffix Begins with a Vowel

ban	—banned	hit	—hitting	rid	—riddance
bid	—biddable	hop	—hopping	Scot	—Scottish
dig	—digger	quit	—quitter	stop	—stoppage
drag	—dragged	["qu"-consonant]		wet	—wettest

Accented on Last Syllable—Suffix Begins with a Vowel

abhor	—abhorrence	equip	—equipping
acquit	—acquitted	occur	—occurrence
allot	—allotted	omit	—omitted
begin	—beginner	prefer	—preferring
commit	—committing	regret	—regrettable
control	—controlled	repel	—repellent

Not Accented on Last Syllable—Suffix Begins with a Vowel

differ	—different	open	—opener
happen	—happening	prefer	—preference
hasten	—hastened	sharpen	—sharpened

Suffix Begins with a Consonant

allot	—allotment	mother	—motherhood
color	—colorless	sad	—sadness
equip	—equipment	sin	—sinful

(See Supplement 1.)

An apparent exception to this rule affects a few words formed by the addition of *ing*, *ed*, or *y* to a word ending in *c*. To preserve the hard sound of the *c*, a *k* is added before the vowel of the suffix, resulting in such spellings as *frolicking, mimicked, panicked, panicky, picnicked,* and *trafficking*.

Another irregularity applies to such spellings as *quitting* and *equipped.* One might think that the consonant should not be doubled, reasoning that the final consonant is preceded by two vowels, not by a single vowel. But because *qu* is phonetically the equivalent of *kw,* the *u* is a consonant when it follows *q.* Therefore, because the final consonant is actually preceded by a single vowel, the consonant is doubled before the suffix.

Rule 4: Words ending in *y* preceded by a vowel retain the *y* before a suffix; most words ending in *y* preceded by a consonant change the *y* to *i* before a suffix.

Ending in Y Preceded by a Vowel

boy	—boyish	coy	—coyness	enjoy	—enjoying
buy	—buys	donkey	—donkeys	stay	—staying

Ending in Y Preceded by a Consonant

ally	—allies	easy	—easiest	pity	—pitiable
busy	—busily	icy	—icier	study	—studies
cloudy	—cloudiness	mercy	—merciless	try	—tried

The Y is Unchanged in Words Like the Following:

baby	—babyish	lady	—ladylike
carry	—carrying	study	—studying

Words Similar in Sound

Accept. I should like to accept your first offer.
Except. He took everything except the rugs.

Advice. Free advice [noun] is usually not worth much.
Advise. Ms. Hull said she would advise [verb] me this term. (Similarly, de*vice* [noun] and de*vise* [verb], prophe*cy* [noun] and prophe*sy* [verb].)

Affect. His forced jokes affect [verb] me unfavorably.
Effect. His humor has a bad effect [noun]. Let us try to effect [verb] a lasting peace.

All ready. They were all ready to go home.
Already. They had already left when we telephoned the house.

All together. Now that we are all together, let us talk it over.
Altogether. They were not altogether pleased with the results.

Altar. In this temple was an altar to the Unknown God.
Alter. One should not try to alter or escape history.

Canvas. We used a piece of canvas to shelter us from the wind.
Canvass. The candidate wanted to canvass every person in her precinct.

Capital. A capital letter; capital gains; capital punishment; state capital.
Capitol. Workers are painting the dome of the Capitol.

Cite. He cited three good examples.
Site. The site of the new school has not been decided on.

Sight. They were awed by the sight of so much splendor.

Coarse. The coarse sand blew in my face.
Course. We discussed the course to take. Of course he may come with us.

Complement. Your intelligence is a complement to your beauty.
Compliment. It is easier to pay a compliment than a bill.

Consul. Be sure to look up the American consul in Rome.
Council. He was appointed to the executive council.
Counsel. I sought counsel from my friends. They counseled moderation. He employed counsel to defend him.

Decent. The workers demanded a decent wage scale.
Descent. The descent from the mountain was uneventful.
Dissent. The voices of dissent were louder than those of approval.

Desert. Out in the lonely desert [noun—desert], he tried to desert [verb— desert] from his regiment.
Dessert. We had apple pie for dessert.

Dining. We eat dinner in our dining room. Dining at home is pleasant.
Dinning. Stop dinning that song into my ears!

Formerly. He was formerly a student at Beloit College.
Formally. You must address the presiding judge formally and respectfully.

Forth. Several witnesses came forth to testify.
Fourth. We planned a picnic for the Fourth of July.

Incidence. Better sanitation lowered the incidence of communicable diseases.
Incidents. Smugglers were involved in several incidents along the border.

Instance. For instance, she was always late to class.
Instants. As the car turned, those brief instants seemed like hours.

Its. Your plan has much in its favor. [Possessive of *it*.]
It's. It's too late now for excuses. [Contraction of *it is, it has.*]

Later. It is later than you think.
Latter. Of the two novels, I prefer the latter.

Lead. Can you lead [lēd—verb] us out of this jungle? Lead [lĕd—noun] is a heavy, soft, malleable metallic element.
Led. A local guide led us to the salmon fishing hole.

Loose. He has a loose tongue. The dog is loose again.
Lose. Don't lose your temper.

Passed. She smiled as she passed me. She passed the test.
Past. It is futile to try to relive the past.

Personal. Write him a personal letter.
Personnel. The morale of our company's personnel is high.

Pore. For hours they pored over the mysterious note.
Pour. Ms. Cook poured hot water into the teapot.

Precedence. Tax reform takes precedence over all other legislative matters.
Precedents. The judge quoted three precedents to justify his ruling.

Presence. We are honored by your presence.
Presents. The child received dozens of Christmas presents.

Principal. The principal of a school; the principal [chief] industry; the principal and the interest.
Principle. He is a man of high principles.

Quiet. You must keep quiet.
Quite. The weather was quite good all week.

Rain. A soaking rain would help our crops greatly.
Reign. Samuel Pepys was briefly imprisoned during the reign of William III.
Rein. Keep a tight rein when you ride this spirited horse.

Shone. The cat's eyes shone in the dark.
Shown. He hasn't shown us his best work.

Stationary. The benches were stationary and could not be moved.
Stationery. She wrote a letter on hotel stationery.

Statue. It was a statue of a pioneer.
Stature. Athos was a man of gigantic stature.
Statute. The law may be found in the 1917 book of statutes.

Than. She sings better than I.
Then. He screamed; then he fainted.

Their. It wasn't their fault. [Possessive pronoun.]
There. You won't find any gold there. [Adverb of place.]
They're. They're sure to be disappointed. [Contraction of *they are.*]

Thorough. We must first give the old cabin a thorough [adjective] cleaning.
Through. The thief had entered through [preposition] a hole in the roof.

To. Be sure to speak to her. [Preposition.]
Too. He is far too old for you. [Adverb.]
Two. The membership fee is only two dollars. [Adjective.]

Whose. Whose book is this? [Possessive pronoun.]
Who's. I wonder who's with her now. [Contraction of *who is.*]

Your. I like your new car. [Possessive pronoun.]
You're. You're not nervous, are you? [Contraction of *you are.*]

Supplement 1

(Rule 1): A few common adjectives with the suffix *able* have two correct spellings:

likable/likeable, lovable/loveable, movable/moveable, sizable/sizeable, usable/useable.

(Rule 3): Dictionaries show two spellings for the *-ed* and *-ing* forms (and a few other derived forms) of dozens of verbs ending in single consonants preceded by single vowels. In general, the single-consonant spelling is usually found in American printing; some of the dictionaries label the double-consonant spelling a British preference.

biased/biassed, canceling/cancelling, counselor/counsellor, diagraming/diagramming, equaled/equalled, marvelous/marvellous, modeled/modelled, totaling/totalling, traveler/traveller.

Practice Sheet **27**

Spelling Rules; Words Similar in Sound

NAME _____ SCORE _____

Directions: Each of the following sentences contains three italicized words, one of which is misspelled. Underline each misspelled word and write it, correctly spelled, in the space at the left.

_____ 1. Two *diferent pieces* of *equipment* are needed to complete that part of the paint job.

_____ 2. *Accept* for Audrey, everyone in the club had a *preference* for that new *colorless* cola drink.

_____ 3. The sailmaker will *alter* that piece of *canvass* to make it run *past* the end of the cockpit.

_____ 4. The *opening* of that *writting* lesson was *altogether* too difficult for most people in the class.

_____ 5. "Is it *conceivable* that Tom can do a *thorough* job in the time *alloted*?" asked Andrea.

_____ 6. Two of the men are *too* short to play the *role* opposite Ms. France, who is *extremly* tall.

_____ 7. A *removable* cover would be a *desireable* feature for a billiards table, if it is not *excessively* expensive.

_____ 8. The architects will *advice* the board about selecting a *site* for the stable for the *donkeys*.

_____ 9. It is *regretable* that we do not have the *capital* needed to fund the construction of a new *dining* hall.

_____ 10. Jan's *references* made her the *preffered* candidate; therefore, the *personnel* office offered her the job.

_____ 11. Any change in our *hireing policies* seems *unlikely* at this time.

_____ 12. One of Raymond's favorite *activities* is a *leisurely* walk along the lakeshore among *it's* beautiful trees.

_____ 13. After the two *incidence,* the *duties* of the *cashiers* were simplified considerably.

_____ 14. "*Your* not likely to find better *opportunities* for *studying* migratory birds," said the guide.

_____ 15. *There fourth* attempt to climb the mountain failed at the *iciest* part of the trail.

255

_____ 16. New cars are *fitted* with very *servicable batteries.*

_____ 17. She was an *adorable* baby, but she seemed to *loose* all her charming *qualities* as she grew older.

_____ 18. The firefighters made the difficult *dissent* from the top floor by *rappelling* down the outside *past* the fire zone.

_____ 19. Anne has *committed* herself to taking an *extremely* technical *coarse* in mechanical engineering.

_____ 20. One of the *presence* Marty *received* for his birthday contained large *quantities* of various chocolate candies.

_____ 21. Winning that tournament against such *fierce* competitors was *quiet* an *achievement.*

_____ 22. The *principle* reason Arline is *quitting* that job is that she finds it very *boring.*

_____ 23. The people *living* on Shorewood Road hope that the city *counsel* will provide funds for *repaving* its surface.

_____ 24. All the team members had a different reaction to the *weird, unforgetable occurrences* at the season's end.

_____ 25. The students who took that course have *shone* a *noticeable improvement* in their math scores.

_____ 26. *Latter* that day the three *buddies* gathered at the *desert* campsite for a steak dinner.

_____ 27. In his *journeys* around the West, Martin collected large *quantities* of *fascinateing* relics.

_____ 28. "Those were the *noisiest,* most *irritable* children we've ever had *picnicing* with us," said the guide.

_____ 29. The race leaders were *adversely effected* by the *changeable* winds and the high waves.

_____ 30. In all *likelihood* this year's team will *lose* more games *then* last year's.

EXERCISE 27

SPELLING RULES; WORDS SIMILAR IN SOUND

NAME _____ SCORE _____

Directions: Each of the following sentences contains three italicized words, one of which is misspelled. Underline each misspelled word and write it, correctly spelled, in the space at the left.

_____ 1. Intensive *studies* of that problem by *you're committee* have provided no solution up to this point.

_____ 2. *Unmanageable* salary demands by that *fameous* player did not cause the owner to *alter* her position.

_____ 3. I do not know *whose* book that is *lying forgoten* on our living room table.

_____ 4. The *changable* weather did not have any great *effect* on the size of the crowd *coming* to see the game.

_____ 5. *Writting* reports is fast *becoming* the only way people use *their* computers.

_____ 6. "Wally, for *instance,* is only the *forth* person today to ask for the *allotted* travel money," said Al.

_____ 7. *Happyness* and joy *reigned* in the office after Mr. Alcott explained the *desirable* terms of the contract.

_____ 8. Those *presence* at the birthday party produced a *noisy* kind of *excitement* among the children.

_____ 9. A *lifelike* statue of the three boyish heroes of the *dessert* war was unveiled today.

_____ 10. *Dinning* in our ears through the entire morning was the *altogether* horrible sound of the *begining* trumpet class.

_____ 11. Any *descent* effort on her part probably would have earned a *different* response from the *hopeful* crowd.

_____ 12. We *poured* over our notes for hours, but we found nothing *notably* important about work *stoppages*.

_____ 13. Does new federal law take *precedents* over *personnel* policies *formerly* in effect in our company?

_____ 14. Denice seemed *knowledgeable* about computers, but she has *shown* no ability at *compilling* reports.

257

————————— 15. After the *festivities* my *neice* took my wife and me out for a *quiet* meal at a local restaurant.

————————— 16. The new *management counsel* has met several times but has *expressed* no opinion on quality control.

————————— 17. The *studious priest* went to the *capital* building to testify in the hearings.

————————— 18. "Jim *denies* that his view of the incident is *biased* by his *earlyer* experiences," said Yolanda.

————————— 19. The *attorneys councilled* us to move rapidly to correct that *regrettable* mistake.

————————— 20. Everyone *complimented* the girls in the *brideal* party on the beauty of their *dresses*.

————————— 21. We replaced the office *stationary* because our new printer is not *equipped* to handle odd-sized *envelopes*.

————————— 22. The crew is *all ready removing* the tarpaulin although the rain has not yet completely *stopped*.

————————— 23. We were *lead* to *believe* that we had not used up our *allotment* of funds for studying the election results.

————————— 24. If Jim is forced to choose between his *studies* and a nap, he *usualy* chooses the *latter.*

————————— 25. As a beginning golfer, Julie *preferred coarses* which had the *easiest* finishing holes.

————————— 26. The *exciteable* crowd responded *immediately* to the *imaginative* story told by the lecturer.

————————— 27. The staff has made every *conceivable* effort to find a more *servicable copier* for the office.

————————— 28. Isn't that *they're equipment gathering* dust on that shelf in the back room?

————————— 29. No one is *happier then* Joan about the *arrival* of the new office manager.

————————— 30. A person of your *statute* in the community could *easily* obtain *complimentary* tickets to that playoff game.

LESSON 28 ■

Plurals and Capitals

Plurals

Plurals of most nouns are regularly formed by the addition of *s*. But if the singular noun ends in an *s* sound *(s, sh, ch, x, z)*, *es* is added to form a new syllable in pronunciation:

crab, crabs	foe, foes	kiss, kisses	tax, taxes
lamp, lamps	box, boxes	church, churches	lass, lasses

Nouns ending in *y* form their plurals according to the spelling rule. (See Lesson 27.)

toy, toys	army, armies	fly, flies	attorney, attorneys
key, keys	lady, ladies	sky, skies	monkey, monkeys

Some words ending in *o* (including all musical terms and all words having a vowel preceding the *o*) form their plurals with *s*. But many others take *es:*

alto, altos	folio, folios	tomato, tomatoes
piano, pianos	hero, heroes	potato, potatoes

For several nouns ending in *o,* most modern dictionaries give both forms. Here are some examples; they are printed here in the order found in most dictionaries. The first spelling is the more common one:

banjos/banjoes buffaloes/buffalos cargoes/cargos frescoes/frescos grottoes/grottos halos/haloes lassos/lassoes mottoes/mottos tornadoes/tornados volcanoes/ volcanos zeros/zeroes

Some nouns ending in *f* or *fe* merely add *s;* some change *f* or *fe* to *ves* in the plural; and a few *(hoofs/hooves, scarfs/scarves, wharves/wharfs)* use either form. Use your dictionary to make sure:

leaf, leaves	life, lives	half, halves	wolf, wolves
roof, roofs	safe, safes	gulf, gulfs	elf, elves

A few nouns have the same form for singular and plural. A few have irregular plurals:

deer, deer	ox, oxen	child, children	goose, geese
sheep, sheep	man, men	foot, feet	mouse, mice

Many words of foreign origin use two plurals; some do not. Always check in your dictionary:

alumna, alumnae	bon mot, bons mots
alumnus, alumni	crisis, crises
analysis, analyses	criterion, criteria
appendix, appendixes, appendices	datum, data
basis, bases	thesis, theses
beau, beaus, beaux	focus, focuses, foci
curriculum, curriculums, curricula	fungus, funguses, fungi
memorandum, memorandums, memoranda	index, indexes, indices
tableau, tableaus, tableaux	

WARNING: Do *not* use an apostrophe to form the plural of either a common or a proper noun.

Wrong: Our neighbor's, the Allen's and the Murray's, recently bought new Honda's.
Right: Our neighbors, the Allens and the Murrays, recently bought new Hondas.

Capitals

A capital letter is used for the first letter of the first word of any sentence, for the first letter of a proper noun, and often for the first letter of an adjective derived from a proper noun. Following are some reminders about situations that cause confusion for some writers.

1. Capitalize the first word of every sentence, every quoted sentence or fragment, and every transitional fragment. (See Lesson 14.)

> The building needs repairs. How much will it cost? Please answer me. Mr. James said, "We'll expect your answer soon." She replied, "Of course." And now to conclude.

Traditionally, a capital letter begins every line of poetry. This convention, however, is not always followed by modern poets; when you quote poetry, be sure to copy exactly the capitalization used by the author.

2. Capitalize proper nouns and most adjectives derived from them. A proper noun designates by name an individual person, place, or thing that is a member of a group or class. Do not capitalize common nouns, which are words naming a group or class:

> Doris Powers, woman; France, country; Tuesday, day; January, month; Christmas Eve, holiday; Shorewood High School, high school; Carleton College, college; *Mauretania,* ship; Fifth Avenue, boulevard; White House, residence

> Elizabethan drama, Restoration poetry, Chinese peasants, Indian reservation, Red Cross assistance

3. Do not capitalize nouns and derived forms that, although originally proper nouns, have acquired special meanings. When in doubt, consult your dictionary:

> a set of china; a bohemian existence; plaster of paris; pasteurized milk; a mecca for golfers; set in roman type, not italics

4. Capitalize names of religions, references to deities, and most words having religious significance:

Bible, Baptist, Old Testament, Holy Writ, Jewish, Catholic, Sermon on the Mount, Koran, Talmud

5. Capitalize titles of persons when used with the person's name. When the title is used alone, capitalize it only when it stands for a specific person of high rank:

I spoke briefly to Professor Jones. He is a professor of history.
We visited the late President Johnson's ranch in Texas.
Jerry is president of our art club.
Tonight the President will appear on national television.

6. Capitalize names denoting family relationship but not when they are preceded by a possessive. This rule is equivalent to saying that you capitalize when the word serves as a proper noun:

At that moment Mother, Father, and Aunt Lucy entered the room.
My mother, father, and aunt are very strict about some things.

7. Capitalize points of the compass when they refer to actual regions but not when they refer to directions:

Before we moved to the West, we lived in the South for a time.
You drive three miles west and then turn north on the Pacific Highway.

Do not capitalize adjectives of direction modifying countries or states:

From central Finland the group had emigrated to northern Michigan.

8. Capitalize names of academic subjects as they would appear in college catalog listings, but in ordinary writing capitalize only names of languages:

I intend to register for History 322 and Sociology 188.
Last year I took courses in history, sociology, German, and Latin.

9. In titles of books, short stories, plays, essays, and poems, capitalize the first word and all other words except the articles *(a, an, the)* and short prepositions and conjunctions. (See Lesson 19 for the use of italics and quotation marks with titles.)

Last semester I wrote reports on the following: Shaw's *The Intelligent Woman's Guide to Socialism and Capitalism,* Joyce's *A Portrait of the Artist as a Young Man,* Pirandello's *Six Characters in Search of an Author,* Poe's "The Fall of the House of Usher," Yeats's "An Irish Airman Foresees His Death," Frost's "Stopping by Woods on a Snowy Evening," and Muriel Rukeyser's "The Soul and Body of John Brown."

Practice Sheet 28
Plurals and Capitals

NAME _____ SCORE _____

Directions: Write the plural form or forms for each of the following words. When in doubt, consult your dictionary. When two forms are given, write both of them.

1. analysis _____ _____

2. assembly _____ _____

3. auditorium _____ _____

4. bistro _____ _____

5. buttonhole _____ _____

6. cry _____ _____

7. commando _____ _____

8. datum _____ _____

9. father-in-law _____ _____

10. fiasco _____ _____

11. fungus _____ _____

12. giraffe _____ _____

13. handful _____ _____

14. Jones _____ _____

15. kidney _____ _____

16. lily _____ _____

17. louse _____ _____

18. moose _____ _____

19. motto _____ _____

20. proof _____ _____

21. radio _____ _____

22. sleeve _____ _____

23. thesis _____ _____

24. workman _____ _____

25. zero _____ _____

263

Directions: The following sentences contain fifty numbered words. If you think the word is correctly capitalized, write C in the space at the left with the corresponding number. If you think the word should not be capitalized, write W in the space.

```
____  ____  ____
  1     2     3

____  ____  ____
  4     5     6

____  ____  ____
  7     8     9

____  ____  ____
 10    11    12

____  ____  ____
 13    14    15

____  ____  ____
 16    17    18

____  ____  ____
 19    20    21

____  ____  ____
 22    23    24

____  ____  ____
 25    26    27

____  ____  ____
 28    29    30

____  ____  ____
 31    32    33

____  ____  ____
 34    35    36

____  ____  ____
 37    38    39

____  ____  ____
 40    41    42

____  ____  ____
 43    44    45

____  ____  ____
 46    47    48

____  ____
 49    50
```

(1) "Please send this letter to Senator Paul Robinson who is
    [1]   [2]   [3]   [4]
the Senator from my home state," said Al.
    [5]

(2) Early in the Fall my Brother heard a special lecture by
             [6]   [7]
John Adams, Professor of History at the University Of The
    [8]   [9]   [10] [11]
South.
[12]

(3) My Father-in-Law, Larry Keeler, was a General in the U.S.
        [13]   [14]   [15]
Army before he became the President of a consulting firm.
[16]   [17]

(4) The Players' Theater, located on Dunleavy Street, is
        [18]   [19]   [20]
presenting *Guys And Dolls,* a popular musical.
            [21] [22] [23]

(5) The local Police Chief reports the theft of 100 Hymnbooks
              [24]   [25]   [26]
from the Lutheran Church over on Sixth Street.
         [27]   [28]

(6) Yolanda is required to take History 221, Physics 331, and
    [29]   [30]   [31]
a Course in Math, Sociology, and French Literature.
  [32]   [33]   [35]   [36]

(7) My Uncle, Sam Talbot, flies for Northern Airways, a
       [37]   [38]   [39]
Commuter Airline flying from Chicago to several Cities
[40]   [41]   [42]   [43]
in the Northern States.
        [44]   [45]

(8) Sometimes the college President eats in the cafeteria in
                        [46]
Ralston Hall, but usually he eats lunch in the Faculty Club.
[47]   [48]   [49]   [50]

Exercise 28

PLURALS AND CAPITALS

NAME _____ SCORE _____

Directions: Write the plural form or forms for each of the following words. When in doubt, consult your dictionary. When two forms are given, write both of them.

1. analogy   _____   _____

2. attorney   _____   _____

3. beau   _____   _____

4. crisis   _____   _____

5. condominium   _____   _____

6. dwarf   _____   _____

7. gulf   _____   _____

8. hero   _____   _____

9. fresco   _____   _____

10. key   _____   _____

11. mouse   _____   _____

12. nucleus   _____   _____

13. podium   _____   _____

14. potato   _____   _____

15. princess   _____   _____

16. roomful   _____   _____

17. sheriff   _____   _____

18. sheep   _____   _____

19. silo   _____   _____

20. sister-in-law   _____   _____

21. taxi   _____   _____

22. turkey   _____   _____

23. vortex   _____   _____

24. wolf   _____   _____

25. yo-yo   _____   _____

Directions: The following sentences contain fifty numbered words. If you think the word is correctly capitalized, write C in the space at the left with the corresponding number. If you think the word should not be capitalized, write W in the space.

1	2	3
4	5	6
7	8	9
10	11	12
13	14	15
16	17	18
19	20	21
22	23	24
25	26	27
28	29	30
31	32	33
34	35	36
37	38	39
40	41	42
43	44	45
46	47	48
49	50	

(1) The high school Principal told Dad and Uncle Rob that the
graduation ceremony would be held in Easton Hall of the
County Auditorium.

(2) My friend Jim went to college for one year in Cedar
Rapids, Iowa, but he transferred here to the State
University as a Sophomore.

(3) In the Southwest, farmers consult *The Old Farmers'*
Almanac to determine when Spring will begin.

(4) In Mellon County, the Mayor of the County Seat, Vernon
City, is my Uncle Jim's brother-in-law.

(5) To take Computer Programming, a student must first take
Data Processing 1101 and two courses in Mathematics.

(6) "We found no one home," said Holly, "And so We went
down to The Stop-And-Shop and bought a couple of sodas."

(7) My Aunt Jessie left me a set of China, two French
Porcelain figurines, and a $500 U.S. Savings Bond.

(8) In English 2101 we read *The Return of The Native* and
A Tale of Two Cities, two classics of English Literature.

LESSON 29 ■
Spelling List

This list includes words frequently misspelled by high school and college students. Each word is repeated to show its syllabic division. Whether this list is used for individual study and review or in some kind of organized class activity, your method of studying should be the following: (1) Learn to pronounce the word syllable by syllable. Some of your trouble in spelling may come from incorrect pronunciation. (2) Copy the word carefully, forming each letter as plainly as you can. Some of your trouble may come from bad handwriting. (3) Pronounce the word carefully again. (4) On a separate sheet of paper, write the word from memory, check your spelling with the correct spelling before you, and, if you have misspelled the word, repeat the learning process.

abbreviate	ab-bre-vi-ate	audience	au-di-ence
absence	ab-sence	auxiliary	aux-il-ia-ry
accidentally	ac-ci-den-tal-ly	awkward	awk-ward
accommodate	ac-com-mo-date	barbarous	bar-ba-rous
accompanying ac-	ac-com-pa-ny-ing	basically	ba-si-cal-ly
complish	ac-com-plish	beneficial	ben-e-fi-cial
accumulate	ac-cu-mu-late	boundaries	bound-a-ries
acknowledge	ac-knowl-edge	Britain	Brit-ain
acquaintance	ac-quaint-ance	bureaucracy	bu-reauc-ra-cy
acquire	ac-quire	business	busi-ness
across	a-cross	calendar	cal-en-dar
additive	ad-di-tive	candidate	can-di-date
admissible	ad-mis-si-ble	cassette	cas-sette
aggravate	ag-gra-vate	category	cat-e-go-ry
always	al-ways	cemetery	cem-e-ter-y
amateur	am-a-teur	certain	cer-tain
among	a-mong	chosen	cho-sen
analysis	a-nal-y-sis	commission	com-mis-sion
analytical	al-a-lyt-i-cal	committee	com-mit-tee
apartheid	a-part-heid	communicate	com-mu-ni-cate
apparatus	ap-pa-ra-tus	communism	com-mu-nism
apparently	ap-par-ent-ly	comparative	com-par-a-tive
appearance	ap-pear-ance	competent	com-pe-tent
appreciate	ap-pre-ci-ate	competition	com-pe-ti-tion
appropriate	ap-pro-pri-ate	completely	com-plete-ly
approximately	ap-prox-i-mate-ly	compulsory	com-pul-so-ry
arctic	arc-tic	computer	com-put-er
argument	ar-gu-ment	concede	con-cede
arithmetic	a-rith-me-tic	condominium	con-do-min-i-um
association	as-so-ci-a-tion	conference	con-fer-ence
astronaut	as-tro-naut	confidentially	con-fi-den-tial-ly
athletics	ath-let-ics	conscience	con-science
attendance	at-tend-ance	conscientious	con-sci-en-tious

conscious	con-scious	foreign	for-eign
consistent	con-sist-ent	forty	for-ty
continuous	con-tin-u-ous	frantically	fran-ti-cal-ly
controversial	con-tro-ver-sial	fundamentally	fun-da-men-tal-ly
convenient	con-ven-ient	generally	gen-er-al-ly
counterfeit	coun-ter-feit	ghetto	ghet-to
criticism	crit-i-cism	government	gov-ern-ment
criticize	crit-i-cize	graffiti	graf-fi-ti
curiosity	cu-ri-os-i-ty	grammar	gram-mar
curriculum	cur-ric-u-lum	grievous	griev-ous
decision	de-ci-sion	guarantee	guar-an-tee
definitely	def-i-nite-ly	guerrilla	guer-ril-la
describe	de-scribe	harass	ha-rass
description	de-scrip-tion	height	height
desperate	des-per-ate	hindrance	hin-drance
dictionary	dic-tion-ar-y	humorous	hu-mor-ous
difference	dif-fer-ence	hurriedly	hur-ried-ly
dilapidated	di-lap-i-dat-ed	hypocrisy	hy-poc-ri-sy
dinosaur	di-no-saur	imagination	im-ag-i-na-tion
disappear	dis-ap-pear	immediately	im-me-di-ate-ly
disappoint	dis-ap-point	impromptu	im-promp-tu
disastrous	dis-as-trous	incidentally	in-ci-den-tal-ly
discipline	dis-ci-pline	incredible	in-cred-i-ble
dissatisfied	dis-sat-is-fied	independence	in-de-pend-ence
dissident	dis-si-dent	indispensable	in-dis-pen-sa-ble
dissipate	dis-si-pate	inevitable	in-ev-i-ta-ble
doesn't	does-n't	influential	in-flu-en-tial
dormitory	dor-mi-to-ry	initiative	in-i-ti-a-tive
during	dur-ing	intelligence	in-tel-li-gence
efficient	ef-fi-cient	intentionally	in-ten-tion-al-ly
eligible	el-i-gi-ble	intercede	in-ter-cede
eliminate	e-lim-i-nate	interesting	in-ter-est-ing
embarrass	em-bar-rass	interpretation	in-ter-pre-ta-tion
eminent	em-i-nent	interrupt	in-ter-rupt
emphasize	em-pha-size	irrelevant	ir-rel-e-vant
enthusiastic	en-thu-si-as-tic	irresistible	ir-re-sist-i-ble
entrepreneur	en-tre-pre-neur	irritation	ir-ri-ta-tion
environment	en-vi-ron-ment	knowledge	knowl-edge
equipment	e-quip-ment	laboratory	lab-o-ra-to-ry
equivalent	e-quiv-a-lent	laser	la-ser
especially	es-pe-cial-ly	legitimate	le-git-i-mate
exaggerated	ex-ag-ger-at-ed	library	li-brar-y
exceed	ex-ceed	lightning	light-ning
excellent	ex-cel-lent	literature	lit-er-a-ture
exceptionally	ex-cep-tion-al-ly	livelihood	live-li-hood
exhaust	ex-haust	loneliness	lone-li-ness
existence	ex-ist-ence	maintenance	main-te-nance
exorbitant	ex-or-bi-tant	marriage	mar-riage
experience	ex-pe-ri-ence	mathematics	math-e-mat-ics
explanation	ex-pla-na-tion	memento	me-men-to
extraordinary	ex-traor-di-nar-y	miniature	min-i-a-ture
extremely	ex-treme-ly	miscellaneous	mis-cel-la-ne-ous
familiar	fa-mil-iar	mischievous	mis-chie-vous
fascinate	fas-ci-nate	misspelled	mis-spelled
February	Feb-ru-ar-y	mortgage	mort-gage

mysterious	mys-te-ri-ous	remembrance	re-mem-brance
naturally	nat-u-ral-ly	repetition	rep-e-ti-tion
necessary	nec-es-sar-y	representative	rep-re-sent-a-tive
ninety	nine-ty	respectfully	re-spect-ful-ly
ninth	ninth	respectively	re-spec-tive-ly
nowadays	now-a-days	restaurant	res-tau-rant
nuclear	nu-cle-ar	rhetoric	rhet-o-ric
obedience	o-be-di-ence	rhythm	rhythm
oblige	o-blige	ridiculous	ri-dic-u-lous
obstacle	ob-sta-cle	robot	ro-bot
occasionally	oc-ca-sion-al-ly	sacrilegious	sac-ri-le-gious
occurrence	oc-cur-rence	sandwich	sand-wich
omission	o-mis-sion	satellite	sat-el-lite
opportunity	op-por-tu-ni-ty	satisfactorily	sat-is-fac-to-ri-ly
optimistic	op-ti-mis-tic	schedule	sched-ule
original	o-rig-i-nal	scientific	sci-en-tif-ic
pamphlet	pam-phlet	secretary	sec-re-tar-y
parallel	par-al-lel	separately	sep-a-rate-ly
parliament	par-lia-ment	sergeant	ser-geant
particularly	par-tic-u-lar-ly	significant	sig-nif-i-cant
partner	part-ner	similar	sim-i-lar
pastime	pas-time	sophomore	soph-o-more
performance	per-form-ance	spaghetti	spa-ghet-ti
permissible	per-mis-si-ble	specifically	spe-cif-i-cal-ly
perseverance	per-se-ver-ance	specimen	spec-i-men
perspiration	per-spi-ra-tion	speech	speech
persuade	per-suade	strictly	strict-ly
politics	pol-i-tics	successful	suc-cess-ful
possession	pos-ses-sion	superintendent	su-per-in-tend-ent
practically	prac-ti-cal-ly	supersede	su-per-sede
preceding	pre-ced-ing	surprise	sur-prise
prejudice	prej-u-dice	suspicious	sus-pi-cious
preparation	prep-a-ra-tion	syllable	syl-la-ble
prevalent	prev-a-lent	synonymous	syn-on-y-mous
privilege	priv-i-lege	synthetic	syn-thet-ic
probably	prob-a-bly	technology	tech-nol-o-gy
procedure	pro-ce-dure	temperament	tem-per-a-ment
proceed	pro-ceed	temperature	tem-per-a-ture
processor	pro-ces-sor	together	to-geth-er
professional	pro-fes-sion-al	tragedy	trag-e-dy
professor	pro-fes-sor	truly	tru-ly
pronunciation	pro-nun-ci-a-tion	twelfth	twelfth
propaganda	prop-a-gan-da	unanimous	u-nan-i-mous
psychiatrist	psy-chi-a-trist	undoubtedly	un-doubt-ed-ly
psychological	psy-cho-log-i-cal	unnecessarily	un-nec-es-sar-i-ly
pursue	pur-sue	until	un-til
quantity	quan-ti-ty	usually	u-su-al-ly
questionnaire	ques-tion-naire	various	var-i-ous
quizzes	quiz-zes	vegetable	veg-e-ta-ble
realize	re-al-ize	video	vid-e-o
really	re-al-ly	village	vil-lage
recognize	rec-og-nize	villain	vil-lain
recommend	rec-om-mend	Wednesday	Wednes-day
regard	re-gard	whether	wheth-er
religious	re-li-gious	wholly	whol-ly

Spelling

NAME _____ SCORE _____

Directions: Each sentence contains two words from the first half of the spelling list. In each one of these words at least one letter is missing. Write the words, correctly spelled, in the spaces at the left.

_____ 1. Em—nent scholars did not give her presentation a very enthu-
_____   sia—tic evaluation.

_____ 2. The h—pocrisy of those silly politicians is genuinely hu-
_____   mor—s.

_____ 3. The graf—ti on the walls in my neighborhood do not follow
_____   all the rules of gram—r.

_____ 4. It is difficult to critici—e Jim's consist—nt efforts at studying
_____   his math.

_____ 5. That can—date successfully overcame his early life in a
_____   gh—to and became a businessman before he ran for office.

_____ 6. Gener—ly speaking, our employees are all very compet—t.

_____ 7. The lifelike qualities of the dinos—rs in that movie were
_____   extr—rdinary.

_____ 8. Her decis—n to spend f—rty dollars on a scarf seems a little
_____   silly, doesn't it?

_____ 9. The regular cur—culum in a Japanese grade school would be
_____   contr—versial in this country.

_____ 10. Oil companies now provide special equi—ent to protect the
_____   envir—ment in case of oil spills.

_____ 11. The emotional exper—nce of watching that movie ex—usted
_____   me completely.

_____ 12. Can you accom—date an acqu—ntance of mine as a guest at
_____   your dinner party?

271

_____
_____

13. In some cities, condomin—ms are appar—ntly almost impossible to buy for a reasonable price.

_____
_____

14. Jon is dis—atisfied with the performance of his new comput—r.

_____
_____

15. The counterf—t jeans seized by the police will be admiss—ble as evidence in the trial of those men.

_____
_____

16. I think you exag—rated when you reported the h—ght of the mountain you climbed last summer.

_____
_____

17. Attend—nce at the meetings of our planning com—ittee has been very low lately.

_____
_____

18. Ronald's absen—e from history class this morning will make a differ—nce in his grade.

_____
_____

19. Audrey accident—lly created an awkw—rd situation by inviting both Barbara and Carol to her party.

_____
_____

20. The bound—ries of Martin Township have remained basi—lly unchanged for two hundred years.

_____
_____

21. Life in a dormit—ry do—sn't offer much privacy.

_____
_____

22. Today's aud—nce is filled with owners of small bus—nesses.

_____
_____

23. The president is on a confer—nce call concerning gover—ent regulation of the power industry.

_____
_____

24. The debaters refused to conc—e even one point in my arg—ent.

_____
_____

25. The calend—r accompan—ng this letter will give you the schedule for this week.

EXERCISE 29

SPELLING

NAME _____ SCORE _____

Directions: Each sentence contains three italicized words from the first half of the spelling list. One of the three words is misspelled. Underline the misspelled word and write it, correctly spelled, in the space at the left.

_____ 1. "*Confidentialy,* the president's *calendar* is empty *during* the middle of this next week," said the secretary.

_____ 2. *Efficient* use of your time will *eliminate* the need to complete your work *hurredly.*

_____ 3. The *amateurs amoung* the *arctic* explorers made a major contribution to the expedition.

_____ 4. The *casette* you have *chosen* is *completely* sold-out at this time.

_____ 5. *Certian* members of the *bureaucracy* want to make attendance at the Friday staff meeting *compulsory.*

_____ 6. My grandmother wants to *comission* a painting of that *dilapidated* cabin before the last trace of it *disappears.*

_____ 7. Tom was *especially fascinated* by the ideas of that young *entrepeneur.*

_____ 8. *Competition* for that scholarship from outside the campus was neither *appropriate* nor *apreciated.*

_____ 9. The natives' *desparate* demands for help *accomplished* little or nothing to improve their *existence.*

_____ 10. The *appearance* at the stadium of a soccer *association* from *Britian* did nothing to quiet the crowd.

_____ 11. "I need your *analysis* of the *criticisms* of the report *accompaning* the plans for the new building," said Robin.

_____ 12. The coach is *dissappointed* by the *disastrous* lack of *discipline* among the members of the team.

273

_____ 13. Marge's *description* of the land *across* the river failed to *co-municate* its true beauty to anyone.

_____ 14. At *exhorbitant* cost, the highway department has *acquired* an old *cemetery* to add to the highway's right-of-way.

_____ 15. The *arithmetic* in that first *category* of sales figures shows we *exeded* our quota by a wide margin.

_____ 16. Her *abbreviated* efforts to *discribe February's* weather fell far short of the truth.

_____ 17. We *always* need to *acknowlege* the contributions of *astronauts* and test pilots to airline safety.

_____ 18. That *dissident* group from the *athaletic* dorms *aggravated* an already difficult situation.

_____ 19. The new fire *apparatus* will be delivered to the *auxilary* fire company at a *convenient* time this weekend.

_____ 20. "Were you *consciouos* of the *continuous* roar of the fans during that *exceptionally* long rally?" asked the coach.

_____ 21. *Concientious* efforts by *approximately* one hundred men proved to be *extremely* successful against the floods.

_____ 22. The *incredable* courage of the *guerrilla* forces helped them win their *independence* from their oppressors.

_____ 23. The *impromptu* speech only *embarassed* students who were not *familiar* with the special techniques required.

_____ 24. Both *comparative* and *analytical* studies demonstrate the *fundamentelly* sound nature of your conclusions.

_____ 25. "We want to *emphasize* the need to resolve that *grievos* problem *immediately*," said the Prime Minister.

Practice Sheet 29A
Spelling

NAME _____ SCORE _____

Directions: Each sentence contains two words from the second half of the spelling list. In each of these words at least one letter is missing. Write the words, correctly spelled, in the spaces at the left.

_____
_____   1. Can you tell from my transcript w—ther I will be a soph—ore or a junior next year?

_____
_____   2. A las—r printer can satisfact—rily produce all types of documents.

_____
_____   3. I am not w—olly satisfied with my sc—edule this term.

_____
_____   4. Last Wed—sday the weather was particul—rly nasty.

_____
_____   5. The new tech—logy will broaden the uses for sat—lite dishes.

_____
_____   6. S—nthetic materials have made maint—nance on my new sailboat much simpler than it was on my first boat.

_____
_____   7. It is difficult to p—rsuade many qualified people to enter pol—tics today.

_____
_____   8. "My new word proces—r catches most, but not all of the mi—spelled words in my papers," said Alice.

_____
_____   9. Mor—age rates will probably go up in the next nin—ty days.

_____
_____   10. Now—days it is permis—ble for a man to wear his hat inside a building.

_____
_____   11. Will nuc—ear power someday super—ede power generated by steam or hydroelectric plants?

_____
_____   12. Marge was always very suc—essful in math—matics classes.

275

_____ 13. Practic—ly speaking, there is no specific prep—ration for tak-
_____   ing the LSAT or the GRE.

_____ 14. "I don't have the temper—ment to work with Jane; she is al-
_____   ways bringing up irrelev—nt ideas," said Marvin.

_____ 15. The fire alarm inter—upted the boss's wonderfully exciting
_____   sp—ch on profit margins.

_____ 16. Jennie has decided to p—rsue a degree in lib—ry science.
_____

_____ 17. Earning a livel—hood in the rest—rant business is very hard
_____   work.

_____ 18. In most classes pop qui—es are thought of as an obst—cle to
_____   success.

_____ 19. "It's often a surpr—e," observed Al, "that the temper—ture in
_____   the desert is very cool at night."

_____ 20. We should put that memo in the "miscellan—s" file; it deals
_____   with var—ous subjects that are not at all related.

_____ 21. Julie usu—ly shows up about ten minutes late for class, thus
_____   annoying the profes—r a great deal.

_____ 22. The origin—l of that document should be filed sepa—tely in
_____   a safe place.

_____ 23. Spag—tti and linguine are simil—r but not identical.
_____

_____ 24. The par—ners in that firm are all passionate about the same
_____   pa—time, fly-fishing.

_____ 25. "Although we were suspic—ous of his actions, we did not
_____   have any tr—ly incriminating evidence," said the detective.

EXERCISE 29A

SPELLING

NAME _____ SCORE _____

Directions: Each sentence contains three italicized words from the second half of the spelling list. One of the three words is misspelled. Underline the misspelled word and write it, correctly spelled, in the space at the left.

_____ 1. "Careful *preperation* and *perseverance* can help your *performance,*" said Coach Morton.

_____ 2. *Occassionally* my father likes to pick up a *video* of an old detective movie with a classic *villain* in it.

_____ 3. "I need a word with two *syllables* that begins with S and is *synonimous* with *ridiculous,*" said Susan.

_____ 4. The *tragedy* is that the injured boy was not *truly* bad, he was simply *mischevious.*

_____ 5. The *inevitible interpretation* of that comment will be that it was based on little or no *knowledge.*

_____ 6. "*Naturally,* the desk *seargent* reported a *wholly* wrong version of my story," said Marge.

_____ 7. It was absolutely *necessary* to watch that *interesting laberatory* experiment yesterday.

_____ 8. *Knowlege* of ancient mythology and *literature* is a valuable tool for a *psychiatrist.*

_____ 9. Not until the *twelth* vote did the selection of our *representative* become *unanimous.*

_____ 10. Jill's favorite *memento* of that trip is a *miniature villiage* set in a field of snow.

_____ 11. "I *really* didn't *reconize* the *scientific* importance of that simple event," said Raymond.

_____ 12. "My little nephew does not *regard vegtables* as a *legitimate* food group," said Ronnie.

277

_____ 13. People in ancient civilizations thought *lightening* made a *significant religious* statement.

_____ 14. The *superintendant* on that job *specifically* told those two men not to work *together.*

_____ 15. *Until* the police became *suspisious,* the *mysterious* phone calls were only an annoyance to Barbara.

_____ 16. The lab manual *recommends* several *repititions* of that *procedure* to insure accuracy.

_____ 17. "We must *procede* quickly through that *questionnaire* and read the *pamphlet* before we leave," said the leader.

_____ 18. Some people do not *realize* that *propeganda* often creates an *irresistible* attraction to certain ideas.

_____ 19. Silly *prejudices* are *probobly influential* in decisions that ought to be made on the basis of facts.

_____ 20. "*Initiative, intelligence,* and large doses of *persperation* can lead to success," said my grandmother.

_____ 21. The *secratary's sandwich* was *intentionally* taken from the refrigerator sometime during the morning.

_____ 22. The *prevalent* belief is that *robots* will soon seize the *oppertunity* to take over most of the jobs in the country.

_____ 23. The *ninth* puppy in the ring is a *specamen* of the Rottweiler breed, admired for *obedience* to one master.

_____ 24. It was a *privalege* to watch the *professional* golfers, who were *undoubtedly* enjoying the Pro-Am Tournament.

_____ 25. The *preceding* memo said that we are *obligded* to avoid using the fax machine *unnecessarily.*

EXERCISE 29B
SPELLING REVIEW

NAME _____ SCORE _____

Directions: A sentence may have no misspelled words, one misspelled word, or two misspelled words. Underline the misspelled words and write them, correctly spelled, in the spaces at the left.

_____ 1. Accept for James, everyone at the performance was disa-
_____   pointed by the work of the vocalists.

_____ 2. Early fans thought it almost sacreligious to play the national
_____   pastime, baseball, at night or in the rein.

_____ 3. "Whose going to interrupt such an eminant scholar and tell her
_____   that her time is up?" asked Marv.

_____ 4. Two quizzes and a questionnaire from the personnel depart-
_____   ment took up most of this morning's class time.

_____ 5. The decent from the top of the cliff demanded very technical
_____   procedures and specialized equiptment.

_____ 6. Maria exagerated the importance of her role in the preparation
_____   of the coarse in modern dance.

_____ 7. The site of the new auxiliary power station has been selected
_____   by the Public Utilities Commission.

_____ 8. The city consul will hear arguments tomorrow about the om-
_____   mission of the Opera Guild from next year's budget.

_____ 9. The company formally guaranteed to correct any problems,
_____   but today it dropped the promise without any explanation.

_____ 10. Attendence at the first session is necessary if you want to see
_____   the movie that will be shone later.

_____ 11. The waiter said quite clearly, "The wine you have chozen does
_____   not compliment the entree; please select another."

_____ 12. Jack accidentally deleted the original file from the hard disk in
_____   the computer.

_____ 13. The front carrying the artic air apparently did not move passed
_____   the northern part of the state.

_____ 14. We now abbreviate the names of states in a way designed
_____   specifically to make mail sorting more efficient.

_____ 15. The President dosen't want to disipate the good will accumu-
_____   lated during the first half of his term.

_____ 16. The statue of limitations does not apply to a few extremely
_____   grevious crimes.

_____ 17. The guerrillas, lead by a young woman, harrassed the peasants
_____   and small farmers in that country unmercifully.

_____ 18. Joan has all ready asked the morgage company to proceed
_____   with the processing of her application.

_____ 19. Rosa's forth request for a schedule from the registrar's office
_____   was ignored, so she sought help from a profesor.

_____ 20. "My word processer cannot do a thorough analysis of spelling
_____   and punctuation in my essays," said Mario.

Writing Paragraphs and Essays

SECTION 1 ▪

An Overview of College Writing

Although it may come as a surprise to you, you will be called on to do a great deal of writing in college and in your career. Lecture notes, essays, research papers, and tests are the very stuff of which college courses are made. Memorandums, letters, reports, and proposals are basic tools in almost any career you can name. And all this writing, whether in or out of college, is in great measure a key to your progress and success. In fact, in many large organizations, people are known to those in other areas more through their written work than through personal contact, and progress and promotion ride as much on the quality of that written work as on any other factor. Writing skills will be a major factor in your success.

Beyond such practical benefits, writing is a very effective tool for learning. Writing about a subject produces two good results: greater understanding and control of the material itself, and new connections to other facts and concepts. Writing out lecture notes and textbook materials in your own words will give you better control of those materials and will help you to connect the new materials with facts and concepts you learned earlier.

In the previous sections of this book, you examined the operating principles of the language and applied those principles to writing correct, effective sentences. Now you need to learn to combine those sentences into paragraphs, and the paragraphs into papers that will fulfill your college writing assignments.

The assignments you receive in college may be widely varied, ranging from a single paragraph narrating an event in your life to a complex research paper. Look briefly at a list of these possible assignments:

1. *Personal Essays*
   - Recount an event in your life, explaining its importance.
   - Discuss your position on the approaching presidential election.
2. *Essay Tests*
   - Answer two of the following three questions, using well-developed paragraphs and complete sentences in your answer.
3. *Essays and Discussions*
   - Explain the causes of structural unemployment in our country today.
   - Discuss the work of Jonas Salk in disease prevention.

4. *Critical Papers*
   - Evaluate the enclosed proposal for the construction of a new dam.
   - Assess the work of the Thatcher administration in Britain.
5. *Persuasive or Argumentative Papers*
   - Argue for or against the use of government spending to retrain displaced workers.
   - Discuss the arguments against universal military training in the United States.
6. *Documented Papers*
   - After thorough research into the subject, write a paper discussing the use of nuclear power in this country. Be sure to discuss the history, the current situation, and the arguments for and against continued use and further development.

Although this list seems extremely diverse and the types of writing quite varied, you can take comfort in the fact that underneath this diversity and complexity lies a fairly straightforward process that can be applied to all types of writing. You need only to learn one set of steps, the basic writing process, in order to deal effectively with any writing project you might face.

The Writing Process

Writing is a process, a set of steps, not a project that is started and finished in a single session. Often people believe that successful writers have in some way happened onto a secret method of production that allows them, almost by magic, to sit down and write out a nearly perfect draft on the first try. This happens only rarely, and always to writers with long experience; most people can assume that good writing always rises out of slow, painstaking, step-by-step work.

The steps in the writing process group themselves naturally into two phases, and each phase requires an approach, a mind-set, that is quite different from the other.

In the first phase, composing, you should be very free and creative. Think of this phase as a search, an adventure, an opportunity to try out many possibilities for ideas, content, and strategies.

In the second phase, editing, you must be very critical of the materials you composed earlier. This is the time when you must evaluate, rewrite, reject, and correct the materials you developed while composing.

You must be careful not to mix the modes of operation. Don't edit when you should be composing. Don't delete materials, or decide not to pursue an idea, or ponder the correctness of a mark of punctuation. Such distractions will almost certainly stop your flow of ideas.

But don't allow yourself to be free and creative when you are working as an editor. Keeping a word that is not quite right or failing to cut out a section that does not fit will produce papers that lack focus and are full of distractions.

Remember that each phase in the process is separate and distinct. Each one requires separate and distinct attitudes toward the work at hand.

The following brief explanation provides a general introduction to the steps in the writing process. In later sections you will see these steps applied to different types of writing; those applications will illustrate minor changes to suit specific types of writing.

COMPOSING

Step 1. Select or identify the subject.

Basic Question: What should I write about? Or (if the assignment is very specific): What does the assignment require me to write about?

Strategy: Select the subject on the basis of these questions:
  • Are you and your reader interested in it?
  • Do you have enough knowledge to write on it? If not, can you locate enough?
  • Can you treat the subject completely within the length allotted for the assignment?

Step 2. Gather information on the subject.

Basic Question: What do I know about the subject? More importantly, what do I need to know in order to write about this subject fully and effectively?

Strategy: Organize what you already know about the subject. Identify areas for which you will need additional information. ("A Few Words Before Starting," pp. 286–291, will give you helpful hints with this process.) Continue exploring and writing about the subject until you bring the work naturally to Step 3.

Step 3. Establish a controlling statement or thesis for the paper.

Basic Question: Exactly what can I say about this subject on the basis of the information and ideas I developed in Step 2?

Strategy: Continue to gather information and write about the subject until a specific idea develops. Write out that idea in a single sentence.

Step 4. Select specific items of support to include in the paper.

Basic Question: What ideas, facts, and illustrations can I use to make the thesis completely clear to the reader?

Strategy: Review the stockpile of materials gathered in Step 2. Select from these materials only those ideas, facts, and illustrations that will develop and support the thesis.

Step 5. Establish an order for presenting the materials you have selected.

Basic Question: What is the most effective order for presenting the materials that I have selected?

Strategy: Choose from among the possible arrangements—most to least important, least to most important, chronological, or any others mentioned in the section on paragraphs (pages 303–320)—and follow that order in writing the draft.

Step 6. Write the first draft.

Basic Question: What will the materials look like when presented in the order I have chosen?

Strategy: Write out a complete version of the paper, following the plan developed in the first five steps.

EDITING

Before you begin to edit the first completed draft of the paper, be sure that you shift from the role of composer/writer to the role of editor. You have before you a completed product, not a perfect product. You must examine that product with a very critical eye, testing and weighing each part to be sure that it is as good as it can be.

Step 7. Revise the draft.

Basic Question: What changes can I make to improve the organization and content of the draft?

Strategy: Make the necessary changes in the draft. Examine first the largest elements of the paper (thesis and outline) and work down through the paragraphs and sentences.

Step 8. Correct the draft.

Basic Question: What errors in mechanics and grammar do I need to correct?

Strategy: Read each sentence as an independent unit. It is best to read the sentences in reverse order from the end of the paper or section where you are working. Reading "backward" in this fashion ensures that you will see each sentence as it actually appears and will not make silent mental corrections or assumptions as you read.

Step 9. Write the final draft.

Basic Question: What form shall I use for the final copy of the paper?

Strategy: Follow the guidelines for manuscript form given by your instructor and copy the paper neatly and carefully, making sure to include all the revisions and corrections you made on the rough draft. Proofread the final draft carefully.

This nine-step process can be followed with only minor changes for any writing assignment. Study it carefully as we apply it to various types of assignments. Make the process second nature to you, a set of habits followed anytime you write. The more you practice, the greater will be your facility in writing.

Before we begin to examine the writing process as it applies to specific projects in college writing, let's take a few moments to study the results that a professional writer can achieve using this process—or a similar one—in writing a publishable article about a personal experience.

The setting for the experience and the article is Australia; the writer is an editor of *Car and Driver,* a magazine for auto enthusiasts. The occasion is a trip across the Outback, a sparsely settled region in the interior of Australia. The author and a passenger are driving on a 1500-mile trip to survey Australian methods of improving auto safety. They have been driving in desolate country almost all day when, late in the afternoon, they encounter a washed-out bridge and must double back to find a new route. They have been driving fast; the detour seems to urge them to increased speed.

A Drive in the Outback, with Second Chances

DAVID ABRAHAMSON

It took less than two seconds. The stab of oncoming headlights, a blur of looming sheet-metal in the center of the windshield, a jabbing reaction at the steering wheel and then that awful, indelible noise. And then an unearthly silence, as if nature itself knew that something irrevocable had happened and that a moment—maybe much more—was needed for the reality to be dealt with.

I had been driving fast most of the afternoon. Not really at the car's limit, but well above the posted speed. I enjoy fast driving for its own sake, and this new and isolated environment seemed to urge me on. After all, Australia's wide open spaces are exactly that, and we'd encountered less than one car an hour in either direction of the towns. And besides, Baker, my passenger, didn't seem to mind. We were in the middle of a long, sweeping right-hander when suddenly the windshield was filled with another set of headlights. Coming at us, in the middle of the road, was a monstrous truck. The left front corner of the truck cab buried itself in the left front door of our car. The sound was absolutely deafening. Bits of metal and glass were everywhere. The impact ripped the watch off my wrist and the lenses out of my glasses. But I was lucky. Because it was a righthand-drive car, as the driver I was at least three feet away from the point of impact. Passenger Baker, however, was not. The true violence of the crash took place almost in his lap. Part of his seat was torn up and out of its mount. The door and a section of the roof were battered in toward his head and left shoulder. We were both wearing lap-and-shoulder seat belts at the time. Mine saved my life, Baker's did too, but in the process broke his collarbone and badly bruised a few essential internal organs. A grisly tradeoff.

How and why had the accident happened? What exactly had been my mistake? Long after I'd returned to the United States, long after Baker had recovered from his injuries, I was still asking myself those questions. Now, almost a year later, the answers are clear. And they go far beyond any chance encounter on a strange road in a strange land, even beyond the crushing sense of remorse I felt at the time. And they tell me something about who I was and what I might be. I enjoyed driving, and a big part of that enjoyment came from taking a number of risks. Risks I thought were calculated, but in truth were not. Rather they were part of a glorious game, imbued with notions of independence, willful mobility and a heavy dose of virility. I'd had more than my share of near misses, but they merely served to prove the range of my skills at the wheel—my ability to judge relative speed and distance, the speed of my reflexes, the correctness of my kinesthetic instincts. In my car at speed, there was never any hint of my own mortality. Or of anyone else's. So the accident had to happen. Maybe not with that truck on that blind curve on the far side of the Earth, but somewhere. It has less to do with the law of averages than the laws of physics. Roads are a decidedly hostile environment, peopled with an unknown number of other drivers who are certain to do the wrong thing at the wrong time. And no amount of skill, real or imagined, can save you. Sweet reason is the only defense. Prudence, moderation and caution are not the stuff of grand illusions, unbridled exuberance and youthful panache. But they're great for survival.

And that, in the end, is what my experience boils down to. I now see, as I did not before, that my survival (and that of others who choose to ride with me) is at stake. I've never seen myself as a particularly courageous person, but I've always enjoyed sports containing an element of risk: parachuting, scuba diving, alpine skiing and the like. Strange that something as mundane as an auto accident should, at age 30, give me my first glimpse of my own mortality. Thinking back to that evening south of Bombala, I am certain that I never want to hear that awful sound again. But I also never want to forget it.

Following the process as we have outlined it, the writer would have asked himself these questions:

1. What should I write about?

> My Australian trip, or some part of it. The most memorable and important part of the trip was the terrible accident near Bombala, in which my passenger Bill Baker was injured.

2. What do I know or remember about the trip and, more specifically, about the accident?

> Beginning with the plane ride from San Francisco, I can record as background material all the things we did on the flight, in Sidney, and on the trip itself. I will record in greatest detail the auto trip, focusing as closely as possible on the moments before and after the crash. I'll continue to write until I reach a statement or conclusion about that accident and its meaning to me now.

3. Exactly what can I say about this subject, the accident? What impression has it made on me?

> The accident changed my view of my driving skills and the importance of those skills in pre-serving my safety while I drive. I never want to hear the awful sound of the crash again, but I never want to forget it, either.

4. What details, facts, illustrations, and observations can I use to make that thesis clear to my reader?

> I will use visual details and facts surrounding the crash itself. I'll include the aftermath of the crash, the time while we wait to take Baker to the hospital. Finally, I'll record my thoughts on and impressions of the importance and meaning of the accident.

5. What order will most effectively present these supporting materials?

> Because this piece is basically a narrative, I'll follow chronological order, but I'll use a few details of the actual crash to catch my readers' interest in the introduction.

6. What will the materials look like when I actually write out a first completed version of the article?

> [You have read the final draft of the essay. The rough draft contained much more material.] I will cut out distracting material that weakens my statement.

A Few Words before Starting

Getting started is often the most difficult part of writing. We all have a tendency to avoid the blank page and the work involved in filling it meaningfully. Writing will always be hard work, but a few preliminary exercises will help make getting started a little easier.

First: Strengthen your muscles so that you can write with ease. You would not go mountain climbing or run a marathon without getting in shape; you should not expect writing to be enjoyable unless you are in shape for it. Do the following exercises once each day:

- Sit in a place where you can watch people passing by. Writing as rapidly as possible, jot down a description of all that occurs, noting sizes, shapes, descriptions, and other visual details.
- Writing continuously, sign your name or copy other words down as many times as you can in two minutes.
- Without stopping, write everything that comes into your head when you read the following words:

submarine
photosynthesis
chocolate milkshake

The goal of these exercises is to be able to write for fifteen minutes without any discomfort and for an hour with two short breaks.

Second: Free your mind to write without constraints. As you work in the first phase of the writing process, composing, you need to learn to write freely without editing what you write. This "freewriting," or "stream-of-consciousness writing," will allow you to record at random all the ideas that come to mind on your subject. In fact, you will probably bring to mind ideas that are technically off the subject of your paper. Don't be afraid to record these stray ideas, as they will often lead in circular fashion back to the subject from a direction you had not imagined before. Writing in this free way becomes a way of learning about your subject, a way of making new connections within it.

Freewriting is especially valuable when you are writing a paper based on personal experience because it allows you to make something important out of that experience. It is also valuable in writing papers of opinion or papers stating a personal position on a controversial subject. Only through extensive writing can you define your opinion or position clearly and firmly. A would-be comic once said, "I don't know what I think until I see what I've written." He probably intended the statement as a joke, but it is, in fact, the truth. Writing about opinions and ideas forms the ideas as you write about them. Be sure to write extensively, randomly, freely, on all such writing assignments before you formulate your thesis.

Freewriting also has an important place in writing more objective papers, papers based on research and written notes. After you have completed your research and put your note cards in reasonably good order, you should read through them two or three times to get a sense of the content. After reading the notes, set them aside and begin to write freely about the subject.

At least two good things should come out of this freewriting. First, freewriting on the subject will help you to formulate a position on the subject that is specially your own and not the opinion of the writers you covered in your research. You learn about your subject when you write about it.

Second, freewriting will allow you to write about your subject in your own voice rather than in the voices of the writers you read during your research. Without this freewriting, your writing will sound like every other research paper ever written because we tend to take on the tone and style of the writers we have recently read. Through freewriting you can move away from the voices of those other writers and into your own voice. Freewriting will allow you to produce a paper that is uniquely "you," rather than a generic, sounds-like-all-the-other-papers-ever-written sort of production.

Freewriting will develop both ideas and a voice that are uniquely yours.

Third: Explore your topic extensively. You can employ specialized techniques to help you gather information and formulate your ideas on your writing projects.

One technique most closely allied to freewriting is called **brainstorming** or **clustering.** Clustering is a *nonlinear, free association* drill. In this drill, the writer sits quietly with pen and pencil, or at a typewriter, and records words and phrases as they come to mind. Write the name of the subject

American Politics

and then record the words and ideas that come to mind—without editing or limiting the list.

American Politics

Democrat   Republican   liberal   conservative   neo-liberal

Constitution   Bill of Rights   John F. Kennedy

radicalism   William F. Buckley   The Boston Tea Party

The Sixties   The Civil Rights Movement

This brainstorming will not work in a vacuum. If you have never studied, or even thought about, American politics, you will not have any associations to make. But you will have a store of ideas and concepts to work on if you have been studying American history or political science.

If you have the background to make constructive associations, clustering or brainstorming can help you in two ways.

Brainstorming can help to isolate a manageable topic within a subject area.

An assignment in an American history course that simply says:

Write a paper on American politics.

requires a good deal of probing and restriction before a workable topic for a paper emerges. Clearly, you can't write a paper fully exploring American politics in ten pages, or even in a whole semester. To write a successful paper, you will need to restrict and focus your thinking to a single aspect of the subject area. Brainstorming can help to make that restriction.

> Thus you can move from John F. Kennedy to the idea that he became president in 1960 to the idea that the Civil Rights Movement began in the late fifties and early sixties to the idea that there must have been some relationship between his administration and the Civil Rights Movement. At that point you might suspect that you have hit on a workable topic and move off to the library to do some preliminary work on bibliography and some background reading.

Brainstorming can also help you to make connections between ideas within a subject area.

Writing about one concept causes you to remember a second concept. Writing about the second concept can lead to a third and then a fourth.

So you might begin to think on a general subject—grades

and then about grades in high school

and then about your greater motivation in college

and then about your lack of real effort in high school

and then about your much better grades in college

and then about the marked improvement in your grades

Then you can make a connection between better grades and greater motivation. From there you might move to a possible comparison between low motivation in high school and higher motivation in college, and then, **by brainstorming again on that concept,** you might develop several reasons why those conditions existed.

At that point, you can choose a direction for the paper, depending on the focus required in the assignment. If the assignment asks for a personal paper—observations on your grades and experiences in high school and college—then you must continue into additional brainstorming and then into freewriting and other techniques on gathering information on the topic.

If, on the other hand, you can move into an objective examination of motivation and grades in high school and college, you can go to the library for bibliography work and preliminary reading.

For papers on personal experience, you can employ the five questions used by journalists to develop articles:

1. **WHO** is involved?
2. **WHAT** happens?
3. **WHEN** does it happen?
4. **WHERE** does the event occur?
5. **WHY** does it happen?

In this exercise, don't limit yourself to one-word or brief answers. Employ freewriting techniques when you answer the questions. Don't answer the question "Who?" by saying, "John and Mr. Smith." Write about John and Mr. Smith. Explore the answers to each question extensively in a freewriting mode.

Next, you can explore your topic by asking questions that focus on parts and relationships that exist in and around your topic. Suppose that your assignment asks you to explore some aspect of business in modern Japan. After examining the general subject, you discover that Japanese business executives use a special style of management that has sparked considerable interest among managers in the United States. You might begin your exploration by looking at the topic in three ways.

Examine the discrete parts of the topic itself: What are the *distinctive features* of Japanese management style?
Examine the topic as a whole.
How do these features *work together as a system?*
Examine the place of the topic within the general subject matter.
How does Japanese management style *fit into the overall subject* we call management?

Or, phrased in a different way,

> How do we identify this subject?
> How do we differentiate it from others in the same general area?
> What are the important parts or aspects of this subject?
> What is the physical appearance of these parts?
> What examples of this subject occur in real life?
> How does this subject compare and/or contrast with others of the same general type?

Some writers find it useful to construct *analogies* and *metaphors* on a subject. When you make an analogy, you examine ways in which an unknown concept is like a well-known concept.

> My brother, who plays Little League baseball, is a ballplayer out of the Rickey Henderson mold: he is quick on his feet, aggressive, a singles hitter most of the time, and, above all, he loves the game more than anything else in his life.

This brother is unlike Rickey Henderson in a thousand ways, including age, size, and success in the game. But a person who knows a little bit about Rickey Henderson will be able to know a little more about your brother. And so will you, when you recognize the similarities between the two people.

In the same way, on personal topics, it is possible to construct metaphors and similes, figures of speech that establish comparisons.

> Red Grange was *like a will-o'-the-wisp,* dancing and dodging his way through opposing teams to become the greatest running back in the early history of football.

> The invading army *was a tornado,* moving where it wished and destroying everything in its path.

Sometimes even metaphors that seem ridiculous can be productive.

> If your father were an automobile, what make and model would he be?

> He might be a 1938 Cadillac, very classy, but a trifle old-fashioned in some ways.

Images such as these can provide insight that can lead to new information and new insights, **if you follow them up with additional reading and writing on the subject.**

Certain subjects can be explored by **approaching them through the senses.** Recording visual aspects (shapes, sizes, and colors, for example) or recording words that describe sounds, smells, and textures might offer insights into the subject.

All these methods of exploring a subject and refining a subject into manageable parts simply open areas for reading and writing on a subject. They help you with Step 2 of the writing process, gathering materials. The resulting notes and written materials must not be confused with a first, complete draft or the final draft of a paper. They constitute the raw material of a paper, material that must be evaluated, accepted, rejected, placed in order in the draft, and written out for revision. They are not the finished product; they are background to help with production of that finished product.

So don't wait for inspiration or good beginnings. Write what you can write as well as you can write it. If you can't think of a good way to start, start any way you can. If you can't think of exactly the right word, use a close approximation. Time and condition and the freedom to write without editing will improve your ideas; careful attention to revision and correction will improve the quality of your written expression. Practice and more practice will lead to success.

In the next section we will examine closely a very important type of college writing, the essay test.

Writing Exercises for an Overview of College Writing

1. Each day for the first two weeks of your experience in using the writing sections of this book, follow the instructions for getting in shape to write.
2. Follow the steps in the writing process illustrated with "A Drive in the Outback, with Second Chances," and write about an experience in your own life.
3. Find an example of personal writing about an experience or an attitude. Read it to locate the thesis statement or core idea (Step 3 in composing). Then outline the supporting details to show how they develop (or fail to develop) the core idea.

SECTION 2 ■
Taking Essay Tests

Essay tests provide an excellent opportunity to apply your writing skills to college writing assignments. Working on test taking is very practical; success on tests will improve your grades. Beyond that practical consideration, and perhaps more important, essay test answers require you to work within a very narrow subject area to produce a concise, complete written statement. These tight limitations of time and space require you to be very precise in the formulation of a topic statement and to distinguish carefully between materials essential to your answer and those that are only related to it. Finally, essay tests often require that you present your answer in a single well-developed paragraph. Practice in writing essay test answers will develop your ability to write successful paragraphs.

Getting Ready

The best preparation for taking any test is consistent, effective study throughout the term. In addition, however, you need special strategies for the last few days before the test to improve your chances of success.

Begin your final preparations for the test a few days in advance so that you will have ample time to study and assimilate the material. Follow these suggestions as you study.

Step 1. Make an overview or survey of the materials you have covered for the test. Look for periods, trends, theories, and general conclusions. Try to pinpoint important concepts and basic ideas in the materials. You may find it useful to consult a general encyclopedia for an overview or a summary of the subject areas to be covered by the test. If the subject is technical or complex or is part of an advanced course, consult an appropriate specialized encyclopedia or reference work in that field.

Step 2. Write a series of questions encompassing the major items that you have located. Cover broad areas of material. Try to concentrate on questions that begin with such words as compare, trace, outline, *and* discuss. *(See the discussion of instruction words on pages 296–298.) In six to ten broad-scope questions of your own, you can cover all the possible questions that the teacher may ask. If you have covered all the material in your own questions, you will not be surprised by any questions on the exam.*

Step 3. Read your outline, notes, and other materials, looking for answers to the questions you have composed. As you read and review, outline the answers, commit the outlines to memory, and use them as guides during the test. Write out answers to any questions that are difficult for you.

Step 4. Review the outlines, the materials, and the answers to your questions the afternoon before the test. Then put the whole thing aside and get a good night's rest.

Final Preparation

Just before going in to take the test:

- Eat a high-energy snack; fruit is a good choice. Coffee or tea will also help. Do some calisthenics or whatever else is necessary to make you alert.
- Get your equipment ready: pens, pencils, erasers, paper or examination booklets, and scratch paper. Take what you will need so that you will not worry about supplies once you enter the room.
- Arrive two minutes early for the test. Get yourself and your equipment arranged. Relax for a few seconds before the work begins.

Taking the Test

Your success in taking tests depends on your study habits and preparation; no student—or at least not very many students—can earn a high grade on a test without proper preparation. But good preparation alone will not guarantee success. You need a strategy for taking tests, a strategy that will help you to decide which questions to answer, what order to use in answering the selected questions, and what organization to use for each question.

When you have made the best possible preparations for taking the test and are in the classroom with the test in your hands, do two things before you write:

First, read the test from start to finish, beginning with the directions. Decide which questions you know the most about. Determine the point value of each question. Answer first the questions you know the most about. Answering them first will ease you into the test, develop your confidence, and keep you from wasting time on questions you can't answer well anyway. Do first what you can do best. Use the remaining time to do the best you can on the rest of the questions.

Be sure to select the most valuable questions from among those you can answer. Don't waste time on a question of low point value when you could be answering a question with a high point value.

Always follow the directions. If options allow you to choose certain questions from a group, be sure you understand the options and make your choices based on your knowledge and on the point value of the questions. Invest your time wisely.

Second, make careful preparations before you write. Adapt the first four steps in the writing process to guide you in writing the answers.

Step 1. Identify the subject. The first step in the writing process is the selection of a subject. On a personal paper narrating an event in your life, your range of choices is wide. On a test, clearly, you have no such choice. The teacher has selected the subject for each question. Your job is to identify that subject correctly. A question that asks for a discussion of the causes of the Great Depression is not properly answered by a discussion of the characteristics of the Roaring Twenties. Make sure you answer the question that is asked.

Step 2. Review what you know about the question. Recall your outlines and notes. Bring to mind the practice answers you wrote in your review exercises. Make notes of these on a sheet of paper. Try to remember as much material as you can. List any special or technical words related to the subject.

Step 3. Decide exactly what the question asks for and what overall statement you are able to make and support in response to the question. Before you write, construct a specific statement of the idea or concept that you intend to develop in writing your answer. This point, or main idea, will come out of the materials you reviewed in Step 2.

Step 4. Carefully select supporting materials, examples, explanations, and other data that will serve to establish and clarify the main idea. You will have pulled together a considerable amount of material in your quick mental review. Not all of it will fit exactly the statement you are making; not all of it will be especially effective in your answer. Select materials that will establish and reinforce your point as effectively as possible within the constraints of time and space.

Now that you have looked at the basic steps in writing essay test answers—or any paragraph, for that matter—let us examine each of these steps in greater detail. Assume that you have read the test carefully, have selected your questions, and are now ready to start on the question you'll answer first.

Let us set up a brief example and follow it through these steps. Suppose you pick up a test and find on it a problem such as this:

Select one of the seven species of sea turtles and discuss its physical appearance, its habitat and geographic distribution, and its status in both present numbers and population trends.

Step 1 requires careful identification of the subject matter covered in the question. The sample question refers to sea turtles, not to all kinds of turtles. It also asks for a discussion of just one of the seven species of sea turtles. It asks for only three rather simple pieces of information about that species:

1. What is the physical appearance of that species?
2. In what type of habitats is the species found, and where are these habitats located?
3. How many individuals of this species are estimated to be alive, and is that number increasing or decreasing?

Only the last point is at all tricky. *Status* has in this question a somewhat specialized meaning referring to the species' survival potential based on what the estimated living population is and on whether it is increasing or decreasing worldwide. So the subject of that question is information about a particular species of sea turtle.

Step 2 is to collect material, to recall what you know about one species of sea turtle. From the textbook, your lecture notes, and a brief outside reading assignment, you remember this about sea turtles and jot down the following notes:

Actually 7 species—only three much covered in class. One stood out because commercial importance (food & other products)—green turtle.
Large: 3 to 6 feet from front to back over curve of upper shell (carapace; lower shell, plastron).
Weighs 200–300 lb. average but reaches 850 lb. some specimens. Color from green-brown to near black. Scutes (bony plates) clearly marked. Head small compared to body.

Occurs almost worldwide in warmer waters shallow enough to allow growth of sea grass turtles eat.

Present status questionable. Not endangered because lrg. pops. in remote areas—under pressure and declining in pop. areas. Needs protection. First protective law in Caribbean,
passed 1620. Used extensively for food by early sailors, who killed mainly females coming on shore to lay eggs. Now used for cosmetics and jewelry.

Large green turtles make good zoo exhibits. W. Indian natives make soup of them.

Nesting habits: Female beaches and lays approx. 100 eggs in shaped hole. First hatchlings
on top of nest push out sand covering them and leave. Those on bottom crawl out using
sand first hatchlings displaced and crushed shells of vacated eggs as platform. 100 eggs
right number—fewer places top of nest too low in hole, more requires nest too deep for
last hatchling to escape. Recent increase in ecological pressure because women use more
cosmetics based on turtle oil.

This quick mental review, jotted down hastily (perhaps more sketchily on an actual test
than in the example), has produced enough information to allow you to move to the
next step.

In Step 3 you must determine what you can say in response to the question. Before
you can make that determination, you must know exactly what the question directs you
to do. These directions are usually given at the beginning of the question, and, although
their exact wording may vary, they generally fall into one of several categories.

The following list of instruction words covers most standard types of essay questions. Read this list carefully; note that each type of instruction requires a different type
of answer.

• List, name, identify

These words require short-answer responses that can be written in one or two complete
sentences. Do exactly what the question asks; don't try to expand the scope of the question.

Example: Name the presidents who served in the military prior to becoming president.

The word *identify* suggests that you ought to mention the two or three most important
facts about a person or a subject area, not just any facts that come to mind. You would
thus identify Eisenhower as a military commander and U.S. President, not as a West
Point graduate who played golf.

• Summarize, trace, delineate

An instruction to summarize asks that you give an overview or a capsule version of the
subject.

Example: Summarize Senator Smith's position on tax reform.

An answer to this question would provide a three- or four-sentence statement of the
main points of Smith's position.

The words *trace* and *delineate* usually ask that you describe the steps or process that
brought some event to pass.

Example: Trace the life cycle of the monarch butterfly.

The answer requires a listing of the steps in the development of the butterfly from egg to adulthood.

• Define

The instruction *define* usually asks that you establish the term within a class and then differentiate it from the other members of the class. "A parrot is a bird" establishes the word *parrot* in a class, and "found in the tropics and capable of reproducing human speech" is an attempt at differentiation. You should be careful to add enough elements of differentiation to eliminate other members of the class. For instance, as the myna is also a tropical bird capable of reproducing speech, you must complete your definition of *parrot* by specifying such items as size, color, and habitat.

• Analyze, classify, outline

These command words imply a discussion of the relationship that exists between a whole and its parts.
Analyze asks that you break an idea, a concept, or a class down into its integral parts.

Example: Analyze the various political persuasions that exist within the Republican party.

This question asks that you look at the party and identify the various categories of political belief ranging from right to left.
Classify asks that you position parts in relation to a whole.

Example: Classify the following parts of an automobile as to location in engine, steering, or drive shaft:
1. Ball joint
2. Piston ring
3. Pinion gear

Outline requires that you break down an idea or a concept into its parts and show how the parts support and reinforce each other. Whether you arrange your sentences in the form of a whole paragraph or in a listing of main headings and subheadings, your outline must show how the idea or concept is made up of smaller parts and how these parts relate to the idea and to each other.

Example: Outline Senator Random's position on emission controls for automobiles.

This question requires that you state the position and its supporting points.

• Discuss, explain, illustrate

This type of command word is probably the most general of all the possible directions for essay tests. The request here is that you expose, in detail, the idea, concept, or process in question. Single simple sentences will not suffice to answer such instructions. You must provide all pertinent information and write enough so that your readers have no questions, no gaps left in their information, when they've finished reading. Often such questions can be answered by making a statement of the idea or process and providing examples to illustrate your statements. In fact, if the instruction is *illustrate,* examples are required.

> **Example:** Discuss the effect of depriving a child of physical affection in the first three years of its life.

The answer could be given by making a statement or statements of the effects and giving examples of each.

• Compare, contrast

A question that asks you to compare, or to compare and contrast, is simply asking that you discuss the similarities and differences between two or more subjects.

> **Example:** Compare the military abilities of Grant and Sherman. Make a comparison between Smith's plan and Jones's plan for shoring up the value of the dollar overseas. What are the similarities and differences between racketball and squash?

All these example questions ask you to establish categories—for example, skill in tactics, ability to motivate, and so on, as they relate to Grant and Sherman—and to explain how the subjects are alike or different in the areas you establish.

• Evaluate, criticize

This type of question is probably the most difficult because it requires that you know what is correct or best or ideal and that you assess the assigned topic against that ideal. So you must know the subject *and* the ideal equally well.

> **Example:** Evaluate Eisenhower as a leader in foreign affairs.

The question is, then, "What are the characteristics of a leader in foreign affairs and how does Eisenhower measure up in each of these categories?"

When you have clarified the instruction for a question, determine exactly what subject you must deal with in your answer. Focus on the limited area of the subject specified by the question.

A question asking you to deal with *the qualities of Willa Cather's prose* does not ask for a discussion of her life or her early efforts at poetry. The question asks for treatment of a limited area: *the qualities of Willa Cather's prose.*

Examine the subject area and the instructions of the question very carefully. Be sure to get both clear in your mind before you begin to write. An answer that *evaluates* will get little credit if the question says *define.* A discussion of the care and feeding of peregrine falcons will get few points if the question asks for a classification of birds of prey in North America.

Examine now the sample problem presented earlier:

> Select one of the seven species of sea turtles and discuss its physical appearance, its habitat and geographic distribution, and its status in both present numbers and population trends.

The direction, the instruction word, is *discuss,* which means make a statement and support it. The subject area is clear: any one of the seven species of sea turtles. The direction is clear: discuss

the physical appearance
the habitat and general distribution
the current status

You have collected information on the subject. Now determine exactly what you can say on that subject. For this sample question, your statement might read:

The green turtle is a large green-to-black sea turtle residing in warm, shallow waters all over the world; it is numerous but is declining in populated areas.

Keep the statement simple and direct. It need not state all the facts and details; indeed, it should not try to. It is designed to serve only as a guide for the development of your answer. If you follow the outline of the answer suggested by this controlling statement, you will select in Step 4 only the materials that serve to answer the question, and you will not be tempted to add irrelevant materials. When you have completed a controlling statement for the answer, move to the next step.

Step 4 requires that you select from the collected materials those items that will develop the statement. Select specific details to explain each area within the statement. For the first section, physical appearance, your notes contain the following concrete details:

1. Size—three to six feet from front to back over the shell; average weight—200–300 pounds, record is 850 pounds.
2. Coloration—greenish brown is lightest color, almost black when splotches are close together.
3. Shape of flippers, head, tail. [Note that these items are not in the original list. New materials often come to mind during preparations.]

You can fill in the other sections by selecting from the collection of materials. Do not include any materials that do not specifically develop or illustrate the statement that controls the answer. Provide ample development, but do not pad.

In the collection of supporting materials for the sample question, the long discussion of the nesting habits and the number of eggs ordinarily laid by the green turtle does not fit into the answer. The material is interesting, it is concerned with the green turtle, but it does *not* fit any of the three categories in the question. Don't use materials simply because they relate to the general subject. Use only materials that support the answer to the specific question.

Writing the Answer

At this point you have before you on scratch paper:

1. A basic idea.
2. Supporting materials for that basic idea.

These will be useful in writing the answer, but they are not the answer. They are the *content* for the answer. The answer requires content, but it also requires form: grammatically correct, complete sentences that present the material in a logical, relevant order.

The best way to provide order for your answer is to modify your controlling statement to suggest the order that you intend to follow. This modification will help your reader to follow your answer.

A sentence combining elements of the question with a suggestion of your answer's focus offers a good beginning and adequate control:

Of the seven species of sea turtles, the green turtle is the largest and the most widely distributed, but it is nearing endangered status because it has commercial value.

Note that the sentence establishes your topic, the green turtle, and defines the aspects that you will discuss by using key words from each of those areas:

1. *Largest* leads to a physical description.
2. *Most widely distributed* leads naturally to a discussion of habitat and distribution.
3. *Nearing endangered status* opens the discussion of population size and trends. The sentence relates your answer to the question and will keep you from wandering into irrelevancy. Try to make your first sentence as specific as possible, but be sure that you can expand on it. A statement that the green turtle is "an interesting species" is little help in controlling the answer because it does not focus on the question. You are not concerned with how interesting the species is; you are concerned with its appearance, its habitat and distribution, and its status. The entire answer to this sample question might read as follows:

Of the seven species of sea turtles, the green turtle is the largest and the most widely distributed, but it is nearing endangered status because it has commercial value. It is a large turtle, measuring between 3 and 6 feet in length over the top of the shell and weighing on the average 200–300 pounds. The largest specimens are over 5 feet in length and weigh 800–1000 pounds. The upper shell (carapace) is light to dark brown, shaded or mottled with darker colors ranging to an almost black-green. The lower shell (plastron) is white to light yellow. The scales on the upper surface of the head are dark, and the spaces between them are yellow; on the sides of the head, the scales are brown but have a yellow margin, giving a yellow cast to the sides of the head. The shell is broad, low, and more or less heart-shaped. The green turtle inhabits most of the warm, shallow waters of the world's seas and oceans, preferring areas 10–20 feet deep where it can find good sea grass pastures for browsing. The turtles prefer areas that have many potholes, because they sleep in the holes for security. In numbers and population trends, the status of the green turtle is in doubt. It is under great pressure in highly populated areas such as the Caribbean Sea, where it is avidly hunted for food and for use in making jewelry and cosmetics. However, because it occurs in large numbers in remote areas, it is not technically an endangered species at this time. It needs better protection in populated areas so that its numbers will not decline any further.

Assignments and Exercises

The suggestions offered in this section will not improve your ability to take tests unless you practice applying them in your own work. Here are some suggested exercises to apply the principles:

1. Analyze your performance on a recent essay test and discuss the ways in which following the suggestions in this chapter might have improved your performance.

2. Assume that you are enrolled in a course in American history and must take an essay test on the Revolutionary War. The materials covered include the textbook, your lecture notes, your outside readings, and two films. Write a paragraph describing your preparations for the test.

3. As a practice test, write answers to the following questions on the chapter you have just read on essay-test taking.

- Discuss the preparations for taking a test up to the point where you enter the test room.
- Describe the process by which you would decide which questions to answer (if given options) and in which order you would answer them.
- Name and define four of the seven command-word categories often found in test questions, discussing the kinds of materials that each word requires in its answer.
- Describe the final form of the answer, including a discussion of thesis statement and development as it occurs in this chapter.

SECTION 3 ■
Writing Effective Paragraphs

The Paragraph

A paragraph is a group of sentences (or sometimes just one sentence) related to a single idea. Each paragraph begins on a new line, and its first word is indented a few spaces from the left margin. The last line of a paragraph is blank from the end of the last sentence to the right margin.

The function of a paragraph is to state and develop a single idea, usually called a **topic.** The topic is actually the subject of the paragraph, what the paragraph is about. Everything in the paragraph after the statement of the topic ought to **develop the topic.** *To develop* means to explain and define, to discuss, to illustrate and exemplify. From the reader's point of view, the content of the paragraph should provide enough information and explanation to make clear the topic of the paragraph and the function of the paragraph in the essay or the chapter.

The Topic Sentence

The first function of the paragraph is to state what it is about, to establish its topic; therefore the first rule of effective paragraph writing is as follows:

Usually, declare the topic of the paragraph early in a single sentence (called the *topic sentence***).** You remember that the first sentence of our sample answer to an essay test question related the answer to the question by paraphrasing a significant part of the question. This sentence also provided direction for the answer by telling briefly what the answer would contain. Each paragraph should contain such a point of departure, a sentence that names what the paragraph is about and indicates how the paragraph will proceed. It may do so in considerable detail:

Although the green turtle—a large, greenish-brown sea turtle inhabiting warm, shallow seas over most of the world—is not yet generally endangered, it is subject to extreme pressure in populated areas.

or rather broadly:

The green turtle is one of the most important of the seven species of sea turtles.

Both statements name a specific topic: the green turtle. But neither sentence stops with a name. A sentence that reads:

This paragraph will be about green turtles.

is not a complete topic sentence because it does not suggest the direction that the rest of the paragraph will take. Note that both the good examples are phrased so that a certain type of development must follow. The first sentence anticipates a discussion that will mention size, color, habitat, and distribution but will focus on the green turtle's chances for survival. The second sentence will develop the assertion that the species is one of the most important of the sea turtles. Note that neither example tries to embrace the whole idea of the paragraph. The topic sentence should lay the foundation for the paragraph, not say everything there is to be said.

As a general rule, make the topic sentence one of the first few sentences in the paragraph. Sometimes a paragraph has no topic sentence; occasionally the topic sentence occurs at the end of the paragraph. These exceptions are permissible, but the early topic sentence is more popular because it helps in three ways to produce an effective message:

1. It defines your job as a writer and states a manageable objective—a single topic.

2. It establishes a guide for your development of the basic idea. You must supply evidence of or support for any assertion in the topic sentence. The topic sentence is only a beginning, but it predicts a conclusion that the paragraph must reach.

3. It tells your reader what the paragraph is going to contain.

Notice how the topic sentence (italicized) in the following paragraph controls it and provides clear direction for the reader:

> Of all the inventions of the last one hundred years, *the automobile assembly line has had the most profound effect on American life.* The assembly line provided a method for building and selling automobiles at a price many could afford, thus changing the auto from a luxury item owned by the wealthy few to an everyday appliance used by almost every adult in America. Universal ownership and the use of the automobile have opened new occupations, new dimensions of mobility, and new areas of recreation to everyone. In addition, the automobile assembly line has provided a model for the mass production of television sets, washing machines, bottled drinks, and even sailboats. All these products would have been far too expensive for purchase by the average person without the introduction of assembly-line methods to lower manufacturing costs. With the advent of Henry Ford's system, all Americans could hope to possess goods once reserved for a select class, and the hope changed their lives forever.

The italicized sentence states the topic and the purpose of the paragraph: The paragraph is going to argue that the assembly line, more than any other invention, changed America's way of life. The writer is controlled by this sentence because everything in the paragraph should serve to support this argument. Readers are assisted by the sentence, for they know that they can expect examples supporting the position stated in the sentence.

Writing a good topic sentence is only the first step in writing an effective paragraph, for an effective paragraph provides complete development of the topic; that is, it tells the readers all they need to know about the topic for the purposes at hand. This principle is the second basic rule of effective paragraph writing:

Always provide complete development in each paragraph. Complete development tells the readers all that they need to understand about the paragraph itself and the way the paragraph fits into the rest of the essay or chapter. Complete development does not necessarily provide all the information the reader *wants* to know; rather, the reader receives what is *needed* for understanding the internal working of the paragraph (the topic and its development) and the external connection (the relationship between the paragraph and the paper as a whole). As an illustration of that rather abstract statement, read the following paragraph, which gives a set of instructions for a familiar process:

Another skill required of a self-sufficient car owner is the ability to jump-start a car with a dead battery, a process that entails some important do's and don't's. First, make certain that the charged battery to be used is a properly grounded battery of the same voltage as the dead one. Put out all smoking material. Connect the first jumper cable to the positive terminal of each battery. Connect one end of the second cable to the negative terminal of the live battery, and then clamp the other end to some part of the engine in the car with the dead battery. DO *NOT* LINK POSITIVE AND NEGATIVE TERMINALS. DO *NOT* ATTACH THE NEGATIVE CABLE DIRECTLY TO THE NEGATIVE TERMINAL OF THE DEAD BATTERY. Choose a spot at least 18 inches from the dead battery. A direct connection is dangerous. Put the car with the live battery in neutral, rev the engine, and hold it at moderate rpm while starting the other car. Once the engine is running, hold it at moderate rpm for a few seconds and disconnect the NEGATIVE cable. Then disconnect the positive cable. It is wise to take the car to a service station as soon as possible to have the battery checked and serviced if necessary.

The instructions in this paragraph are clear, and they will enable anyone to start a car with a dead battery. The curious reader, however, will have certain questions in mind after reading the paragraph:

1. What is a properly grounded battery?
2. Why is it necessary to extinguish smoking materials?
3. To what parts of the engine may one attach the negative cable? [After all, attaching it to the fan will have exciting results.]
4. What is the danger of making a direct connection?

Also, there are at least two important steps left out of the process:

Before connecting the two batteries,
1. Remove the caps to the cells of both batteries.
2. Check the fluid levels in the cells of both batteries.

Without these steps in the process, the car with the dead battery will start, but there is still a chance of explosion.

A paragraph that lacks material, that is not fully developed, probably won't explode. But it probably won't succeed, either. Questions raised in the mind of the reader will almost always weaken the effect of the paragraph. Sometimes the omissions are so important that the reader will miss the point or give up altogether in frustration. Remember the second rule for writing effective paragraphs:

Always provide complete development in each paragraph. Never leave your reader with unanswered questions about the topic.

Most of the time, you can write a well-developed paragraph by following three very simple steps:

Step 1. Make the topic statement one clear, rather brief sentence.

Step 2. Clarify and define the statement as needed.

Step 3. Illustrate or exemplify the topic statement concretely where possible.

As an example of the use of this three-step process, follow the development of a paragraph in answer to the question, "What is the most important quality that you are seeking in an occupation?" The student's answer, found after much preliminary writing and a good bit of discussion, led to the following topic sentence:

> Above all other qualities, *I want to have variety in the tasks I perform and in the locations where I work.*

Clarification and Definition {

I know I must do the general line of work for which I'm trained, but I want to do different tasks in that work every day if possible. Repeating the same tasks day after day must be a mind-numbing experience. Our neighborhood mechanic does one tune-up after another, five days a week. A doctor friend tells me that 90 percent of her practice involves treating people ill with a virus, for which she prescribes an antibiotic against secondary infection. I want no part of that sort of humdrum work. Variety means doing a different part of a job every day, perhaps working on the beginning of one project today and the completion of another tomorrow, or working on broad concepts one day and details the next. I'd also like to work at a dif-

Concrete Example {

ferent job site as often as possible. The field of architecture is one area that might suit me. I could work in drafting, and then switch to field supervision, and move from that task to developing the overall concepts of a large project. By doing this, I could vary my assignments and the locations of my work.

A revised version of such a paragraph might read this way:

Topic Sentence {

Some people want salary and others want big challenges, *but in my career I want variety, in both assignment and work location,* more than any other single quality. As much as possible, I want

Clarification and Definition {

to do a different part of a job every day. Perhaps I could work on the beginning of one project and shift to the completion of another, or work on details for a while and then shift to broad concepts involved in planning. For this reason architecture looks like a promising field

Concrete Example {

for me. I could work in drafting and detailing, move next to on-site supervision, and then shift to developing the design concepts of a major project. I know that doing the same task in the same place would be a mind-numbing experience for me. Our family doctor says that 90 percent of her practice consists of treating patients who have a routine virus infection, for which she routinely prescribes an antibiotic against secondary infection. Our neighborhood mechanic spends all his time doing tune-ups. I want none of that humdrum sort of work. Variety is the spice of life; it is also the ingredient that makes work palatable for me.

These general guidelines will help you to provide complete development of your paragraphs:

1. Write a topic sentence.
2. Define and clarify that statement.
3. Provide concrete examples and illustrations.

Patterns for Paragraphs

In addition to the method of development by topic sentence/discussion/example, writers over the years have developed several recognizable patterns for paragraphs. These patterns are useful for presenting certain types of information for specialized purposes within an essay. You should recognize and practice these patterns so that you can use them in your own writing.

Comparison/Contrast

When you are asked to compare, to contrast, or to compare and contrast two or more people, ideas, attitudes, or objects, you are being asked to examine items that fall within the same general group or class and, after this examination, to point out ways in which the items are similar and dissimilar. Common test questions read as follows:

> Compare the attitudes of General Patton and Bertrand Russell toward war and the mainte-nance of a standing army.
> Compare the effects of heroin and marijuana on the human body.
> Compare orange juice and lemon juice in respect to taste, vitamin C content, and usefulness in cooking.

Note that in each question there is a large class that includes the subjects of the com-parison:

> Patton and Russell were both famous people who held carefully developed attitudes toward war. [If one had no attitude on war, the comparison couldn't be made.]
> Heroin and marijuana are both drugs that act on the human body.
> Orange juice and lemon juice are both citrus products.

The point of comparison/contrast is that the items share certain qualities but can be separated or distinguished by other qualities that they do not share. The identification of these like and unlike qualities is the aim of comparison/contrast. One of the most useful ways to employ comparison/contrast is to create an understanding of an unfa-miliar concept by showing how that concept is like or unlike a more familiar concept.

> If you know the stereotype of the Texan—loud, boisterous, bragging about his state and his own possessions—you could appreciate my friend Jack because he is the exact antithesis of that stereotype. He is quiet. . . .

In a course in business or investments you might be asked to compare stocks and bonds as investment instruments. Begin by listing the qualities of a common stock and the qualities of a bond side by side.

A bond is	A stock is
1. an instrument used by investors.	1. an instrument used by investors.

Note how this first point in each list establishes that the two objects of comparison are members of the same large class and can therefore be compared and contrasted.

2. a certificate of indebtedness.

2. a representation of ownership of a fraction of a company.

3. a promise to repay a specific number of dollars.

3. worth the selling price on any day, whether more or less than the purchase price.

4. payable on a specified date.

4. sold anytime, but not ever payable as is a bond.

5. sold at a specific rate of interest.

5. not an interest-drawing instrument; rather, it earns a share of profits.

In geology rocks can be divided into three groups:

Igneous	*Sedimentary*	*Metamorphic*
Formed when molten rock material called *magma* cools and solidifies.	Formed from deposits of older rocks or animal or plant life. Are deposited on each other and joined by pressure or natural chemicals.	Formed when old rocks change under heat or pressure. They do not divide easily into subgroups.
One type (extrusive) is forced out by pressure from within the earth; for example, a volcano erupts and spews out lava, which, if cooled quickly, becomes glassy or forms small crystals such as obsidian or pumice.	Three types: Classic—formed of older rock pieces. Chemical—formed of crystallized chemicals. Organic—formed of plant and animal remains.	

However, a detailed comparison of the three basic types of rocks is impossible in a single paragraph because of the enormous complexity of the subject. Certain qualities exist in each of the three groups—smooth surfaces, for example—but what caused the smooth surfaces in one case or another may not be particularly relevant to the factors that determine what group a rock belongs to. About all that can be dealt with in a single paragraph is a very broad comparison of the three major groups of rocks.

In the study of human anatomy, the two muscle groups—skeletal and smooth—offer a sufficient number of common points to make the exercise of comparison possible. The two groups can be compared on the basis of

	Skeletal	*Smooth*
1. Location	Attached to skeleton.	Found in blood vessels, digestive system, and internal organs.
2. Function	To move legs, arms, eyes, and so on.	To move food for digestion, contract or expand blood vessels—varies by location.

| 3. Structure | Long, slender fibers bundled together in parallel, contain many nuclei. | Arranged in sheets or in circular fashion, contain one nucleus. |
| 4. Contraction | Rapid, only when stimulated by nerve; stimulus can be voluntary or involuntary. | Slow, rhythmic; cannot be controlled consciously (voluntarily); stimulated by nerves or by hormones. |

It is possible to develop a paragraph of comparison/contrast in two different ways. The first pattern is clearly illustrated in the list of muscle characteristics: The qualities of both muscle groups are listed numerically in the same order. This pattern is useful if you are comparing only a limited number of characteristics. A second pattern, because it focuses the comparison point by point, provides better control of longer or more complicated topics. A paragraph comparing stocks and bonds in this way might read as follows:

> Although stocks and bonds are both common investment instruments, they differ in several important aspects and thus appeal to different types of investors. A bond is a certificate of indebtedness; a share of stock represents ownership of a percentage of a company. A bond involves a promise to repay a specified amount of money on a day agreed on in advance. Because it represents ownership, stock must be sold to obtain its value, and it is worth only the selling price on a given day, never a guaranteed amount. A bond earns money in the form of interest at a fixed rate, but stocks share in the profits, partial distributions of which are called *dividends*. Thus the value of a bond, if held to its date of maturity, is fixed, and the periodic interest paid by many bonds is relatively secure. A stock, on the other hand, changes its value on the basis of market conditions and its rate of return on the basis of the profitability of the company. The risk in a bond is the risk that inflation will reduce the value of its fixed number of dollars and its fixed rate of return; stocks risk a possible decline in the general market and a possible reduction of profits that might erode the sale price and the dividends. So bonds are useful where security of investment is a high priority and protection against inflation is not vital. Stocks fit an investment portfolio in which some risk is acceptable and a hedge against inflation is very important.

So in this pattern we see bonds and stocks compared in respect to the following categories:

1. The nature of the instrument itself.
2. The way the value of the instrument is established.
3. The method of earning money.
4. The relative security of the two instruments.
5. The risks inherent in each one.
6. The situations in which each might be useful as an investment.

As an exercise in comparison/contrast, you might try following each of the two patterns in writing a paragraph on the two groups of muscles described earlier.

Definition

We have all read definitions; they are the subject matter of dictionaries, which we customarily use to find the meaning of an unfamiliar word. But definition, as a process, is also a useful device in writing; it can serve to establish meaning for words, concepts, and attitudes. You have often written paragraphs of definition on tests and in essays. On tests, you might find instructions such as these:

> Define the *sonata-allegro form* and give examples of it in twentieth-century music.
> Define *conservatism* as it is used in American politics.
> Define a *boom-vang* and describe how it is used in sailing.

The correct responses to such instructions are paragraphs of definition. Such paragraphs ought to follow the same rules of presentation and development that the dictionary does. Let us examine two definitions in the pattern used in dictionaries and discover how they are formed.

> Basketball is a game played by two teams on a rectangular court having a raised basket at each end. Points are scored by tossing a large round ball through the opponent's basket.

> Football is a game played with an oval-shaped ball by two teams defending goals at opposite ends of a rectangular field. Points are scored by carrying or throwing the ball across the opponent's goal or by kicking the ball over the crossbar of the opponent's goalpost.

These two definitions concern games familiar to most of us. Notice that they both follow the same pattern:

First, they identify both words as the names of games.
Second, they specify

1. the number of teams in a game.
2. the number of players on each team.
3. the type of playing area.
4. the way in which scoring occurs.
5. the shape of the ball.

The examples illustrate the classic pattern of definition: The first step is to classify the word within a class or group; the second step is to differentiate the word from other members of its class:

> Football is a game ... [Establishes in a class.]
> played by two teams
> of eleven players each
> on a rectangular field.   [Differentiates from other games.]
> Scoring occurs by crossing
> opponent's goal in a special way.

When you write a paragraph of definition, follow the same method: Classify the term, then distinguish it from other members of its class.

However, your paragraph of definition ought to offer more than just the basic points of differentiation. You should also provide illustrations, examples, and comparisons of the term being defined to terms that might be familiar to your reader. This additional information helps your reader to understand and assimilate the information that you are offering. The process is often called **extending the definition.** Examine the following paragraph defining football and note how basic definition and extension are combined to make an effective presentation:

On any Saturday or Sunday afternoon in the fall, hundreds of thousands of Americans betake themselves to stadiums, and millions more hunker down before television sets to witness the great American spectator sport, football. In simplest form, a definition of football states that it is a game played on a large field by two teams of eleven players and that scoring is accomplished by carrying or throwing an oval ball across the opponent's goal line or by kicking the ball between two uprights called *goalposts*. But such literal definition scarcely does justice to the game or to its impact on Americans. For it is more than a game or a sport; it is a happening, a spectacle, a ritual that is almost a religious experience for its devotees. The game catches them with its color: a beautiful green field surrounded by crowds dressed in a galaxy of hues, teams uniformed in the brightest shades ever to flow from the brush of deranged artists. It holds these fans with its excitement: the long pass, the touchdown run, the closing-minutes drive to victory. But above all the game seems to captivate them with its violence, with dangers vicariously experienced, with a slightly veiled aura of mayhem. This element of danger draws casual viewers and converts them into fanatic worshippers of the great American cult-sport, football.

Finally, a word of warning about constructing definitions: A fundamental rule is that a definition must not be circular. A useful definition does not define a term by using a related form of the term itself. To define the word *analgesic* by saying that it causes analgesia means nothing unless the reader knows that *analgesia* means absence or removal of pain. To define *conservatism* as a philosophy that attempts to conserve old values doesn't really add much to a reader's understanding. Thus the rule:

Do not construct circular definitions; i.e., do not use in the definition a form of the word being defined.

Analysis

Chemists analyze compounds to isolate and identify their components. Economists analyze the financial data of the nation to determine the factors contributing to recessions. Sports commentators analyze games to explain the strengths leading to a victory.

Analysis is the act of breaking down a substance or an entity into its components. It is possible to analyze a football team and to point out the various positions: ends, tackles, guards, and the rest. An army can be broken down into infantry, artillery, and engineers. A piano is made up of parts: keys, strings, sounding board, and so on.

A paragraph of analysis provides information derived from this act of breaking down into parts, usually by listing, defining, and explaining the parts of the whole in question. As an example, take the elements or characteristics that make up that rarest of animals, the good driver:

The good driver possesses
1. technical competence.
2. physical skills.
3. sound judgment.
4. emotional stability.

A paragraph analyzing the qualities of a good driver might read this way:

Every American over age fourteen wants to drive, does drive, or just stopped driving because his or her license was revoked. Not every American—in fact, only a very few Americans—can be counted in the ranks of good drivers. Good drivers must possess technical competence in the art of driving. They must know the simple steps, starting, shifting, and braking, and the highly sophisticated techniques, feathering the brakes and the power slide, for example. In addition they must possess physical skills, such as exceptional eye–hand coordination, fast reflexes, outstanding depth perception, and peripheral vision. They must also possess good judgment. What speed is safe on a rain-slick highway? How far can a person drive without succumbing to fatigue? What are the possible mistakes that the approaching driver can make? And besides the answers to these questions and the technical and physical skills listed above, good drivers possess steel nerves to cope with that potentially lethal emergency that one day will come to everyone who slips behind the wheel of a car. Only with these qualities can a person be called a good driver and be relatively sure of returning home in one piece.

A suggestion about analysis: When you divide or break down an entity into its elements, be sure that you establish parallel categories. It is not proper, in analyzing an automobile's main systems, to list

frame
body
drive train
engine
piston rings

Although the first four items could possibly be called major systems in an automobile, piston rings are a small part of a large system, the engine, and cannot be included in a list of major systems.

The rule for analysis is
Keep categories parallel.

Process Analysis

A process paragraph is a form of analysis that examines the steps involved in an action or a sequence of actions. The most common sort of process analysis is the recipe: To make a rabbit stew, first catch a rabbit, and so forth. Instructions for building stereo receivers or flying kites or cleaning ovens are all process analyses. In addition to instructions, process analysis can be used to trace the steps involved in a historical event. Such analysis would be required to answer an essay test question that begins with the word *trace* or *delineate*.

The following paragraph provides a set of instructions:

Changing the oil and the filter in your car is a simple process, and "doing it yourself" can save several dollars every time you change the oil. First, go to an auto parts store or a discount store and buy the oil and the oil filter specified for your car. At the same time, buy an oil filter wrench, the only specialized tool necessary for this job. Don't buy these items at your gas station; prices are lower at the other stores. In addition, you will need an adjustable wrench and a pail or bucket low enough to fit under the car to catch the old oil as it drains from the crankcase. Don't lift the car on a bumper jack. Simply crawl under the car and locate the drain plug for the crankcase. From the front of the car the first thing you see underneath will be the radiator—the thing with the large hose running from the bottom. That hose runs to the engine, the next piece of equipment as you work your way back. On the bottom surface is the drain plug, usually square with a few threads visible where it screws into the oil pan. Place the pail or bucket beneath this plug. Fit the wrench to the plug by adjusting its size. Turn the plug counterclockwise until it falls out of its hole into the pail. Don't try to catch it; the oil may be hot. While the oil drains into the pail, find the oil filter on one side of the engine, usually down low. (It will look exactly like the one you bought.) Reach up (or perhaps down from the top, whichever is easier) and slip the circle of the filter wrench over it. Pull the wrench in a counterclockwise direction and take off the old filter. Put the new filter on in exactly the opposite way, tightening it clockwise by hand until it is snug. Put the drain plug back in place, tightening it firmly with the adjustable wrench. Now find the oil filler cap on the top of the engine and pour in the new oil. Tighten the filler cap firmly. Dispose of the old oil at a collection station and wipe your hands clean. Finally, record the mileage for this change somewhere so that you will know when the next change is due.

A process paragraph that traces a historical development might be somewhat more difficult to write than a set of instructions. Essentially, however, tracing the steps in a historical process follows the same form as instructions; the major difference is that the historical event has already occurred and the paragraph is written in the past tense. Examine the following paragraph, which traces the transformation of the computer from mainframe to microcomputer, and notice how its pattern (this happened, then that, then another thing) follows very closely the pattern of the instructions in the previous example (do this, then that, then the other thing):

> The first computer was made from vacuum tubes about as big as a bread box, and the collection of them filled up a room the size of a classroom. The tubes were inordinately sensitive to changes in temperature and humidity, and the smallest speck of dust caused them to go berserk. They were expensive to build and expensive to maintain; therefore they were operated only by highly trained technicians. Anyone who wished to use the computer was forced to deal with the people in the white lab coats, an inconvenient arrangement at best. The first step in reducing the size and increasing the reliability of the computer was the invention of transistors, small, inexpensive devices that control the flow of electricity. They are solid and durable, and, most important, they can be made very small. Scientists soon discovered that they could also be hooked together into integrated circuits known as *chips;* the chips could contain tremendous amounts of circuitry, an amount comparable to the wiring diagram of an office building, on a piece of silicon no bigger than your thumbnail. Finally, scientists and computer experts developed the microprocessor, the central works of a computer inscribed on a chip. Presto! The way was opened for the development of a microcomputer about the size of a bread box.

Causal Analysis

Causal analysis, as the name implies, is a discussion of the causes leading to a given outcome. On an essay test, you might be asked to explain or discuss the reasons for a lost war, a victory in an election, a depression, or the collapse of a bridge. In your life outside school, you might be called on to explain why you have selected some occupation or particular college or why you wish to drop out of school to hike the Appalachian Trail for four or five months.

Causal analysis differs from process analysis in that it does not necessarily involve a chronological sequence. Instead, it seeks the reasons for an outcome and lists them (with necessary discussion) in either ascending or descending order of importance. A process analysis concerned with the growth of inflation in the last seventy-five years might trace the fall of the dollar's value and the actions and reactions of government and consumers at intervals of ten years. On the other hand, a causal analysis on the same subject would give the reasons why the dollar has declined in value and why the reactions of government and consumers have produced progressively worse conditions. Causal analysis might also be used to explain why a course of action has been taken or ought to be taken.

It is important that the United States curb inflation over the next few years. Inflation at home is reducing the value of the dollar overseas, making it very difficult for Americans to purchase products from other countries. German automobiles, even those that once were considered low-cost transportation, have increased in price dramatically in the last few years. At home, rapid price increases have made it very difficult for salary increases to keep pace with the cost of living. In spite of large pay increases over the past few years, factory workers have shown little or no gain in buying power; prices have climbed as their wages have increased, leaving them with nothing to show for a larger paycheck. Inflation has been especially hard on retired people who live on a fixed income. They receive only a set number of dollars and do not benefit from pay increases as do wage earners. But while their income has remained the same, prices have increased; thus they cannot buy the same amounts as they could previously. Unchecked inflation works a hardship on all of us, but it is especially hard on those whose income does not increase to match the increases in prices.

Causal analysis might also be used to explain the reasons why someone holds a particular position or opinion. A student explained her love of sailing as follows:

A sailboat, a broad bay, and a good breeze form the most satisfying combination in the world of sport. To be sailing before a brisk wind across an open expanse of water allows—no, requires—cooperation with the forces of nature. Working with the wind in moving the boat provides us one of the few times when we are not forced to ignore, or work against, or even overcome the natural rhythms and functions of the universe. Too much of daily life pits us against those forces; finding them on our side, aiding us in a worthwhile project, is indeed a pleasure. The boats used are in themselves very pleasant. They do not bang or clank, nor do they spout vile fumes or foul the air, suddenly explode, or cease to function altogether. Instead, they offer the soft, sliding sounds of the bow slipping through the sea, the creak of ropes and sails, and the gentle, soothing hum of the standing rigging pulled tight by the pressure of wind on sails. Most important, sailing puts us in close contact, in communion, with that most basic element, the sea. The sea remains constant; winds or storms may stir the surface, but the depths are never moved. The sea always has been and always will be, or so it seems. It offers constancy and permanence in the midst of a world where flux and change are the only constants. Is it any wonder that sailing is such a delight, such a joy?

Use of Examples

One of the simplest yet most effective paragraphs states an idea and uses examples to illustrate and explain the idea. The following paragraph explains an idea by using examples:

Youth and beauty are grand attributes, and together they are a wonderful possession. But television commercials and programs extol youth and beauty to such an extreme that those not so young and less than beautiful are made to feel inferior. Cars, beer, clothes, and even lawn mowers are almost always pictured with lithe, beautiful women of tender age or well-muscled young men with luxuriant, well-groomed hair. Cosmetics are always portrayed in use by people who have almost no need of them. Beauty, and especially youthful beauty, sells goods, we surmise, and those who do not become young and beautiful after buying the car or ingesting the iron supplement are obviously unfit to share the planet with the favored ones. And the programs themselves emphasize youthful beauty. There are few homely, few truly decrepit people who play regularly in any series. Any family, and any individual, who cannot compare with those perfect people ought to be exiled from the land of the lovely. We are left to believe that only the beautiful young are acceptable.

Description and Narration

Two important orders of development remain: development by space and development by time, more commonly called *description* and *narration*. Each of these patterns involves a direction or a movement. Description requires that you move your writer's eye through a given space, picking out selected details in order to create an effect. Narration demands that you create a progression through time, providing details selected to convey a story and its impact. The success of each pattern depends on the careful selection of details of physical qualities or of action and on the vivid presentation of these details.

In *Huckleberry Finn* Mark Twain has Huck give a beautiful description of a sunrise on the Mississippi:

... we run nights, and laid up and hid day-times; soon as night was most gone, we stopped navigating and tied up—nearly always in the dead water under a tow-head; and then cut young cottonwoods and willows and hid the raft with them. Then we set out the lines. Next we slid into the river and had a swim, so as to freshen up and cool off; then we set down on the sandy bottom where the water was about knee deep, and watched the daylight come. Not a sound, anywhere—perfectly still—just like the whole world was asleep, only sometimes the bull-frogs a-cluttering, maybe. The first thing to see, looking away over the water, was a kind of dull line—that was the woods on t'other side—you couldn't make nothing else out; then a pale place in the sky; then more paleness, spreading around; then the river softened up, away off, and warn't black any more, but gray; you could see little dark spots drifting along, ever so far away—trading scows, and such things; and long black streaks—rafts, sometimes you could hear a sweep screaking; or jumbled up voices, it was so still, and sound come so far; and by-and-by you could see a streak on the water which you know by the look of the streak that there's a snag there in a swift current which breaks on it and makes that streak look that way; and you see the mist curl up off the water, and the east reddens up, and the river, and you make out a log cabin in the edge of the woods, away on the bank on t'other side of the river, being a wood-yard, likely, and piled by them cheats so you can throw a dog through it anywheres; then the nice breeze springs up, and comes fanning you from over there, so cool and fresh, and sweet to smell, on account of the woods and the flowers; but sometimes not that way, because they've left dead fish laying around, gars, and such, and they do get pretty rank; and next you've got the full day, and everything smiling in the sun, and the song-birds just going it!

Two qualities of this description are important to your writing. Note first the direction or movement of the unfolding picture. Beginning with the dim view of the far bank, the narrator observes traces of paleness in the sky. He then notes that the river has softened up "away off"; notice the logical progression from sky to horizon to river. After he gives details of the changing sights and sounds at river level, the mist curling up from the river focuses his attention again on the sky as the "east reddens up." Then he returns to the river and develops the picture as new details become visible in the light of morning. This movement from mid-picture to background to foreground to background to foreground follows a sensory logic, an order of increasing visibility as the sun rises and the light increases. It is important to select an order of presentation (or, as here, a logic) and to stick with the order, whether it be left-to-right, right-to-left, middle-to-left-to-right, or any other easily followed combination.

Second, Twain provides details that appeal to the senses:

Color:	dull line of woods
	pale sky
	river changing from black to gray
	dark spots and black streaks
	east reddening
Sound:	complete absence of sound
	bullfrogs a-cluttering
	sweep screaking
	jumbled up voices
	song birds
Smell:	woods
	flowers
	dead fish
Motion:	dark spots drifting
	snag in swift current
	mist curling up off the water
Touch:	cooling off in water
	sitting on sandy bottom of river
	cool breeze springing up

Supply your reader with sensory appeal. Keep your description lively and colorful.

Twain provides us with a heart-stopping piece of narration in *Huck Finn,* the killing of the old drunk, Boggs:

So somebody started on a run. I walked down the street a ways, and stopped. In about five or ten minutes, here comes Boggs again—but not on his horse. He was a-reeling across the street towards me, bareheaded, with a friend on both sides of him aholt of his arms and hurrying him along. He was quiet, and looked uneasy; and he warn't hanging back any, but was doing some of the hurrying himself. Somebody sings out—"Boggs!"

I looked over there to see who said it, and it was that Colonel Sherburn. He was standing perfectly still, in the street, and had a pistol raised in his right hand—not aiming it, but holding it out with the barrel tilted up towards the sky. The same second I see a young girl coming on the run, and two men with her. Boggs and the men turned round, to see who called him, and when they see the pistol the men jumped to one side, and the pistol barrel came down slow and steady to a level—both barrels cocked. Boggs throws up both of his hands, and says, "O Lord, don't shoot!" Bang! goes the first shot, and he staggers back clawing at the air—bang goes the second one, and he tumbles backwards onto the ground, heavy and solid, with his arms spread out. That young girl screamed out, and comes rushing, and down she throws herself on her father, crying, and saying, "Oh, he's killed him, he's killed him!" The crowd closed up around them, and shouldered and jammed one another, with their necks stretched, trying to see, and people on the inside trying to shove them back, and shouting, "Back, back! give him air, give him air!"

Colonel Sherburn he tossed his pistol onto the ground, and turned around on his heels and walked off.

Again, two aspects of the narrative are important. The order is simple, straight chronology. But notice the action words. The girl comes on the run, the men jump, Boggs staggers. Few forms of the verb *to be* intrude to slow the action, and no statements of thought or emotion stop the progression. All of the impact and emotion is conveyed through action, and that use of action is the essence of good narrative.

A FINAL NOTE

Good paragraphs are not necessarily restricted to a single pattern of development. Quite often it is useful to combine patterns to produce a desired effect. The following paragraph on spider webs illustrates such a combination of patterns. The predominant device used here is analysis: The larger unit, spider webs, is broken down into three separate types or categories. But the writer uses an additional strategy; he clarifies his analysis by comparison/contrast, pointing out like and unlike details of the three kinds of spider webs:

> Web-spinning spiders construct three kinds of webs. The first type is the tangled web, a shapeless helter-skelter jumble attached to some support such as the corner of a room. These webs are hung in the path of insects and serve to entangle them as they pass. The second type of web is the sheet web. This web is a flat sheet of silk strung between blades of grass or tree branches. Above this sheet is strung a sort of net, which serves to knock insects into the sheet. When an insect hits the sheet, the spider darts out and pulls it through the webbing, trapping the insect. Finally, perhaps the most beautiful of the webs, is the orb. The orb web consists of threads that extend from a center like a wheel's spokes and are connected to limbs or grass blades. All the spokes are connected by repeated circles of sticky silk, forming a kind of screen. Insects are caught in this screen and trapped by the spider.

Unity

An essential quality that you need to develop in good paragraphs is unity. A very simple rule says everything necessary to make clear the concept of unity in paragraph writing:

Handle only one idea in the paragraph. Second and subsequent ideas should be handled in separate paragraphs.

The paragraph originated as a punctuation device to separate ideas on paper and to assist readers in keeping lines separate as they read. Introducing more than one idea in a paragraph violates the basic reason for the existence of the paragraph.

It would seem to be easy to maintain unity in a paragraph, but sometimes ideas can trick you if you don't pay close attention to your topic sentence. A student wrote this paragraph on strawberries some years ago:

> Strawberries are my favorite dessert. Over ice cream or dipped in powdered sugar, they are so good they bring tears to my eyes. My uncle used to grow strawberries on his farm in New Jersey. Once, I spent the whole summer there and my cousins and I went to the carnival. . . .

Things went pretty far afield from strawberries as the paragraph continued, and you can see how one idea, "used to grow strawberries on his farm," led to a recollection of a delightful summer on that farm and opened the door to a whole new idea and a change in form from discussion to narration. "Strawberries" and "that summer on the farm" are both legitimate, interesting, and perfectly workable topics for a paragraph.

But they are probably not proper for inclusion in the same paragraph. Unity demands that each topic be treated in a separate paragraph. One paragraph handling one idea equals unity.

Coherence

Coherence is another important quality that you need to develop in your paragraphs. The word *cohere* means "to stick together," "to be united." It is a term used in physics to describe the uniting of two or more similar substances within a body by the action of molecular forces. In paragraph writing, the term *coherence* is used to describe a smooth union between sentences within the paragraph. In other words, the sentences in a coherent paragraph follow one another without abrupt changes. A good paragraph reads smoothly, flowing from start to finish without choppiness to distract the reader.

The first step in establishing coherence occurs when you select a pattern for developing the paragraph. The selection of a pattern is based on the assignment that the paragraph is going to fulfill. You learned in the study of essay test answers that a question asking for discussion requires one sort of development and a question asking for comparison demands another. Review the discussions of essay tests and of paragraph patterns to keep this idea fresh in your mind.

(Note, however, that it is sometimes necessary to include more than one pattern of development in a paragraph. A narration, for example, may demand a passage of description. Don't hesitate to shift methods where a switch is useful. Do so with care, and with the possibility in mind that a new method of development might suggest the need for a new paragraph.)

The pattern you select will help to establish coherence because it produces a flow and a movement in the paragraph and because it serves as a frame for providing details of development. Select the pattern according to the demands of the assignment and follow that pattern through the whole paragraph.

The selection of a development pattern is perhaps the most important step in achieving a coherent paragraph. There are, however, various other writing strategies contributing to the same end.

1. Repetition of nouns and use of reference words.

> My father asked me to dig some postholes. After I finished that, he told me the truck needed washing. It is Father's pride and joy, but I'm the one who has to do such jobs.

These three short sentences show a fairly clear pattern of development that in itself establishes coherence. There is the beginning of a story, suggesting that narration will carry the paragraph further. Events occur one after another, setting a pattern of straight chronology. But note how strongly the repeated nouns and reference words knit the sentences together:

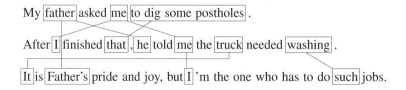

2. Use of temporal words: conjunctions and adverbs.

A series of short, abrupt sentences, although following a rigid chronological pattern, does not read as though it has coherence:

> I drove to the corner. I stopped for a light. A car smashed into the back of mine. I got out rubbing my neck. The driver of the other car sat behind the wheel and wept. I realized that the other driver was an elderly, gray-haired man.

The writer, sensing that something is lacking from the paragraph, might revise it this way:

> I drove to the corner. *While* I was stopped for a light, a car smashed into the back of mine. *As* I got out, rubbing my neck, the driver of the other car sat behind the wheel and wept. Only *then* did I realize that the other driver was an elderly, gray-haired man.

Two features of the revision have improved on the original draft. The first and most obvious is the addition of the words *while, as,* and *then* to connect the sentences by declaring the chronological sequence. Second, *while* and *as* convert short sentences into dependent clauses, thus replacing four choppy sentences with two longer ones and eliminating the jog-trot rhythm that gave the reader hiccups.

3. Use of transitional words and phrases at or near the beginning of sentences.
The coordinating conjunctions*; adverbs like *however, moreover, therefore, consequently, similarly,* and *thus;* and expressions like *on the other hand, in addition,* and *for example*—all can produce a subtle transitional effect rather like that of reference words. They force the reader to recollect the preceding material, thus making a tie between the thoughts they introduce and what has already been stated. When you read *But* at the beginning of a sentence, the author is declaring to you in loud tones, "You are to interpret the forthcoming statement as being in opposition or in contrast to what you have just read." *Moreover,* in the same place, suggests that what is coming is an addition to the last remarks; *consequently* means "as a result of what I have just stated."

The ploy of cementing the parts of a paragraph together with these words and phrases is used by nearly every writer. It is a perfectly good device, but unfortunately it is also a seductively easy one. The unwary writer larding sentences with *however*'s and *therefore*'s in search of elegance and poise may get into trouble with logic. "Sam drank too much on our dinner date. Consequently he threw up," may leave one wondering whether the nausea stemmed from the liquor or the date.

Exercises for Patterns for Paragraphs

1. Examine the following facts and observations about two methods for recording and playing music and other sound:
   • Cassette tapes can stretch and lose sound quality.
   • Compact discs are resistant to damage.
   • Compact discs maintain their sound quality.
   • Cassette tapes are less expensive than compact discs.

---

*Disregard the myth that there is something wrong with starting a sentence with *and, but, for, or,* or *nor.* Do realize, however, that these words at the opening of a sentence provide a special effect and call attention to themselves and to what follows them. Don't overuse them, and be sure of your purpose when you do launch a statement with one.

- Cassette tapes can be damaged by tangling or unwinding.
- In general, sound quality on compact discs is higher than sound quality on cassette tapes.

Write a paragraph of comparison/contrast discussing the merits of these two media.

2. Write a paragraph giving directions for preparing your favorite dessert. Include every step and provide enough detail and information for a beginning cook to be able to make the dessert successfully. Check your work by preparing the dessert following your instructions.
3. Write a description of one of the buildings on your campus. Provide sufficient detail so that a person can identify the building that you are describing. Do not use the name, the location, or any identifying colors in the description.

SECTION 4 ■
Writing Longer Essays

Once you have mastered the steps in the writing process by creating paragraphs, you will need to make only a few adjustments to follow that same process in writing a longer essay, the sort of essay you might be assigned in a college class in biology, business, or English.

In earlier sections you have practiced writing essay tests and special paragraph arrangements; each piece of writing required the use of the writing process applied to a rather short project. In each case the process was the same. Considered as a series of questions, the process looks like the following:

Composing

1. What is my subject? What have I been assigned, or what do I wish to write on?
2. What do I know, what can I learn, about that subject?
3. What specific statement can I make about that subject on the basis of what I know or can learn?
4. Of all I know on the subject, what specific items will best support and illustrate that specific statement?
5. What is the best order for presenting the support and illustration?
6. What does a first attempt (draft) at writing that paper produce?

Revising

7. What changes must be made in content and organization to improve the draft and make it acceptable to my reader?
8. What corrections must be made in grammar, mechanics, and usage to make the paper acceptable to my reader?
9. What form must the final version take?

The same writing process works well on a structured class assignment or on an assignment in which some leeway is given on topic selection. Here is how you might develop a paper assigned in your English class.

1. Select the subject. Because this paper is a class assignment, the first step requires a look at the nature of class assignments and the problems of defining the subject and limiting it to an appropriate, manageable length.

The nature of an assignment for a paper can vary, but you will find that writing assignments usually fall into one of three categories.

1. *GENERAL:* Write a two-page paper on something we've covered in this course.
2. *SOMEWHAT SPECIFIC:* Write a two-page paper on some aspect of the novel *Huckleberry Finn.*
3. *VERY DIRECTIVE:* Write a two-page paper explaining why Huck Finn's experiences led him to make his final statement: "Aunt Sally's going to adopt me and sivilize me and I can't stand it. I been there before."

The first example, the general assignment, grants considerable latitude in the selection of a subject for your paper. Often this latitude will provide more of a problem than a blessing because it is necessary to find something to write about that you *and* the teacher consider interesting and worthwhile. It is of little value to write a fine paper and find that the teacher (the grader) thinks the topic so insignificant that the whole effort can't be worth more than a C. The best approach here is to review the textbook, your lecture notes, and previous tests (if any); to select from these an important content area, concept, or personality; and to use that selection as a starting point for your work. Be sure to choose an area that interests you, an area about which you have some knowledge and some readily accessible sources of information. Once you have made this initial selection, you have converted the type of assignment from "general" to "somewhat specific." Next, you need to restrict the area you selected or were assigned so that you can develop it fully within the assigned length of the paper. Suppose, for example, the assignment names the novel *Huckleberry Finn* as the subject for a two-page paper. Several areas are open to you:

1. Autobiographical aspects of the novel.
2. Problems of plot and structure.
3. Problems of characterization.
4. Philosophical aspects of the novel.

For the selection or restriction process, choose one of the areas and make a final selection of a topic within that area. The final selection should be fairly small in scope, something manageable within two pages. In the example of *Huckleberry Finn,* the process of restriction might look like this:

1. Philosophical aspects of the novel.
2. The relationship between individuals and society.
3. Huck Finn's attitude toward the world as he saw it.
4. Why Huck's experiences led him to say that he couldn't stand to be "sivilized."

The final version of the topic (Number 4) is probably limited enough for it to be treated adequately within the assigned length. The topic asks a single question about one person, and that question—"Why?"—can be answered: "because his experiences with civilization were unpleasant or terrifying." That statement and the unpleasant or terrifying experiences can be illustrated efficiently by the use of three or four examples. The statement of this restricted topic results in a "very directive" assignment and provides the basis for organizing and writing a two-page paper.

The process just detailed is designed to help you derive a topic that is manageable within the scope of a given assignment. There are three stages in this restriction process:

• Selection of a general subject area.
• Selection of a portion or phase of this general area to form a limited subject area.
• Final selection of a specific limited topic within the limited subject area.

Note that the way in which your teacher states the assignment dictates the starting point for your work. A general assignment requires that you go through all three stages. A somewhat specific assignment completes the first two stages for you by limiting you to a general area. You need deal with only the third stage to complete the restriction process for this assignment. A very directive assignment accomplishes all three stages and leaves you free to begin work on the organization of the paper itself.

The final version of the restricted topic is the same as that "very directive" assignment already listed:

> Explain why Huck's experiences led him to make his final statement: "Aunt Sally's going to adopt me and sivilize me and I can't stand it. I been there before."

2. Gather materials. You need to establish what you know about this particular topic. What were Huck's experiences? Why did they make him want to avoid Aunt Sally's attentions? List some of the experiences he had in the "sivilized" world. Here are some possibilities:

1. The confining life at the Widow Douglas's home and Miss Watson's efforts to teach Huck manners and religion.
2. The brutal shooting of Boggs by Colonel Sherburn and the mob violence of the attempted lynching that was faced down by Sherburn's single-handed capacity for even greater violence.
3. The Grangerford—Shepherdson feud.
4. Huck's obvious pleasure at living outside civilization with Jim on Jackson's Island and on the raft.

Others may come to mind as you work on the paper. The immediate conclusion that you can draw from these experiences is that all of what Huck saw of civilization was unpleasant or bad or dangerous. The list of experiences leads directly to Step 3.

3. Establish a controlling statement. The thesis serves the longer essay much as the topic sentence serves the paragraph. The topic sentence states the subject of the paragraph and tells what will be said about it. The thesis statement does exactly the same thing for the longer paper. The statement controls the writer by defining the subject and what is to be said about the subject. It keeps the writer from wandering away from the subject; sometimes it is so specific that it establishes the order in which the essay will be arranged.

The thesis statement for the *Huckleberry Finn* paper is obvious:

> Huck could not stand to be "sivilized" because his experiences in civilization were frightening, dangerous, or confining.

4. Select specific items of support. Keeping the thesis statement in mind, you need to select from the book experiences and observations that will clearly illustrate the conditions in civilization. All the possible pieces of evidence listed above can be used to point out the conditions that Huck wanted to avoid. Even the pleasant experiences with Jim on Jackson's Island serve to make the bad experiences more vivid. The strange episode at the end of the book, dealing with the mock freeing of Jim, who is being held as a runaway slave at the home of Tom Sawyer's Aunt Sally, is pretty clear evidence that civilized people often act in an uncivilized fashion.

5. Establish an order of presentation. Several orders are possible, but the easiest one to follow is to take the materials in the order in which they occur in the book.

6. Write the first draft. Begin by writing an introduction and continue into the supporting paragraphs. The introduction might read this way:

> At the close of the novel *Huckleberry Finn,* Huck concludes his story by saying that he intends to "light out for the Territory" because Aunt Sally intends to "sivilize" him, and he feels that he can't stand any more efforts to make him an upstanding, moral, and

religious citizen. His attitude is understandable, for his experiences in society as it existed along the Mississippi were confining, unpleasant, or downright terrifying.

(We will discuss introductions again in the second example in this section.)

Continue now to the paragraphs of development. The paragraphs of development might read this way:

> Huck's experiences of "home," or at the two places where he lives at the opening of the novel, are decidedly unpleasant. The home of Widow Douglas and Miss Watson tends to oppress and constrict a boy's natural energy and interests. Regular meals eaten with careful manners and polite small talk work against Huck's tendency to roam at will through the woods. Lectures on morality and religion tend to confuse him. If one can obtain his or her desires through prayer, why are folks poor, or sick, or crippled? If being good makes one blessed, why is Miss Watson so sour and seemingly unhappy? Life with Pap may be more free from the repressions of etiquette, but it also has its frightening side of drunkenness, violence, and delirium tremens. So Huck decides to leave these situations behind to look for something better.
>
> Something better turns out to be life on the river with Jim, the runaway slave. They meet on Jackson's Island and camp there for a time. Their experiences on the island are mostly pleasant: loafing, camping, fishing, and generally hanging out, all of which suit Huck just fine. The idyll is interrupted by a snakebite (from which Jim recovers) and is ended by the threat of a search party coming out to find Jim. Jim is a slave and, by all the measures of that day, less than human, but in reality he is the only truly civilized person Huck meets in his travels. Jim loves Huck and cares for him, in spite of Huck's tendency to play cruel jokes on him. He shelters Huck from the knowledge of Pap's death and doesn't reject Huck after he discovers the hoax of Huck's dream fabrication when they have been separated in a fog. It is ironic that the only civilized person Huck meets is not considered truly human by those who regard themselves as civilized.
>
> The other people Huck meets in his travels do very little to improve his suspicious view of the world. He and Jim happen upon some fairly terrible people as soon as they venture out on the river: slave hunters, the gamblers who are trying to kill their partner, and a nonhuman agent of civilization, a steamboat that runs them down and puts Huck back on shore. There he meets the Grangerfords, gentlemen and ladies all, living in a fine house and enjoying prosperity. The Grangerfords are aristocrats and moral churchgoing people who have only one fault: They are engaged in a murderous, generations-old feud with the Shepherdsons. One Sunday afternoon Huck witnesses an outbreak of this feud that leaves most of the people from both families dead.
>
> Fleeing from the killing, Huck returns to the river and finds Jim. They continue down the river. Later they meet the King and the Duke, two great con artists who dupe the people in a nearby town and are eventually tarred and feathered for their efforts. During the adventures with the King and the Duke, Huck witnesses the shooting of the harmless drunk Boggs and the attempted lynching of Colonel Sherburn, the man who shot him. Taken on balance, most of Huck's experiences on shore are grim and frightening, good reasons for his lack of enthusiasm for civilization.
>
> Even the last episode of the book does little to increase Huck's desire to live in the civilized world. Huck comes by chance on the home of Tom Sawyer's Aunt Sally and adopts Tom's identity. When Tom shows up, he is introduced as Cousin Sid. Jim is also on the plantation, being held as a runaway slave. The two boys, with Tom leading, enter an incredible plot to free Jim, although, as Tom knows but conceals, Jim has already been freed. After a series of cops-and-robber antics, the plot resolves into what looks like a happy ending. It is revealed that Jim is free, Pap is dead, and Huck's personal fortune, presumed lost, is intact. Aunt Sally offers to adopt Huck and raise him properly so that he can become a successful, civilized adult. At this point Huck reviews his situation. Life in town and his misadventures on shore with the Grangerfords, the King and the Duke,

Sherburn, and others suggest only bad experiences to come if he accepts Aunt Sally's offer. His time with Jim, living free and easy on the river, seems wonderfully pleasant, compared to those recollections. Little wonder, then, that he decides to "light out for the Territory."

This completes the writing process through the writing of the rough draft. The remaining steps in the process will be covered in the second example of this section.

With this review of the process fresh in your mind, follow how you might want to apply it in writing a paper of six to eight paragraphs that might be assigned in a business course.

Your class has been studying business leaders, past and present, and the assignment is to write a paper of about eight hundred words discussing the contributions of one of these leaders to American business.

1. Select the subject. Several names come to mind from the history of American business: F. W. Taylor, Thomas Watson, Douglas McGregor, Alfred Sloan, Frederick Herzberg. But perhaps the most interesting and certainly one of the most important contributors to the theory and practice of business in America is Peter F. Drucker. His contributions are famous and respected in this country and abroad, and they have been cataloged and discussed in two well-respected books. Thus Drucker's contributions meet the criteria for selection as a subject. They are important and interesting, and information on them is readily available.

2. Gather materials. What is there to know about Peter Drucker?

He has written twenty-seven books and many articles on business. He was born in Vienna, Austria. Father was a college teacher in America. Drucker started career as a bookkeeper and a writer. He left Germany early in WWII. Went to London and worked in a bank. Then worked for American newspapers as a British correspondent. Worked for the U.S. government during the war, then taught at two colleges, moving in 1950 to New York University, where he taught till 1970.

His first consulting job was a massive study of General Motors Corporation, a study highly critical of its management systems. From this work he wrote *The Concept of the Corporation,* a book that was the beginning of management thought in the modern sense of the word. His latest book, *Management: Tasks—Responsibilities—Practices,* is a very broad study of modern management philosophy and practices.

He continues to consult for major corporations, but he requires that the client come to him in California. He charges $1,500 a day and still manages to stay booked up far in advance.

Drucker is well known as a teacher. He taught first at NYU in a special program for active business people. He now teaches in the Claremont Graduate School in California, a position he has held since 1971. Drucker loves teaching so much that some believe he would pay to do it if necessary. He especially enjoys teaching those who are currently employed in management positions. He uses a case-study method of his own invention, not following accepted case-study methods from other colleges. His case studies are short and are not loaded with data and statistics. Instead they concentrate on analysis and on finding the right questions to ask in a given situation. Often high-level executives attend his classes for enrichment and pleasure, even though they do not need any further course work or degrees to augment their careers. His associations in the classroom often ripen into rich and enduring friendships.

Much more information could be collected about Drucker, and more probably would be needed to fill an essay of eight hundred words. But this is enough material to allow us to move to the next step.

3. Establish a controlling statement. It is clear from the information gathered about Peter Drucker that he is active in three general areas of business: He is a teacher, a consultant, and a writer. But it is important to note that the key word in the assignment is not *activity;* rather, it is *contributions.* The fact that Drucker has been active as a writer does not automatically mean that he has made a contribution to the theory and practice of American business in his writings. That remains to be determined; you must return to the information gathered in Step 2 to see what is known about his *contributions.* (NOTE: It is not uncommon to discover that writing the statement for a paper [Step 3] requires a return to the information-gathering stage [Step 2] to find additional information to use in formulating the thesis statement.)

The information already collected provides only a suggestion of Drucker's contributions: the phrase that says he wrote a book that was the "beginning of management thought in the modern sense of the word." Now the job is to collect much information directly related to that idea.

Further reading in books and articles about Peter Drucker indicates two very important areas of contribution, one theoretical and the other practical.

> In the theory of management, Drucker was the first to identify the corporation as a whole as something that needed management and that could be managed. Prior to his work, discussions of corporation management were rather fragmented, dealing with isolated problems such as accounting and materials handling. Drucker developed a theory for the operation of the entire corporation.
>
> On the practical side, Drucker developed the concept of the manager and his or her role in the corporation, and he has written guides to the day-to-day functions of those in management. He has worked as a consultant for major corporations, and the solutions to their problems have filtered to other companies and influenced institutions such as schools and hospitals. He also did initial work on ideas that later were more fully developed by others: The "hygiene" theory of the effects of wages on motivation and the theories of motivation often labeled X and Y were initially discussed in Drucker's works, at least in concept, and were developed by other writers, Herzberg and McGregor in particular.

The addition of these ideas to the information collected provides a solid basis for working on Step 3, establishing the statement.

The nature of Drucker's contributions is now clear enough for you to try writing a statement about them. Such a statement might read:

> Peter Drucker has made both a theoretical and a practical contribution to American business.

> *or*

> Peter Drucker was the first to develop a theory of the nature and function of the corporation, and he has made practical application of that theory to the day-to-day work of the manager through his writings and his work as a consultant. He also did initial work on concepts fully developed by others.

The second version captures most of what needs to be said, but the order is jumbled and the statement is too wordy. A better version is

> Peter Drucker developed the overall concept of the corporation, its place in society, and its operation; he also began work on specific concepts that were later developed by

other men. His practical work as writer and consultant has provided direction to many managers.

You can shape that statement into a general outline for a paper and get an idea of the kinds of materials you will need to support the statement.

Drucker's Contributions

1. Developed theory and concept of the corporation.
2. Began work on concepts later fully developed by others.
3. Provided practical applications of those theories in writings and in consulting work.

Now you are ready to move to Step 4.

4. Select specific items of support. To develop the first point in the outline, you will need to discuss the state of management theory when Drucker began his work. Then you will need to explain how he developed his theory, where he first began to publish it, and, in general terms, what that theory of the corporation and its management is. For the second point, you need to identify the concepts that Drucker began to develop, the people who completed that development, and the name or the final form of those concepts. A discussion of his more practical books and some of the guidelines in them can be joined with a brief discussion of his work as a consultant to present the third point in the outline.

5. Establish an order of presentation. There is an order already built into the outline from the materials collected in Step 2: first, theories and concepts of the corporation as a whole, then specific theories, and then practical applications of those theories. This order also seems to arrange the contributions in descending order of importance, taking the larger, more global contributions first and moving to less important theories and practical matters next. It would be possible to reverse that order and work from least important to most important, from practical to theoretical. But such a progression does not seem to suit the materials as well as the first order, so you should present the materials in the draft in the order suggested by the outline.

6. Write the first draft. It might seem logical to begin writing a draft of a paper with the beginning, the introduction. If a clear, effective introduction comes to mind rather handily, begin with the introduction. But do not wait with pen in hand for the perfect introduction to appear on the page. Make one attempt at an introduction; if nothing comes of that first attempt, begin to write the body of the paper wherever you find the writing easiest, even if you begin with what is actually the last paragraph in the essay. Get the material written and *then* put the paper in the proper order. Write, don't wait for the inspiration.

When you do write the introduction, be sure to make it serve the two important functions of an introduction. First, and more important, an introduction must catch the interest of the reader. Second, the introduction must give the reader an idea of the direction the paper will take. This sense of direction may come from an explicit statement of the core idea or thesis of the paper, a paraphrase of the result of your work in Step 3. On the other hand, it may be given as a general identifying statement of the topic. For the paper on Peter Drucker a paraphrase of the Step 3 statement might read:

> Peter Drucker developed a philosophy of the corporation, devised specific concepts within that philosophy, and showed managers how to make a practical application of that philosophy.

Identifying the topic and making a general statement of the ideas to be covered might produce:

> Of all those who have helped to develop our ideas of the nature and workings of the corporation, Peter Drucker is among the most important.

With this effort to provide a sense of direction, you must also catch the reader's interest. If you have trouble thinking of methods for developing introductions, you might try one of the following strategies:

- Use a quotation or a paraphrase of a striking statement:

> Peter Drucker is, in the words of C. Northcote Parkinson, "preeminent among management consultants and also among authors of books on management."

- Cite an important fact or statistic:

> Prior to the writing of *The Concept of the Corporation,* the idea of the corporation as an entity that needed management did not exist. Drucker invented the corporate society.

- Recount an anecdote:

> "What *is* your business?" the famous consultant asked the directors of a firm that made bottles. "Everyone knows," responded the chairman, "that we make bottles for soft drinks and other foods." "I disagree," replied the consultant to the astounded board. After a pause to let his words sink in, he continued, "Your business is not the making of bottles; you are in the packaging business." With that one question Peter Drucker, America's foremost business consultant, opened the board's eyes and provided new direction for a foundering company.

- Use a dictionary definition:

> The dictionary defines a corporation as a group of individuals legally united to conduct business. Peter Drucker defines the corporation as the cornerstone of our society.

- Set up a contrast between two ideas:

> The original management consultant was really an efficiency expert, timing workers on an assembly line and suggesting ways of improving their speed and productivity. Peter Drucker's work is as far removed from that practice as the supersonic transport is from the Wright brothers' first plane.

As you become a more experienced writer, you will find less and less need for those strategies. Use them now, but feel free to experiment as your confidence grows.

Always provide a conclusion for your paper. As a rule, a short sentence of summary or a restatement of the topic will suffice. The function of a conclusion for a short paper is to let the reader know that the paper has been completed, to provide a sense of "finishedness." Don't leave the reader with the impression that he or she ought to be looking for more material. Don't try to provide an extensive restatement or summary for a short paper. And be very careful that you never use the conclusion to introduce a new point or add additional information. A one-sentence conclusion should be ample for most college essays.

The first completed draft of the paper on the contributions of Peter Drucker might read this way:

Of the business people, scholars, and writers who have attempted to analyze and influence the business world of the twentieth century, none has made a greater contribution or been more interesting to observe than Peter Drucker. Drucker is a teacher, a consultant, and a writer who has drawn from each role to construct a philosophy or theoretical concept of the corporation and a workable application of the theory to actual business problems and challenges. In theory and in practice, Drucker has been a major influence on American business for the last fifty years.

In the minds of many, Drucker is the person who almost single-handedly invented the idea of the corporation. Prior to Drucker's introduction of the idea in *The Concept of the Corporation,* the study of business management was the study of individual problems such as accounting or materials handling. Drucker changed that view and suggested that the corporation was an entity, a whole, and needed to be managed as a whole, not as a series of isolated services or problems. Much of this book, and the ideas within it, arose from a massive study of General Motors undertaken in 1943. Having examined the operation of that company in great detail, and having reported that he thought it was managed chaotically, he set about developing a unified view of the corporation and its management. He did develop such a view and, in the process, suggested that the key institution and the chief influence on the future of the Western world would be the corporation, complete with assembly lines. This view of the corporation as a whole and his realization that the corporation was a major political, social, *and* economic force have made Drucker a major contributor to the present-day theory of business.

Drucker has written extensively in the area of management and has been a leader in the development of important concepts in specific areas of management. He was a leader, or at least an important forerunner, of the management system commonly called *management by objectives* (MBO). He first used the term in his book *The Practice of Management* and says he first heard it used by Alfred Sloan in the 1950s. Essentially, MBO tries to focus the attention of managers on their objectives. Managers of the old school had always asked themselves, "What do I do?" Drucker turned their attention from the process to the product or objective and said that the proper question is "What do I wish to accomplish?" That principle of management is now so commonplace in business and government that it seems always to have existed. Two concepts in the area of motivation were suggested by Drucker and developed by others. The first is the now famous "hygiene" theory of compensation, which says that wages and certain other conditions of employment do not cause high morale and motivation; instead they prevent low morale and allow other positive motivators to have an impact on the workers. These *hygiene factors* do not increase motivation and production, but motivation and the accompanying higher production cannot occur without them. Drucker also was an early contributor to the theories of motivation commonly called *Theory X* and *Theory Y,* which are widely discussed by writers such as Douglas McGregor. Theory X says that people are motivated best by threat and fear, by negative or extrinsic motivation; Theory Y counters that people are better and further motivated by satisfaction of their basic needs and by appeals to their sense of participation and involvement. These ideas are well known and widely used today; Drucker was a major contributor to their early development.

But Drucker is no airy theorist incapable of practical work. He is a consultant whose services are heavily sought by industry and government. He is in such demand that he can charge $1,500 a day for his services and never lack clients. He is a consultant who does not try to provide clients with an answer to their problems. Rather, he tries to point out what the proper questions are and to help the clients find the answers. In early work with a manufacturer of glass bottles, he shocked the executive committee by asking them what business the firm was in. Silence followed the question, and then the chairman replied with a hint of anger in his voice, "We make glass bottles for soft-drink makers and others," "No," replied Drucker, "your business is not making bottles. You are in the packaging business." That answer, coming from an unusual perspective, greatly altered the executives' view of the company and its problems and led to solutions never suspected by the executive committee. Drucker constantly advises his clients to build from strength, to use the abilities that each person possesses, and to structure assignments so that no manager is forced to work long in an area where she or he is weak. Managers of the old school always looked at weaknesses and worked for their correction. Drucker said, "Forget the weaknesses. Put the person in a position where his weaknesses will not matter; use and develop the strengths of each employee."

Drucker has raised the art of consulting to new heights, making practical applications of the theories of management he developed. As a writer he has been an important contributor to the practical side of management. *The Effective Executive* is full of good advice to managers, advice useful on a day-to-day basis. His later book, *Management: Tasks—Responsibilities—Practices,* has in it long sections that are intensely practical. Even his more theoretical works have a practical bent. Arjay Miller, former president of Ford Motor Company, says that *The Concept of the Corporation* was "extremely useful in forming my judgments about what was needed at Ford. It was, by considerable margin, the most useful and pragmatic publication available and had a definite impact on the postwar organizational development within the Ford Motor Company" (*Drucker: The Man Who Invented the Corporate Society,* 1976, p. 32). Peter Drucker, philosopher, theorist, and practical authority, is, without doubt, a major figure in the history of American business and a man who helped to shape and form the corporation as we know it today.

Materials for this essay were taken from John J. Tarrant, *Drucker: The Man Who Invented the Corporate Society* (Boston: Cahners Books, Inc., 1976) and from Tony H. Bonaparte and John E. Flaherty, eds., *Peter Drucker: Contributions to Business Enterprise* (New York: New York University Press, 1970). Drucker's latest book is *Managing for the Future* (Truman Talley Books/Dutton, 1992).

The completed version of the paper that comes out of Step 6 is *not*—repeat, *not*—the version of the paper that you ought to turn in. Step 6 produces a rough draft, a version suitable for revision and not much else. Think of that draft as a good start, but remember that it is still a long way from completion. Use the remaining steps of the writing process in revising your draft. Wait a day or two (if possible) between completing the draft and undertaking the revision.

7. Revise the rough draft. Read the draft all the way through twice. Then ask the following questions:

- Will the introduction interest the reader? Does it provide a sense of direction for the paper?
- Does the Step 3 statement in the introduction accurately reflect what you intend to say on the topic?
- Does the rest of the paper, does each supporting paragraph, serve to develop the statement you intend to make in the paper?
- Are the supporting points presented in the best order?
- Is there an adequate conclusion?

Read each paragraph of support very carefully.

- Is the point of support developed completely? Will readers have any questions on the point when they finish reading the paragraph? Is the paragraph *complete*?
- Is each paragraph unified? Does any paragraph treat more than one idea?
- Is each paragraph coherent? Does it read smoothly, tying the sentences together with transitional devices?

8. Correct the draft. Check the paper sentence by sentence to improve its style and to correct errors.

- Check each sentence for errors in completeness (Lesson 13), subject–verb agreement (Lesson 22), pronoun–antecedent agreement (Lesson 23), pronoun case (Lesson 24), dangling or misplaced modifiers (Lesson 14), and the use of prepositions (Lesson 25). (NOTE: As you find errors in your papers and as marked errors appear on papers returned to you, keep a record of them—either by putting a check in the appropriate lessons of this book or by marking your reference handbook. You will soon discover whether you have a tendency to repeat certain kinds of errors, and you can simplify your proofreading by checking first for these errors. In a short time, you should be able to eliminate repeat faults from your writing.)
- Check each sentence for errors in punctuation; check for missing punctuation marks *and* for unneeded marks.
- Check for errors in mechanics, capitalization, and spelling.

9. Write the final draft. Copy the paper in its final, corrected form. Be sure to observe correct margins, and to write or type neatly. Make a copy of the paper before you turn it in.

# Progress Tests

SUBJECTS AND VERBS; PARTS OF SPEECH
(LESSONS 1, 2)

NAME _____ SCORE _____

Directions: Copy the subject of the sentence on the first line at the left and the verb on the second line.

_____   1. Our first sight of the dilapidated house depressed us.
_____

_____   2. There was no sign of life about the farm.
_____

_____   3. Each of the tourists carried a small camera.
_____

_____   4. Beyond the pines grew a few dwarf junipers.
_____

_____   5. This was only the first of a long series of interruptions.
_____

_____   6. Close to the summer camp is a nine-hole golf course.
_____

_____   7. He's the only one of my teenage friends with an unlisted
_____   phone number.

_____   8. By this time next week most of the vacationers will have left
_____   the island.

_____   9. Not one of the villagers had received the proper legal notice.
_____

_____   10. One of the bored clerks perfunctorily rubber-stamped Jane's
_____   passport.

_____   11. Moments later a covey of quail rose from the large patch of
_____   weeds.

_____   12. Next on the program will be three songs by the junior-high
_____   mixed chorus.

_____   13. Finally, shortly before midnight, the last of the guests drove
_____   away.

_____   14. On the kitchen table lay the remnants of a quick lunch.
_____

_____   15. Behind the shed was a short row of plum trees in full bloom.
_____

Directions: Each sentence contains two italicized words. In the space at the left, write one of the following numbers to identify the part of speech of each italicized word:

1. Noun	3. Verb	5. Adverb
2. Pronoun	4. Adjective	6. Preposition

_____ 1. The *address on* the letter was almost illegible.
_____

_____ 2. The general *addressed* the troops and urged them *on*.
_____

_____ 3. More money will be available at *some later* date.
_____

_____ 4. *Later, some* of the guests washed the dishes.
_____

_____ 5. In a firm *voice,* the sergeant demanded an *apology.*
_____

_____ 6. The teacher *voiced* the opinion that Joe's speech was needlessly *apolo-*
_____ *getic.*

_____ 7. *Beyond* a doubt, the *arrival* of the Marines saved the day.
_____

_____ 8. *Doubtlessly* a large crowd will await the candidate's *arrival.*
_____

_____ 9. A *lovely* park is *close* to the campus.
_____

_____ 10. The *alert* dog guarded the prisoner *closely.*
_____

_____ 11. The sentinel was commended *for* his *alertness.*
_____

_____ 12. *Everyone* thinks your action deserves a *reward.*
_____

_____ 13. *Every* member of the squad must work *harder.*
_____

_____ 14. The children *like* an *occasional* visit to the zoo.
_____

_____ 15. *Occasionally* Julia's practical jokes *annoy* me.
_____

_____ 16. We consider these interruptions only a minor annoyance.
_____

_____ 17. We *worked throughout* the hot afternoon.
_____

_____ 18. You should be commended for your *enthusiastic work* on the project.
_____

_____ 19. *This* plan sounds completely *workable.*
_____

_____ 20. *This* improvement cannot be made *without* additional funds.
_____

PROGRESS TEST 2
COMPLEMENTS (LESSONS 3–6)

NAME _____ SCORE _____

Directions: Identify the italicized word by writing one of the following abbreviations in the space at the left:

    S.C. [subjective complement]   I.O. [indirect object]
    D.O. [direct object]   O.C. [objective complement]

If the italicized word is *not* used as one of these complements, leave the space blank.

_____ 1. Next Thursday afternoon might be a good *time* for our next meeting.

_____ 2. You should have looked up the correct *spelling* of the word in your dictionary.

_____ 3. I can have your meal *ready* for you in half an hour.

_____ 4. The truck had been standing out in the sub-zero *weather* all week.

_____ 5. One in high political office must avoid even a *hint* of scandal.

_____ 6. In a hard-fought eighteen-hole playoff, Jeremy emerged the *winner.*

_____ 7. The injured woman could give the *police* only a sketchy account of the accident.

_____ 8. You should send the personnel *officer* a list of your previous employers.

_____ 9. These vacuum-packed bags will keep the potato chips *crisp.*

_____ 10. How *old* is that noisy, gas-guzzling car of yours?

_____ 11. How many *miles* per gallon do you get from your car?

_____ 12. The children were happily making sand *castles* on the beach.

_____ 13. Henry made *me* an attractive offer for my used camcorder.

_____ 14. A fresh coat of paint would make this dingy room more *attractive.*

_____ 15. The Chinese consider dried sea cucumber a great *delicacy.*

_____ 16. When will you send *me* a bill for your professional services?

_____ 17. Our new state officers are taking on an awesome *responsibility.*

_____ 18. "I want every one of these windows *spotless* by noon," said the sergeant.

_____ 19. "I want every one of these *windows* spotless by noon," said the sergeant.

_____ 20. Later the picture frames will be given three *coats* of varnish.

_____ 21. In his youth he had been looked upon as the town *buffoon.*

_____ 22. How *certain* can we be of the mayor's support for our project?

_____ 23. Which of these three samples do you consider the best *buy*?

_____ 24. *Which* of these three samples do you consider the best buy?

_____ 25. During the cook's testimony the accused man appeared *worried.*

_____ 26. After a noticeable pause the umpire called the pitch a *strike.*

_____ 27. All of us wish *you* a prosperous New Year.

_____ 28. The influx of refugees brought our *city* new problems.

_____ 29. How *wide* should we make the new path?

_____ 30. How wide should we make the new *path*?

_____ 31. Susan had been putting off a *visit* to her dentist.

_____ 32. Did Mrs. Camp offer you *any* of her famous blueberry pie?

_____ 33. Did Mrs. Camp offer *you* any of her famous blueberry pie?

_____ 34. I now feel *rested* enough for the climb to the summit.

_____ 35. How *cold* do the winters get in Anchorage?

_____ 36. *Whom* has the chairwoman chosen as her assistant?

_____ 37. This dessert must be kept very *cold* until serving time.

_____ 38. First of all, someone will give *you* an aptitude test.

_____ 39. First of all, you will be given an aptitude *test.*

_____ 40. You will find the climate here quite *moderate.*

PROGRESS TEST 3

SUBORDINATE CLAUSES (LESSONS 8–10)

NAME _____ SCORE _____

Directions: Each of the following sentences contains one subordinate clause. Use square brackets ([ ]) to mark the beginning and the end of each subordinate clause. Circle the subject and underline the verb of each subordinate clause. Identify the clause by writing in the space at the left one of the following abbreviations:

     Adv. [adverb clause]   Adj. [adjective clause]   N. [noun clause]

_____ 1. As the chorus marched onto the stage, a small dog followed.

_____ 2. There is much merit in what you propose.

_____ 3. The scenery collapsed at the moment when Gene stepped out from the wings.

_____ 4. Have you told your family of the plans you have made?

_____ 5. Anyone as old as your niece should know the alphabet.

_____ 6. Were I you, I'd apply for the scholarship.

_____ 7. It's unfortunate that you missed the class picnic.

_____ 8. We had nothing to eat except what was left over from lunch.

_____ 9. Theodore Roosevelt did several things that restored presidential leadership over Congress.

_____ 10. According to the legend, Medusa could change a man to stone as he was looking at her.

_____ 11. The dormitory where Julie lived housed several students from India.

_____ 12. This pamphlet explains on what bases the student essays should be judged.

_____ 13. The diamond ring Alice is wearing came originally from her aunt in Holland.

_____ 14. Do you sometimes wonder if you could handle a confining job in an office?

_____ 15. Beth looks after two small children whose mother works afternoons on the campus.

_____ 16. Mark's lawyer argued that his client was not financially liable for the damages.

_____ 17. An argument that Mark's lawyer presented questioned the financial liability for the damages.

_____ 18. Mark's lawyer's argument was that his client was not financially liable for the damages.

_____ 19. Mark's lawyer's argument that his client was not financially responsible for the damages impressed the jury.

_____ 20. Some of us wonder if you would be interested in the job.

339

Directions: The italicized material in each of these sentences is a subordinate clause. In the first space at the left, write Adv., Adj., or N. to identify the clause. Within the italicized clause the word printed in boldface type is a complement. Identify it by writing in the second space at the left one of the following:

      S.C. [subjective complement]   I.O. [indirect object]
      D.O. [direct object]   O.C. [objective complement]

_____ 1. One of Jeff's difficulties is *that he is painfully **shy** in the presence of*
_____   *strangers.*

_____ 2. *If you follow these **directions,*** you will avoid really heavy traffic.
_____

_____ 3. After you leave this class, I hope that you will practice ***what** you have*
_____   *learned here.*

_____ 4. The letter of introduction *that you sent **me*** proved very helpful.

_____ 5. The car was registered in the name of Charles Albertson, a Britisher ***whom***
_____   *the FBI had been investigating.*

_____ 6. Beth has as yet told no one ***who** her bridesmaids will be.*

_____ 7. We are living in a period *when crises are almost daily **occurrences.***
_____

_____ 8. I'm afraid *that I caused my **parents** some real embarrassment.*
_____

_____ 9. The substitute teacher devised some activities *that kept the youngsters*
_____   ***busy** for half an hour.*

_____ 10. Uncle Jake sputtered indignantly *when the waiter reminded **him** that the*
_____   *customary gratuity is fifteen percent.*

_____ 11. The first fish ***that** Laura caught* was only five inches long.
_____

_____ 12. Several friends commented on *how **happy** Elaine looked.*
_____

_____ 13. I am sure *that the best seats for the concert are no longer **available.***
_____

_____ 14. I think you should tell the mechanic *that you consider his bill unreason-*
_____   *ably **high.***

_____ 15. Although Sue has shown me *where I had been making **mistakes,*** I'm still
_____   not entirely comfortable with my new computer.

_____ 16. The board approved Mr. Barnes' suggestion *that the club make Ms.*
_____   *Thompson an honorary **member.***

_____ 17. An actress ***whom** none of us had ever seen before* played the part of the
_____   prosecuting attorney.

_____ 18. The contractor could only guess at ***what** the total cost will be.*

_____ 19. Ted has been studying the pamphlet *the traffic officer gave **him.***
_____

_____ 20. Your theme will be improved, I think, *if you make your introductory para-*
_____   *graph somewhat **shorter.***

PROGRESS TEST 4

VERBAL PHRASES (LESSONS 11, 12)

NAME _____ SCORE _____

Directions: Each sentence contains one verbal phrase. Underline the phrase and, in the space at the left, write one of the following letters to identify the phrase:
    G. [gerund phrase]   P. [participial phrase]
    I. [infinitive phrase]   A. [absolute phrase]

_____ 1. It might be a good idea to look into the Acme Company's offer more carefully.

_____ 2. Tomorrow being a holiday, I shall loaf most of the day.

_____ 3. Wayne's daily chores included looking after the boss's collection of African violets.

_____ 4. Do you think that granting Larsen another extension on the loan is wise?

_____ 5. I'll send you a ten-page brochure describing this tremendous real-estate opportunity.

_____ 6. Dad would sometimes let me sit on his lap while he was steering the car.

_____ 7. Troubled by these inaccuracies, one board member demanded that new auditors be hired.

_____ 8. Hatchwood was found guilty of sending an abusive, threatening letter to the mayor.

_____ 9. Can you show me how to put this new ribbon into my printer?

_____ 10. Over the weekend I did little except review my geology notes for the midterm examination.

_____ 11. Dad has done most of the cooking this week, Mother having been called for jury duty.

_____ 12. Perhaps your client might consider buying a somewhat larger piece of property.

_____ 13. The substitute teacher's first mistake was assigning the class some additional homework.

_____ 14. Another possibility would be to rent a car at the airport.

_____ 15. Three men found guilty of espionage were deported.

_____ 16. One of Paula's unusual hobbies is collecting old theater programs.

_____ 17. Keeping the younger children quiet during the long ceremony will tax your ingenuity.

_____ 18. One of the ushers will tell you when to march to the platform for your diploma.

_____ 19. Johnson returned to Memphis, having been unsuccessful in his search for a job in Atlanta.

_____ 20. Being a charitable person, Bascom graciously accepted the apology.

Directions: Each of the italicized words in the following sentences is used as a complement within a verbal phrase. In the first space at the left, write one of the following letters to identify the phrase:

      G. [gerund phrase]   P. [participial phrase]
      I. [infinitive phrase]   A. [absolute phrase]

In the second space, write one of the following numbers to identify the complement:

      1. Subjective complement   3. Indirect object
      2. Direct object   4. Objective complement

_____   1. You can help the committee most by providing *transportation* for the out-
_____   of-town delegates.

_____   2. It might be to our advantage to make *Chapman* a second offer for his prop-
_____   erty.

_____   3. There will be celebrating in Coalville this week, the local baseball team
_____   having won the league *pennant.*

_____   4. The excited children raced to the backyard, leaving the kitchen door wide
_____   *open.*

_____   5. These graphic pictures succeeded in making the legislators *aware* of the
_____   need for immediate action.

_____   6. The clerk, looking extremely *annoyed* by our insistence, finally sum-
_____   moned his supervisor.

_____   7. How may *signatures* were you able to get for our petition?
_____

_____   8. "Remember, jurors," said the attorney, "that no one actually heard my
_____   client threaten the police *officer.*"

_____   9. Beth's aunt looked after the children yesterday, our regular sitter being *un-
_____   available.*

_____ 10. A new regulation making students *eligible* for membership on college
_____   committees is being considered.

_____ 11. Having already sent the *bank* the February payment, Tracy was puzzled by
_____   the delinquent notice.

_____ 12. Spending time with Uncle Josh is almost as unpleasant as visiting the *den-
_____   tist.*

_____ 13. Feeling *sorry* for the embarrassed clerk, Mother paid for the broken cook-
_____   ies.

_____ 14. Have you ever thought of becoming an airline *steward*?
_____

_____ 15. I must find a new handball partner, Jeff Toner having left *town.*
_____

PROGRESS TEST **5**

DANGLING MODIFIERS (LESSON 14)

NAME _____ SCORE _____

Directions: If a sentence is correct, write C in the space at the left. If you find a dangling modifier, underline it and write W in the space.

_____ 1. In purchasing a dog for a family pet, its background is as important to consider as its appearance.

_____ 2. A boat as light as this one can be upset by sitting on the side the way you are doing now.

_____ 3. Turning the car into the driveway, my purse fell to the floor and the contents scattered all over.

_____ 4. Dad is certainly busy enough this morning without asking him to drive us to the gym.

_____ 5. Dad is certainly busy enough this morning without being asked to drive us to the gym.

_____ 6. Upon reaching nine years of age, my family moved again, this time to Omaha.

_____ 7. Having bruised her ankle while taking inventory this morning, the boss told Edith to take the afternoon off.

_____ 8. I think I'll splurge tonight and order an expensive dessert, tomorrow being payday.

_____ 9. The tapes may be used again after rewinding them.

_____ 10. The tapes may be used again after being rewound.

_____ 11. After filing away all the loose magazines and pamphlets that I have acquired this year, my shelves look quite tidy.

_____ 12. To be assured of a capacity audience, the price of the tickets must be kept low.

_____ 13. The weather having turned cold and windy, we decided to take along our parkas.

_____ 14. Exhausted after the long hours of studying, Luke's head slowly nodded and finally came to rest on the open book.

____ 15. Notice also that, by being reversed, this coat can be used in rainy weather.

_____ 16. Notice also that, by reversing it, this coat can be used in rainy weather.

_____ 17. Notice also that, by reversing it, you can use this coat in rainy weather.

_____ 18. Meeting Lois after work, she suggested that we see a movie.

_____ 19. Yesterday, while eating lunch on the patio, a flock of crows made a raucous racket.

_____ 20. Instead of leaving the lawn mower out in the rain, it should be put away in the carport.

Directions: Rewrite each of the following sentences twice:
    a. Change the dangler to a complete clause with subject and verb.
    b. Begin the main clause with a word that the dangler can logically modify.

1. Having been in the army for five years, my serious reading has been neglected.

    a. _____

    b. _____

2. While mowing the grass, the long-lost gold chain was found.

    a. _____

    b. _____

3. Before applying the first coat of paint, the surface should be sanded well.

    a. _____

    b. _____

4. To be assured of a successful cake, the flour must be sifted thoroughly.

    a. _____

    b. _____

5. Having turned the horses loose, they raced for the cool, inviting stream.

    a. _____

    b. _____

PROGRESS TEST 6

SENTENCE BUILDING (LESSONS 13–16)

NAME _____   SCORE _____

Directions: Study these paired sentences for incompleteness, misplaced modifiers, faulty parallelism, and faulty comparisons. In the space at the left, write the letter that identifies the correct sentence.

_____ 1. A. Our service department uses only factory-approved materials.
        B. Our service department only uses factory-approved materials.

_____ 2. A. One of the laboratory assistants having had enough presence of mind to rush the injured student to the infirmary.
        B. One of the laboratory assistants had enough presence of mind to rush the injured student to the infirmary.

_____ 3. A. Although a sergeant's pay is lower than a commissioned officer, an officer has several additional expenses.
        B. Although a sergeant's pay is lower than a commissioned officer's, an officer has several additional expenses.

_____ 4. A. Our company specializes in cars of conservative design and which get good gas mileage.
        B. Our company specializes in cars that are conservatively designed and get good gas mileage.

_____ 5. A. Last semester Johnny had a better grade-point average than any other fellow in his fraternity.
        B. Last semester Johnny had a better grade-point average than any fellow in his fraternity.

_____ 6. A. Gladys only approves of a movie if it has a gloriously happy ending.
        B. Gladys approves of a movie only if it has a gloriously happy ending.

_____ 7. A. What started the argument was Fran's casual remark that hers was the fastest of any speedboat on the lake.
        B. What started the argument was Fran's casual remark that hers was the fastest of all the speedboats on the lake.

_____ 8. A. Jan had to reluctantly admit that all college students are not vitally interested in modern dance.
        B. Jan had to admit reluctantly that not all college students are vitally interested in modern dance.

_____ 9. A. It was one of the greatest thrills, if not the greatest thrill, of my life.
        B. It was one of the greatest, if not the greatest, thrill of my life.

_____ 10. A. Minnesota, I have been told, has more lakes than any state in the Union.
         B. Minnesota, I have been told, has more lakes than any other state in the Union.

_____ 11. A. The road is wide, hard-surfaced most of the way, and very few sharp curves.
         B. The road is wide and hard-surfaced most of the way and has very few curves.

_____ 12. A. The survey revealed that the salaries of the janitors were equal, and in some cases higher than the beginning teachers.
         B. The survey revealed that the salaries of the janitors were equal to, and in some case higher than, those of the beginning teachers.

_____ 13. A. The receptionist told me to return the questionnaire to her as soon as I finished it.
         B. The receptionist told me to, as soon as I finished the questionnaire, return it to her.

_____ 14. A. Some of the more vocal fans, still complaining about Coach Driscoll's lack of imagination and new ideas.
         B. Some of the more vocal fans are still complaining about Coach Driscoll's lack of imagination and new ideas.

_____ 15. A. "I admire neither the mayor's politics nor the people he associates with," said Ms. Ames.
         B. "I neither admire the mayor's politics nor the people he associates with," said Ms. Ames.

_____ 16. A. The predicted rainfall will be as heavy as that of the last few days, if not heavier.
         B. The predicted rainfall will be as heavy, if not heavier than, the last few days.

_____ 17. A. One unusual bit of information being that Hong Kong boasts of more Rolls Royces per square foot than any city on earth.
         B. One unusual bit of information is that Hong Kong boasts of more Rolls Royces per square foot than any other city on earth.

_____ 18. A. Danny managed by December to pay off nearly half of his father's debts.
         B. Danny managed to by December nearly pay off half of his father's debts.

_____ 19. A. The accident happened because the street was icy and the other driver was inexperienced and careless.
         B. The accident happened because the street was icy and because of the other driver's inexperience and carelessness.

_____ 20. A. Whose SAT scores were best, yours or your twin brothers?
         B. Whose SAT scores were better, yours or your twin brother's?

PROGRESS TEST 7

SUBORDINATION (LESSON 15)

NAME _____ SCORE _____

Directions: Change the italicized sentence to the form indicated in the parentheses and rewrite enough of the new sentence to illustrate the construction.

1. The Jensens were in Hawaii on vacation. They missed the dedication of the new courthouse. (adverbial clause of reason) _____

   _____

2. *The Jensens were in Hawaii on vacation.* They missed the dedication of the new courthouse. (absolute phrase) _____

   _____

3. *Brush the movable metal parts lightly with oil.* This will protect them against rust. (gerund phrase) _____

   _____

4. Brush the movable metal parts lightly with oil. *This will protect them against rust.* (infinitive phrase) _____

   _____

5. The survivors were flown to Ellertown by Ben Towle. *He is a local helicopter pilot.* (adjective clause) _____

   _____

6. The survivors were flown to Ellertown by Ben Towle. *He is a local helicopter pilot.* (appositive) _____

   _____

7. *I had read the editorial.* I decided to write a letter to the editor. (adverbial clause of time) _____

   _____

8. *I had read the editorial.* I decided to write a letter to the editor. (participial phrase)

   _____

   _____

9. *I had read the editorial.* I decided to write a letter to the editor. (prepositional phrase with gerund phrase object) _____

   _____

10. With our sandwiches we drank warm ginger ale. *Our meager supply of ice had melted.* (absolute phrase) _____

    _____

Directions: Rewrite each of the following numbered sections as one complex sentence; show enough of the new sentence to illustrate the construction. In each case use the italicized subject and verb for the main clause. Use a variety of the subordinating units listed on the first page of Lesson 15.

1. I knew Stan Whipple in college. He is now a successful art auctioneer. *I was surprised* to learn this. _____

2. I spent five hours typing my research paper and *I was* exhausted and so I went to bed before nine o'clock. _____

3. This *quilt* has been in our family for over sixty years. It *was made* by my grandmother. She was twenty years old when she made it. _____

4. I finished high school in June. I didn't find a job that I liked. *I returned* to summer school for a course in typing. Typing is a valuable skill for anyone. _____

5. The recipe called for chopped pecans. *I used* chopped peanuts instead. Chopped peanuts are more fitted to my limited budget. _____

6. Hank and I attended college together. That was twenty years ago. *He seemed* completely lacking in ambition. But he was intelligent. _____

7. Jackson is not a very strong student, but he is a good basketball player and so *I suppose* he'll have no trouble getting into college somewhere. _____

8. Mother is usually easygoing. She rarely raises her voice. *She surprised* the family. She announced that this year she was not cooking a big Thanksgiving Day dinner. _____

9. Duncan graduated from college in pharmacy. But now *he manages* a seed company. The company is large. It is located near Lompoc, California. _____

10. Laura's uncle learned that she was majoring in journalism. *He sent* her a letter. It was stern and unequivocal. It ordered her to change her major to law. _____

PROGRESS TEST **8**

COMMAS AND SEMICOLONS: COMPOUND UNITS (LESSONS 7, 17)

NAME _____   SCORE _____

Directions: In each sentence a *V* marks a point of coordination between (1) two verbs with a coordinating conjunction, (2) two independent clauses with a coordinating conjunction, or (3) two independent clauses without a coordinating conjunction. In the space at the left, write one of the following:
  0 [no punctuation is needed]
  C [a comma is needed]
  S [a semicolon is needed]

_____ 1. "I have a new machine here," said the mechanic *V* "in two minutes it will analyze your car's exhaust."

_____ 2. Dr. Ellis's lecture must have impressed her audience *V* for dozens of people with questions crowded around her after she finished.

_____ 3. Many years ago Jerome had fished for bass and muskellunge in northern Minnesota *V* in those days no one worried about polluted lakes and streams.

_____ 4. Ms. Brady's comments on student themes were sometimes cruel *V* and did not endear her to the fellows in pre-engineering.

_____ 5. The living conditions of the people are improving slowly *V* but there is little hope for significant change.

_____ 6. The party must have been rather unexciting *V* for my roommate was home and in bed by ten o'clock.

_____ 7. The day-long meeting was routine and uneventful *V* for the visiting students from India it must have seemed quite dull.

_____ 8. Under the new law automobile drivers over seventy years of age must pass a test *V* otherwise their current licenses will be revoked.

_____ 9. This set of matched golf clubs normally sells for $350 *V* but during our anniversary sale it is available for only $265.

_____ 10. This set of matched golf clubs normally sells for $350 *V* during our anniversary sale, however, it is available for only $265.

_____ 11. This set of matched golf clubs normally sells for $350 *V* but during our anniversary sale is available for only $265.

_____ 12. A teenager carrying a noisy boom box lurched past Mrs. Howe *V* and sat down in the only unoccupied seat in the bus.

_____ 13. For several months General Benham had been receiving anonymous threats over the telephone *V* but had not reported them to the police.

_____ 14. For several months General Benham had been receiving anonymous threats over the telephone *V* but he had not reported them to the police.

_____ 15. The ill-mannered guard neither answered Marcy's question *V* nor invited her to step inside out of the rain.

_____ 16. The ill-mannered guard did not answer Marcy's question *V* nor did he invite her to step inside out of the rain.

_____ 17. The ill-mannered guard did not answer Marcy's question *V* moreover, he did not invite her to step inside out of the rain.

_____ 18. This television by itself sells for $672 *V* with its matching stand the price is $730.

_____ 19. The advertised price is $730 *V* but without the matching stand the price is only $672.

_____ 20. Ms. Shaw has used these films in her seventh-grade class *V* she reports that the student response was good.

_____ 21. Ms. Shaw has used these films in her seventh-grade class *V* and reports that the student response was good.

_____ 22. Ms. Shaw has used these films in her seventh-grade class *V* the student response, she reports, was good.

_____ 23. Our special this week is the four-head video receiver pictured in our advertisement *V* we are offering it at the low price of $299.

_____ 24. You'll like its on-screen menu system *V* and inexperienced users will appreciate its easy-to-understand panel display.

_____ 25. Ms. Stern comes to our firm well-recommended *V* for the past four years she headed a workforce of nearly seventy people.

_____ 26. Ms. Stern should go far with our firm *V* for she is intelligent and hard-working.

_____ 27. Dean Lewis accepted the students' petition *V* and promised that he would study it carefully.

_____ 28. *Ilex opaca* is an American holly with glossy leaves and red berries *V* the foliage and berries are often used for Christmas decorations.

_____ 29. Juniors in this program normally take History 350 *V* however, Dean Tate has allowed me to substitute Political Science 107.

_____ 30. A limited number of viewers have called this movie a masterpiece *V* but many others are bothered by its ambiguities.

PUNCTUATION: ALL MARKS
(LESSONS 17–20)

NAME _____ SCORE _____

Directions: The following sentences contain fifty numbered spots between words or beneath words. (The number is beneath the word when the punctuation problem involves the use of an apostrophe in that word.) In the correspondingly numbered spaces at the left, write C if the punctuation is correct or W if it is incorrect.

1. _____   (1) Had we known that the lecture would attract such a large audience;$_1$

2. _____   we would have scheduled it for Farwell Hall,$_2$ which has three hun-

             dred seats.

3. _____   (2) The average tourists'$_3$ equipment consists of:$_4$ a camera, a raincoat,

4. _____   dark glasses, and a guidebook.

5. _____   (3) Geoffrey Chaucer, who wrote *The Canterbury Tales,*$_5$ is known for his

6. _____   realism, his humor, and$_6$ his accurate observation.

7. _____   (4) The 1928 Olympic Games,$_7$ by the way, made history$_8$ for competitive

8. _____   events for women were introduced.

9. _____   (5) Mother was not amused when she discovered that the children had

10. _____   made a snowman$_9$ and had used one of her new golf balls for it's$_{10}$ nose.

11. _____   (6) Frank Duveneck, a portrait painter who was born in Kentucky on

12. _____   October 9, 1848,$_{11}$ eventually settled in Cincinnati$_{12}$ where he died in

             1919.

13. _____   (7) "I distinctly heard someone say, 'What's$_{13}$ that guy talking about?' "$_{14}$

14. _____   said the new teacher.

15. _____   (8) If you didn't draw this hilarious caricature of me, I wonder who's$_{15}$

16. _____   responsible for it?$_{16}$

17. _____   (9) "Please remember, my dear Miss.$_{17}$ Scroggs," said the secretary, "that

18. _____   a neat tidy$_{18}$ appearance is one of the best recommendations."

19. _____   (10) Dark clouds crept up from the west,$_{19}$ and the hot,$_{20}$ sultry air was omi-

20. _____   nously quiet.

21. _____   (11) When Mr. Davis finally does resign$_{21}$ the position will probably be

22. _____   filled by one of the boss's$_{22}$ nephews.

351

23. _____ (12) When we lived there, the village was peaceful and restful, now it has
24. _____   been ruined by noisy ill-mannered tourists.

25. _____ (13) Mr. Oldham's assessment for the new paving on Elm Street being, in
26. _____   his opinion, too high; he protested to Ned Lane, a member of the
            Council.

27. _____ (14) "Responsibility for the seating arrangement at the banquet will be
28. _____   someone else's, not your's," the chairperson told Edith.

29. _____ (15) A short, quite pathetic appeal was made to the mayor by an elderly
30. _____   woman whose property tax had been nearly doubled.

31. _____ (16) A fiery, political speech was made by our senior county commis-
32. _____   sioner who hopes to be reelected.

33. _____ (17) "This car seems to be pulling slightly to the left, I wonder if one of
34. _____   the tires is going flat?" said Marge.

35. _____ (18) Epictetus, a Greek Stoic who was originally a slave, taught in Rome
36. _____   until 90 A.D. when the emperor Domitian banished all philosophers.

37. _____ (19) This week you'll find real bargains at Woodward's Department Store
38. _____   in: light fixtures, paint, linens, and childrens' shoes.

39. _____ (20) "My briefcase isn't here in the car," said McCall; "I wonder if I could
40. _____   have left it in your office."

41. _____ (21) "We had a bad storm when I was out fishing in the bay two week's
42. _____   ago," said Mark, who knew that Jo was a nervous landlubber.

43. _____ (22) The last bus from Lawrenceville having arrived with no passengers,
44. _____   Jim and Trudy walked slowly to their car and drove back to the farm.

45. _____ (23) "Let's drop the matter," said Anne impatiently. "After all these prob-
46. _____   lems are nobody's business but mine."

47. _____ (24) Louisa is writing a book about her paternal grandmother who was a
48. _____   vigorous worker for womens' rights.

49. _____ (25) From the very first difficulties beset the planned expansion; finally
50. _____   resulting in the withdrawal of funds by the two principal backers.

PUNCTUATION: ALL MARKS
(LESSONS 17–20)

NAME _____ SCORE _____

Directions: The following sentences contain fifty numbered spots between words or beneath words. (The number is beneath the word when the punctuation problem involves the use of an apostrophe in that word.) In the correspondingly numbered spaces at the left, write C if the punctuation is correct or W if it is incorrect.

1. _____   (1) The treasurer's report was so long, so disorganized, and so dull that

2. _____   some of the listeners dozed off at times.

3. _____   (2) At daybreak a crow parked itself outside our balcony and kept us

4. _____   awake with it's loud raucous scolding.

5. _____   (3) The dodo and the roc, both commonly found only in crossword puz-

6. _____   zles, are similar in some respects, and different in others.

7. _____   (4) The dodo, a bird that is now extinct, actually lived in Mauritius but

8. _____   the roc lived only in people's imagination.

9. _____   (5) Rotary International was founded in Chicago, Illinois, in 1905, it

10. _____   now has chapters in more than seventy countries.

11. _____   (6) The Jensens sat in the airport for six long, tedious hours; their flight

12. _____   being delayed by what was called an equipment shortage.

13. _____   (7) Your equipment should consist of: heavy hiking boots, a waterproof

14. _____   tarpaulin, and plenty of warm clothing.

15. _____   (8) Today I received from a travel agency a new calendar; on the cover

16. _____   theres a beautiful picture of the Bay of Naples.

17. _____   (9) "A team that wont be beaten can't be beaten," said Coach Wellby,

18. _____   who is hopelessly addicted to clichés.

19. _____ (10) In the outer lobby is a huge oil portrait of the founder of the firm; his

20. _____   stern humorless face adding to the austerity of the surroundings.

21. _____ (11) The midterm test will cover the following materials: the class lec-

22. _____   tures to date and chapters 2, 3, 4, and 5 of the text.

23. _____ (12) The play has received good reviews from the critics, I suppose it's

24. _____   impossible to get tickets at this late date.

25. _____ (13) "You agree with me, dont you," Jean answered, "that my suggestion
25

26. _____ was a reasonable one."
26

27. _____ (14) For most of this summer Martha has been borrowing one of my

28. _____ bikes; her's is now too old and too rusty to be safe.
27   28

29. _____ (15) Flight 723, which is scheduled to arrive here at 4:12 P.M. has been
29

30. _____ delayed at Topeka, Kansas, because of bad weather.
30

31. _____ (16) Coleman, the third baseman, threw down his glove, and screamed
31

32. _____ that the runner hadn't touched the base.
32

33. _____ (17) The art teacher, Miss. Philbrick, asked Janey if she had ever done any
33

34. _____ professional modeling?
34

35. _____ (18) Our neighbors, the Thomas's, have a new television set that has a
35

36. _____ much larger picture than our's.
36

37. _____ (19) The notice on the bulletin board announced the new schedule: break-
37

38. _____ fast at six-thirty, lunch at eleven-thirty, and dinner at six.
38

39. _____ (20) "After all my friends will help me out of this, they know that my
39   40

40. _____ word is as good as my bond," said Mr. Winther.

41. _____ (21) Julia's cousin Larry studied at Heidelberg, where he became well ac-
41

42. _____ quainted with Judge Coleman's only grandson Herman.
42

43. _____ (22) "Judd shouldn't have taken offense at my remark, I merely asked him
43

44. _____ if he was made up for a masquerade party?" said Eugene.
44

45. _____ (23) Dr. Andrews has written articles about child psychology but his own
45

46. _____ childrens' behavior in a group is far from admirable.
46

47. _____ (24) "The story line, the costumes, the music—everything must be
47

48. _____ changed," said Cecil Burbank, the new director.
48

49. _____ (25) Laura is the kind of person who shops downtown until five oclock,
49   50

50. _____ and then complains about the crowded condition of the bus on her

ride home.

PROGRESS TEST 11
VERBS (LESSONS 21, 22)

NAME _____ SCORE _____

Directions: Study these sentences for (1) the correct form of a principal part of a verb, (2) the correct subject–verb agreement, and (3) the correct tense of a verb. Underline every incorrect verb and write the correct form in the space at the left. No sentence contains more than two incorrect verb forms. Some sentences may be correct.

_____ 1. After setting in the hot sun all day, every one of the petunia plants I put out this morning has wilted badly.

_____ 2. Neither Dr. Alterton nor his assistant were able to make sense of the peculiar symbols written on the wooden slab.

_____ 3. Has either of your two roommates begun to be interviewed for a job after graduation?

_____ 4. One story that I've heard is that Judge Trowbridge payed back to the bank all of the money that his nephew had stole.

_____ 5. The mayor, along with three of her top aides, has been asked to set at the head table with the visiting dignitaries.

_____ 6. "I been hunting in these woods for fifty years but never before seen a critter like that one," said the guide.

_____ 7. Stan walked into the principal's office, laid his books on the table, and says, "I've come to the end of my rope."

_____ 8. There was only seven seconds left in the game when Pete West let fly from midcourt and sank the game-winning three-pointer.

_____ 9. A news story reports that the appearance of mysterious patterns in wheat fields have become a summer diversion in southern England.

_____ 10. After the eight-o'clock bell had rang, Mr. Towle said, "The fact that the weather is bad don't mean that we won't hold classes today."

_____ 11. I would have liked to have gone to the movie with you, but I saw that show last month in Dallas.

_____ 12. Don't it worry you that the price of your shares of stock have fallen by nearly thirty percent in four months?

_____ 13. Seated behind us were a woman with four children who noisily ate candy and drunk pop during the entire movie.

_____ 14. After the other officers had given their reports, the colonel said, "The evidence has shown that neither of the two incidents were the result of equipment failure."

355

_____ 15. There's been so many improvements made at the Lakeside Inn
_____ that it has became one of the most popular resorts in the state.

_____ 16. As we rose to leave the auditorium, Bart remarked, "I think
_____ our speaker could have chose a livelier topic to discuss."

_____ 17. In July heat records were broke on two days, but during Au-
_____ gust the range of temperatures were normal for the season.

_____ 18. Julie had just lain down for a short rest when her neighbor
_____ came running over and tells her that there was a couple of rac-
coons in her vegetable garden.

_____ 19. The Associated Press reports that the search for possible sur-
_____ vivors of the earthquake have been slowed because of repeated
aftershocks that have shaken the area.

_____ 20. The magnitude of our budgetary problems have left a shadow
_____ across the legislative process; no wonder that the confidence
in our lawmakers has sank to new low levels.

_____ 21. The advertisement announcing that our entire stock of Na-
_____ ture's Own Vitamins are on sale has drawn huge crowds.

_____ 22. "It's been a hectic day," said Beth. "The two-o'clock bell has
_____ already rung, and I haven't eaten a bite of lunch yet."

_____ 23. "Commissioner Bunker's standards for the behavior of public
_____ servants, including himself," the editor had written, "has always been minimal."

_____ 24. "Neither of the two Ford trucks in our lot have been drove
_____ more than forty thousand miles," said the salesperson.

_____ 25. The number of fatal accidents at the corner of Fifth and Oak
_____ has risen alarmingly over the past two years.

_____ 26. In the lobby there is a davenport and several overstuffed chairs
_____ where patients can set and read while waiting to see the dentist.

_____ 27. The leader of the gang, along with two of his followers, were
_____ lying wounded on the floor of the garage.

_____ 28. Not one of the paintings that were taken from the museum
_____ during the robbery last summer have been recovered.

_____ 29. The girls abandoned the sinking canoe and swam safely to
_____ shore, but unfortunately their pet dog was drownded.

_____ 30. Has either your teacher or the school counselor spoke to you
_____ about applying for a scholarship?

PRONOUNS (LESSONS 23, 24)

NAME _____ SCORE _____

Directions: Study the following sentences for poorly used pronouns. Look for wrong case forms, misspelled possessives, vague or inexact references. Circle each incorrect pronoun. In the space at the left of each pair of sentences, write the letter that identifies the correct sentence.

_____ 1. A. Usually the personnel director of the laboratory will inquire about an applicant's personal life, including such things as whom your associates are.
   B. Usually the personnel director of the laboratory will inquire about an applicant's personal life, including such things as who his or her associates are.

_____ 2. A. Every fellow at the dorm except Jacobs, Peterson, and me has already had his spring-term class schedule approved.
   B. Every fellow at the dorm except Jacobs, Peterson, and I has already had their spring-term class schedule approved.

_____ 3. A. Four of us girls got in line for the ticket sale at seven in the morning, and then we were told that the office wouldn't open until noon.
   B. Four of we girls got in line for the ticket sale at seven in the morning, and then they told us that the office wouldn't open until noon.

_____ 4. A. "I'm supposed to ride in Phil's car," said Lew, "but, just between you and I, I'd prefer to ride in someone elses."
   B. "I'm supposed to ride in Phil's car," said Lew, "but, just between you and me, I'd prefer to ride in someone else's."

_____ 5. A. "I plan to become a forester," said Tom, "because it allows you to do your bit for saving the environment."
   B. "I plan to become a forester," said Tom, "because work in forestry allows a person to do his or her bit for saving the environment."

_____ 6. A. It said on television that the finalists, whomever they are, will meet for five games in Las Vegas.
   B. According to a television report, the finalists, whoever they are, will meet for five games in Las Vegas.

_____ 7. A. Ginny told her best friend, Marge, that she should lose at least five pounds.
   B. Ginny told her best friend, Marge, "I should lose at least five pounds."

_____ 8. A. "Dad is a dedicated fisherman, and he keeps trying to get my sister and me interested in fishing," said Mary Jane.
   B. "Dad is a dedicated fisherman, and he keeps trying to get my sister and I interested in it," said Mary Jane.

_____ 9. A. Mr. Capri's lawyer produced two witnesses who he said had been present when the alleged bribe offer was made.
   B. Mr. Capri's lawyer produced two witnesses whom he said had been present when the alleged bribe offer was made.

357

_____ 10. A. "All of us administrators are pleased," said Dean Powers, "that the college is attracting many adults into its Homemakers' Program."
B. "The college is attracting many adults into their Homemakers' Program, which pleases all of we administrators," said Dean Powers.

_____ 11. A. A tourist whom we met at a filling station in Plainview told us that the highway for the next two miles is being resurfaced.
B. A tourist who we met at a filling station in Plainview told us that they are resurfacing the highway for the next two miles.

_____ 12. A. My younger brother is a better mathematician than me, principally because he has taken several courses in it.
B. My younger brother is a better mathematician than I, principally because he has taken several courses in mathematics.

_____ 13. A. It clearly states in the application form that you must provide a recent three-by-five picture of yourself.
B. The application form clearly states that applicants must provide three-by-five pictures of themselves.

_____ 14. A. The person whom the Speaker of the House appoints to make this investigation must reconcile himself or herself to a thankless chore.
B. The person who the Speaker of the House appoints to make this investigation must reconcile themself to a thankless chore.

_____ 15. A. The car ahead of our's was weaving so erratically that I didn't want to try to pass him.
B. The car ahead of ours was weaving so erratically that I didn't want to try to pass it.

_____ 16. A. At the first pep rally the cheerleaders told we freshmen to wear our green beanies at every game.
B. At the first pep rally the cheerleaders told us freshmen to wear our green beanies at every game.

_____ 17. A. "Is there anyone who you really think might get more votes than I in the primary election?" asked ex-Senator Wiley.
B. "Is there anyone whom you really think might get more votes than me in the primary election?" asked ex-Senator Wiley.

_____ 18. A. The three new owners of the Busy Bee Store maintain that you can't find another merchant in town who's prices are lower than their's.
B. The three new owners of the Busy Bee Store maintain that there isn't another merchant in town whose prices are lower than theirs.

_____ 19. A. Your brother likes to tease you. If it wasn't he who sent you the comic valentine, who do you think it might have been?
B. Your brother likes to tease you. If it wasn't him who sent you the comic valentine, whom do you think it might have been?

_____ 20. A. "This notebook must be someone else's," said Martin. "Mine has an American flag stenciled on its cover."
B. "This notebook must be someone elses," said Martin. "Mine has an American flag stenciled on it's cover."

PROGRESS TEST 13

MODIFIERS: APPROPRIATE USE (LESSONS 25, 26)

NAME _____ SCORE _____

Directions: In the space at the left, write the *number* of the correct form given in parentheses.

_____ 1. I (1. couldn't have, 2. couldn't of) finished typing my term paper even if
_____   I had worked on (1. steady, 2. steadily) until midnight.

_____ 2. (1. Let us, 2. Let's us) put in an extra hour on this project and finish it
_____   (1. faster, 2. more faster) than in the time allotted for it.

_____ 3. "(1. Where, 2. Where at) can I buy some of (1. them, 2. those) huge sun-
_____   glasses like the ones you are wearing?" Ms. Tower asked Letty.

_____ 4. "I have no doubt," said Mrs. Lathrop, "(1. but what, 2. that) my daugh-
_____   ter will finally select the (1. more, 2. most) expensive of the two dresses."

_____ 5. Our committee got a (1. real, 2. really) early start, and by noon we had
_____   addressed (1. most, 2. almost) all of the political pamphlets.

_____ 6. Coach Treadwell is (1. sure, 2. surely) happy about the large (1. amount,
_____   2. number) of junior-college transfers who turned out for the team.

_____ 7. "Old Hank Jones (1. use to, 2. used to) appear (1. regular, 2. regularly)
_____   at our church functions," said Mrs. Walker, "but I haven't seen him in
        months."

_____ 8. Frankly, I am (1. kind of, 2. rather) surprised that our girls' team did as
_____   (1. good, 2. well) as they did in the regional tournament.

_____ 9. As I stood up ready to get (1. off, 2. off of) the bus, a fire engine swerved
_____   around the corner and came (1. awful, 2. very) close to us.

_____ 10. (1. Due to, 2. Because of) his bad eyesight, Mel didn't do very (1. good,
_____   2. well) on the map-reading part of the test.

_____ 11. "I know that your uncle will feel (1. bad, 2. badly) if he doesn't receive
_____   an (1. invite, 2. invitation) to the wedding," said Aunt Yolanda.

_____ 12. "I think (1. this, 2. this here) purple scarf would look (1. good, 2. well)
_____   with your new suit," said the salesperson.

359

_____ 13. Judged on (1. this, 2. these) new and stricter criteria, Ludlow's essay is
_____ clearly the (1. better, 2. best) of the two finalists.

_____ 14. From his report, Jack sounded (1. as if, 2. like) he had a (1. real, 2. re-
_____ ally) good time on his trip to Florida.

_____ 15. I wish Professor Lynn would talk (1. more slower, 2. more slowly); I
_____ (1. can hardly, 2. can't hardly) take notes when he is racing to finish his
lecture.

_____ 16. The thing (1. that, 2. what) really surprised the firefighters is that no one
_____ was injured (1. bad, 2. badly) in the spectacular fire.

_____ 17. A (1. couple, 2. couple of) friends and I work out (1. regular, 2. regu-
_____ larly) at the company's gymnasium.

_____ 18. (1. Lots of, 2. Many) of the native people have (1. emigrated, 2. immi-
_____ grated) because of the crop failures in their homeland.

_____ 19. That flower that you call an evening primrose (1. sure, 2. surely) smells
_____ (1. sweet, 2. sweetly).

_____ 20. The reason the deal fell through is (1. because, 2. that) at the last minute
_____ the seller increased the price (1. considerable, 2. considerably).

_____ 21. (1. Light-complexioned, 2. Light-complected) people like you and me
_____ (1. shouldn't, 2. hadn't ought to) stay out in the hot sun on a day like
today.

_____ 22. (1. Because of, 2. Due to) the infection in his eye, Darrell hasn't been
_____ able to study very (1. good, 2. well) this week.

_____ 23. Now that he has lost weight, Graham looks quite (1. different, 2. differ-
_____ ently) (1. from, 2. than) the way he looks in these old photographs.

_____ 24. "I'm (1. enthused, 2. enthusiastic) about my new job," said Malcolm. "It
_____ is interesting, and, best of all, it pays (1. good, 2. well)."

_____ 25. By your answer to Mike's question, did you mean to (1. imply, 2. infer)
_____ that you feel (1. bad, 2. badly) about the election results?

PROGRESS TEST 14
USAGE (LESSONS 21–26)

NAME _____ SCORE _____

Directions: Each sentence has two italicized words or expressions. If you think that a word or expression is inappropriate in serious writing, write a correct form in the space at the left. If a word or expression is correct, write C in the space.

_____ 1. *Lying* at the side of the road was a plastic bag full of garbage
_____   that some tourist had apparently thrown from *their* car.

_____ 2. In this senior class there *are* only four or five people *whom* I
_____   think are capable of successful work at the graduate level.

_____ 3. The reward money was divided *among* four of *we* hikers who
_____   had turned in the fire alarm.

_____ 4. The mechanic *lay* down the wrench and explained to Roger
_____   and *I* what had to be done and what it would cost.

_____ 5. We were *plenty* surprised when we learned that there *was* only
_____   one teacher and eighteen pupils in the entire school.

_____ 6. "I doubt that fellows as short as you and *me* can play basket-
_____   ball *good* enough to earn a letter," Al said to Jeremy.

_____ 7. No one at headquarters was *suppose to* know *who* the new
_____   agent was reporting to in Berlin.

_____ 8. Sergeant Gross did not *suspicion* that quite a few of *we* men
_____   had been sneaking off to the movies in the village.

_____ 9. A gregarious person like Andy seems able to make *themself*
_____   feel right at home almost *anywheres.*

_____ 10. By the end of the second week every freshman should have
_____   *chosen* which social club *they* will join.

_____ 11. "Who can be *enthused* about *those kind* of video games?"
_____   asked Claire.

_____ 12. Just *like* I had predicted, after the speech there *wasn't* more
_____   than three or four questions from members of the audience.

_____ 13. Dan was *sure* surprised to learn that everyone in class except
_____ Marcia Lerner and *him* would have to take another test.

_____ 14. The reason there is a critical shortage is *because* neither of the
_____ two state-supported universities *is* turning out qualified engineers.

_____ 15. The thief, *whoever* he was, had apparently left the warehouse
_____ parking lot in a small truck that he had *stolen* earlier in the
day.

_____ 16. "These people speak a language that is strange to us," said the
_____ guide, "but in truth they are really not much different *from* you
and *I.*"

_____ 17. *Has* either of the two plum trees you planted *began* to bear
_____ fruit yet?

_____ 18. *Due to* the icy condition of the roads, all of *we* latecomers
_____ were given excuses today.

_____ 19. The sale of season tickets for basketball games this year *has*
_____ declined *considerable.*

_____ 20. The missing climber's rucksack was found *lying* at the bottom
_____ of a small crevasse, where it had apparently *lain* for several
days.

_____ 21. Every one of the stocks that you recommended to my wife and
_____ *me* last year *has* declined in value.

_____ 22. All of us agree that *whoever* took the money from the Christ-
_____ mas Fund was *real* desperate.

_____ 23. The committee's choice for chairperson was Marge Bingham,
_____ not *I,* in spite of the fact that my experience is much broader
than *her's.*

_____ 24. Just between you and *me,* my parents don't approve of *me*
_____ postponing my senior year of college.

_____ 25. *Whom* do you suppose could have written *them* insulting
_____ anonymous letters to the superintendent?

PROGRESS TEST 15

SPELLING RULES; WORDS SIMILAR IN SOUND (LESSON 27)

NAME _____ SCORE _____

Directions: In the spaces at the left, copy the correct forms given in parentheses.

_____   1. We took a cab to the auditorium, but when we arrived the
_____   (conference, conferrence) had (already, all ready) begun.

_____   2. The homemade warning device, although far from perfect, is
_____   (quiet, quite) (servicable, serviceable).

_____   3. The fast-talking salesman maintained that he was a (personal,
_____   personnel) friend of several New York (financeirs, financiers).

_____   4. "In my lifetime I (seized, siezed) many golden (opportunities,
_____   opportunitys) but couldn't hold on to them," Mr. Caldwell
                         answered.

_____   5. "I'd hardly call this an (unforgetable, unforgettable) (dining,
_____   dinning) experience," said Sal as she set aside the bowl of
                         lukewarm soup.

_____   6. "(Neither, Niether) of your two laboratory experiments was
_____   (completely, completly) satisfactory," said the lab assistant.

_____   7. The Acme Corporation has donated to the city a very (desir-
_____   able, desireable) building (cite, sight, site) for the proposed
                         convention center.

_____   8. "Just to be in the (presence, presents) of such a (fameous, fa-
_____   mous) basketball star is a great honor," said the youngster.

_____   9. I haven't seen my neighbors lately; in all (likelihood, likely-
                         hood, liklihood, liklyhood) (their, there, they're) out of town.

_____   10. Some people (beleive, believe) that the city engineer will
_____   (altar, alter) the specifications in order to attract more bidders.

_____   11. Remember, (its, it's) considered good manners to (comple-
_____   ment, compliment) the hostess after a good meal.

_____   12. With my two time-consuming jobs, I assure you that I have no
_____   (leisure, liesure) time (activities, activitys) to speak of.

363

_____ 13. "Our negotiators managed to (affect, effect) an (advantageous,
_____ advantagous) settlement with the union," said Mr. Siebert.

_____ 14. (Unfortunately, Unfortunatly), similar (incidence, incidents)
_____ are being reported to the police with increasing frequency.

_____ 15. The judge (adviced, advised) the quarreling neighbors to set-
_____ tle their problem (peacably, peaceably) without outside help.

_____ 16. This semester Sherwood's work in mathematics has (shone,
_____ shown) a (noticable, noticeable) improvement.

_____ 17. The (principal, principle) of the school was not (deceived, de-
_____ cieved) by young Thompson's outlandish story.

_____ 18. After confessing to the theft, the man (lead, led) the officers to
_____ the place in the barren (desert, dessert) where he had buried
the loot.

_____ 19. "I think (your, you're) being very (courageous, couragous),"
_____ said Belinda to the young fire fighter.

_____ 20. "Frankly, Alice," said Marlene, "I think that your new friend
_____ is (outrageously, outragously) (conceited, concieted)."

_____ 21. The three (attornies, attorneys) representing our competitor
_____ were much younger (than, then) I had expected.

_____ 22. The bank president rewarded the (casheir, cashier) (who's,
_____ whose) quick thinking had thwarted the holdup.

_____ 23. For her (neice's, niece's) birthday Ms. Simpson sent her a box
_____ of monogramed (stationary, stationery).

_____ 24. "I predict that our (cheif, chief) of police will (loose, lose) his
_____ job after the next election," said Alderman Whiteside.

_____ 25. After (poring, pouring) over dozens of books in the library, I
_____ feel that I have done a (thorough, through) job of researching
the matter.

PROGRESS TEST 16
SPELLING (LESSON 29)

NAME _____ SCORE _____

Directions: Each sentence contains two words from the first half of the spelling list. In each of these words at least one letter is missing. Write the words, correctly spelled, in the spaces at the left.

_____
_____
1. The new dorm—tory, which will be finished by next fall, will ac—modate three hundred students.

_____
_____
2. I am cer—n that you and your family will enjoy your tour of Great Brit—n.

_____
_____
3. The results of most of our school's ath—tic contests for the past two seasons have been dis—pointing.

_____
_____
4. In class were between thirty-five and fo—ty enthu—tic students.

_____
_____
5. The careless, a—ward boy accident—y broke one of the jars.

_____
_____
6. The new clerk in the office is sometimes embar—sed by his glaring mistakes in gram—r.

_____
_____
7. We were dis—atisfied with the poor service and the ex—rbitant price of the meals.

_____
_____
8. Caldwell is building a large apartment complex ac—oss the street from a large cem—tery.

_____
_____
9. Janice is an exception—y good student of for—n languages.

_____
_____
10. Delegates are arriving for an international confer—nce concerned with protecting the env—nment.

Directions: These sentences contain thirty italicized words from the first half of the spelling list. A sentence may have no misspelled words, one misspelled word, or two misspelled words. Underline each misspelled word and write it, correctly spelled, in a space at the left.

_____
_____
1. *Confidentially,* Mr. Burke's resignation *dosen't* make any real *difference* in our company's long-range plans.

_____
_____
2. Although only an *amateur,* Ms. Davis has *aquired* a collection of early-American pewter that is *amoung* the best in the nation.

_____
_____
3. *Finally,* late in *Febuary,* an *eminent* retired general spoke out strongly against the proposed treaty.

_____
_____
4. One of the *candidates* for mayor gave the *committee* a lengthy *explaination* of his financial dealings.

_____
_____
5. This applicant is an *efficient* worker whose wide *experience* makes her *especialy* well equipped to replace Thornton.

_____
_____
6. *Apparently* the new *apparatus* will cost the county *approximately* three thousand dollars.

_____
_____
7. *During* your college days, ownership of an *excellent dictionary* is a necessity.

_____
_____
8. The visitor's harsh *criticism* of our *goverment* was, we all agreed, not *appropriate.*

_____
_____
9. "I *allways* went to chapel when I was in school," said Uncle James. "*Attendance,* I might add, was not *compulsory.*"

_____
_____
10. *Accompaning* the letter was a brochure with a *discription* of the proposed *condominium.*

PROGRESS TEST 17
SPELLING (LESSON 29)

NAME _____ SCORE _____

Directions: Each sentence contains two words from the second half of the spelling list. In each of these words at least one letter is missing. Write the words, correctly spelled, in the spaces at the left.

_____   1. Densmore found it nec—sary to borrow money in order to fin-
_____   ish his sop—ore year of college.

_____   2. I can rec—mend Ms. Lukens highly; I am sure that she will
_____   do the work satisfa—ly.

_____   3. After speaking to Prof—r Quigley, I felt more opt—tic about
_____   being able to finish the course.

_____   4. The secr—ry of the local chamber of commerce ordered a
_____   large quan—ty of the booklets.

_____   5. Leonard's parents lost pract—ly all of their pos—sions in
_____   the fire.

_____   6. The three of us left the chemistry lab—atory and walked to a
_____   nearby rest—nt for lunch.

_____   7. The superinten—nt ordered me to return all of the books to the
_____   school lib—ry.

_____   8. The teacher said that Angela's interp—tation of the poem was
_____   highly orig—nal.

_____   9. Oc—sionally Jenny would su—prise the family by offering to
_____   plan and cook a meal for them.

_____ 10. The spe   ch instructor criticized my pron—ciation of a few
_____   historical place names.

Directions: These sentences contain thirty italicized words from the second half of the spelling list. A sentence may have no misspelled words, one misspelled word, or two misspelled words. Underline each misspelled word and write it, correctly spelled, in a space at the left.

_____   1. You must admit that our drama club has put on several *really*
_____   *successful preformances*.

_____   2. Some people look upon *politics* as a somewhat *rediculous pas-*
_____   *time*.

_____   3. Last month I worked overtime on *Wednesday* the *eighth* and
_____   Sunday the *twelfth*.

_____   4. In his writings one can find many *specimans* of *propaganda*
_____   that play upon racial *prejudices*.

_____   5. The *sergeant* and I often go to the gym to exercise on the *par-*
_____   *allel* bars to develop grace and *rythm*.

_____   6. My lack of *preserverence* can *undoubtably* be explained in im-
_____   pressive sounding *psychological* terms.

_____   7. I *regard* it a *privilege* to interview such a prominent member
_____   of the British *Parliament*.

_____   8. My *pardner's schedual* is so full that he never has time for
_____   more than a hurried *sandwich* at noon.

_____   9. "I *usualy* avoid parsnips and *similiar vegetables*," said Mr. Jef-
_____   ferson.

_____   10. I *recognize* the fact that a person of my *temperment* should
_____   *probably* avoid being around small children.

PROGRESS TEST 18
PLURALS AND CAPITALS (LESSON 28)

NAME _____ SCORE _____

Directions: Write the plural form or forms for each of the following words. When in doubt, consult your dictionary. If two forms are given, write both of them.

1. beef   _____   _____

2. child   _____   _____

3. curio   _____   _____

4. donkey   _____   _____

5. fox   _____   _____

6. graffito   _____   _____

7. handkerchief   _____   _____

8. hippopotamus   _____   _____

9. knife   _____   _____

10. mouse   _____   _____

11. oasis   _____   _____

12. opportunity   _____   _____

13. phenomenon   _____   _____

14. portico   _____   _____

15. process   _____   _____

16. roomful   _____   _____

17. species   _____   _____

18. stadium   _____   _____

19. syllabus   _____   _____

20. trout   _____   _____

21. valley   _____   _____

22. variety   _____   _____

23. waltz   _____   _____

24. witch   _____   _____

25. workman   _____   _____

Directions: The following sentences contain fifty numbered words. If a word is correctly capitalized, write C in the space with the corresponding number. If a word should not be capitalized, write W in the space.

1	2	3
4	5	6
7	8	9
10	11	12
13	14	15
16	17	18
19	20	21
22	23	24
25	26	27
28	29	30
31	32	33
34	35	36
37	38	39
40	41	42
43	44	45
46	47	48
49	50	

(1) My advisor, Professor Samuels, suggested that during my Sophomore year I take Accounting 194 and elective courses in Economics, English History, Sociology, and German.

(2) On their recent trip to the East, Mother and Aunt Lydia visited the Museum Of The City Of New York, which is on Fifth Avenue at 104th Street.

(3) Bob's Indian fishing guide gave him a photograph of Mount Baker, a snow-capped Mountain of the Cascade Range Northeast of Seattle.

(4) The day after the Fourth Of July holiday the Professor of my class in American Literature tested us on our reading of Poe's *Fall Of The House Of Usher.*

(5) Formerly a Captain in the United States Coast Guard, Linda's Father is now an assistant to Secretary Watkins of the Department Of The Interior.

PROGRESS TEST 19

GENERAL REVIEW: PROOFREADING

NAME _____ SCORE _____

Directions: If you find a misspelled word, underline it and write it correctly at the left. (Consider an omitted or misused apostrophe a punctuation error, not a spelling error.) In the column of figures at the left, circle numbers that identify errors in the sentence. Each sentence contains at least one of the following errors:

1. The group of words is a sentence modifier.
2. There is a dangling or misplaced modifier.
3. There is a misused verb (wrong number, tense, or principal part).
4. There is a poorly used pronoun (wrong number or case form, or inexact reference).
5. There is an error in punctuation.

_____
1 2 3 4 5
(1) A car that was backing out of the restaurant parking lot had a breifcase setting on its top but when I tried to signal them they just waved and drove off.

_____
1 2 3 4 5
(2) Last Sunday, while looking out the window of my new condominium, an ugly rat come out from some bushes and ran across the lawn.

_____
1 2 3 4 5
(3) "The simple construction of the five opening lines of the poem result in an especially pleasing rythm," Professor Quigley told his class of literature majors.

_____
1 2 3 4 5
(4) The boss's inability to make quick decisions, as well as her often faulty judgment, have certainly brought about most of our companys really serious problems.

_____
1 2 3 4 5
(5) The chair of the board, to use an obvious example, a person with admireable instincts and real dedication but little skill in management.

_____
1 2 3 4 5
(6) "The fact that advance ticket sales have been dissappointing don't mean that the concert will be postponed, does it," the worried young sophomore asked.

_____
1 2 3 4 5
(7) "The preformance of our defensive backs in the last three games have been less than outstanding," said our head coach who sometimes uses understatement to emphasize his points.

_____
1 2 3 4 5
(8) Trying to decide on our route, it was pointed out that the shorter one was quite hilly and winding, therefore the shorter one would very likely take more time than the longer one.

_____
1 2 3 4 5
(9) Theres not more than three or four people in this entire city goverment whom I'd say are capable of leadership in difficult times.

_____
1 2 3 4 5
(10) The three older women always arrived at the class earlier than the other students, they also managed to quickly, carefully, and throughly complete every assignment.

_____
1 2 3 4 5
(11) Assembling in the superintendent's office at ten o'clock, Mr. Swift asked we seven freshmen if we wanted to form an honors class?

371

_____ (12) My neighbor's oldest son, for example, who confidently se-
1 2 3 4 5   lected a course in engineering, in spite of the fact that his
                  knowledge of mathmatics and physics were slight.

_____ (13) Apparently the mischievous youngsters choice of compan-
1 2 3 4 5   ions have given him many oppertunities to get into real trou-
                  ble.

_____ (14) Although both Thelma and Mary Lou were named in the
1 2 3 4 5   grandmother's will neither one of them have as yet received
                  their share of the inheritance.

_____ (15) How can you maintain that this dictionery is yours when
1 2 3 4 5   someone else's name and address is stamped on its inside
                  cover.

_____ (16) Their delay in making shipments, in addition to their higher
1 2 3 4 5   prices, have lost business for them, they're no longer serious
                  compitition for us.

_____ (17) "Just between you and I," said Eddie, "there's to many peo-
1 2 3 4 5   ple in this elevator; let's wait for the next one."

_____ (18) The amateur entrepreneur explained to my partner and I that
1 2 3 4 5   the influx of orders from small investors have undoubtedly
                  effected the market unfavorably.

_____ (19) Bruce's face turned flaming red upon hearing that his grade
1 2 3 4 5   on the literature midterm test was higher then anyone elses.

_____ (20) I'm quiet sure that I won't get the job, I was told that to be
1 2 3 4 5   hired a person either had to be a union member or have their
                  apprentice card.

_____ (21) The article concluded with the following sentence; "Part of
1 2 3 4 5   the credit should go to whomever supplies the restaurant with
                  its incredibly fresh vegetables."

_____ (22) People in our neighborhood are extremely dissatisfied with
1 2 3 4 5   the maintainence work of the Highway Department, there's
                  still several deep chuckholes in our street.

_____ (23) We were unhappily supprised to hear the mayor say, "Neither
1 2 3 4 5   of these projects, although desperately needed, have been
                  funded, our repair fund only has four thousand dollars left in
                  it."

_____ (24) There having been, if I remember correctly, two or three pro-
1 2 3 4 5   ductions of our drama association that many in the audience
                  nearly thought were of professional quality.

_____ (25) After crossing the boundary into the next country, bad dri-
1 2 3 4 5   ving conditions can be expected for approximately fourty
                  miles; the government having neglected the roads and
                  bridges outrageously.

PROGRESS TEST 20

GENERAL REVIEW: PROOFREADING

NAME _____ SCORE _____

Directions: If you find a misspelled word, underline it and write it correctly at the left. (Consider an omitted or misused apostrophe a punctuation error, not a spelling error.) Circle at least one of the numbers at the left:
   1. The sentence is correct.
   2. There is a dangling or misplaced modifier.
   3. There is a misused verb.
   4. There is a misused pronoun.
   5. There is an error in punctuation.

_____
1   2   3   4   5

(1) While walking down the slippery wooden steps to the beach, a most embarassing thing happened to my escort and I.

_____
1   2   3   4   5

(2) In the margin of my theme Professor Jenkins had written this note: "You can now see, can't you, that the omission of two commas from this sentence have produced a humerous effect."

_____
1   2   3   4   5

(3) The eminent critic nearly spent forty-five minutes giving us an extraordinary explaination of one of the short poems we had read.

_____
1   2   3   4   5

(4) Clancy, a chunky, pleasant sophomore whom I had known in high school, stopped me and said, "Tell me, friend, what you thought about that last test we took in mathematics."

_____
1   2   3   4   5

(5) "The usual procedure," explained the receptionist, "is that Ms. Stanton's secretary or one of her assistants are on duty until five oclock on Wednesdays."

_____
1   2   3   4   5

(6) I could hardly believe what I had just heard, the superintendent had never before ever spoke so harshly to any of we students.

_____
1   2   3   4   5

(7) The frightened little boy told Mother and me that he had become separated from his parents, had wandered away from the other picnickers, and had been chased by a fierce dog.

_____
1   2   3   4   5

(8) Beyond the village of Greenville the motorist must procede cautiously, I have been told that they are resurfacing the highway for approximately ninety miles.

_____
1   2   3   4   5

(9) If anyone tells me that any child can learn to, with patient teaching, play a musical instrument, I'll give them a real arguement.

_____
1   2   3   4   5

(10) On the last night of Homecoming Week there is usualy a banquet at which the college president or the football coach give the alumni an inspirational speech.

_____
1   2   3   4   5

(11) Apparently every boy in our dormitory except you and I has already had a conference with their academic adviser.

373

_____ (12) "The *Santa Maria* wasn't Columbus's favorite ship," ex-
1 2 3 4 5   plained Dr. Slade. "After its destruction he is quoted as say-
                     ing that it was 'too weighty and not suitable for making
                     discoveries.' "

_____ (13) "There's probably only three or four boys on this team whom
1 2 3 4 5   I think stand a chance of receiving college atheletic scholar-
                     ships," said Coach Wills who is normally quite optimistic.

_____ (14) "I'm absolutely sure that the suspected troublemakers about
1 2 3 4 5   whom the principal of the school has been talking are not you
                     and I," Jacklin confidently told his pal Barnhart.

_____ (15) After reading the pamphlet you brought me from the library,
1 2 3 4 5   my understanding of the history, purpose and accompolish-
                     ments of the United Nations have been broadened.

_____ (16) Unfortunately, many intelligent and conscientious high
1 2 3 4 5   school graduates lack enough funds to go directly to college,
                     which is an outrageous situation.

_____ (17) The person whom I was referred to told me that I would have
1 2 3 4 5   to only wait a few more days before learning whether I or one
                     of the other contestants have won the first prize.

_____ (18) Having paid my fine at the local sheriff's office, our next des-
1 2 3 4 5   tination was Centerville where I understand they also have
                     extreamly strict laws relating to speeding.

_____ (19) The personnel director replied, "Our company plans to within
1 2 3 4 5   a month or so hire a new financial adviser whom we all hope
                     will solve these troublesome problems for us."

_____ (20) "Dont it seem unusual that every one of us five trainees re-
1 2 3 4 5   ceived the same letter of recommendation from the boss?"
                     asked Stan.

_____ (21) The police sergeant approached my roommate and me,
1 2 3 4 5   opened his notebook, and asked, "Has either one of you ever
                     before seen the hammer that was found lying near the front
                     door?"

_____ (22) Miss Perkins was a truely dedicated teacher, she seemed al-
1 2 3 4 5   ways ready to graciously and uncomplainingly give her time
                     to whomever came to her for help.

_____ (23) The members of the planning committee have studied these
1 2 3 4 5   problems and have become convinced that neither of the two
                     suggested remedies has been satisfactorily researched.

_____ (24) This applicant has only been studying Russian for three se-
1 2 3 4 5   mesters, his knowledge of the grammar, literature, and pro-
                     nounciation are quite limited.

_____ (25) The fact that your niece's careless handling of money could
1 2 3 4 5   result in her loosing the property to the mortgage holder
                     don't seem to trouble either she or her husband.

Study Skills: Basic Tools for College Work

The ability to write well is a great advantage to a college student. But there are other skills that you should master early in your college career. Using the dictionary, outlining, paraphrasing, and summarizing written material will be necessary almost from the first day of class. Managing your time is extremely important for success in college. The following sections will serve as an introduction to these very important skills.

Use of the Dictionary

You will soon find that a desk dictionary is as necessary to your writing as pen and paper. A good one is worth every cent of its cost; don't economize on a paperback pocket version and expect it to serve you adequately. Your instructor will probably recommend any of the following:

The American Heritage Dictionary, Third Edition
The Random House Webster's College Dictionary
Webster's Tenth New Collegiate Dictionary
Webster's New World Dictionary of the American Language, Third College Edition

Make your dictionary earn its price. Use it. Keep it near you when you study or write. It's a trove of information and will tell you much more than the mere meanings of words. Before you begin to use your dictionary, look inside the covers to see what is printed on the endpapers. It may be something you'll want to refer to often. Browse through the first few pages—especially those that explain the dictionary's system of pronunciation symbols, indication of preferred spellings and pronunciations, treatment of alphabetical order, usage notes, arrangement of multiple meanings, and notation for parts of speech. Then turn to the back pages. Does the dictionary have separate listings for geographic and biographical names? Does it give tables of weights and measures, rules for punctuation and mechanics? If you know what extra content your dictionary holds, you may be able to save yourself time, bother, and even cold cash when the need arises for some odd little fact.

1. Spelling. The dictionary will, of course, give the correct spelling of a word— sometimes two correct spellings, of which the first entry is usually the more widely used spelling.

---

high profile to H.I.M.

hi·jack or **high·jack** (hī´ jak´), *v.,* **-jacked, -jack·ing,** *n.* —*v.t.* **1.** to seize (an airplane or other vehicle) by threat or by force, esp. for ransom or political objectives. **2.** to steal (cargo) from a truck or other vehicle after forcing it to stop: *to hijack a load of whiskey.* **3.** to rob (a vehicle) after forcing it to stop: *They hijacked the truck outside the city.* —*n.* **4.** an act or instance of hijacking. [1920-25, *Amer.;* of uncert. orig.]
hi·jack·er or **high·jack·er** (hī´ jak´ ər), *n.* a person who hijacks. [1920-25, *Amer.*]

The *Random House Webster's College Dictionary* by Random House, Inc. Copyright © 1991 by Random House, Inc. Reprinted by permission of Random House, Inc.

The dictionary will also give you information on how compounds or near-compounds should be written. Of the ten entries in the following excerpt, three are written solid, two may be solid or hyphenated, two are hyphenated, and three appear as two separate words.

> **fly ball** *n. Baseball.* A ball that is batted in a high arc, usually to the outfield.
> **fly·blow** (flī´ blō´) *n.* The egg or larva of a blowfly, usually deposited on meat. **—flyblow** *tr.v.* **-blew** (-blōō´), **-blown** (-blōn´), **-blow·ing, -blows. 1.** To deposit flyblows on. **2.** To contaminate; taint.
> **fly·blown** (flī´ blōn´) *adj.* **1.** Contaminated with flyblows. **2.a.** Tainted; corrupt: *a flyblown reputation.* **b.** Dirty or rundown; squalid: *a flyblown bar on the edge of town.*
> **fly·boat** (flī´ bōt´) *n. Nautical.* Any of various small, swift boats. [Alteration and partial translation of Dutch *vlieboot: Vlie,* a channel off the island of Vlieland in the northern Netherlands + *boot,* boat.]
> **fly book** *n.* A case, usually in the form of a book, in which artificial flies for fishing are carried.
> **fly·boy** or **fli-boy** (flī´ boi´) *n. Slang.* A member of an air force, especially a pilot.
> **fly bridge** *n. Nautical.* See **flying bridge.**
> **fly·by** also **fly-by** (flī´ bī´) *n., pl.* **-bys.** A flight passing close to a specified target or position, especially a maneuver in which a spacecraft or satellite passes sufficiently close to a body to make detailed observations without orbiting or landing.
> **fly-by-night** (flī´ bī-nīt´) *Informal adj.* **1.** Unreliable or unscrupulous, especially with regard to business dealings: *"fly-by-night telephone companies that open up shop, sell some systems, then disappear when service is needed"* (Mary Ellen Jordan). **2.** Of an impermanent or insubstantial nature: *fly-by-night fashions in clothing.* **—fly-by-night** also **fly-by-night·er** (-nī´ tər) *n.* **1.** An unscrupulous or undependable person, especially one who leaves secretly without paying creditors. **2.** Something of a shaky or impermanent nature.
> **fly-cast** (flī´ kăst´) *intr.v.* **-cast, -casting, -casts.** To cast artificial flies with a fly rod, as in fishing. **—fly´ -cast´ er** *n.*

Can you look up the spelling of a word in the dictionary if you can't spell the word to begin with? Yes, almost always. Words like *phobia, pneumatic, rhyme, xylophone,* and a few others in which the first or second letter is the doubtful point may give trouble, but one or two searches under likely combinations will usually turn up the answer.

2. Pronunciation. Before you can use your dictionary effectively, you must understand its pronunciation symbols. In the following entry, the material within parentheses gives other information besides a representation of the sounds of the letters. (1) There is an alternate pronunciation of the second syllable. (2) The primary stress is on the third syllable and the secondary (or lesser) stress is on the first syllable. (3) Although the boldface entry shows that the word has five syllables, the pronunciation transcription shows two hyphens, indicating the two permissible points where the word may be broken at the end of a line.

> **in·di·gest·i·ble** (ĭn´ dĭ-jĕs´ tə-bəl, -dī-) *adj.* Difficult or impossible to digest: *an indigestible meal.* **—in´ di·gest´ i·bil´ i·ty** *n.* **— in´ di·gest´ i·bly** *adv.*

The presence of more than one pronunciation means that different people in different parts of the country pronounce the word differently. It does not mean that one is right and the other wrong.

Look up the pronunciations of the following:

1. acclimate	4. decadent	7. exquisite	10. pianist
2. adult	5. desperado	8. neither	11. processes
3. Caribbean	6. drama	9. pejorative	12. sonorous

3. Plurals. If you are not sure about the correct plural of a noun, your dictionary will settle the question.

> **cur·ric|u·lum** (kə rik´ yoo ləm, -yə-) **n.**, *pl.* **-lu·la** (-lə) or **-lu·lums** [L, lit., a running, course, race, career < *currere*, to run: see CURRENT] **1** a fixed series of studies required, as in a college, for graduation, qualification in a major field of study, etc. **2** all of the courses, collectively, offered in a school, college, etc., or in a particular subject—**cur·ric´ |u·lar** *adj.*
> **curriculum vi·tae** (vīt´ ē) *pl.* **cur·ric´ |u·la vi´ tae** [L, course of life] a summary of one's personal history and professional qualifications, as that submitted by a job applicant; réesumé

Webster's New World Dictionary of the American Language, Third College Edition, Copyright © 1988 by Simon and Schuster, Inc. Reprinted by permission.

Look up the correct plurals of the following:

1. adieu	4. bus	7. genus	10. radius
2. appendix	5. crocus	8. mother-in-law	11. solo
3. beau	6. cupful	9. ox	12. species

4. Capitalization. Problems of capitalization may also be referred to your dictionary. You know, of course, that proper nouns—that is, names of persons and places—are capitalized. You know that common nouns are not capitalized. But often the real question is whether a noun is used in its proper sense or its common sense. With the help of your dictionary, try to determine whether the italicized words in the following sentences should be capitalized:

1. She ordered *french fries* with her steak.
2. This should be set up in *roman* type.
3. Many students do not understand *roman* numerals.
4. Later in life he was attracted to the *christian* religion.
5. He brought back some very fine *china* from *china*.

5. Principal parts of verbs. If you are not sure whether to say, "His coat was laying on the bed" or "His coat was lying on the bed," whether to say, "My sister growed," or "My sister grew," the dictionary will help you.

> **grow** \´ grō)\ *vb* **grew** \grü\; **grown** \´ grōn\; **grow·ing** [ME *growen,* fr. OE *grōwan;* akin to OHG *gruowan* to grow] *vi* (bef. 12c) **1 a :** to spring up and develop to maturity **b :** to be able to grow in some place or situation <trees that ~ only in the tropics> **c :** to assume some relation through or as if through a process of natural growth <ferns ~*ing* from the rocks> **2 a :** to increase in size by addition of material either by assimilation into the living organism or by accretion in a nonbiological process (as crystallization) **b :** INCREASE, EXPAND <~*s* in wisdom> **3 :** to develop from a parent source <the book *grew* out of a series of lectures> **4 a :** to pass into a condition : BECOME <*grew* pale> **b :** to have an increasing influence <habit ~*s* on a person> **c :** to become increasingly acceptable or attractive <didn't like it at first, but it *grew* on him> ~ *vt* **1 :** to cause to grow : PRODUCE <~ wheat> **2 :** DEVELOP **5** — **grow·er** \´ grō(-ə)r\ *n* — **grow·ing·ly** \´ grō-in-lē\ *adv*

Webster's Ninth New Collegiate Dictionary © 1991 by Merriam-Webster Inc., publisher of the Merriam-Webster ® dictionaries. Reprinted by permission.

Because *grow* is an irregular verb and does not form the past by adding *ed,* clearly, "My sister *grew*" is the correct choice. Note that *grow* is identified as both *vi* and *vt,* that is, as an intransitive verb and a transitive one. An intransitive verb does not act on an object; a transitive verb does. Now look up *lay* and *lie* in the dictionary. Why is "His coat was *lying* on the bed" the better sentence?

You should know the principal parts of the following troublesome verbs:

1. bring	5. do	9. hang
2. burst	6. drag	10. see
3. buy	7. drown	11. shine
4. dive	8. eat	12. take

6. Meaning. Many words, some of them very ordinary words, have a variety of meanings. The dictionary lists and separates all the definitions and gives their applications.

lead¹ (lēd), *v.*, **led, lead·ing,** *n., adj.* —*v.t.* **1.** to go before or with to show the way; conduct or escort; guide: *to lead a group on a hike.* **2.** to conduct by holding and guiding: *to lead a horse by a rope.* **3.** to influence or induce; cause: *What led her to change her mind?* **4.** to guide in direction, course, action, opinion, etc.; bring: *You can lead him around to your point of view.* **5.** to go through or pass (time, life, etc.): *to lead a full life.* **6.** to conduct or bring (water, wire, etc.) in a particular course. **7.** (of a road, passage, etc.) to serve to bring (a person) to a place: *The next street will lead you to the post office.* **8.** to take or bring: *The visitors were led into the senator's office.* **9.** to be in control or command of; direct: *He led the British forces during the war.* **10.** to go at the head of or in advance of (a procession, list, body, etc.); proceed first in: *The mayor will lead the parade.* **11.** to be superior to; have the advantage over: *The first baseman leads his teammates in runs batted in.* **12.** to have top position or first place in: *Iowa leads the nation in corn production.* **13.** to have the directing or principal part in: *Who is going to lead the discussion?* **14.** to act as leader of (an orchestra, band, etc.); conduct. **15.** to begin a hand in a card game with (a card or suit specified). **16.** to aim and fire a weapon ahead of (a moving target) in order to allow for the travel of the target while the missile is reaching it.
—*v.i.* **17.** to act as a guide; show the way. **18.** to afford passage to a place: *That path leads directly to the house.* **19.** to go first; be in advance. **20.** to result in; tend toward (usu. fol. by *to*): *The incident led to her resignation.* **21.** to take the directing or principal part. **22.** to take the offensive. **23.** to make the first play in a card game. **24.** to be led or submit to being led, as a horse. **25.** (of a runner in baseball) to leave a base before the delivery of a pitch (often fol. by *away*). **26. lead off, a.** to being; start. **b.** *Baseball.* to be the first player in the batting order or the first batter in an inning. **27. lead on,** to mislead.
—*n.* **28.** the first or foremost place; position in advance of others: *to take the lead in the race.* **29.** the extent of such an advance position. **30.** a person or thing that leads. **31.** a leash. **32.** a suggestion or piece of information that helps to direct or guide; tip; clue. **33.** a guide or indication of a road, course, method, etc., to follow. **34.** precedence; example; leadership. **35. a.** the principal part in a play. **b.** the person who plays it. **36. a.** the act or right of playing first in a card game. **b.** the card, suit, etc., so played. **37.** the opening paragraph of a newspaper story, serving as a summary. **38.** an often flexible and insulated single conductor, as a wire, used in electrical connections. **39.** the act of taking the offensive. **40.** *Naut.* **a.** the direction of a rope, wire, or chain. **b.** Also called **leader.** any of various devices for guiding a running rope. **41.** an open channel through a field of ice. **42.** the act of aiming a weapon ahead of a moving target. **43.** the distance ahead of a moving target that a weapon must be aimed in order to hit it. **44.** the first of a series of boxing punches.
—*adj.* **45.** most important; principal; leading; first: *a lead editorial.* **46.** (of a runner in baseball) nearest to scoring.
-*Idiom* **47. lead someone on a (merry) chase** or **dance,** to entice someone into difficulty and confusion by behaving unpredictably. **48. lead up to, a.** to prepare the way for. **b.** to approach (something gradually. [bef. 900; ME *leden,* OE *lǣdan* (causative of *lithan* to go, travel), c. OS *lē djan,* OHG *leiten,* ON *leitha;* akin to LODE]

Random House Webster's College Dictionary by Random House, Inc. Copyright © 1991 by Random House, Inc. Reprinted by permission of Random House, Inc.

7. Appropriate use. A certain word, either in all of its uses or in some of its special meanings, is effective if it is appropriate to the occasion, the purpose, the time, and the place of its use. By means of usage labels, such as *Slang, Colloq., Dial., Archaic, Obs., Illit.,* a dictionary tries to indicate that a certain word has a restricted appropriateness. (Note that dictionaries may vary in their application of these labels.)

Examine this selection from *Webster's New World Dictionary,* in which four uses are labeled *Colloq.* (see page 227), four *Slang,* and one *Archaic.* Some dictionaries use *Substandard* for *Slang* and *Informal* for *Colloq.* Words without any usage label are usually appropriate at all times, on every occasion, in every situation.

goodly¹ (good´ ē) *n., pl.* **good´ ies** [Colloq.] **1** something considered very good to eat, as a piece of candy *2 GOODY-GOODY —*adj.* [Colloq.] GOODY-GOODY —*interj.* a child's exclamation of approval or delight
goodly² (good´ ē) *n., pl.* **good´ ies** [<GOODWIFE] [Archaic] a woman, esp. an old woman or housewife, of lowly social status: used as a title with the surname
Good·year (good´ yir'), **Charles** 1800-60; U.S. inventor: originated the process for vulcanizing rubber
goodly-goodly (good´ ē good´ ē) *adj.* [redupl. of GOODY¹] [Colloq.] moral or pious in an affected or canting way—*n.* [Colloq.] a goody-goody person Also **goodly-two-shoes** (-too ´ shooz´)
***gooley** (goo´ ē) *adj.* **goo´ li·er, goo´ li·est** [GOO + -EY] [Slang] **1** sticky, as glue **2** sticky and sweet **3** overly sentimental
goof (goof) *n. prob. < dial.* [goff < Fr goffe, stupid < It goffo] **1** a stupid, silly, or credulous person **2** a mistake; blunder —*vi.* [Slang] **1** to make a mistake; blunder, fail, etc. **2** to waste time, shirk one's duties, etc.: (usually with *off* or *around*)
***goof·ball** (-bôl´) *n.* [prec. + BALL¹] [Slang] a pill containing a barbiturate, or sometimes a stimulant drug, tranquilizer, etc., esp. when used nonmedicinally Also **goof ball**
goof-off (-ôf´) *n.* a person who wastes time or avoids work; shirker
goofly (goof´ ē) *adj.* **goof´ li·er, goof´ li·est** [Slang] like or characteristic of a goof; stupid and silly —**goof´ li·ly** *adv.* —**goof´ li·ness** *n.*

Webster's New World Dictionary of the American Language, Third College Edition. Copyright © 1988 by Simon and Schuster, Inc. Reprinted by permission.

Where the labels *Slang, Colloq.,* and so on are inapplicable, a dictionary may give, at the end of the entry, a short paragraph or two of usage information. (For this purpose *American Heritage* makes use of a panel of consultants.)

dec·i·mate (dĕs´ ə-māt´) *tr.v.* **-mat·ed, -mat·ing, -mates. 1.** To destroy or kill a large part of (a group). **2.** *Usage Problem.* **a.** To inflict great destruction or damage on: *The fawns decimated my sister's rose bushes.* **b.** To reduce markedly in amount: *a profligate heir who decimated his trust fund.* **3.** To select by lot and kill one in every ten of. [Latin *decima¯re, decima¯t-,* to punish every tenth person, from *decimus,* tenth, from *decem,* ten. See **dekm** in Appendix.] —**dec´ i·ma´ tion** *n.*
USAGE NOTE: *Decimate* originally referred to the killing of every tenth person, a punishment used in the Roman army for mutinous legions. Today this meaning is commonly extended to include the killing of any large proportion of a group. Sixty-six percent of the Usage Panel accepts this extension in the sentence *The Jewish population of Germany was decimated by the war,* even though it is common knowledge that the number of Jews killed was much greater than a tenth of the original population. However, when the meaning is further extended to include large-scale destruction other than killing, as in *The supply of fresh produce was decimated by the accident at Chernobyl,* the usage is accepted by only 26 percent of the Panel.
WORD HISTORY: *Decimate* comes from the Latin word *decimāre,* which meant "to punish every tenth man chosen by lot, as in a mutinous military unit," *decimāre* being derived from *decimus,* "tenth." Our word *decimate* is first recorded in this sense in 1600 in *A Treatise of Ireland,* written by John Dymmok: "All . . . were by a martiall courte condemned to dye, which sentence was yet mitigated by the Lord Lieutenants mercy by which they were onely decimated by lott." *Decimate* then passed beyond the military context and came to be used rhetorically or loosely with reference to more than a tenth. Charlotte Brontë, for example, stated in a letter of 1848 that "Typhus fever decimated the school periodically," although typhus fever certainly did not always kill exactly a tenth of the school's population.

Copyright © 1992 by Houghton Mifflin Company. Reproduced by permission from the *American Heritage Dictionary of the English Language,* Third Edition.

en·thuse \in-´ th(y)üz\ *vb* **en·thused; en·thus·ing** [back-formation fr. *enthusiasm*] *vt* (1827) **1 :** to make enthusiastic **2 :** to express with enthusiasm ~ *vi* : to show enthusiasm <a splendid performance, and I was *enthusing* over it Julian Huxley>
usage *Enthuse* is apparently American in origin, although the earliest known example of its use occurs in a letter written in 1827 by a young Scotsman who spent about two years in the Pacific Northwest. It has been disapproved since about 1870. Current evidence shows it to be flourishing nonetheless on both sides of the Atlantic esp. in journalistic prose.

Webster's Ninth New Collegiate Dictionary, © 1991 by Merriam-Webster Inc., publisher of the Merriam-Webster ® dictionaries. Reprinted by permission.

8. Synonyms and antonyms. Although it is impossible for a dictionary to give differentiated synonyms for every word it contains, most dictionaries do group relatively common words that have similar definitions to demonstrate particular qualities and various shades of meaning. Some also give words of opposite meanings (antonyms) as an aid to distinctions in meaning.

> **mon·strous** \ˊmän(t)-strəs\ *adj* (15c) **1** *obs* : STRANGE, UNNATURAL **2** : having extraordinary often overwhelming size ; GIGANTIC **3 a** : having the qualities or appearance of a monster **b** *obs* : teeming with monsters **4 a** : extraordinarily ugly or vicious : HORRIBLE **b** : shockingly wrong or ridiculous **5** : deviating greatly from the natural form or character : ABNORMAL **6** : very great—used as an intensive—**mon·strous·ly** *adv*—**mon·strous·ness** *n*
> **syn** MONSTROUS, PRODIGIOUS, TREMENDOUS, STUPENDOUS mean extremely impressive, MONSTROUS implies a departure from the normal (as in size, form, or character) and often carries suggestions of deformity, ugliness, or fabulousness <the imagination turbid with *monstrous* fancies and misshapen dreams —Oscar Wilde> PRODIGIOUS suggests a marvelousness exceeding belief, usu. in something felt as going far beyond a previous maximum (as of goodness, greatness, intensity, or size) <made a *prodigious* effort and rolled the stone aside> <men have always reverenced *prodigious* inborn gifts —C. W. Eliot> TREMENDOUS may imply a power to terrify or inspire awe <the spell and *tremendous* incantation of the thought of death —L. P. Smith> but in more general and weakened use it means only very large or great or intense <success gave him *tremendous* satisfaction> STUPENDOUS implies a power to stun or astound, usu. because of size, numbers, complexity, or greatness beyond description <all are but parts of one *stupendous* whole, whose body Nature is, and God the soul —Alexander Pope>

Webster's Ninth New Collegiate Dictionary, © 1991 by Merriam-Webster Inc., publisher of the Merriam-Webster ® dictionaries. Reprinted by permission.

Note in the example that each synonym is illustrated by a quotation. Not all dictionaries provide this particularly helpful feature.

You can use synonyms in two ways to improve your writing. The first use simply prevents repetition. The same word used again and again may look more important to the message than it really is; it may also make the message dull. The second use of synonyms, possibly the crucial one, is the matter of precision, of discovering just the right word for the sense. By the "right" word we mean no more than a word apt or suitable in its context. There are bookish or literary words that may be suitable in some formal contexts, in serious books. There are simple and homely words that are right in more informal writing. The distinctions between them are learned slowly, it is true, and all we can do here is give a few examples:

Bookish Words	*Simple Words*
impecunious	poor
opulent	rich, wealthy
discoursed	talked, spoke
dolorous	sad, painful, mournful
emolument	pay, wages, salary, fee
sustenance	support, food

9. Denotation and connotation. A dictionary definition will establish the meaning of a word, but that definition does not necessarily include all the information about meaning that you need to use the word. The first definition in a dictionary for the adjective *fat* could be something like "having an unusual amount of fat" or "made up of too much adipose [fatty] tissue." Definitions such as these, stated in cold, factual, almost clinical analysis, are the *denotative* meanings of the word.

Most dictionaries will also give for such a commonly used word as *fat* a list of synonyms—*American Heritage* (page 664) gives these: *fat, obese, corpulent, fleshy, portly, stout, pudgy, rotund, plump, chubby.* These words share the same denotative meaning: a fat person, a stout person, and a plump person are all overweight. But words in lists of synonyms are not always interchangeable. They have different emotional weights, different associations with the pleasant and the unpleasant; they express different degrees of positive and negative attitude or appeal. This emotional implication of a word is its *connotation.*

A stout man is an overweight man who gives an impression of solidity, strength, good health, and vigor; *stout* thus has a positive connotation. A plump man is also fat, but in a sense of the ridiculous, as though it were more a question of his being too short for his girth than of his being too broad for his height. *Plump* applied to a woman, on the other hand, is usually a term of approval, implying to many readers that the well-rounded woman thus described is also jovial.

Plump describing a cooked turkey awaiting carving at a holiday feast is effective and appropriate. But, because they normally connote qualities of people, *portly* and *stout* would be wrong if used to describe a cooked turkey. A child could well have *chubby* cheeks and *pudgy* fingers, but *corpulent* cheeks and *obese* fingers verge on the ridiculous. Although careful study of synonyms, their definitions, and illustrative sentences will help you find the word that gives the exact meaning you intend, such study may also help you avoid a completely inappropriate choice.

Study the following words, referring to a dictionary as necessary. Which words are usually positive or neutral by connotation? Which negative? Which words have similar denotative meanings?

1. articulate	6. demure	11. liberal	16. proud
2. blunt	7. eloquent	12. officious	17. prudish
3. candid	8. fussy	13. particular	18. reject
4. credulous	9. garrulous	14. profligate	19. trusting
5. decline (refuse)	10. haughty	15. prolix	20. zealous

10. Derivations of words. Your dictionary will tell you the derivation or source of any word. Although there is some danger in assuming that the original meaning of a word is still its exact meaning (meanings change, you know, through long use), quite often a knowledge of the source and the original meaning of a word can illuminate it for you and give it a vividness of meaning that you will never forget. Did you know that *salary* comes from the Latin *salarium,* which meant the money given to Roman soldiers to buy salt with? Or that *tribulation* comes from a Latin word meaning a threshing sledge? Hence a man afflicted with tribulation is like a man beaten with the swinging clubs used to pound out grain on a threshing floor. Or consider *recalcitrant.* A recalcitrant child is an obstinate child. But if you look up the original meaning of the word, you find that the child is really "kicking back," like a mule.

The following words have interesting histories. Look them up in your dictionary.

1. bowery	4. carouse	7. hussy	10. panic	13. scuba
2. boycott	5. chortle	8. jeep	11. quixotic	14. tawdry
3. carnival	6. curfew	9. laser	12. sabotage	15. terrier

11. Persons and places. The most convenient source of information about persons and places is your dictionary. It is true that the information you get there is condensed, but in most cases it is enough to set you on the right track. As a means of finding out where proper names are listed, you might look up some of the names in the following list. Remember that some dictionaries have a special section for geographic names and another for names of persons, whereas others list everything in the regular vocabulary.

    1. Boucicault   3. Cassandra   5. Galen   7. Mount Kosciusko
    2. Casanova   4. Corday   6. Ganges   8. Poseidon

12. Miscellaneous information. Finally, the dictionary contains in easily accessible form a large amount of miscellaneous information about science, geography, biography, history, mythology, and so forth. Test this statement by looking up the following:

1. What sort of person would shed crocodile tears?
2. What were the former names of Zimbabwe, Iran, Sri Lanka, and Namibia?
3. What is a Hobson's choice, and how did the expression originate?
4. What is Mrs. Malaprop noted for?
5. Give an example of a spoonerism.
6. Why did the editor object to the reporter's writing about "the Thursday afternoon soiree at the home of . . ."?
7. How do you pronounce *provost* (1) when it refers to a college official, and (2) when it refers to a military officer?
8. Why is *cheeseburger* a totally illogical name?
9. Translate into American English the following: "My last ten bob went for a few litres of petrol for my lorry."
10. What is the most notable characteristic of a Manx cat?
11. Explain this bracketed insertion: One taxpayer wrote that "the schools don't teach enough grammer [*sic*] and spelling."
12. Look up the four italicized words and explain the meaning of this sentence: The word *radar* is probably *unique* in that it is both an *acronym* and a *palindrome*.

Paraphrasing

You will also find it useful to be able to paraphrase short passages that are particularly important or particularly difficult to read. A paraphrase is a rewriting of the original version in your own words—almost a translation. It simplifies, but does not necessarily shorten, the passage. Read the following technical passage on the description and purpose of an automobile turbocharger:

> Basically turbocharging is a system for increasing engine horsepower by using the exhaust gases to drive a turbine connected by a shaft to a compressor which pumps the fuel/air mixture into the engine. With an increase in engine speed, this compressor forces a greater volume of mixture into the combustion chambers, producing more power. During the cruising or light-load conditions, the turbocharger is essentially quiescent and the volume of mixture ingested is about the same as with any normally aspirated engine. The primary benefit of turbocharging, then, is that a fuel efficient small-displacement engine can have increased performance with little or no sacrifice in fuel economy. (*Road and Track,* February 1978, p. 88)

Two words require immediate definition before any other efforts at simplification can begin:

1. *turbine:* a machine that has a rotor (a system of rotating airfoils) driven by the pressure of moving water, gases, or air. [Sometimes even dictionaries are no help.

Picture a set of blades mounted around a shaft, much as the paddles of a water wheel are arranged. These blades—the rotor—are mounted inside a chamber, and water, gas, or even air moving at high speed flows through the chamber and turns the rotor by pressing on the blades.]

2. *compressor:* a pump or other machine for reducing the volume and increasing the pressure of gases. [Again the dictionary is not a great help. This part of the turbocharger pushes more gas–air mixture into the combustion chamber than would enter under ordinary pressure.]

NOTE: These two definitions offer a classic example of the problems facing a beginner in any field: The dictionary definitions are given in words too technical for a beginner to grasp, forcing the beginner to seek further definitions in the dictionary or to find a person both willing and able to explain the term in simple words. Asking for help from a teacher or a knowledgeable student is the easiest way out of the difficulty.

With these definitions in hand, try the passage in its existing order, making it simpler by substituting simpler words wherever possible.

A turbocharger is a device mounted on an automobile engine to increase the power of the engine. It uses exhaust gases to turn a wheel mounted on a shaft (turbine), which then turns another wheel or pump and forces the fuel–air mixture into the cylinders under pressure. Thus more fuel enters than ordinary pressure would bring in; more fuel mixture produces greater power. At low engine speed the device doesn't turn very fast, and the cylinders receive about as much mixture as they would through an ordinary carburetor. At high speed the compressor greatly increases the efficiency with which the engine uses the fuel–air mixture. The result is that a small engine can produce good performance without sacrificing fuel economy.

Sometimes it is equally useful to shorten a passage and make the basic idea easier to remember. A summary of that same paragraph on the turbocharger might read:

A turbocharger is a compressor driven by a rotor turned by exhaust gases. The compressor forces fuel–air mixture into the cylinders under greater than normal pressure, providing more fuel–air mixture for each detonation; thus the power of a small engine can be increased without a loss of economy.

This new version cuts the number of words in the passage by half and simplifies the wording somewhat. The shorter version ought to prove more manageable during study or review.

Outlining and Taking Notes

As you study, you will need to outline some of the materials you read in order to get an overall view of their scope and direction. Reading, outlining, and taking notes from a chapter of a textbook are not exceptionally difficult, but they constitute a very important skill.

Begin by reading the chapter through once rather quickly, trying to catch the general subject and the direction that the author is taking. Then read the chapter a second time, paying close attention to detail. In this second reading you should look up any words that are unclear to you. Paraphrase short passages that are especially difficult for you to read. This is the time to get complete control of the chapter.

On the third reading, locate the major divisions of the chapter. Note the headings, usually printed in contrasting type; they often indicate major divisions in a chapter. If you do not find headings within the chapter, search the introductory paragraphs for clues or statements that will help you to pick out the major divisions. Quite often the introduction contains some statement of the thesis of the chapter or provides enough direction so that you can find the major divisions.

If the chapter has no headings and the introduction does not offer enough direction to enable you to find the major divisions, work through the chapter paragraph by paragraph, writing a one-sentence summary for each paragraph. Read these sentences and try to group them into topics. If you are able to divide these topics into groups, summarize the ideas in each group and use those summaries as the headings in your chapter outline.

In addition to outlining the chapter, you should take other notes that will give you a complete picture of its content. Write down all the important dates. List the names of people, ideas, and events that figure in the chapter; later on, write out a brief identification of each item in the list. Take from the chapter illustrations and examples that might help to develop an answer on a test or a portion of a paper. Record quotations that seem to state an idea or a concept with exceptional clarity. With an outline and a thorough collection of notes such as these suggested, you should be able to master the material in a chapter without much difficulty.

Planning Your Time and Your Work

Some students do a bare minimum of work during the term and then cram massive amounts of studying into the last few days. Because such cramming requires that you ingest large and potentially harmful doses of coffee, amphetamines, and other stimulants, and because material learned quickly is forgotten quickly, a system of regular, manageable doses of work has much to recommend it.

Such a system of regular work is a necessity for success in college. The time spent in class in a college course is significantly shorter than the class time of a high-school course. New students sometimes fool themselves into believing that this shorter class time means that college is less work than high school. Nothing could be more likely to lead to failure. Many people believe that the average college student ought to spend *at least* an hour in outside work for every hour of class time in a college course. So in a three-credit course you should do three hours of preparation each week. And note that *one hour* is the *minimum* time for an average student. If you wish to make more than an average grade, or if you find a course difficult, you must spend more than the minimum time in outside preparation. Here are a few suggestions that might make your time allotted to preparation more productive:

1. Schedule study (and work, if you have a job) at regular times during the day. Provide enough time to keep up with your course work without cram sessions every two or three weeks to catch up. Allot your time so that the classes needing greater effort will receive extra time. Remember to schedule time regularly for working on long-term assignments and for library work. A large project will be easier and more beneficial if you do it in a number of short sessions than if you cram all the work into one or two marathon sessions.

2. Review your lecture and discussion notes immediately after the class or just before the next session. Consolidate and organize the notes while the material is fresh in your mind.

3. Do outside reading and writing assignments when they are assigned so that work outside the class will relate closely to the lectures and discussions in the class. Use class work and outside preparation to reinforce each other.

4. Work regularly rather than in fits and starts. Your mind needs time to understand new material and to develop new ideas. It does these tasks best in smaller units of time and materials. Trying to pressure-pack four or five weeks of material into a single day's cramming for a test is a very inefficient way to use your time and your mind. The same amount of time, spread out over several weeks, will yield far better results—more learning and better grades—with less strain on you.

5. Work neatly and carefully. Keep your notes and other materials in neat, well-organized folders. Time spent in the regular care and maintenance of these materials will allow you to study productively when test time finally arrives, without the frustration of searching for lost materials and of deciphering unreadable notes.

Regular work, performed with consistent high quality and meticulous care, is the only guarantee of success in college. Good work habits, developed at the beginning of your college career, will pay dividends from the start. It is impossible to emphasize too much the importance of working regularly, as opposed to letting matters slide and trying to catch up in agonized bursts of effort later in the term. A ten-hour project will always take ten hours to complete successfully. You will put in the time one way or another, but ten hours spent in five two-hour sessions will produce far better results than ten hours spent in a single marathon session. Invest your time wisely.

APPENDIX B Diagnostic Tests

DIAGNOSTIC TEST:

PUNCTUATION

NAME _____ SCORE _____

Directions: In the space at the left of each pair of sentences, write the letter that identifies the correctly punctuated sentence.

_____ 1. A. "Whenever I try to study my class notes are almost unreadable," complained Ruth, "I must be more careful about my handwriting."
           B. "Whenever I try to study, my class notes are almost unreadable," complained Ruth; "I must be more careful about my handwriting."

_____ 2. A. Some of the stockholders are now wondering if the company has overextended itself by buying the two new ships.
           B. Some of the stockholders are now wondering, if the company has overextended itself by buying the two new ships?

_____ 3. A. Although the Perkinses live less than a block away from us, we hardly feel that we know them well.
           B. Although the Perkins's live less than a block away from us; we hardly feel that we know them well.

_____ 4. A. The following notice recently appeared on the bulletin board; "The editors of this years Senior yearbook have decided to dispense with the so-called humor section."
           B. The following notice recently appeared on the bulletin board: "The editors of this year's Senior yearbook have decided to dispense with the so-called humor section."

_____ 5. A. I scraped the mud and mashed insects from the windshield and Norma sadly inspected the crumpled, rear fender.
           B. I scraped the mud and mashed insects from the windshield, and Norma sadly inspected the crumpled rear fender.

387

_____ 6. A. After they had cleaned the kitchen, put the children to bed, and locked the front door, Pete and Jane looked forward to a quiet, peaceful evening.

B. After they had cleaned the kitchen, put the children to bed and locked the front door; Pete and Jane looked forward to a quiet peaceful evening.

_____ 7. A. Some neighbors asked questions about Jim's strange friends but Mother told them that it was nobodys concern except our family's.

B. Some neighbors asked questions about Jim's strange friends, but Mother told them that it was nobody's concern except our family's.

_____ 8. A. "Tryouts for the class play have been completed," Miss. Lowe, the drama coach, announced, "this year we are blessed with almost too much talent."

B. "Tryouts for the class play have been completed," Miss Lowe, the drama coach, announced; "this year we are blessed with almost too much talent."

_____ 9. A. My office mate claims to understand horse racing, but his bets every month usually cost him a week's pay.

B. My office mate claims to understand horse racing but his bets every month usually cost him a weeks pay.

_____ 10. A. The childrens' father made a good impression, the presiding judge, in fact, commended him for his handling of the matter.

B. The children's father made a good impression; the presiding judge, in fact, commended him for his handling of the matter.

_____ 11. A. Coach Stannard scheduled volleyball tryouts for February 16, 1988 and nearly two dozen eager, young women turned out.

B. Coach Stannard scheduled volleyball tryouts for February 16, 1988, and nearly two dozen eager young women turned out.

_____ 12. A. "How can we foreigners learn English," complained Carmen, "when you give different pronunciations to words like *bough, cough, dough, plough* and *slough.*"

B. "How can we foreigners learn English," complained Carmen, "when you give different pronunciations to words like *bough, cough, dough, plough,* and *slough?*"

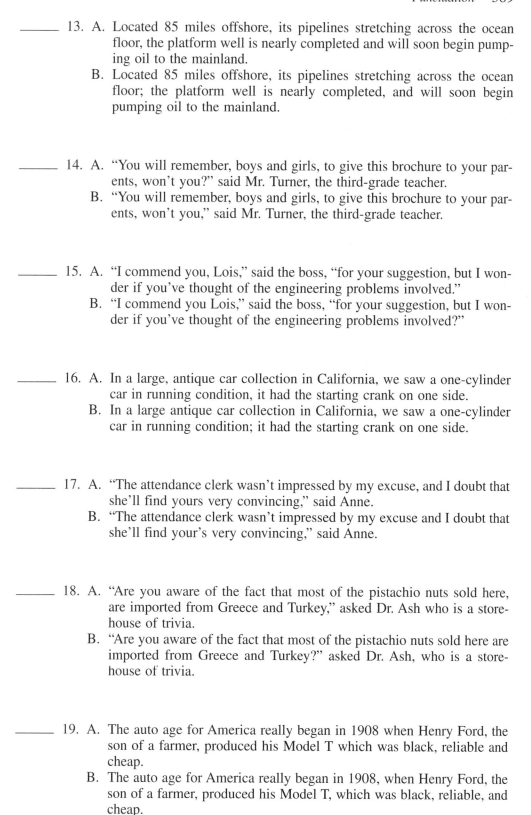

_____ 13. A. Located 85 miles offshore, its pipelines stretching across the ocean floor, the platform well is nearly completed and will soon begin pumping oil to the mainland.

        B. Located 85 miles offshore, its pipelines stretching across the ocean floor; the platform well is nearly completed, and will soon begin pumping oil to the mainland.

_____ 14. A. "You will remember, boys and girls, to give this brochure to your parents, won't you?" said Mr. Turner, the third-grade teacher.

        B. "You will remember, boys and girls, to give this brochure to your parents, won't you," said Mr. Turner, the third-grade teacher.

_____ 15. A. "I commend you, Lois," said the boss, "for your suggestion, but I wonder if you've thought of the engineering problems involved."

        B. "I commend you Lois," said the boss, "for your suggestion, but I wonder if you've thought of the engineering problems involved?"

_____ 16. A. In a large, antique car collection in California, we saw a one-cylinder car in running condition, it had the starting crank on one side.

        B. In a large antique car collection in California, we saw a one-cylinder car in running condition; it had the starting crank on one side.

_____ 17. A. "The attendance clerk wasn't impressed by my excuse, and I doubt that she'll find yours very convincing," said Anne.

        B. "The attendance clerk wasn't impressed by my excuse and I doubt that she'll find your's very convincing," said Anne.

_____ 18. A. "Are you aware of the fact that most of the pistachio nuts sold here, are imported from Greece and Turkey," asked Dr. Ash who is a storehouse of trivia.

        B. "Are you aware of the fact that most of the pistachio nuts sold here are imported from Greece and Turkey?" asked Dr. Ash, who is a storehouse of trivia.

_____ 19. A. The auto age for America really began in 1908 when Henry Ford, the son of a farmer, produced his Model T which was black, reliable and cheap.

        B. The auto age for America really began in 1908, when Henry Ford, the son of a farmer, produced his Model T, which was black, reliable, and cheap.

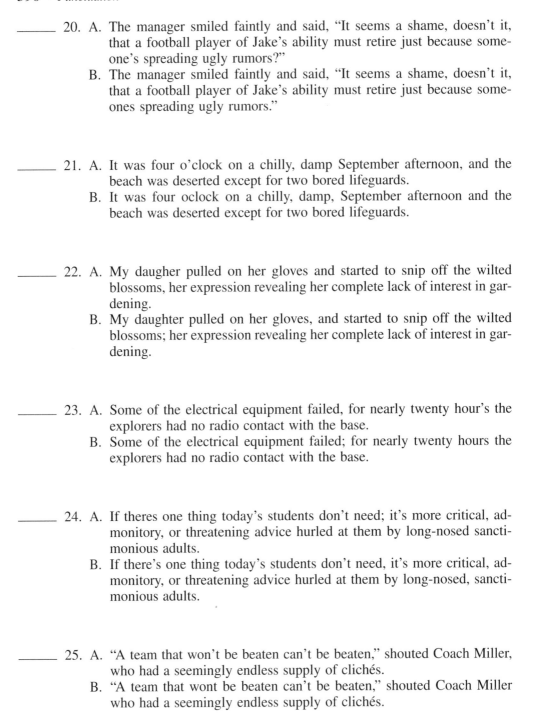

_____ 20. A. The manager smiled faintly and said, "It seems a shame, doesn't it, that a football player of Jake's ability must retire just because someone's spreading ugly rumors?"
        B. The manager smiled faintly and said, "It seems a shame, doesn't it, that a football player of Jake's ability must retire just because someones spreading ugly rumors."

_____ 21. A. It was four o'clock on a chilly, damp September afternoon, and the beach was deserted except for two bored lifeguards.
        B. It was four oclock on a chilly, damp, September afternoon and the beach was deserted except for two bored lifeguards.

_____ 22. A. My daugher pulled on her gloves and started to snip off the wilted blossoms, her expression revealing her complete lack of interest in gardening.
        B. My daughter pulled on her gloves, and started to snip off the wilted blossoms; her expression revealing her complete lack of interest in gardening.

_____ 23. A. Some of the electrical equipment failed, for nearly twenty hour's the explorers had no radio contact with the base.
        B. Some of the electrical equipment failed; for nearly twenty hours the explorers had no radio contact with the base.

_____ 24. A. If theres one thing today's students don't need; it's more critical, admonitory, or threatening advice hurled at them by long-nosed sanctimonious adults.
        B. If there's one thing today's students don't need, it's more critical, admonitory, or threatening advice hurled at them by long-nosed, sanctimonious adults.

_____ 25. A. "A team that won't be beaten can't be beaten," shouted Coach Miller, who had a seemingly endless supply of clichés.
        B. "A team that wont be beaten can't be beaten," shouted Coach Miller who had a seemingly endless supply of clichés.

DIAGNOSTIC TEST:

SPELLING

NAME _____   SCORE _____

Directions: Each of the following sentences contains three italicized words, one of which is misspelled. Underline each misspelled word and write it, correctly spelled, in the space at the left.

_____ 1. "There are limitations on the length, breadth, and *heighth* of packages we ship, and the weight must not *exceed forty* pounds," the agent said.

_____ 2. My present was a box of fancy *stationery;* I was *dissappointed* that I didn't *receive* something more practical.

_____ 3. The food served at this rural inn is *becoming fameous* throughout Great *Britain.*

_____ 4. Lathrop sought the *advise* of an *eminent psychiatrist.*

_____ 5. This may sound *unbelievable* to you, but our city *library* has been struck three times by *lightening.*

_____ 6. Jerry is *dissatisfied* with his new *schedual* because it does not allow him time for studying *during* the afternoons.

_____ 7. In her *sophmore* year Joyce took a course in *speech* and two courses in *literature.*

_____ 8. The play had *it's* first *performance* in Hartford last *February.*

_____ 9. "An *acquaintance* of mine *reccommended* your *restaurant* to me," said Mrs. Watkins to the receptionist.

_____ 10. The applicant attempted to flatter the interviewer by saying, "You are *undoubtably knowledgeable* about the latest *technology* in our field."

_____ 11. "Your *humorous* remarks were not *appropriate* for a serious *occassion* such as this one," said the chairperson.

_____ 12. I admit that my new dog behaved *deploreably* last *Wednesday* at *obedience* school.

_____ 13. The data we get from these *questionnaires* could have an *effect* on next year's hiring *proceedures.*

_____ 14. *Reference* to a *dictionary* could have quickly settled the *arguement* the two of you were having.

_____ 15. We must all *recognize* the fact that tourism is the *principle* source of income in our quaint *village.*

_____ 16. Yesterday one of the arrested men *lead* the police officers to the place where the *equipment* stolen from the *laboratory* had been hidden.

_____ 17. A *goverment* spokesperson announced that the new *satellite* will provide weather forecasters with *indispensable* data.

_____ 18. The coach happily announced a *noticeable improvement* in batting averages, *especialy* in those of our outfielders.

_____ 19. A serious accident on the highway caused us to *loose approx-imately ninety* minutes of valuable time.

_____ 20. A senior *pardner* of the firm *conceded* that further meetings would very likely be *necessary.*

_____ 21. "This *pamphlet* is full of the most *rediculous propaganda* I've ever read," shouted the incumbent.

_____ 22. "*Neither* of these two small countries could withstand a long *seige,*" replied *Sergeant* Lewis.

_____ 23. As he presented Enid with the award, the *superintendent* said, "Here is a young person *who's courageous* fight has inspired all of us."

_____ 24. When arrested, Elaine had in her *possession* a large *quanity* of *counterfeit* money.

_____ 25. "Serving on this *committee* has been a *priviledge* and a won-derful *experience,*" said the retiring chairperson.

DIAGNOSTIC TEST:

USAGE

NAME _____ SCORE _____

Directions: In the space at the left, copy from within the parentheses the form that would be appropriate in serious writing.

_____ 1. Bert was surprised to learn that everyone in the class except Maria and (he, him) had to take another test.

_____ 2. The thief apparently had crept through the broken ventilator grill and had (laid, lain) quietly in the storeroom until nightfall.

_____ 3. Mary Ellen wasn't at the park yesterday; it hardly could have been (she, her) who tore your scarf.

_____ 4. Anyone selected for the acting presidency must prepare (himself or herself, themself, themselves) for a short and thankless term of office.

_____ 5. The reason I'm looking so pale is (because, that) my sunlamp needs repairing.

_____ 6. Some fellow who had occupied the room before I arrived had left some of (his, their) old clothes in the closet.

_____ 7. I wish someone on the school paper would write an editorial in (regard, regards) to the noise in the library reading room.

_____ 8. Just between you and (I, me), Luke shouldn't expect to get off with only a lecture from the judge.

_____ 9. You're convinced now, aren't you, that you (hadn't ought to, shouldn't) leave your garage unlocked?

_____ 10. My sister once studied the alto saxophone but never played it (good, well) enough to be chosen for the school band.

_____ 11. The robbers, (whoever, whomever) they were, must have known exactly when the workers would be paid.

_____ 12. The school's new program must be effective, for there (has, have) been surprisingly few complaints from parents.

_____ 13. Not many jobs are available, (because, being that) the government has curtailed operations at the navy yard.

393

_____ 14. After speaking into the microphone, Laura played back the tape and commented on how (different, differently) her voice sounded.

_____ 15. "Vote for (whoever, whomever) you think is the best candidate," answered Anita's father.

_____ 16. In a political campaign every candidate makes promises that (they know, he or she knows) cannot possibly be kept.

_____ 17. Also included in the packet (is, are) a travel guide, some special trip tips, and two exceptional bonus prizes.

_____ 18. Someone should have told (we, us) ushers that the main door had not been unlocked.

_____ 19. Do you know who the man is who is (setting, sitting) at the head table next to the guest speaker?

_____ 20. As everyone knows, neither DDT nor any other insecticide (has, have) the ability to distinguish between good and bad insects.

_____ 21. If the helicopter pilot had not dropped blankets to the men stranded on the ice floe, they probably would have (froze, frozen) to death.

_____ 22. After a few months Carrie (began, begun) to have doubts about her nephew's ability to manage her investments.

_____ 23. No one could have been more surprised than (I, me) to learn of your recent marriage.

_____ 24. The gratification resulting from working on the school newspaper and other publications (outweighs, outweigh) the demands on one's time.

_____ 25. After a person has sat for five hours in the blazing sunlight listening to this kind of music, (he or she feels, they feel) numb and beaten.

DIAGNOSTIC TEST:
SENTENCE STRUCTURE

NAME _____ SCORE _____

Directions: Study these paired sentences for incompleteness, dangling or misplaced modifiers, faulty parallelism, and faulty comparisons. In the space at the left, write the letter that identifies the correct sentence.

_____ 1. A. The cotton crop this year, we all hope, will be much better than last years.
 B. The cotton crop this year, we all hope, will be much better than last year's.

_____ 2. A. Because we are the parents of five active children, our washing machine is running much of the time.
 B. Being the parents of five active children, our washing machine is running much of the time.

_____ 3. A. Searching the area carefully, we finally found the tunnel entrance, expertly covered by underbrush and which the other searchers had overlooked.
 B. Searching the area carefully, we finally found the tunnel entrance, which had been expertly covered by underbrush and which the other searchers had overlooked.

_____ 4. A. The group's intention, surely a noble one, to constantly and relentlessly encourage the protection of the environment.
 B. The group's intention, surely a noble one, is to encourage constantly and relentlessly the protection of the environment.

_____ 5. A. Believing me to be a better public speaker than anyone else in the class, my parents told all the relatives that I would be the valedictorian.
 B. Being a better public speaker than anyone in the class, my parents told all the relatives that I would be the valedictorian.

_____ 6. A. Malaysia and other countries proved incapable of sheltering or unwilling to shelter all of the refugees.
 B. Malaysia and other countries proved incapable or unwilling to shelter all of the refugees.

_____ 7. A. "I neither intend to withdraw from the race nor to in any degree stop pointing out my opponent's shortcomings," Ms. Hawley replied.
 B. "I intend neither to withdraw from the race nor in any degree to stop pointing out my opponent's shortcomings," Ms. Hawley replied.

_____ 8. A. When seen from a distance, the white cliffs seem to resemble icebergs.
 B. When seen from a distance, one might think that the white cliffs were icebergs.

_____ 9. A. This popular young actor lives high in the Hollywood hills in a small apartment decorated with posters of auto races and bullfights.
　　　 B. This popular young actor lives in a small apartment decorated with posters of auto races and bullfights high in the Hollywood hills.

_____ 10. A. The relatively small amount of flood water has not and probably won't cause any major damage.
　　　 B. The relatively small amount of flood water has not caused and probably won't cause any major damage.

_____ 11. A. When we replaced the wooden shingles with a composition roof, the insurance company agreed to lower our annual premium quite considerably.
　　　 B. By replacing the wooden shingles with a composition roof, the insurance company agreed to quite considerably lower our annual premium.

_____ 12. A. Commissioner Reed stated that our downtown streets are as clean, if not cleaner than, other cities.
　　　 B. Commissioner Reed stated that our downtown streets are as clean as, if not cleaner than, those of other cities.

_____ 13. A. I already have a full enough schedule of work today without being asked to listen to you practice your speech.
　　　 B. I already have a full enough schedule of work today without asking me to listen to you practice your speech.

_____ 14. A. The reason for our moving being that the security system at Elmhurst Manor is more modern than the old apartment.
　　　 B. The reason for our moving is that the security system at Elmhurst Manor is more modern than that at the old apartment.

_____ 15. A. Sylvia Andrews is a self-sufficient and talented person who, since her husband died, has supported herself and her family tutoring students in mathematics.
　　　 B. Sylvia Andrews, a self-sufficient and talented person who has supported herself and her family since her husband died tutoring students in mathematics.

_____ 16. A. My mother's paternal grandmother was one of the very few, if not the only, woman to study veterinary medicine in the early 1900s.
　　　 B. My mother's paternal grandmother was one of the very few women, if not the only woman, to study veterinary medicine in the early 1900s.

_____ 17. A. You must either return these books to the library or pay a substantial fine.
　　　 B. Either you must return these books to the library or pay a substantial fine.

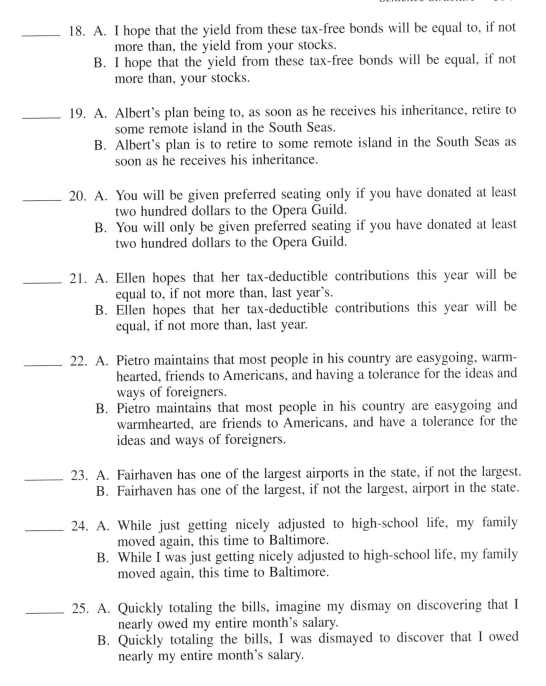

_____ 18. A. I hope that the yield from these tax-free bonds will be equal to, if not more than, the yield from your stocks.
       B. I hope that the yield from these tax-free bonds will be equal, if not more than, your stocks.

_____ 19. A. Albert's plan being to, as soon as he receives his inheritance, retire to some remote island in the South Seas.
       B. Albert's plan is to retire to some remote island in the South Seas as soon as he receives his inheritance.

_____ 20. A. You will be given preferred seating only if you have donated at least two hundred dollars to the Opera Guild.
       B. You will only be given preferred seating if you have donated at least two hundred dollars to the Opera Guild.

_____ 21. A. Ellen hopes that her tax-deductible contributions this year will be equal to, if not more than, last year's.
       B. Ellen hopes that her tax-deductible contributions this year will be equal, if not more than, last year.

_____ 22. A. Pietro maintains that most people in his country are easygoing, warm-hearted, friends to Americans, and having a tolerance for the ideas and ways of foreigners.
       B. Pietro maintains that most people in his country are easygoing and warmhearted, are friends to Americans, and have a tolerance for the ideas and ways of foreigners.

_____ 23. A. Fairhaven has one of the largest airports in the state, if not the largest.
       B. Fairhaven has one of the largest, if not the largest, airport in the state.

_____ 24. A. While just getting nicely adjusted to high-school life, my family moved again, this time to Baltimore.
       B. While I was just getting nicely adjusted to high-school life, my family moved again, this time to Baltimore.

_____ 25. A. Quickly totaling the bills, imagine my dismay on discovering that I nearly owed my entire month's salary.
       B. Quickly totaling the bills, I was dismayed to discover that I owed nearly my entire month's salary.

APPENDIX C Answer Key to Practice Sheets

P.S. 1, p. 5

1. is   2. accompanied   3. came   4. sought   5. attended
6. are   7. stood   8. seems   9. stands   10. whitewashed
11. was   12. was   13. helped   14. is   15. are   16. found
17. taped   18. was   19. approached   20. is

P.S. 1, p. 6

1. neither   2. boos   3. one   4. shorter   5. reform   6. one
7. time   8. all   9. guard   10. daughter   11. one
12. explanation   13. most   14. three   15. one   16. stamps
17. cottage   18. some   19. series   20. guide

P.S. 2, pp. 15, 16

1. 5, 1   2. 3, 4   3. 5, 6   4. 3, 4   5. 2, 5   6. 4, 1   7. 5, 5
8. 6, 1   9. 4, 2   10. 3, 2   11. 5, 1   12. 6, 5   13. 4, 4
14. 2, 4   15. 1, 6   16. 3, 6   17. 1, 5   18. 4, 1   19. 5, 3
20. 6, 4   21. 3, 4   22. 2, 1   23. 5, 1   24. 5, 4   25. 3, 4
26. 4, 1   27. 4, 1   28. 2, 3   29. 4, 5   30. 4, 4   31. 5, 6
32. 3, 4   33. 2, 1   34. 3, 5   35. 6, 1   36. 6, 5   37. 1, 3
38. 4, 5   39. 4, 1   40. 5, 6

P.S. 3, p. 25

1. friends   2. event   3. help   4. Wednesday   5. driver
6. power   7. one   8. necessity   9. yours   10. one
11. suspect   12. salesman   13. time   14. mine   15. guess
16. addition   17. comfort   18. fan   19. optimist   20. resorts

P.S. 3, p. 26

1. ready   2. brown   3. tired   4. shy   5. inexperienced
6. relaxed   7. frozen   8. active   9. This   10. unworthy
11. usable   12. tinny   13. salty   14. fresh   15. suspicious
16. implausible   17. puzzled   18. listless   19. qualified
20. cold

P.S. 4, p. 33

1. response 2. history 3. one 4. account 5. value 6. room
7. letter 8. chores 9. reason 10. lights 11. many 12. piece
13. luxuries 14. desserts 15. endings 16. all 17. everything
18. meals 19. all 20. larger

P.S. 4, p. 34

1. I.O. 2. I.O. 3. O.C. 4. D.O. 5. I.O. 6. O.C. 7. D.O.
8. I.O. 9. I.O. 10. D.O. 11. O.C. 12. I.O. 13. O.C. 14. D.O.
15. D.O. 16. O.C. 17. I.O. 18. O.C. 19. D.O. 20. D.O.

P.S. 5, pp. 41, 42

1. 3 2. 2 3. 2. 4. 4. 5. 5 6. 2 7. 1 8. 2 9. 5 10. 3
11. 4 12. 1 13. 3 14. 5 15. 4 16. 1 17. 2 18. 5 19. 3
20. 2 21. 2 22. 2 23. 3 24. 4 25. 2 26. 3 27. 3 28. 4
29. 1 30. 3 31. 2 32. 4 33. 1 34. 1 35. 5 36. 4 37. 2
38. 3 39. 3 40. 4

P.S. 6, p. 51

1. 5, was called 2. 4, will be sent 3. 3, is appreciated
4. 3, had been called 5. 4, was told 6. 3, is being talked about
7. 4, was allowed 8. 3, is delivered 9. 3, was composed
10. 5, should have been made

P.S. 6, p. 52

1. pancakes 2. taxis 3. What 4. applicants 5. notes 6. these
7. mistakes 8. whom 9. Who 10. officer 11. whom 12. color
13. Who 14. What 15. Whom

P.S. 7, pp. 59, 60

1. O 2. S 3. C 4. O 5. C 6. S 7. C 8. O 9. C
10. S 11. O 12. C 13. O 14. C 15. S 16. C 17. S
18. S 19. C 20. S 21. C 22. O 23. S 24. C 25. S

P.S. 8, pp. 67, 68

1. 1 2. 2 3. 3 4. 4 5. 5. 6. 6. 7. 7 8. 8 9. 9.
10. 10 11. 9 12. 8. 13. 7 14. 6 15. 5 16. 1 17. 2
18. 3 19. 4 20. 10 21. 1 22. 2 23. 3 24. 4 25. 5
26. 6 27. 7 28. 8 29. 9 30. 10 31. 10 32. 9 33. 8
34. 7 35. 6 36. 5 37. 4 38. 3 39. 2 40. 1

P.S. 9, pp. 75, 76

1. books   2. high school   3. flight   4. watch   5. Dick Lee   6. road
7. someone   8. Dallas   9. mystery   10. spot   11. Julie Ross
12. theme   13. report   14. house   15. 1938   16. woman   17. fellow
18. those   19. dog   20. friends   21. man   22. person
23. Speech 301   24. scouts   25. sofa   26. time   27. everything
28. James   29. table   30. subject   31. Guthrie Center   32. father-in-law
33. place   34. bus   35. van   36. pickles   37. articles   38. plays
39. person   40. fall

P.S. 10, p. 83

1. S.   2. S.   3. D.O.   4. D.O.   5. S.C.   6. S.   7. O.P.   8. S.C.
9. S.   10. S.   11. D.O.   12. Ap.   13. Ap.   14. D.O.   15. Ap.
16. D.O.   17. D.O.   18. D.O.   19. S.C.   20. O.P.

P.S. 10, p. 84

1. D.O. (where he had left his keys)
2. S.C. (that the price we had paid was too high)
3. D.O. (where the county courthouse is)
4. D.O. (that Fran will ever marry again)
5. S.C. (that he resists those who try to help him)
6. S.C. (what I had purchased at the store)
7. S. (that I should have studied harder for the exam)
8. D.O. (that I should have studied harder for the exam)
9. Ap. (that I should have studied harder for the exam)
10. D.O. (that voters who live in farming areas will defeat the referendum)
11. D.O. (that you were being overcharged)
12. S.C. (that Jackson could not pay the initiation fee)
13. S. (Whoever owns the Buick that is blocking my driveway)
14. S. (that the report you got the figures from)
15. O.P. (how you will pay for these luxuries)
16. S. (Why Mary Ellen still works when she could retire with a good pension)
17. D.O. (that the receptionist was surprised by the request I made)
18. Ap. (that the school levy was defeated)
19. D.O. (if he had any inherited wealth)
20. D.O. (he had never voted)

P.S. 11, p. 93

1. 1   2. 4   3. 2   4. 1   5. 4   6. 3   7. 4   8. 2   9. 1   10. 3
11. 4   12. 2   13. 1   14. 4   15. 3   16. 4   17. 2   18. 3   19. 4
20. 4

P.S. 11, p. 94

1. Adv.   2. N.   3. N.   4. N.   5. Adj.   6. N.   7. Adv.   8. Adj.
9. Adj.   10. Adv.   11. Adv.   12. N.   13. N.   14. N   15. Adv.
16. Adv.   17. Adj.   18. Adv.   19. N.   20. Adj.

P.S. 12, pp. 101, 102

1. commercials   2. those   3. __   4. epichondylitis   5. __   6. John
7. __   8. she   9. memo and note   10. Harry   11. __   12. brother
13. you   14. __   15. Anyone   16. merchandise   17. students
18. __   19. __   20. Martha James   21. __   22. monkey   23. Anita
24. __   25. __   26. woman   27. prison   28. one   29. __   30. __
31. I   32. road   33. __   34. Tom   35. guard   36. Angela
37. plant   38. __   39. Jim   40. Helen

P.S. 13, pp. 111, 112

1. F   2. S   3. F   4. S   5. F   6. S   7. S   8. F   9. S   10. S
11. F   12. S   13. S   14. S   15. F   16. S   17. S   18. F
19. S   20. S   21. S   22. F   23. S   24. F   25. S   26. S
27. F   28. S   29. S   30. F   31. S   32. F   33. S   34. S
35. S

P.S. 14, p. 121

1. B.   2. B.   3. B.   4. A.   5. A.   6. A.   7. A.   8. B.   9. A.
10. A.

P.S. 14, p. 122

1. B.   2. A.   3. A.   4. B.   5. B.   6. A.   7. B.   8. B.   9. B.
10. B.   11. A.   12. B.   13. B.   14. B.   15. B.

P.S. 14A, pp. 125, 126

1. B.   2. A.   3. B.   4. B.   5. B.   6. A.   7. A.   8. B.   9. B.
10. B.   11. B.   12. A.   13. A.   14. A.   15. A.   16. B.   17. B.
18. A.   19. B.   20. B.

P.S. 15, pp. 135, 136

1. 1   2. 7   3. 4   4. 2   5. 3   6. 6   7. 2   8. 1   9. 5   10. 1
11. 4   12. 1   13. 2   14. 6   15. 1   16. 5   17. 1   18. 4   19. 7
20. 1   21. 2   22. 1   23. 2   24. 1   25. 3

P.S. 16, p. 147

1. A   2. B   3. B   4. A   5. B   6. A   7. B   8. B   9. A
10. B

P.S. 16, p. 148

1. B   2. B   3. B   4. B   5. A   6. B   7. B   8. A   9. B
10. B

P.S. 17, pp. 155, 156

1. 4, 3   2. 2, 1   3. 2, 3   4. 5, 1   5. 3, 4   6. 2, 1   7. 4, 1   8. 4, 3
9. 4, 3   10. 4, 1   11. 2, 1   12. 4, 2   13. 4, 3   14. 1, 3   15. 2, 3
16. 4, 3   17. 2, 1   18. 4, 2   19. 2, 1   20. 5, 3

P.S. 18, p. 165

1. 2   2. 4   3. 6   4. 5   5. 2   6. 6   7. 3   8. 1   9. 2   10. 1
11. 2   12. 6   13. 1   14. 1   15. 1   16. 5   17. 6   18. 1   19. 1
20. 5

P.S. 18, p. 166

1. R   2. N   3. N   4. N   5. R   6. N   7. R   8. N   9. N
10. R   11. N   12. R.   13. R   14. N   15. R   16. R   17. N
18. N   19. R   20. N

P.S. 19, p. 175

1. C   2. W   3. W   4. C   5. W   6. W   7. W   8. C   9. W
10. C   11. W   12. C   13. W   14. C   15. W

P.S. 19, p. 176

1. The caller told us, "The owner's manual for the new car is not very clear."
2. Marian says, "I intend to look for a new job unless I get a raise."
3. Julia said, "I worked for weeks on the report, and I was disappointed by the boss' lack of enthusiasm for it."
4. Jim said, "I am leaving for my vacation in two days and won't be back for four weeks."
5. Do the instructions say, "You are supposed to leave that valve open 24 hours a day?"
6. The announcement said that the airport would be closed for departures after midnight until the weather clears.
7. Randolph said that he would need a ride home from class tomorrow afternoon.
8. The child asked when she could go back to the zoo to see the tigers.
9. Mr. Watson complained that the mysteries he had read lately were too gory and their plots were too simple.
10. Did you hear Professor Lopez say that there would be a test on the first two chapters in the text next Tuesday?

P.S. 20, pp. 183, 184

1. W   2. W   3. C   4. C   5. C   6. W   7. W   8. C   9. W
10. C   11. C   12. W   13. W   14. W   15. C   16. C   17. C
18. C   19. W   20. C   21. W   22. W   23. W   24. C   25. C
26. W   27. C   28. W   29. W   30. C   31. W   32. W   33. W
34. W   35. W   36. W   37. W   38. W   39. W   40. W   41. C
42. W   43. C   44. W   45. W   46. C   47. W   48. W   49. W
50. C

P.S. 21, p. 195

1. rose, raised   2. began, dug   3. withdrawn, grown   4. sought, set
5. swum, lay   6. built, spent   7. swung, flew   8. fell, froze
9. crept, spent   10. set, laid   11. spoken, wrote   12. drew, threw
13. lent, paid   14. begun, broken   15. drowned, dragged   16. stung, took
17. worn, shone   18. gave, stolen   19. seen, went   20. taught, forgotten

P.S 21, p. 196

1. were, driven   2. C, ridden   3. have been, have seen   4. lying, fallen
5. C, rang   6. has been, C   7. C, chosen   8. grew, C   9. lent, forgotten
10. knew, shone   11. threw, swore   12. brought, ate   13. drowned, ran
14. frozen, swam   15. dragged, taken   16. clung, shook   17. C, spent
18. taught, torn   19. C, burst   20. skinned, C

P.S. 22, p. 203

1. was   2. were   3. do   4. were   5. seems   6. know   7. has
8. is   9. has   10. was   11. plays   12. goes   13. was   14. was
15. is

P.S. 22, p. 204

1. is   2. was   3. are   4. is   5. correct   6. have   7. are   8. has
9. correct   10. are   11. has   12. were   13. correct   14. has
15. Has

P.S. 23, pp. 213, 214

1. B   2. A   3. B   4. A   5. B   6. B   7. A   8. B   9. B
10. A   11. A   12. B   13. B   14. A   15. B   16. B   17. A
18. B   19. B   20. A

P.S. 24, p. 223

1. 4   2. 3   3. 6   4. 1   5. 1   6. 5   7. 1   8. 4   9. 2   10. 4
11. 1   12. 6   13. 2   14. 5   15. 2   16. 2   17. 4   18. 5   19. 4
20. 1

P.S. 24, p. 224

1. Whom   2. who   3. us   4. me   5. she   6. yours   7. he
8. whoever   9. whomever   10. her   11. anybody's   12. us   13. who's
14. I   15. who   16. whom   17. me   18. who   19. me
20. whoever

P.S. 25, p. 233

1. looked, Adj.   2. Tim, Adj.   3. thought, Adv.   4. road, Adj.
5. watched, Adv.   6. Jan, Adj.   7. went, Adv.   8. chance, Adj.
9. distribution, Adj.   10. distributed, Adv.   11. exciting, Adv.
12. debaters, Adj.   13. Bart, Adj.   14. results, Adj.   15. works, Adv.
16. walk, Adv.   17. pace, Adj.   18. Kelly, Adj.   19. time, Adj.
20. room, Adj.

P.S. 25, p. 234

1. well   2. bright   3. considerably   4. true   5. loosely   6. correctly
7. harder   8. bad   9. differently   10. gently   11. shortest   12. well
13. poorly   14. well   15. good   16. Surely   17. properly   18. better
19. wonderful   20. Almost

P.S. 26, p. 245

1. 2, 2   2. 1, 1   3. 2, 2   4. 2, 1   5. 1, 2   6. 2, 1   7. 2, 1   8. 2, 1
9. 2, 1   10. 2, 2   11. 1, 1   12. 2, 2   13. 2, 2   14. 2, 2   15. 1, 2
16. 2, 2   17. 2, 1   18. 1, 1   19. 2, 1   20. 1, 1

P.S. 26, p. 246

1. should have, C   2. off, C   3. Almost, really   4. that, because of
5. wants to get out of, suspects   6. those, surely   7. Many, C
8. couple of, C   9. from, not very   10. has no response, in regard
11. further, C   12. have, C   13. C, delete at   14. Let's, quite
15. Besides, used   16. Since, way   17. number, C   18. These kinds, annoy
19. try to, C   20. Because, quite

P.S. 27, pp. 255, 256

1. different   2. Except   3. canvas   4. writing   5. allotted
6. extremely   7. desirable   8. advise   9. regrettable   10. preferred
11. hiring   12. its   13. incidents   14. you're   15. their
16. serviceable   17. lose   18. descent   19. course   20. presents
21. quite   22. principal   23. council   24. unforgettable   25. shown
26. later   27. fascinating   28. picnicking   29. affected   30. than

P.S. 28, p. 263

1. analyses   2. assemblies   3. auditoriums, auditoria   4. bistros
5. buttonholes   6. cries   7. commandos, commandoes   8. data
9. fathers-in-law   10. fiascoes   11. fungi, funguses   12. giraffes
13. handfuls, handsful   14. Joneses   15. kidneys   16. lilies   17. lice
18. moose   19. mottoes, mottos   20. proofs   21. radios   22. sleeves
23. theses   24. workmen   25. zeros, zeroes

P.S. 28, p. 264

1. C   2. C   3. C   4. C   5. W   6. W   7. W   8. C   9. C
10. W   11. W   12. C   13. W   14. W   15. W   16. C   17. W
18. C   19. C   20. C   21. C   22. W   23. C   24. W   25. W
26. W   27. C   28. W   29. C   30. C   31. C   32. W   33. W
34. W   35. C   36. W   37. W   38. C   39. C   40. W   41. W
42. C   43. W   44. W   45. W   46. W   47. C   48. C   49. C
50. C

P.S. 29, p. 271-272

1. eminent, enthusiastic   2. hypocrisy, humorous   3. graffiti, grammar
4. criticize, consistent   5. candidate ghetto   6. generally, competent
7. dinosaurs, extraordinary   8. decision, forty   9. curriculum, controversial
10. equipment, environment   11. experience, exhausted
12. accommodate, acquaintance   13. condominiums, apparently
14. dissatisfied, computer   15. counterfeit, admissible
16. exaggerated, height   17. attendance, committee   18. absence, difference
19. accidentally, awkward   20. boundaries, basically   21. dormitory, doesn't
22. audience, businesses   23. conference, government
24. concede, argument   25. calendar, accompanying

P.S. 29A, pp. 275-276

1. whether, sophomore   2. laser, satisfactorily   3. wholly, schedule
4. Wednesday, particularly   5. technology, satellite   6. synthetic, maintenance
7. persuade, politics   8. processor, misspelled   9. mortgage, ninety
10. nowadays, permissible   11. nuclear, supersede
12. successful, mathematics   13. practically, preparation
14. temperament, irrelevant   15. interrupted, speech   16. pursue, library
17. livelihood, restaurant   18. quizzes, obstacle   19. surprise, temperature
20. miscellaneous, various   21. usually, professor   22. original, separately
23. spaghetti, similar   24. partners, pastime   25. suspicious, truly

Index